KINGDOM, OFFICE, AND CHURCH

The Historical Series of the Reformed Church in America
no. 53

KINGDOM, OFFICE, AND CHURCH
A Study of A. A. van Ruler's Doctrine of Ecclesiastical Office

Allan J. Janssen

William B. Eerdmans Publishing Company
Grand Rapids, MI / Cambridge, U. K.

Wm. B. Eerdmans Publishing Co.
255 Jefferson Ave. S. E., Grand Rapids, Michigan 49503/
P.O. Box 163, Cambridge, CB3 9PU U.K.
www.eerdmans.com

Printed in the United States of America

To
Jonathan, Sarah, and Emily

The Historical Series of the Reformed Church in America

The series was inaugurated in 1968 by the General Synod of the Reformed Church in America acting through the Commission on History to communicate the church's heritage and collective memory and to reflect on our identity and mission, encouraging historical scholarship which informs both church and academy.

Contents

Acknowledgements

Scholarly work is done apart; the scholar works in library and at desk. But he or she is never alone. The work is always done in a larger community. The bibliography at the end of this volume is testament to the community of scholars, living and dead, on whose shoulders I am privileged to stand.

Nonetheless, gratitude compels me to acknowledge a closer circle whose contributions have made my offering possible. First, I recognize my promoters, A. van de Beek and C. Lombard, whose encouragement and suggestions have made this a far better work than it otherwise could possibly have been. I remain indebted to them as colleagues and friends. To Paul Fries, teacher, friend, and colleague, who introduced me to Van Ruler as I was becoming theologically aware. As director of New Brunswick Theological Seminary's International Summer School in the Netherlands, he provided me the space and the place by which I grew in interest and appreciation of modern and contemporary Dutch theology and church life.

The staff of the Bijzonder Collecties at the library of the University of Utrecht under the direction of K. van der Horst provided invaluable assistance with access to the Van Ruler Archives, the source of much of the original research in this volume. They have my deepest gratitude.

Special thanks goes to my friend, colleague, and fellow pastor-theologian, Okke Postma who read and provided helpful suggestions to a manuscript in process. He also provided the translation for the Dutch summary. Ans van der Veen also assisted in that translation.

I also thank Donald Bruggink and Russell Gasero of the Historical Series, whose invaluable help saw this into print. They worked tirelessly and graciously with tight deadlines and the inevitable bumps in the road.

A number of persons and institutions have contributed to making the publication of this research possible. I acknowledge and offer my thanks to Carol and David Myers; the Stichting Nederlands Protestants Covent; the First Reformed Church of Bethlehem in Selkirk, New York; and the Community Church in Glen Rock, New Jersey. I also enter my deepest appreciation for the latter two institutions as those places where I have been privileged to serve as pastor and teacher, and who have supported scholarship in their ministers.

Finally, I extend my deepest appreciation to my wife, Colleen. It was and is her constant encouragement and support that has made not only my work possible, but also my life delightful. It is in her company that I have begun to know what Van Ruler was on about as together we discover creation as God's kingdom.

Preface

This book was prepared as a dissertation submitted to the faculty of the Free University in Amsterdam, the Netherlands. It is intended as a contribution to the continuing discussion on ecclesiastical office as it particularly explores the unique and evocative theology of A.A. van Ruler. It finds its place in the now venerable Historical Series of the Reformed Church in America because Van Ruler has influenced significantly both the discussion and the shape of the Reformed Church in America over the past fifty years. Indeed, this is particularly the case in the matter of ecclesiastical office itself.

Evidence for this claim is found by examining a variety of sources. Throughout that remarkable period following the Second World War, when the Netherlands Reformed Church found itself in a theological and ecclesiastical renaissance, with its new church order, its draft confession, new liturgical service books, and the like, leaders of the Reformed Church in America followed those developments with interest. I discovered in the libraries of two leaders a number of books from the Netherlands that were clearly well read. If one were to restrict oneself to the subject of this book, I found in the library of James Eelman, a professor of practical theology at New Brunswick Theological Seminary, an annotated copy of Van Ruler's *Bijzonder en algemeen ambt.* And it was a copy of Van Ruler's *Het apostolaat der kerk en het ontwerp kerkorde* in Howard Hageman's library that reignited my own interest in church order as a theological discipline.

This interest was being translated—sometimes literally—into print. Isaac Rottenberg, who became an influential church bureaucrat in the position of secretary of communication, had received a grant to study with Van Ruler for several months. (It was Rottenberg who translated *Fundamenten en perspectieven* into English). Following his service in church headquarters, he became an elder statesman of the church. He wrote a number of books that reflect clearly Van Ruler's theology of the kingdom.[1]

In 1974, the Reformed Church in America proposed a new confession, entitled *Our Song of Hope*. Its principal author, Eugene Heideman, who had studied in Leiden, was himself influenced deeply by Van Ruler. That draft confession betrays its Van Rulerian influence in its eschatological shape. It opens, "We are a people of hope, waiting for the return of the Lord." Its longest section is that on the Holy Spirit, which constitutes twelve of its twenty-one stanzas. Included is a major section, "Our Hope in Daily Life," that echoes Van Ruler's insistence that the locus of God's salvific and redemptive work is this earthly life.[2] The draft was not received by the church as a new confession, but it was approved as "a statement of the church's faith for use in its ministry of witness, teaching, and worship."[3]

A second place where Van Ruler's influence is clearly seen is in a recent revision to the denomination's *Book of Church Order*. The church order was seen as too static, as missing the dynamic of the church's task in God's mission. The *Book of Church Order* is unique among church orders with its rather lengthy preamble. It is the preamble that sets out the theological foundation for the church order. The paragraph on the "nature of the church" was rewritten. Principal in the drafting of the new section were this author and a colleague, the Rev. P. Okke Postma, who is also influenced (although not solely) by Van Ruler. That section now reads:

> The church, which Scripture represents with many images, is a gathering of persons chosen in Christ through the Holy Spirit to profess faith in Jesus Christ as Lord and savior in order to embody God's intentions for the world. Gathered by the Spirit around Word and sacrament, the church fulfills its call within the expectations of the reign of God as it participates in mission, in calling all persons to life in Christ, and in proclaiming God's promise and commands to all the world.[4]

1 To my knowledge Rottenberg was the first to introduce Van Ruler to North America in print. See his *Redemption and Historical Reality* (Philadelphia: Westminster Press, 1964), 162-179.

2 *Our Song of Hope* (Grand Rapids: Eerdmans, 1975).

3 *Minutes of the General Synod*, 1978, 36-37.

4 *The Book of Church Order* (New York: 2003), 2.

The insertion of "God's intentions for the world" and the claim that the church "fulfills its call within he expectation of the reign of God" particularly as it "participates in mission, in calling all persons to life in Christ, and in proclaiming God's promise and commands to all the world," are Van Rulerian in origin.

This is not to maintain that Van Ruler's was the only voice, nor even the strongest voice in the life of the Reformed Church in the past fifty years. Quite the opposite is the case. Counter-movements can be detected (this is especially true in the case of church office). It is, to the contrary, to show that his influence was active in the continuing conversation.

This is particularly the case with office. As noted in chapter 7 of this book, the Reformed Church in America has been engaged in a discussion of office for decades. As early as 1957, in a discussion of the ordination of women to office, G.T. Vander Lugt, later a professor at New Brunswick Theological Seminary, published a study for the General Synod that included reflection on the context and function of office. He cites Van Ruler's *Bijzonder en algemeen ambt* claiming that

> A too soteriological emphasis does not do full justice to the Biblical meaning of the significance of Christ, His Church, and the offices. The full context is always eschatological—God's kingdom already present and coming. Only in this context will the significance and nature of the offices become clear.[5]

This introduces clear Van Rulerian understanding into the Reformed conversation.

The above-mentioned Eugene Heideman published his book on the church order of the Church of South India, *Reformed Bishops and Catholic Elders*, in which he clearly introduces Van Ruler's understanding of ecclesiastical office.[6] Heideman himself both taught at the Reformed Church's Western Theological Seminary and served in a central position on the church's national staff.

Paul Fries, noted in this volume as one of the principal interpreters of Van Ruler's thought particularly in North America (although not only there), has weighed in with a number of studies on

5 "The Offices and the Ordination of Women," in *Proposed Revision of the Constitution and Report on Ordination of Women* (Office of the Stated Clerk: June, 1957), 64.

6 (Grand Rapids: Eerdmans, 1970), see especially 123-24.

ecclesiastical office. One in particular has been of significant influence, the paper, "Faithful Consistories." His voice, with colleagues whom he has taught (this author among them), continues within the church. Further evidence is found in the *Reformed Review*, where the proceedings of an important consultation on office held in Holland, Michigan in November 2002, can be found. There, Fries's keynote lecture displays Van Ruler's continuing influence.[7] In addition, I contributed a lecture that included reference to Van Ruler's understanding of church office.[8]

This volume intends to bring to the surface the significant theological underpinning of these contributions to the ongoing discussion. The theology behind what has been offered is rooted deeply within the Reformed theological tradition itself. But it also displays a freshness of vision that is not bound to a stultifying orthodoxy. Indeed, Van Ruler himself considered that his theology would not find echo until the new century. We are in that century now. May this book be a contribution to the Reformed Church in America as it understands itself, drawn by the God who calls it into existence, and who calls it forward to God original and ultimate intentions, not for the church, but for God's delightful creation.

7 "Coordinates of a Theology of Office: Footnotes for an Emerging Narrative," in *Reformed Review*, Spring 2003, 197-210.

8 "The Future of Offices in the Future of God," in *Reformed Review*, Spring 2003, 273-80.

CHAPTER 1

Introduction

Two moments in ecclesiastical life illustrate my personal inclination to undertake a detailed study of ecclesiastical office. The first occurred in a meeting of a committee of the council of churches in Albany, New York. A minister proposed that the churches gather for a common eucharistic celebration at a New Year's observance in that city. The conversation among the participants took grateful notice of the growing agreement on the doctrine of the Lord's Supper. However, the discussion very quickly ran aground, not on eucharistic theology, but on the question of the acknowledged validity of the celebrant. We had run into the ecumenical impasse on office. The salutary result was to be the beginning of a several-year conversation among Protestant, Catholic and Orthodox representatives on the nature of the ministry. That conversation, however, was limited to representatives of a local council of churches and could not, therefore, directly resolve the problem that was itself the occasion for the dialogue.

Second, a classis in the Reformed Church in America, the communion in which I am a minister of Word and sacrament, requested of the General Synod that it begin a study to create an "office of evangelist" in the church. In further discussions in the synod's Commission on Church Order (of which I was a member) it quickly became evident that before the synod could discuss whether it was advisable to add a new office to the offices of the church, the church needed to answer the question of office. The church is not clear why it has offices at all. The result was to commission yet another study on ministry and office in the church.

Personal anecdotes are not sufficient reason to offer a study to the academy and to the church. However, three reasons do stand as occasion and motivation for this study. First, ministry, particularly ministry understood within the category of "office," has been and continues to be a major stumbling block in the ecumenical quest of the churches to express the unity they confess as one of the essential attributes of the church. This is made clear in recent ecumenical texts that attempt to articulate a convergence on the "nature and purpose" of the church. This study will venture an answer to why the issue remains apparently intractable. Second, "office" raises particular issues of Reformed identity. Do the Reformed churches bring a particular understanding of office to the ecumenical table? And if so, what is that understanding? Third, the Dutch theologian A.A. van Ruler proposed and offered a coherent doctrine of office from a Reformed perspective that, this study suggests, offers insights and perspectives that evoke a clearer understanding of office among the Reformed and provoke possibilities in the discussion hitherto under-represented.

1.1 The Ecumenical Motivation

The document, *Baptism, Eucharist and Ministry*, from the Faith and Order Commission of the World Council of Churches, presented to the churches for comment and reception in 1982, signaled a new era in the ecumenical movement.[1] On the historically contentious doctrines of Eucharist and baptism the churches articulated significant agreement. However, the document itself, in the commentary that paralleled the official text, made it clear that convergence in the understanding of ministry was far from having been reached. This was to be confirmed by the responses from the churches to the section on ministry.[2] A later document issued by the

---

[1] *Baptism, Eucharist and Ministry*, Faith and Order Paper No. 111, Geneva: World Council of Churches, 1982. Further citations will be denoted in the text by LM followed by the paragraph number.

[2] See Margriet Gosker, *Het ambt in de oecumenische discussie: De betekenis van de Lima-ambtstekst voor de voortgang van de oecumene en de doorwerking in de Nederlandse SoW-kerken* (Delft: Eburon, 2000). Also, Ed. A.J.G. Van der Borght, *Het ambt her-dacht: De gereformeerde ambtstheologie in het licht van het rapport Baptism, Eucharist and Minisitry (Lima, 1982) van de theologische commissie Faith and Order van de Wereldraad van Kerken* (Zoetermeer: Meinema, 2000). Responses from the churches are contained in Max Thurian, ed., *Churches Respond to BEM: Official Responses to "Baptism, Eucharist*

same commission, *The Nature and Purpose of the Church: A Stage on the Way to a Common Statement*, published in 1998, continued the conversation on office and also articulated where the differences remained.[3] In addition, European churches, particularly Reformed and Lutheran churches, have, since 1973, been working within and toward the framework set out by the Leuenberg Agreement.[4] The working out of the implications of this agreement resulted in consultation toward convergence on the doctrine of ministry.

These ecumenical texts express considerable progress toward agreement among the churches on a common understanding of ministry. Ministry is to be understood from within the ministry of the church, which in turn is set within God's call of the "whole of humanity to become God's people" (LM, 1). The church is called to "proclaim and prefigure the Kingdom of God. It accomplishes this by announcing the Gospel to the world and by its very existence as the body of Christ" (LM, 4). The church lives by the "liberating and renewing power of the Holy Spirit" (LM, 3). The "Spirit bestows on the community diverse and complementary gifts...that are for the common good of the whole people" (LM, 5). How, BEM then asks, "according to the will of God and under the guidance of the Holy Spirit, is the life of the Church to be understood and ordered so that the Gospel may be spread and the community built up in love?" (LM, 6). Likewise, NPC states that

---

and Ministry," 6 vols. Faith and Order Papers 129, 132, 135, 137, 143, 144 (Geneva: World Council of Churches, 1986-1988). A summary of responses from the Reformed churches can be found in Alan P.F. Sell, "Some Reformed Responses to Baptism, Eucharist and Ministry," *Reformed World*, 39, no. 4 (1986), 549-565. See also J.K.S. Reid, "Reformed Responses to Baptism, Eucharist and Ministry: A Commentary," *Reformed World*, 39, no. 5 (1987), 683-692.

[3] *The Nature and Purpose of the Church: A Stage on the Way to a Common Statement* [Hereinafter NPC], Faith and Order Paper No. 181 (Geneva: World Council of Churches, November, 1998). Citations will be to the paragraph in the document, except where otherwise noted.

[4] The *Leuenberg Agreement* can be found in James A. Andrews and Joseph A Burgess, eds., *An Invitation to Action: The Lutheran-Reformed Dialogue, Series III 1981-1983* (Philadelphia: Fortress Press, 1984), 65-73. A number of theses relevant to the discussion of ministry are available in the "Theses on the Consensus on the Question of 'Ministry and Ordination' between the Churches Participating in the Leuenberg Agreement" (the so-called "Neuendettelsaus Theses"), and "Theses on the Current Discussion about Ministry" (the so-called "Tampere Theses"). These documents are available at www.leuenberg.net.

> ...the church, embodying in its own life the mystery of salvation and the transfiguration of humanity, participates in the mission of Christ to reconcile all things to God and to one another through Christ. Through its ministry of service and proclamation and its stewardship of creation, the Church participates in and points to the reality of the kingdom of God. In the power of the Holy Spirit, the Church testifies to the divine mission in which the Father sent the Son to be the Saviour of the world. (NPC, 28)

In this way the church "signifies, participates in, and anticipates the new humanity God wants..." (NPC, 30). Close reading of this and other texts discloses that the discussion on office takes place within the framework of a trinitarian understanding of God. The material *content* of the trinitarian God's action with the world is the kingdom of God. Thomas O'Meara claims that "the kingdom of God is the bestower of ministry. The kingdom of God is the source, the milieu, the goal of ministry."[5]

NPC advances on BEM's claim that the Spirit gives to people the "strength to witness to the Gospel, and empowers them to serve in hope and love" (LM3), and that the Spirit bestows "diverse and complementary gifts" on the community (LM 5), with the statement that the Spirit "bestows gifts on every member of the Body of Christ for the building up of the fellowship of the Church" (NPC, 82). Further, "as the communion of the baptised, the Church is a priesthood of the whole people of God....Derivatively, the Church as a whole can be described as a priestly body" (NPC, 83). Ministry is rooted in the ministry of the whole people of God.

Nonetheless, from "earliest times" some were chosen by the community under the guidance of the Spirit and given specific authority and responsibility. This is denoted as the "ordained ministry." Ordained ministers "serve in the building up of the community, in equipping the saints, and in strengthening the church's witness in the world." They "have special responsibility for the ministry of Word and sacrament. They have a ministry of pastoral care and are leaders in mission" (NPC, 85; cf. LM 8). Thus far a convergence has been expressed.

---

[5] Thomas O'Meara, *Theology of Ministry*, completely revised edition (New York: Paulist Press, 1999), 38. He makes a similar claim later in the same work that the "reign of God is the background, milieu and the goal of the church" (225).

Nonetheless, as remarkable as this convergence has been, profound differences remain and plague further agreement. Anton Houtepen identifies six issues that remain outstanding in the ecumenical discussion on office: (1) apostolic succession; (2) normative nature of the church order of the second century with its three-fold office of bishop/presbyter/deacon; (3) the understanding and form of ordination; (4) the ordination of women; (5) the relation of tasks reserved for office and the tasks of the community of faith—or said another way, the relation of the particular office and the priesthood of believers; and (6) the way that churches at all levels give shape to mutual consultation and decision.[6] Margriet Gosker offers a similar list, but adds the issues of (1) representation in office; (2) whether a certain sacramentality is presupposed in the office; (3) the acceptance of a hierarchical system; and (4) the Petrine office.[7] We shall pay particular attention below to (1) the apostolic nature of the church; (2) the singularity or plurality of office and the particular shape of that plurality; (3) the office of oversight (the episcopal office); (4) the relation of the particular office to the priesthood of believers; (5) the nature of representation in office; (6) the sacramental nature of office, or the question of whether office is functional or ontological; and (7) the question of the relation of ordination to office. The review below of the issues facing the churches will not include discussion of the question of women in office nor of the Petrine office. The subject of this study, A. A. van Ruler, did not have a great deal to say in either of these matters. However, what he does say, often in passing, will be noted in the appropriate places.

1.1.1 The Apostolic Nature of the Church

As BEM puts it, apostolic tradition means:

> ...continuity in the permanent characteristics of the Church of the apostles: witness to the apostolic faith, proclamation and fresh interpretation of the Gospel, celebration of baptism and the Eucharist, the transmission of ministerial responsibilities, communion in prayer, love, joy and suffering, service to the sick

---

[6] Anton Houtepen, *Een asymmetrische dialoog: Historische kanttekeningen bij de onderlinge erkenning van de kerkelijke ambten*. Utrechtse Theologische Reeks, deel 22 (Utrecht: Faculteit der Godgeleerheid, Universiteit Utrecht, 1994), 12.

[7] Gosker, 265.

> and the needy, unity among the local churches and sharing the gifts which the Lord has given to each. (LM, 34)[8]

The "primary manifestation" of apostolic succession is "to be found in the apostolic tradition of the church as a whole. The succession is an expression of the permanence and, therefore, of the continuity of Christ's own mission in which the Church participates" (LM, 35). By such statements BEM moves clearly beyond the notion that the apostolic nature of the church is guaranteed and solely instantiated through personal succession of an office, that of bishop. Apostolicity is present in the "tradition of the Church as a whole." NPC goes a bit further when it claims that in history the church has used several means to hand on the apostolic tradition of the church: scriptural canon, dogma, liturgical order, and structures wider than local communities (NPC, 88). BEM is cautious as it goes on to claim that the ordained ministry has a "particular task of preserving and actualizing the apostolic faith." And the "orderly transmission of the ordained ministry is therefore a *powerful expression* of the continuity of the Church throughout history" (LM, 35, emphasis added). These words opened a way for the churches of the Reformation, for example, to find themselves within the apostolic tradition. The *Neuendettelau Theses* of the Leuenberg churches, for example, could claim that

> Apostolic Succession is understood in our churches as succeeding in the apostolic teaching and mission. This succeeding finds its expression in proclamation, teaching and church life. In this sense the continuity whereby the church ordains to ministry of proclaiming the word and administering the sacraments pertains to this apostolic succession.[9]

Nonetheless, profound differences remain and the nature of apostolic succession remains a critical issue. NPC notes that the question of how apostolicity is to be expressed is one of the issues that remain outstanding.[10] Responses to BEM from the Reformed churches included reservations concerning even BEM's attempt to weave its way through this issue. As one church put it, "What seems to be apostolic succession through bishops is a requirement for church unity even though it is called episcopal succession. This is something which we find unacceptable." Indeed, "fidelity to the gospel is the sign of

---

[8] Cf. NPC, 72.

[9] *Leuenberg*, 33.

[10] NPC, p. 44, commentary.

apostolicity, not the possession of particular forms of ministry."[11] Nor do reservations come only from the Protestant side. The Roman Catholic Church, in its Catechism of 1994, agrees that the entire church is apostolic. Nonetheless, it is built "on a lasting foundation: 'the twelve apostles of the Lamb' (Rev. 21:14)....She is upheld infallibly in the truth: Christ governs her though Peter and the other apostles, who are present in their successors, the Pope and the college of bishops."[12]

1.1.2 The Singularity or Plurality of Office

Is there one office, or are there several? BEM maintains that the three-fold pattern of bishop, presbyter, and deacon, as developed in the second and third centuries and while having undergone changes, continues into the present (LM, 19). This three-fold pattern is proposed as a model for ministry in the *ecumene*. Not surprisingly, this proposal found resistance among the Reformed, in particular, who have had their own version of a three-fold office, that of minister, elder, and deacon.[13] This tri-partite office, while three, does not correspond to the offices of bishop-presbyter (priest)-deacon. In fact, the two offices that share a common name, that of presbyter and deacon, are quite different offices as understood by the two different systems. The Reformed elder, for example, does not exercise a priestly function. And the Reformed deacon is primarily a social deacon and is not a liturgical figure.

But some raise the question: why three offices at all? Is there perhaps one office? This question itself has been asked in a number of different ways. The traditional Lutheran understanding, for example, is of one office, that of minister of the Word.[14] Even a Roman Catholic theology with the three-fold office can understand the offices as fundamentally one. Thomas O'Meara claims that Vatican II restored the offices of bishop, elder, and deacon as three separate offices in contrast to the medieval and Baroque reduction of the three offices to that of the priesthood.[15] And even among the Reformed, questions

[11] Sell, 560.

[12] *Catechism of the Catholic Church* (Liguouri, Missouri: Liguori Publications, 1994), 230.

[13] Sell, 561.

[14] See A.H. Looman-Graaskamp, "Het ambt, in en uit de tijd," in Martien Brinkman and Anton Houtepen, eds., *Geen kerk zonder bisschop?: Over de plaats van het ambt in de orde van de kerk* (Zoetermeer: Meinema, 1997), p. 148.

[15] O'Meara, 172.

have been raised whether its three-fold division of the offices can be maintained. In his sustained study on office, Ed. Van der Borght allows for the offices of elder and deacon, but maintains that they are of a "different order" than that of minister of Word. They belong to the *bene esse* of the church and not to the *esse*. Hence, in his opinion, it is appropriate that elders and deacons not be ordained to office.[16]

1.1.3 The Office of Oversight

The importance of and the difficulty in the exercise of the oversight of the church, or one might say the governance of the church, is made clear by the amount of space that NPC gives to the matter. It dedicates eighteen of its forty-two paragraphs on "Life in Communion" to oversight. Oversight is denoted as *episkopè*. It identifies, however, three different dimensions of the office of oversight—the personal, the collegial, and the communal—and these dimensions find themselves expressed differently among the churches.

The personal dimension is emphasized in those churches that maintain the office of bishop. Other churches, particularly those of the Reformation, exercise this episcopal function in a second way, collegially. That is, their offices or office-bearers gather in synods. The synods (under whatever name) exercise authority within the church. The third dimension of the ministry of oversight, the communal, is most clearly expressed among churches of the congregational type, whereby the gathered believers themselves exercise authority. Documents like NPC describe what it calls the necessary ministry of *episkopè* for the unity of the church (NPC, 89) and the different ways in which that ministry functions among the churches. But it also is clear that the churches remain divided. Is there a particular "office of oversight," that of the bishop? Or is that ministry executed in a different way? Consensus on the nature of that particular ministry may be growing; churches remain far apart on its particular expression in the offices of the church.

Will the church of the future have an office of bishop by whatever name? Discussions of that office as such disclose that it is differently understood in different churches. But however understood, conversations continue whether this personal office is necessary for the church either in an essential sense—the episcopal office is of the

[16] Van der Borght, 492, 493.

esse of the church–or in a contingent sense–no church union will in fact take place without this office.[17]

1.1.4 The Relation of the Particular Office and the Priesthood of Believers

Ecumenical statements express a growing convergence in the notion that the particular, or ordained, ministry of the church is founded in a particular way in the priesthood of all believers. BEM can describe the "church as a whole" as a "priesthood," derivatively of the unique priesthood of Christ (LM, 17). NPC states baldly that "baptism can be considered the 'ordination' of all believers" (NPC, 76). Differences emerge when the nature of the relation between all believers and the particular offices comes to expression.

From one perspective, the particular office *emerges out of* the priesthood of all believers. There can be no "hierarchical" relation between believers and the particular office because God's ministry resides in and among believers themselves. Particular ministry of persons designated by the congregation express only a difference in function. This perspective itself betrays different nuances. At one end of the spectrum it is held that "if the Holy Spirit has equipped believers with spiritual abilities needed to carry out the ministry of the church then it is consistent to accept the authority of the individual so enabled to perform that ministry."[18] From this position, one can go on to argue that final ecclesiastical authority is vested in the local congregation.[19] Reformed theologian G.D.J. Dingemans makes just this argument. The starting point of all ecclesiastical discussion must be the priesthood of all believers and the charismatic giftedness of all members. The authority granted to office in the church is lodged, according to Dingemans, in the believing communion.[20]

E.J. Beker and J. M. Hasselaar take a more complex approach. They maintain that *charisma* given to believers and to the congregation

---

[17] For a helpful and thorough review of the ecumenical discussion see J. Kronenberg, *Episcopus Oecumenicus: Bouwstenen voor een theologie van het bisschopsambt in een verenigde reformatorische kerk* (Zoetermeer: Meinema, 2003), 168-219.

[18] Rodney J. Decker, "Polity and the Elder Issue," *Grace Theological Journal*, 9, no. 2 (1988), 261-262. One might note the logic of this statement. It may be "consistent" to accept the "authority of the individual." Is, however, consistency sufficient to argue for the rightness of the position?

[19] Decker, 262-263.

[20] G.D.J. Dingemans, *Een huis om in te wonen: Schetsen en bouwstenen voor een kerkorde van de toekomst* ('s-Gravenhage: Boekencentrum, 1987), 130.

stands in a tensile relation to office. In summary, they argue that scripture provides a basis for understanding office as that which maintains and proclaims the apostolic word—hence as standing over and against the congregation. At the same time, they maintain, *charisma* emerges from the congregation. Office and charisma presuppose each other and it is only as they point to each other and in their appeal to each other that the congregation of Jesus Christ is built up rightly.[21] The particular office is rooted in the priesthood of believers but it is neither derivative of that "general" office nor can it be reduced to it. Office is founded in *charisma* and without it dissolves. But since office represents scripture it cannot be reduced to *charisma*.

The foundation of ministry in the priesthood of believers is expressed differently from the Lutheran perspective. For the Lutheran churches, "fundamentally each Christian through baptism is capable of the service of proclaiming the word and administering the sacraments."[22] The so-called *Tampere Theses* state that the "proclamation of the gospel and the offer of saving fellowship are entrusted to the congregation as a whole and to its individual members, who through baptism are called to witness to Christ and to serve one another and the world, and who through faith have a share in Christ's priestly office of intercession."[23] From this claim, the Leuenberg churches could describe the relation of particular office to the priesthood of believers:

> The ministry of the word—in the exercise of proclamation, as well as instruction and pastoral care—always depends on the universal priesthood of the congregation and should serve it, as also the universal priesthood of the congregation and everyone baptised depends upon the special service of the proclamation of the word and the administration of the sacraments. Thus, according to Reformation understanding, the ordained office rests upon a particular commission of Christ and at the same time stands together with the whole congregation in his service under the word of God.[24]

Jan Rohls summarizes the Lutheran perspective as he notes that while for Luther office arose out of the priesthood of believers, office

---

[21] E.J. Beker and J.M. Hasselaar, *Wegen en kruispunten in de dogmatiek: Deel 5, Kerk en toekomst* (Kampen: Kok, 1990), 80.

[22] *Leuenberger Text 2*, 32.

[23] *Leuenberger Text 2*, 34.

[24] *Leuenberger Text 2*, 34.

remained. There is a distinction, but the distinction is functional and not ontological.[25]

A second perspective stands in contradistinction to the notion that the particular office emerges from the priesthood of believers. NPC articulates the contrast when it comments on how the different churches understand the "institutional dimension of the Church and the work of the Holy Spirit." NPC notes that for some churches the ordained minister is the effective means, or guarantee, of the presence of the truth and the power of the Word and Spirit, while for others the power and reliability of God's truth is grounded in the sovereignty of his Word and Spirit which comes through, but can run counter to, the institutional structures of the church (NPC, p. 11).

For those churches that understand the minister as a means of grace, the first instance noted by NPC, the particular office stands "over and against" the congregation and is in some manner constitutive of the congregation. M. Gosker comments that those who support the notion that it must be an ordained minister who serves the Lord's Supper do so on the basis of apostolic succession and the nature of office as representative of Christ, and that office is constitutive for the church.[26] This perspective is articulated by the Dutch Commission on the Lord's Supper and Ecclesiastical Office:

> The dynamic of the communion of the church and the peculiar place of ecclesiastical office in that communion are of no value when ecclesiastical office is only approached as a particularization of the general priesthood of all believers. This office is to be received as a particular gift of Christ to his people, as his particular instrument to bring to experience his presence uniquely. The churches [working together in this document] agree....They know themselves called to bring to clearer and more explicit expression by means of particular call and consecration how much Christ is given to the church uniquely as Lord of this supper and as the source of life.[27]

---

[25] Jan Rohls, "Das geistliche Amt in der reformatorischen Theologie," *Kerygma und Dogma*, 31 (April - June, 1985), 136, 144.

[26] Gosker, *Het ambt*, 238.

[27] Commissie maaltijd des Heren en kerkelijk ambt, *Eindrapport-analyse van de liturgische teksten aangaande maaltijd en ambt, een studie*, 1.2.1/ Kerkelijke documentatie, 17 (1989), no. 2, 133, cited in Leo Koffeman, "Het bijzondere van het kerkelijk ambt," *Gereformeerd theologisch tijdschrift*, 91 (March, 1991), 28.

The church is in fact, constituted as "Jesus Christ becomes present in her as Lord in Word and sacrament through the Holy Spirit." In conformity with Christ's institution there "is a ministry [*Amt*] pertaining to word and sacrament, the *ministerium verbi* (Augsburg Confession V) which 'proclaims the gospel and dispenses the sacraments.'"[28]

The issue remains outstanding: does office emerge from the priesthood of believers or does it stand in a relation over and against believers?

1.1.5 The Nature of Representation in Office

The question of representation follows from the previous issue. For those who argue that office comes *to* the church and does not arise *out of* the church, tend to argue further that office represents God in Christ. The report on office in Netherlands Reformed Church, written by Hendrikus Berkhof, maintained that the offices "represent and articulate the salvation of Christ and so determine the church with authority according to his grace and intentions."[29] M.E. Brinkman goes so far as to claim that in every theology of office certain persons are set aside or emerge who are able to stand and to appear in the name of Another, namely, the Lord.[30] In fact, Ed. Van der Borght, who argues in a particular way for a functional view of office, holds to a representational view of office: "The ordained office-bearer represents the Lord because he is called to the proclamation of the story of the Lord in word and sign, to encouragement and admonition in the midst of human events as they occur."[31]

Not all agree. Dingemans, not surprisingly, states simply that "office does not represent Christ."[32] Beker and Hasselaar argue that although since office represents scripture it does in fact stand "over and against" the congregation, nonetheless it does not represent Christ.[33] M. den Dulk even views the representation of Christ as a

---

[28] *Leuenberger Texte 2*, 34.

[29] Cited in C. Graafland, *Gedachten over het ambt: Och of al het volk des Heeren profeten waren...!* (Zoetermeer: Boekencentrum, 1999), 193.

[30] M.E. Brinkman, "Het ambt als heilzaam symbool in onze cultuur," in *Geen kerk zonder bisschop?*, 107.

[31] Van der Borght, 487.

[32] Dingemans, 134.

[33] Beker and Hasselaar, 186.

temptation to the use and the abuse of power through office.[34] In contrast, in fact, office can be said to represent the *congregation*. Office may be viewed as a particularization of the ministries of the church, and what authority adheres to the office is authority granted by the congregation. That is not to argue that God's Spirit cannot and does not work through office in this derivative manner. It is to maintain that office cannot be viewed as standing in the stead of Christ.

Others, like M. Gosker, take a mediating position. She argues that the office represents Christ. In fact, she makes it clear that this representation is not limited to ministers but includes elders and deacons.[35] She is careful to state that this representation is not as a substitution for Christ (*plaastvervanging*), a "second Christ," but as representing Christ (*plaatsbekleding*), and thus functions in more of an ambassadorial role.[36] But she does not stop with office-bearers as representing Christ. All the church represents God (here she expands representation beyond Christ to that of God). "It is the gift and the task which is entrusted by the Holy Spirit to all believers and to all office-bearers as pioneers of the congregation to bear the Word of God and to reflect the Spirit of Jesus in the midst of the congregation and in the midst of all the world around us."[37]

1.1.6 The Sacramental Nature of Office

Churches diverge on whether office-bearers are sacramental in nature. Said another way, the division is often described as between a view of office as *functional* and *ontological*. L.J. Koffeman remarks that the real difference for the Roman Catholic Church is the *sacra potestas* of the consecrated priest.[38] Indeed, the *Catechism* of the Roman Catholic Church puts it clearly: "The ministerial priesthood differs in essence from the common priesthood of the faithful because it confers a sacred power for the service of the faithful."[39] An ontological change

---

[34] M. den Dulk, "De verzoeking Christus te representeren," in *Geen kerk zonder bisschop?*, 115-129.

[35] Gosker, *Het ambt*, 282. She argues directly against Den Dulk. A version of her argument can be found in her "Ambt als Christusrepresentatie" in *Geen kerk zonder bisschop? Over de plaats van het ambt en de orde van de kerk*, Martien E. Brinkman and Henk Witte, ed. (Zoetermeer: Meinema 1997), 130-145.

[36] Gosker, *Het ambt*, 277.

[37] Gosker, *Het ambt*, 284.

[38] Koffeman, 40.

[39] *Catholic Catechism*, 398. In *Lumen Gentium*, par. 10, the Roman Church claims that all the baptized share in the priestly ministry. However, a

takes place with the office-bearer. He or she becomes different in kind from other believers. The office-bearer remains human, but a change is effected in his fundamental humanity. In fact, some Reformed churches responded negatively to BEM's statement on ministry because they think that they find just such a trajectory toward sacerdotal heirarchy, particularly in the use of the term "priest."[40]

The (former) Reformed Churches in the Netherlands take the opposite position. In its 1969 report, *Kerk in Perspectief*, they view the office as functional in nature. Church is not dependent on office, but office on church.[41] This functional understanding of office is represented by G.D.J. Dingmans, who argues that because the church is built from the bottom upward, ministry consists of certain functional tasks of Word, of Communion, and of service.[42] Those who serve as ministers to the church do not undergo a change in being. A. van de Beek represents the same position: "I would plead that office be seen as a function of the congregation: one of many tasks that must take place there, one of many *charismata*, neither greater nor lesser than others."[43] Office-bearers retain their office during the time of their service, or function. They emerge from the congregation and they return to the congregation.

M. Gosker again offers a mediating position. She attempts to find a way between a sacramental and a functional position. She can find no descriptor for her position, but is insistent that while the office is not sacramentally rooted, nonetheless office is representative of Christ.[44]

Ed. Van der Borght agrees that office is functional as it functions in service to the Word. Functionality assures that office does not stand apart from the task of service to the proclamation of the gospel.[45] Nonetheless, functional language is not sufficient. "The ordained office-bearer represents the Lord because he is called to the

---

difference in essence remains. Walter M. Abbott, ed., *The Documents of Vatican II* (The American Press, 1986), 27. See Van der Borght's analysis, 56-57.

[40] Sell, 560.

[41] See Gosker, *Het ambt*, 228.

[42] Dingemans, 121.

[43] A. van de Beek, "Over protestantse reacties op de ambtsvisie van het rapport over doop, eucharistie en ambt van de Wereldraad van Kerken, in *Tussen traditie en vervreemding: Over kerk en christenzijn in een veranderende cultuur* (Nijkerk: G.F. Callenbach, 1985), 131.

[44] Gosker, *Het ambt*, 266-267.

[45] Van der Borght, 484, 485.

proclamation of the story of the Lord in word and sign, to the encouragement and admonition in the midst of human events as they occur."[46] Van der Borght talks about office in the church as "symbol." M.E. Brinkman also describes office under the category of symbol. As symbol it calls to mind that which is not present at first sight. Office is an instance of a "small and modest indicative sign of a greater reality of grace and mercy in a graceless and unmerciful culture."[47] With Gosker, Van der Borght, and Brinkman, office might be said to be functional, but not in the sense that office is a function *of* the congregation. It is a way to acknowledge that office represents Another without acceding to a theology that asserts an ontology redolent of the notion that an alternation in the substance of the office-bearer has taken place.[48]

1.1.7 The Relation of Ordination to Office

BEM articulates a distinction between ministry and ordained ministry. Ministry "denotes the service to which the whole people of God is called, whether as individuals, as a local community, or as the universal Church. Ministry or ministries can also denote the particular institutional forms which this service may take." Ordained ministry, on the other hand, "refers to persons who have received a charism and whom the church appoints for service by ordination through the invocation of the Spirit and the laying on of hands" (LM, 7). The Roman Catholic Thomas O'Meara in his theology of ministry intends to probe what he calls "lay ministry" in the Roman Catholic Church, a ministry not encapsulated by the ordained offices.[49] For this reason, "ministry" is not equivalent for the term "office."

But neither can we equate "ordained ministry" with office. Van der Borght, for example, insists on a distinction between ordained office, which he reserves for ministers of the Word, and the ecclesiastical offices of elder and deacon, which are not ordained. Elders and deacons do not, according to Van der Borght, represent God in Christ to the congregation, but rather represent the congregation itself. He desires to continue to use office to denote the

[46] Van der Borght, 487.

[47] Brinkman, "Het ambt als heilzaam symbool," 107.

[48] I argue elsewhere that ordination does in fact indicate an ontological change, but that it is the *kind* of ontology that is at issue. "Ministry in Context," *Reformed Review*, 50, no. 1 (Autumn, 1997), 15-26.

[49] O'Meara, 9.

"other" Reformed offices. However, he sees these offices of a different order than that of the ordained.

In recent years, the matter of *ordained* ministry in relation to other ministries of the church has taken on a new urgency. A growing number of churches, understood both as communions and as local congregations, employ nonordained ministers either at presidency of the table or as professional leaders of the local congregation, or both. M. Gosker points to this discussion when she reports that the question whether nonministers or the nonordained may administer the Lord's Supper in the churches involved in *Samen op Weg* in the Netherlands had primarily to do with small churches who could not afford to call a full-time, professional minister of the Word.[50]

Peter Steinfels, scholar and newspaper reporter, in his evaluation of the American Roman Catholic Church, discusses the growing phenomenon of nonordained leadership of parishes.[51] This reality brings to the fore the question of the place of the ordained offices at the center of the life of the local parish. Nor is this only a question for the Roman Catholic Church. The Presbyterian Church (U.S.A.), for example, has what it calls a "lay commissioned pastor."[52] The United Methodist Church in the United States ordains what it denotes as a "local pastor." While this involves ordination, it is not ordination that allows that pastor to exercise pastoral functions beyond the local congregation. In all churches, it is often smaller congregations that stand in need of the sort of ministry that has traditionally been reserved for ordained ministry. This state of affairs would seem to present little challenge to a view of ministry that is fundamentally functional and in which the ministers emerge from the congregation. But because the issue presses in churches of a "higher" theology of office, the question presses itself: how does a common theology of office address this changing reality?

---

50 Gosker, *Het ambt*, 237.

51 Peter Steinfels, *A People Adrift: The Crisis of the Roman Catholic Church in America* (New York: Simon and Schuster, 2003), 330-349.

52 *The Constitution of the Presbyterian Church (U.S.A.) Part II Book of Order 2003-2004* (Louisville: The Office of the General Assembly, 2003), G-14.0801. The "commissioned lay pastor" is defined as "an elder of the Presbyterian Church (U.S.A.), who is granted a local commission by the presbytery to lead worship and preach the gospel, watch over the people, and provide for their nurture and service. He or she is authorized to administer the sacraments."

1.2 Office as an Issue among Reformed Churches

The exploration of the contours of the ecumenical discussion of office has exposed not only differences between communions, but differences among the Reformed churches as well. Indeed, these differences can and often do exist within individual communions. In its intention to contribute to a Reformed understanding of the theology of office, this study situates itself specifically within the Reformed discussion. However, it is clear that it is a continuing discussion; no theology of office has achieved a consensus as "Reformed."

That is not to say that the Reformed enter the ecumenical discussion with no commonalities in the matter of office. Many Reformed churches share a presbyterial-synodical polity that includes within itself the three-fold office of minister, elder, and deacon. And as the responses to BEM's statement on ministry demonstrate, Reformed churches tend to hold firmly to those offices. More important than a shared structure of governance, however, is a lack of common theology of the offices, or why, as a matter of theological principle, the churches should display precisely the structure of offices that they do.

In an essay that discusses the contribution that Reformed churches can make confessionally to the universal church, Margit Ernst claims that "a *particular* Reformed church formulates the provisional insight that is given to the *universal* church."[53] She asks, "what are *the* special themes anyway?"[54] She asks the question in the context of confession. In fact, the offices of the church do in fact appear in at least one confession, *The Belgic Confession*, Article 30.[55] One can at least argue, as will become evident in this study, that if not in the confessions themselves, office is deeply related to the confessional

---

[53] Margit Ernst, "We Believe the One Holy and Catholic Church," in Wallace M. Alston, Jr. and Michael Welker, ed., *Reformed Theology: Identity and Ecumenicity* (Grand Rapids: Eerdmans, 2003), 90. Emphasis in original.

[54] Ernst, 93.

[55] "We believe that this true church
ought to be governed according to the spiritual order
that our Lord has taught us in his word.
There whould be ministers or pastors
to preach the word of God
and administer the sacraments.
There should also be elders and deacons,
along with the pastors,
to make up the council of the church." *Ecumenical Creeds and Reformed Confessions* (Grand Rapids: Eerdmans, 1988), 109.

nature of the church. Thus one can extend Ernst's question to include office: do the Reformed churches offer unique perspectives on a theology of office in the ecumenical discussion on office?

As noted, the Reformed do not agree at important points. First, some see the office as emerging "from below." Others view office as coming "from above" or, alternatively, "from without." H. Oostenbrink-Evers, in a review of the 1951 church order of the Netherlands Reformed Church, notes that in response to that order advocates of episcopal elements in the church would like a bishop-like figure in the church while advocates of a more congregationalist view plead for a lower church order with either a more functional or more charismatic vision of the ministries of the church.[56] In fact, as she sees the matter, under the influence of congregationalist and functional thinking a shift has taken place in an understanding of office from the objective to the subjective.[57] That which comes from "without," the objective, is replaced by that which arises from "within," the subjective. Theological reasons are offered for both approaches. Which is warranted?

Second, differences exist on the number of offices. At issue is not "one or three," as though "three" has a particular significance in itself. The issue is, rather, "one or many." If there is one primary office, as we saw Ed. Van der Borght argue, then how do the other offices of elder and deacon relate? But, one must ask, just what are the offices of elder and deacon? If they differ from the old church's offices of presbyter and deacon, how do they differ? Is there a common Reformed vision and what is common about that vision? Such questions force us to ask: how does "office" differ from other ministries in such a way that elders and deacons are designated as offices in the church?

Third, the exercise of an "office" of oversight is present among the Reformed churches. Historically, Reformed churches have maintained that oversight is exercised by the offices as they are gathered in synods, thus emphasizing the collegial nature of oversight, and continues to be maintained among the churches, particularly as embodied in the church order.[58] Nonetheless, there are students of

---

[56] H. Oostenbrink-Evers, "Het ambt in de kerkorde," in W. Balke, A. van de Beek and J.D.Th. Wassenaar, ed., *De kerk op orde? Vijftig jaar hervormd leven met de kerkorde van 1951* (Zoetermeer: Boekencentrum, 2001), 57.

[57] Oostenbrink-Evers, 63.

[58] The church order of the recently united Protestant Church of the Netherlands, for example, is built on the three traditional Reformed offices of minister, elder, and deacon.

office within the Reformed tradition who advocate an episcopal office in one form or another. In his recent doctoral dissertation, J. Kronenberg advocates strongly for a bishop, albeit one that is pastoral in nature, a symbol of church unity, as representative of the doctrinal tradition of the church and as melded into a system that maintains the advantages of both presbyterial and congregational systems of church governance.[59] Ed. Van der Borght and Margriet Gosker offer a more hesitant[60] approach to the consideration of the office of bishop in the Reformed church. Eugene Heideman, arguing from the example of the Church of South India, advocated a place for "Reformed bishops."[61] The Reformed Church of Hungary alone among Reformed bodies has retained the office of bishop. However, that church also retains the Reformed system of classes and synods that themselves perform the ministry of oversight. The issue of just what *kind* of office a bishop would be within the Reformed church and what that office presents to ecumenical partners, of course, remains.

Fourth, the Reformed churches differ on the question of representation. Do the offices represent Christ? Do they represent God in Christ? Or put another way, is what representation that may exist Christological or pneumatological? We noted above (1.1.5) that Gosker, Dingemans, Berkhof and Beker, and Hasselaar take different positions on this matter. Again, it is a question whether the Reformed can come to a theological understanding of office that would adjudicate this matter.

One can respond that the Reformed have no common theology of office. They display certain familiar traits that include a church order that is, at best, rooted in a shared history. Even should that be the case, one wonders whether a common theological warrant did in fact exist for the church order that emerged. Does it express in some way how God interacts with humanity, at least as the Reformed understood it? It is not the purpose of this study to engage in an archeological study of the development of Reformed church order. Such a task, valuable as it is, exceeds the reach of this inquiry.

---

[59] *Episcopus Oecumenicus.* See especially his conclusions, 268-269.

[60] For Van der Borght, see *Het ambt her-dacht*, 344 and 502. For Gosker see *Het ambt in de oecumenische discussie*, 358.

[61] Eugene P. Heideman, *Reformed Bishops and Catholic Elders* (Grand Rapids: Eerdmans, 1970). Heideman's study remains important because like Kronenberg, he argues that both the elder and the bishop are important offices in a united church. He is also interesting because, also like Kronenberg, he was a student of Van Ruler's theology.

However, the question is in large part an occasion for this study. We intend to probe one particular view, that of the Dutch theologian A.A. van Ruler, to inquire whether a coherent theology of office is possible from a Reformed perspective. The intent is not to repristinate a way of thinking about office that would result in a practice neither no longer present nor possible. It is, instead, perhaps to rediscover a way of thinking about office in such a way that it can be examined.

Once examined, we can then ask whether it is of sufficient value to enter the discussion either among the Reformed or ecumenically. Does it offer an understanding of office that is both *usable* and *theologically valid*?

1.3 A Way Forward

The impasse over office in the ecumenical discussion and the lack of unanimity among the Reformed are of themselves not sufficient motive for this study. The description of the nature of the discussion is helpful, but only as it provides the condition for further study. Rather one needs to ask how one might find a way forward. A number of ways have been attempted.

One way is that of *comparative ecclesiology*. Churches and theologians have been forced to offer a clear description of how they understand the nature of the church and, consequently, of the order of the church and the nature of office within the church. This method has had the advantage of forcing theological clarity among the partners to the discussion. This is true not only as partners to the discussion are moved beyond caricature and polemics in their rejection of the offices of other churches; it has compelled the communions themselves to understand and value their own ecclesiological commitments. The discussion can uncover deep commonalities as the partners see in the other's ecclesiology something of their own commitments. More, the conversation can waken communions to forgotten or ignored demands of the gospel as the interchange, for example, highlights the prophetic or the priestly or the royal aspect of the nature of the church.

This approach, however, has not and cannot break the impasse on ministry. The partners in the discussion come to the point where the differences can be described but not resolved. BEM reached that point in its section on ministry when it could only note the areas that require further work by the partner churches. NPC, the further product of the Faith and Order Commission, really advanced little further. Many churches still do not recognize the ministry of other communions. The impasse remains.

A second approach is that of *scripture*. This is particularly attractive to Reformed churches.[62] If a joint inquiry into scripture could find at least certain principles on which a theology of office could be constructed, or at least could construct a framework within which the various churches could acknowledge the view of office that each has taken, then the way would be paved for a mutual recognition of office. And indeed, attempts have been made by the partners in the discussion to root their particular understanding of office in scripture.

This approach has proven to be futile. M.E. Brinkman has maintained that scripture does not resolve the differences and that for a particular reason: "Just as our confessional viewpoint influences our interpretation of the past for interpretation of the historical data, so also our confessional viewpoint influences our exegesis of the New Testament data about the Church's pattern of ministry."[63] The work of C. Graafland illustrates Brinkman's point. Graafland states his approach to office compactly and clearly when he allows that only what appears in scripture will contribute to an understanding of office. It is "*alleen de Schrift en heel de Schrift*" [only what is in scripture and the entire of scripture].[64] Using that approach, Graafland finds little mention of office in scripture. He concludes that there is no biblical basis, let alone necessity, for a doctrine of office that is valid for all ages. Hence there is no theological warrant for either the title nor the number of offices in the church. The result is a minimalist approach to office. What scripture does not require is not necessary for the being of the church. Thus, for example, when he comments on Ephesians 4, he remarks that certain tasks mentioned there can contribute to the *bene esse* of the church but not of the *esse*.[65]

---

[62] See Haitjema, *Nederlands hervormd kerkrecht* (Nijkerk: Callenbach, 1951), 15, 16, where he notes that Reformed church order is built on scriptural principles. See also A.J. Bronkhorst, *Schrift en kerkorde: Een bijdrage tot het onderzoek naar de mogelijkheid van een "schriftuurlijke kerkorde"* (Den Haag: Zuid-Holland Boek- en Handelsdrukkerij, 1947). A recent essay from an American Reformed theologian is offered by James Brownson, "Elder-Pastors and Deacon-Evangelists: The Plurality of Offices and the Marks of the Church," *Reformed Review* 56, no. 3 (Spring, 2003), 235-248.

[63] M.E. Brinkman, "Ministry and Sacrament in a Dutch Context," in Martien E. Brinkman and Henk Witte, ed., *From Roots to Fruits: Protestants and Catholics Towards a Common Understanding of the Church* (Geneva: World Alliance of Reformed Churches, 1998), 145.

[64] Graafland, 256.

[65] Graafland, 329.

Graafland's approach is fair enough, but it has taken a theological decision prior to the inquiry into office. That is, his claim *alleen de Schrift en heel de Schrift* claims that scripture is not only necessary but sufficient for a doctrine of office. That is to betray a prior confessional commitment. And that commitment influences the outcome of the study.

If Brinkman is correct, then the discussion must find a different framework in which to take place. Is it perhaps a *theological* discussion that either needs to take place or in fact does so if albeit at times at a subterranean level? At issue is more than a discrete matter of ministry of the church as it might be institutionalized in one of many possible ways, as though ministry is a sort of "delivery system" for what is of true significance in God's dealings with this world. Ministry is, rather, part and parcel of an entire way of conceiving *God's* way with the world. That is, office has something to do with the nature of God.

If an understanding of office betrays a particular understanding of God, then resistance to alternate views of ministry is understandable. Challenges to a church's understanding of ministry call fundamental confessional commitments into question. A church insists on the shape of its ministry because that shape is deeply connected to the gospel itself.

A theological approach shifts the conversation from immediate concern with offices themselves. It asks of the interlocutors what their particular understanding of office betrays of their theological commitment. This suggests that the discussion on ministry will advance as the discussion becomes a full-bodied theological conversation. For that reason it will be necessary to explore the warrant or sources for theological truth, the nature of God, the way that God engages the world in Christ and through the Spirit, and how God uses the church in God's purposes. If fundamental theological commitments are ignored or passed over in the discussion of office, they will return surreptitiously to impede further progress in discussion. Only as churches engage theologically will a way forward be found.

As the discussion of office takes place within the broader theological conversation, we can then approach a set of theological questions about office itself. What does it mean to call something an "office"? Does office signify something other than ministry in the church? What warrant exists to call some ministry "office" in contrast to other ministries? How and why do we ordain to some offices and not to others? What is the relation of office to the ministry of all believers? Indeed, is office a function of the church? That is does ministry emerge from the church, or does it in some way come to the church? And, as this study will spend a great deal of time exploring, how does office fit within God's actions with this world?

Nonetheless, theological engagement, even when it leads, if not to agreement, to a place where differing theological commitments are not church dividing, still may not be sufficient to break the impasse. George W. Stroup cites the instance of two agreements between representatives from Reformed and Orthodox churches on the central doctrines of the Trinity and of Christology. Will this agreement provide a ground from which the differences in understandings of the church and ministry can be addressed? Stroup doubts that the questions concerning "authority in the life of the church, the church's relation to its social and political context, and the ordination of women" will be easily resolved.[66]

The reason, Stroup advances, is that differences among the churches in ecclesiology and ministry are not only theological differences. They express differences in what Stroup, following Ludwig Wittgenstein, calls "forms of life."[67] It is a matter of the *grammar* and the *habitus* that form and display the identity of particular communions. To shift Stroup's vocabulary, we can think of it as a difference in *religion*, if we understand religion in the sense of an entire way of being. That is, it includes not only confession and theology, but the shape of life that a particular expression of the faith has taken. It includes language, habits, liturgy, the shape of the society in which the church lives as it is been shaped by a particular church. Anton Houtepen articulates the religious world in which ecclesiastical office is viewed:

> We know, whether we intend it or not, a separate clerical class of those freed for the work of the church. The architectonic structure of our church buildings continues to be an imitation of the temple. The liturgy of the temple and the vocabulary of the pilgrimage, purification, atonement, altar, tabernacle, and holy matters continue to determine our view of the sacraments and the area of the tasks of the offices of the church.[68]

---

[66] George W. Stroup, "Reformed Identity in an Ecumenical World," in Wallace M. Alston, Jr. and Michael Welker, ed., *Reformed Theology: Identity and Ecumenicity* (Eerdmans: Grand Rapids, 2003). 269, 270.

[67] Stroup, 264.

[68] Houtepen, 43. A brief but illustrative discussion of the how the offices in the Reformed churches shaped culture can be found in Philip Benedict,

To probe the religious world that divides communions is not to be done separately from theological inquiry. In fact, an attempt to explicate the full religious world as the framework for office is beyond the scope of my project. However, if it is understood that theology both provides a way of understanding religious "forms of life" and that theology has helped to create and to reinforce those ways of life, then theological investigation can assist in finding a way ahead.

This study is intended as a modest contribution to this broader theological investigation. It is modest because it explores the contribution to a theology of office by one Reformed theologian of the mid-twentieth century, A.A. van Ruler. In a discussion of the variety of understandings of office in the Netherlands Reformed Church in the last half of the twentieth century, J. Kronenberg lists a congregational stream, an episcopal "high church" stream, and the presbyterial stream. The later is represented by Van Ruler.[69] This study limits its probe into a Reformed understanding to this stream as represented by one theologian.

At the same time it intends to be a genuine contribution. As will be seen in the following section, Van Ruler wrote and spoke a great deal on office and its theology. However, it is clear that he understood office from within a coherent theological point of view. By listening to Van Ruler as he sets out his theology of the kingdom and by seeing where and how office is to be understood from within that framework, we gain a clearer view of how one (main) stream of Reformed theology views office. More, one meets in Van Ruler an understanding of office as part and parcel of religion or a "way of life" initiated in the Reformation and which can consequently be understood theologically. Van Ruler can assist Reformed thinkers as they come to the ecumenical table both by enabling clarity of thought and by clarifying what is at stake in the conversation.

1.4 A.A. van Ruler

A.A. van Ruler was born on 10 December 1908 in Apeldoorn, the Netherlands, to orthodox-Reformed parents.[70] Apeldoorn is

---

Christ's Churches Purely Reformed: A Social History of Calvinism (New Haven: Yale, 2002), 451-459.

69 Kronenberg, 158. Not only the Netherlands Reformed Church, but the new Protestant Church of the Netherlands adopted a presbyterial-synodical system of church order.

70 Much of the material for this biographical sketch is drawn from Aart de Groot, "Levenschets van Prof. Dr. A.A. van Ruler," in Ellen M.L. Kempers,

located in the Veluwe, a place of natural beauty, of sandhills and forests. It was also characterized by a Calvinism of a heavy "experiential" sort, heir to the so-called "*nadere Reformatie*" ["further Reformation"]. Throughout his life, Van Ruler would engage this mode of being Reformed critically but appreciatively.[71]

A promising student in his early years, he was interested in mathematics, science, and philosophy. Already in gymnasium, he began to read theology, including the works of Kuyper, Bavink, Barth, and Thurneysen. At this early date he also became acquainted with the thinking of Ph. J. Hoedemaker and his later teacher Th. L. Haitjema. In fact, by the time he was seventeen, he had begun to form the theological project that would engage him throughout his life. In response to a question from J.M. Hasselaar whether his thought had developed throughout his career, Van Ruler replied: "No, by my 17th year I knew clearly what I would be about, I had a plan, or to say it dryly, a scheme: it has expanded, deepened, been enriched, but it has remained the same from my 17th year." When asked what that scheme was, he replied: "Theocracy and that it must be that Schleiermacher's question is a genuine question: revelation is service - salvation, but then service and the development of humanity."[72]

In 1927 he enrolled in the University of Groningen as a student in theology. There he continued to follow the developments of dialectical theology, particularly that of Barth and Brunner. He also became deeply acquainted with the thought of H.F. Kohlbrugge. He counted among major influences as teachers, beside Haitjema, the religious historian G. van der Leeuw and W. Aalders. It was with the latter that he prepared for his doctoral examination. His "major" was the philosophy of religion with primary emphasis on Hegel,

---

Inventaris van het archief van Prof.Dr. Arnold Albert van Ruler (1908-1970) (Utrecht: Universiteitbibliotheek, 1997) ix-xvi; and Paul R. Fries, "A Biographical Sketch of A.A. van Ruler," in *Religion and the Hope for a Truly Human Existence: An Inquiry into the Theology of F.D.E. Schleiermacher and A. A. Van Ruler with Questions for America* (n.p., 1979) 214-219.

71 The last article he wrote before he died was a long article entitled "Ultragereformeerd en vrijzinnig," an evaluation of the heretical tendencies in the approach of the "ultra"-Reformed and the liberals. The heresy of the liberals, he argued, was "child's play" in comparison with that of the orthodox Reformed. The article is found, with responses, in *Op het scherp van de snede: Posthuum gesprek met prof. dr. A.A. van Ruler* (Amsterdam: Ton Bolland, 1972). It is also found in *Theologisch Werk III* (Nijkerk: Callenbach: 1971) 98-163.

72 J.M. Hasselaar and H.W. de Knijff, "Arnold Albert van Ruler (1908-1970): Zijn leven. Zijn actualiteit," *Areopagus* 14, no. 2 (1981), 63.

Kierkegaard, and Troeltsch, figures he would engage throughout his theological life. In fact, he planned to write a dissertation on Troeltsch.

First, however, he entered the parish in 1933 as a minister in a Reformed church[73] in Kubaard. Soon after his installation as pastor, he was married to Joanna Adriana Hamelink. She not only became his life partner, but following his death would become active in publication of many of Van Ruler's theological works.

Kubaard was an important beginning for Van Ruler. The congregation was of a "confessional" sort.[74] There Van Ruler followed developments of the national church. He also published his first major work, a study of Abraham Kuyper's doctrine of common grace, *Kuypers idee eener christelijke cultuur.* Van Ruler displayed appreciation for Kuyper, but offered early signal of Van Ruler's clear distancing from Kuyper's antitheoretical approach.

In February 1940 Van Ruler moved to Hilversum where he became pastor. Three months after his arrival, the Second World War broke out. A good part of the normal work of the church came to a halt. The Hilversum period was in part characterized by a group of theological students that Van Ruler gathered at his home one Saturday evening a month for seven years.[75] By all reports Van Ruler was a genial and welcoming host and the evenings were an inviting place where participants learned to develop their own theological views. The group began by reading together Haitjema's *Het erfgoed der Hervorming.* Soon, however, Van Ruler began to read a number of essays and lectures that would be published after the war under the title, *Religie en politiek.*

The Hilversum years were important for another reason, however. It was there that he completed his doctoral dissertation. His original subject, Troeltsch, no longer attracted him. Under the press of

---

[73] The Netherlands Reformed Church.

[74] The "confessional" movement in the Netherlands Reformed Church emerged in the nineteenth century and was characterized by a return to the confessional commitments of the Reformed church from its earliest days of the Reformation. It is often connected with the thought of Ph. J. Hoedemaker (who, however, himself declined to be part of a church "party"). Hoedemaker's thought would have profound influence on Van Ruler's own thinking. On the "confessional" way of thought, see Th. L. Haitjema, *De richtingen in de Nederlandse Hervormde Kerk,* 2nd ed., (Wageningen: Veenman, 1953), 142-170.

[75] See P.F. Th. Aalders, "De Hilversumse theologenklub," *Areopagus* 14, no.2 (1981), 18-20.

the war years and the emergence of national socialism as a theological challenge, he shifted his subject to "church and state." Following Aalders's retirement, now under the supervision of Haitjema, his subject became the relation of God's revelation to human existence. He did much of the work on the dissertation in the "hunger winter" in the last year of the war, in the basement of the Hilversum church, with little heat to keep him warm. The dissertation appeared in 1947 as *De vervulling van de wet*. The work remains as the primary statement of Van Ruler's theological commitments.

It was also during his pastorate in Hilversum that Van Ruler was appointed by the General Synod to the commission that would work on the principles of a new church order. Already in the 1930s Van Ruler had been a member of *Kerkherstel*, a party in the Netherlands Reformed Church that advocated a new church order.[76] The commission prepared a "work order" (a provisional church order) that enabled the gathering of a general synod that was constituted by the entire church. That synod in turn appointed a new commission to prepare a permanent church order. Van Ruler was also a member of this body. In fact, his voice was so prominent that one prominent historian would claim that the church order bears Van Ruler's imprint.[77] Van Ruler would defend the proposed order before the general synod and would write a number of books and articles advocating the principles of this "apostolic" church order. One researcher would say that the secretary for the commission, H.M.J. Wagenaar, was the "pragmaticus and Van Ruler the dogmaticus" for the new church order.[78] Following the adoption of the church order, Van Ruler was appointed as chair of a commission to work out a comprehensive Reformed theology of office. To his regret, that commission could not achieve a consensus. The report for which he was responsible was not submitted to the general synod, and it was not until after his death that the report was distributed.

The years after the war engaged Van Ruler in yet another way. He participated actively in the Protestant Union, a political party established to promote the theocratic ideals of Hoedemaker—the

---

76 Two main groups appeared in the 1930s, *Kerkherstel* ["Church re-establishment"] and *Kerkopbouw* ["Building up the church"]. Both groups were part of a larger struggle to break through the impasse that emerged from the 1816 church order. On this see Bartels, *Tien jaren strijd om een belijdende kerk, de Nederlandsche Hervormde Kerk van 1929 tot 1939* ('s-Gravenhage: W.P. van Stockum, 1946).

77 Otto J. de Jong, *Nederlandse kerkgeschiedenis* (Nijkerk: Callenbach, 1978), 400.

78 H. Oostenbrink-Evers, cited in Groot, xiii.

establishment of society on the principles of scripture and the Reformed confessions.[79] His primary role was as a spokesperson and as chair of a "platform committee." The party had little success; none of its candidates were elected to parliament. Van Ruler continued to work with the party until health forced him to conserve his energy for other work. Eventually he would distance himself somewhat from the party.

In 1947 he was named as church professor at the University of Utrecht. He followed M.J.A. de Vrijer, and his primary areas of responsibility were in biblical theology, Dutch church history, and domestic and foreign missions ("apostolate"). In 1952 he would take over the responsibilities of his colleague at Utrecht, S.F.H.J. Berkelbach van der Sprenkel, by then retired, and assume the areas of dogmatics, Christian ethics, history of the Netherlands Reformed Church (including its liturgical and symbolic literature), and ecclesiastical polity [*kerkrecht*].

By all accounts he was a popular professor. In any case, his lectures were often crowded. Certainly he was a gracious colleague. Fellow professors reported that his study was always open for conversation. Indeed, he was gracious in his dealings with faculty who did not share his theological perspective. Hasselaar tells how when he was appointed to work as Van Ruler's colleague, Van Ruler welcomed him to the faculty. "But I am not a Van Rulerian," Hasselaar replied. To which Van Ruler answered: "That is not so important. I trust that when you speak about me that you will do so honorably and that you will set out what is thematically important for me."[80]

Van Ruler's relation with his students is illustrated by his visits with former students. Every summer for many years, Van Ruler and his wife would visit former students, especially as they struggled in their first pastorates.[81] Until ill health made it too difficult, they would make the visits on bicycles, sharing a meal, listening to questions, but also inquiring as to whether the pastor had kept up his studies. Rumor even had it that some pastors would borrow from the libraries of their colleagues to make their own libraries more presentable for the visit from the professor!

In addition to his work at the university, Van Ruler was well known in the nation for his popular morning meditations broadcast

---

[79] On this see H. van Spanning, *In dienst van de theocratie: Korte geschiedenis van de Protestantse Unie in de Centrumgespreksgroep in het CHU* (Zoetermeer: Boekencentrum, 1994).

[80] Hasselaar and De Knijff, 60.

[81] J.A. van Ruler-Hamelink, "500 Pastorieën," *Areopagus* 14, no. 2 (1981) 8-11.

on the radio. He continued this work until the day he died. Many of his meditations were collected and published in a number of volumes. Always popular but never simplistic, they provide a balance to his more theological works. Indeed, anyone looking for the biblical warrant for Van Ruler's theological positions is advised to consult these works. Nor was he a stranger to the pulpit. He preached, on average, about fifty times a year.[82]

As one who maintained that matter is holy, he enjoyed the beauty of the everyday. He would delight in the playful shock in remarking, for example, that sanctification also is about the enjoyment of a match between Ajax and Feyenoord (two Dutch soccer clubs). And indeed he welcomed the arrival of television as a means of relaxation, especially as it allowed him to watch soccer.[83]

His later years, however, were somber. He felt as though few had traveled with him on his theological journey. "I sometimes feel as though at present I sit with Tito in the mountains and that I lead a complete partisan-existence; I am busy all by myself, battling enormous armies."[84]

After having lived with ill health for many years, he suffered a series of heart attacks. The third attack killed him December 15, 1970, and he died in his book-filled study. He was still a relatively young man with a number of projects left unfinished.

In an article on the "meaning of the institutional (in the church)," Van Ruler considers the ecumenical question of whether Reformed churches should accept the office of bishop for the sake of church unity:

> In view of the numerical relations within the world [Reformed churches together constitute a relatively small part of the world church, AJ], the question becomes ever more insistent to me whether we must not give up the presbyterial-synodical form of church governance and must accept the bishop—with all his authority and thus not purely ornamentally or as historical figure—as a sign of unity. Personally, I am convinced that the presbyterial-synodical form of church governance is the purest,

[82] While most of his sermons remain unpublished, they are catalogued in Kempers and are available in the Van Ruler Archive.

[83] K. van der Zwaag, "Een 'vrijage' met de Bond," at http://out.refdat.nl/series/toonzetters/99042707.html, accessed February 15, 2004.

[84] G.C. Berkouwer and A.S. van der Woude, *In gesprek met Van Ruler* [Hereinafter *Gesprek*] (Nijkerk: Callenbach, 1969), 34.

> the most catholic and the closest to the New Testament that has been reached thus far. I even maintain that its abolition would touch even the structure of religion. Still I maintain that we must seriously consider whether we may still hold on to it or must not give way on this point for the sake of the unity of truth.[85]

Van Ruler was a passionate exponent of the unity of the church. This unity could not be merely conciliar, nor could it be understood as "spiritual." Mutual conversation, worship, and common witness are important gains toward church unity, he argued. But that can be like an "intoxicating drink" that blinds us to the real issue, that the church *is* one. And further, that the church is to be organizationally and institutionally one.[86] This institutional ecumenical commitment would lead to the question of church order. He maintained that it was the church order that is the "unavoidable finishing touch of all ecumenical work."[87]

Nonetheless, while Van Ruler argued passionately for a church union that would find expression in a church order and would thus include the offices of the church, he also offered a coherent and detailed defense of the presbyterial-synodical system. Immediately following the statement we quoted above from his article on the significance of the institutional, he hastens to add:

> The presbyterial-synodical system is a complete form of church governance in itself. It also gives a clear answer to the question where, in the matter of church order, the authority of Christ is to be found. For this reason it appears to me that it is an impossible attempt to graft a bishop onto that system and that a mixture of episcopal and presbyterian facts must come down to an abrogation, or at least a total diminishment of the idea underlying the presbyterial-synodical system. So far as, for example, one has situated the elder and the deacon in their new

---

85 A.A. van Ruler, "De betekenis van het institutaire (in de kerk)" [Herinafter "Institutaire"], in *TW 4*, 195.

86 A.A. van Ruler, "Oecumenisch is: maar één kerk te willen," in *Blij zijn als kinderen: een boek voor volwassenen* [Hereinafter *Blij zijn*] (Kampen: Kok, 1972), 167, 168. In a sermon, "Naar de eenheid van de kerken" (preached January 22, 1961, in Haarlem), Van Ruler Archive, IV, 819, p. 2, Van Ruler claims that the "kernel of the ecumenical question is: how do the existing churches become one church, one visible, spiritual church, confessionally, liturgically, in church order?"

87 A.A. van Ruler, "Na vier en een halve eeuw reformatie," in *Blij zijn*, 171.

> ecumenical synthesis as "lay elements" or "the representatives of the congregation," this underlying ideal is not only completely diminished, but even totally abolished.[88]

Van Ruler is a Reformed theologian who is fully committed to the ecumenical project, so much so that unity must, for him, include structural unity. At the same time, he represents a fully worked-out theology of office from a Reformed perspective. The passages from Van Ruler's article just cited provide a context from which we offer seven reasons why he is of interest for this sustained study on ecclesiastical office.

First, he gave sustained attention to the question of office and its theology. He wrote and spoke on the topic throughout his theological career. As a young man, already in 1930, he delivered a lecture on *Kerk en kerkorganisatie* ["Church and its organization"].[89] His interest coincided with the movement within the Netherlands Reformed Church to establish a new church order, a process that reached its climax in 1951. While writing a number of short books around the discussion of the proposed church order, he also wrote a major monograph on office, *Bijzonder en algemeen ambt* ["Particular and general office"] in 1952. He continued to write and to lecture not only on the theology of office in general, but on the particular offices within the Reformed church as well. His later work includes both a response of a Reformed theologian to the Second Vatican Council, *Reformatorische opmerkingen in de ontmoeting met Rome* ["Remarks from the Reformation in the meeting with Rome"] (1965) and an ecclesiological essay *Waarom zou ik naar de kerk gaan?* ["Why should I go to church?"] (1970). The former includes major sections that expound a doctrine of office. The latter also includes reflections on office from within Van Ruler's mature ecclesiological commitments. His lectures in Reformed polity at Utrecht, his preliminary studies for works on office, and his occasional lectures and essays betray a deep commitment to the topic.

Second, Van Ruler theologizes on office as a *Reformed* theologian. He fully worked out a theology behind the familiar Reformed "triad" of minister-elder-deacon. While he did not view the particular triad of Reformed offices in themselves as sacrosanct, he did maintain that the presbyterial-synodical system was most adequate to a biblical understanding of God's way with the world. As will be clear

[88] Van Ruler, "Institutaire," 195.

[89] Van Ruler, "Kerk en kerkorganisatie," a lecture for the youth organization, "Daniel," Apeldoorn, August 15, 1930, in Van Ruler Archive, I, 35.

from this study, he differed from many of his Reformed colleagues in his theology of office. For example, with his insistence that office stands "over and against" the church he distances himself from those who would view office as emerging from the priesthood of believers. Nor would his notion that the offices are an expression of the apostolic nature of the church win agreement from all Reformed theologians.

The Reformed nature of his theology undoubtedly was in large part due to his intense involvement in the reorganization efforts of the Netherlands Reformed Church. He was very much a theologian of the church who gave unstintingly to the church in which he was a minister and professor. As we have seen in the sketch of his life above, his participation in the commissions that prepared the church order as well as his involvement with office was to result in his chairmanship of a commission of the Netherlands Reformed Church to formulate a theology of office following the adoption of the church order in 1951.[90]

Despite demurs from within Reformed circles, Van Ruler's theology of office appeals to roots in the Reformed branch of the Reformation. For this reason alone his theology deserves attention from within the Reformed family as it wrestles amidst the confusion of its own understanding of office.

Third, although Reformed, Van Ruler understood himself as a theologian of the *church*. His commitment to a theology of office was not to confirm Reformed churches in their particular and peculiar existence, but as a contribution to the ecumenical task. As we have seen from the citations from his 1959 article, he would be deeply troubled by Reformed thinkers ready to cede a Reformed notion of office for the sake of ecclesiastical unity. He would himself not take a back seat to any Reformed in his commitment to the unity of the church. Nonetheless, thinkers who were ready to give in to an episcopal way of ordering the church, for example, had lost sight of the treasures offered by a Reformed view of office.

Van Ruler's approach intended to profile the sharp contours of office within a Reformed church order both for the sake of Reformed churches *and* for the sake of church unity. He gives as his first reason for his study on office in 1952 that within the ecumenical movement, the question of office is at issue in a fundamental and nettlesome

[90] See J. Kronenberg, 130-133, for the background of the commission on ecclesiastical office as response to the Hilversum Convent, a Catholicizing movement within the Netherlands Reformed Church.

way.[91] His commitment to both the Reformed church and to the ecumenical movement make him a particularly important figure within the ongoing conversation.

Fourth, Van Ruler's theology of office can only be understood within his entire theological project. That and how this is so will be a large part of the burden of this study. At this point we can only claim that he gives us a way of seeing how office emerges from a theology that is concerned to show God's way not only with the human but with all creation. Against this background, other theologies of office will have the burden to surface the theological commitments that they betray. However, to see this in each instance requires time and attention to an entire theology.

Fifth, Van Ruler's theology of office is sharp and particular in its own right. As we shall see, office and the offices are to be understood from within an ecclesiology that is itself resolutely eschatological. That is, rooted as they are in the office of the apostle, itself an office not of the church but of the kingdom of God, the offices do not emerge from the church, but come to the church from God's future. They can be understood only as the kingdom is understood, and as the church's place within that kingdom is understood.

Sixth, his theological work on office did not remain theoretical but engaged the offices as they function within the Reformed churches, or at least the Reformed church that he knew, the Netherlands Reformed Church. He wrote and spoke of the everyday work of the elder, the deacon, and the minister, and did so from a resolutely theological perspective. This approach allows the opportunity to see in office an expression of a "form of life" lived out in church and society. It will also enable us to ask whether and how this view might still hold in churches of the early twenty-first century.

Seventh, this study is one of the few studies in English to reflect on an aspect of Van Ruler's theology. A few good studies have introduced him to the English-speaking world; they are noted below in footnotes and in the bibliography. Their number is few, however. They explicate particular areas of his theology; none focuses on his doctrine of office. Furthermore, very little of Van Ruler's theological oeuvre has been translated into English; unfortunately that includes none of his longer major works. To the extent that this study furthers knowledge of and interest in Van Ruler's theology, it has in part succeeded.

---

[91] Van Ruler, *Bijzonder en algemeen ambt* [Hereinafter *Bijzonder*] (Nijkerk: Callenbach, 1952), 9.

1.5 The Approach of this Study

This study is a *dogmatic* inquiry into Van Ruler's doctrine of office and in its implications for ecumenical discussions, particularly in North America. It is, thus, not a theological-historical study that would, for example, probe Van Ruler's theological pedigree. Such an approach would trace the development of doctrine, particularly in a Dutch context, from the nineteenth century and the influences of such figures as J.H. Gunning, Jr., H. Bavink, Ph. J. Hoedemaker, Th. L. Haitjema and others on Van Ruler's thought. It is also not a historical study. Such a study would follow the struggle over office and the order of the church, particularly from early to mid-twentieth century in the Netherlands. One would then pay particular attention to figures like O. Noordmans, H. Kraemer, and later H. Berkhof, to identify a few. Instead, this study attempts to discover the theology of office as it emerges from Van Ruler's theological work thereby to offer a profile of a robust theology of office.

To discover Van Ruler's understanding of office, we consult two types of sources. The first is his published oeuvre. This includes a number of major works, including most importantly, his doctoral dissertation, *De vervulling van de wet.* But it also includes the aforementioned work on office, his response to Rome, and his late work on the church. Other published works include the variety of small books and articles published at the time of the institution of the new church order for the Netherlands Reformed Church. In addition, a number of occasional articles and lectures are published in the six-volume *Theologisch Werk*, most of which was published posthumously.

A second type of source is Van Ruler's unpublished work. This body of work includes a great number of lectures, speeches, preliminary studies for future theological projects, and preparation for courses he taught at the University of Utrecht. It also includes nearly two thousand sermons preached throughout his career as well as correspondence. This study will include the examination of a number of unpublished sermons. This is done to illustrate both that office occupied a central place in Van Ruler's thought, and that his reflection on his theological positions emerged from his work with scripture. Most of these documents are collected by the Van Ruler Archive, housed in the University Library of the University of Utrecht, the Netherlands. This study investigates a number of unpublished documents that disclose Van Ruler's understanding of office.[92]

We noted above that Van Ruler offers a theological approach to office and does so from within a larger theological framework. His understanding determines the three signal concepts of this study: kingdom, church, and office. In fact, his theology sets them in a particular order. We shall investigate first kingdom, then church, and finally office for reasons articulated below. However, that order is only a means of understanding how office is related to the church from the perspective of the kingdom of God. For, in fact, office *precedes* church, and that in several ways. First, office as situated in the kingdom of God is constitutive for the church in that office comes *to* the church as representative of the triune God. Second, office is "ahead" of the church in that office comes to the church from God's future. Office is situated eschatologically. And third, office consequently comes to the church from the past, from events that have already taken place in Palestine. How this works from a future that finds its purchase in the past is to be worked out within this study. Here we simply note that Van Ruler's is an approach of considerable theological reach.

For this reason, while one comes across tantalizing and lucid references to office in a great number of places in his work, they can be understood only as one has a grasp of Van Ruler's entire theological project. The *argument* of this study, then, proceeds as follows:

I. We shall examine Van Ruler's theology of the kingdom of God, describing that kingdom not as other-worldly, but following Van Ruler's contention that reality is one. God works on the plane of history. Van Ruler argues that God takes the human utterly seriously, so much so that God does not intend to elevate the human but to save the human and indeed to engage the human in God's work with the created reality. If God acts in history, God does so eschatologically. That is, God comes to the present from the future. It is a future, however, that reaches into the past. We shall see all of time and history in an eschatological perspective. This does not however, so the argument moves, vitiate the past. God's ultimate intentions are for *creation*. It is creation as the kingdom of God that is to be enjoyed by the human. But the human will be able to do so only as *saved*. The Messiah comes to atone for the sin that the human brings. It will be crucial to note that for Van Ruler, the point of it all is not the Savior, but the saved. The Messiah comes as an "emergency measure" to atone

---

92 Unless otherwise noted, all translations of the Dutch in this study will be the author's.

before God. The ascended Messiah rules as the kingdom of Christ is a manifestation of the kingdom of God. Still it is not the Messiah alone who is at work. God also acts through the Spirit. The Spirit extends and expands what God is about as the Spirit engages the human, fully as human, in the work of the kingdom as it is set toward the future. This, then, is the trinitarian God who is at work, the God who will meet created reality in multifarious ways.

II. The church is a means through which God works in history. We will maintain that Van Ruler views the church as both bearer of the gospel, as it points away from itself *and* as itself a gestalt of the kingdom. The church is itself apostolic in that it has as its task not its own existence but the proclamation of the kingdom. This will express itself in the predestinarian heart of the church, as called and used by the sovereignly free God in achieving God's original and ultimate intentions. If used by God, the church is set within an eschatological horizon. It works within God's historical action of "Christianizing" society and culture; it does so not only with those who find their way into the church, but with a "world" that includes the state, society, indeed the people, or the *volk*. We shall see that this is a church that is confessional, but that is institutional as well. The church as a particular gestalt provides the transition to Van Ruler's later emphasis on the liturgical nature of the church. The church itself is a place where the human comes to his or her own as she experiences creation as God's kingdom and learns to live fully in God's presence. In and with the church, we can see Van Ruler's theology of the kingdom of God take purchase in a particular way.

III. Office now comes to bear as a means that God uses to come to the church, to establish the church, and to work through the church. The theology of office presented here picks up both predestination and eschatology as we will have already seen it at work. Now it is God using persons and coming to the church and humans from God's future. As such, office represents the Messiah, but does so as a moment in the work of the Spirit. As such, we will come to the important conclusion that we have to do with offices as the variegated work of God. We will have seen office as the work of the trinitarian God. This is office as it comes to the church now to establish the human and enable the human to see and experience creation as kingdom. For office "connects" revelation and existence as it communicates to the human what the human cannot know: that atonement takes place before God. This, then will be the office in the economy of salvation.

Office is rooted in the kingdom, and it is so as it has its origin in the office of the apostle. The apostolic nature of the church is, then, borne not by bishops, but by the offices themselves.

At this point in the argument we will be in a position to maintain that the notion of the priesthood of believers is used by Van Ruler in support of his main contention. For it will be clear that office does not emerge from below, as a particularization of the priesthood that all believers share. Rather, what "office" believers have is over and against the nonbeliever.

In this context it will then be possible to make clear just what relation exists between offices and the congregation. For we will have made clear that God, in the Spirit, works through the congregation to elect, ordain, and support the offices. At the same time, the offices establish, encourage, and in some senses embody the church itself.

IV. The apostolic nature of the offices set within the horizon of the kingdom can be made clear through a detailed inventory of how Van Ruler sees the particular offices in their various functions. We will see the elder in his primary task of sanctification, the deacon in his work of justice and mercy, and the minister in the proclamation of the gospel, all set not primarily within the walls of the church, but extra-ecclesia, within the lives and world of those outside the church. We shall see how each of the offices expresses plurality, is centered in the kingdom, gives shape to the church as sign and as its own gestalt, and is used by the Spirit to bring humanity to its goal. This will be so not only as the offices work individually, but as they work together, in synod. For in such arrangement, God's Spirit works pluriformly and yet together. This is a view of office that is both "high" and "horizontal." Office comes to the human from without but does not require that the human enter office to enter a higher or better way of being.

V. With Van Ruler's full theology of office before us, we will use his insights to evaluate the engagement of Reformed churches in the United States in discussions on office. This evaluation will examine one particular venue where the Reformed have been in ecumenical conversation in recent years in North America. In 1997, Reformed and Lutheran churches entered the Formula of Agreement. This unique ecumenical venture followed decades of multilateral discussion. The Reformed churches include the Presbyterian Church (U.S.A.), the Reformed Church in America, and the United Church of Christ. The Evangelical Lutheran Church in America is the Lutheran member of the FOA. Among the points of the agreement was the mutual recognition of ministry. This followed on a joint statement of ministry. How does one evaluate this agreement from a Van Rulerian perspective? And what does Van Ruler's doctrine of office offer to the continuing discussion? At issue is not simply the Reformed/Lutheran discussion, but the ecumenical conversation on office in general. For this reason, our evaluation of the consensus on ministry has an *illustrative* purpose. This conversation will provide a lens through which we hope to see how Van Ruler's doctrine of office remains vital in the twenty-first century.

We shall conclude this study with a short chapter that offers an evaluation of Van Ruler's doctrine of office within the larger ecumenical and theological discussion at the turn into the twenty-first century. There I will argue briefly for a theocentric approach to office from within the American Protestant context.

1.6 Studies of Van Ruler's Doctrine of Office

As mentioned above (1.4), although Van Ruler's doctrine of office is mentioned in Dutch theological and ecclesiological studies, very little extended theological analysis exists. Only two extensive discussions have appeared.

C. Graafland's book on *ambt* gives considerable space to Van Ruler on office.[93] Graafland places Van Ruler's notion of office within the context of his understanding of the kingdom of God. Graafland's exposition is illuminating but finally not helpful. Because his work does not contain detailed citation of Van Ruler's work, it is difficult for the scholar to verify Graafland's exposition. This can be illustrated in a number of instances.

First, Graafland claims that Van Ruler sees the traditional three-fold office in connection with the *munus triplex* of Christ.[94] In fact, Van Ruler's claim in this regard is much more complex. He asks, for example, whether the three offices of the Reformed tradition are rooted in the three offices of Christ. He hesitates to make that claim and states instead that "...in any case: the entire *munus triplex* [is] in each of the three offices—albeit with special accents."[95] He claims that at most he can claim that the *munus triplex* of Christ is a *background* for the three offices of the church.[96]

---

[93] Graafland, 153-189.

[94] Graafland, 167-168.

[95] A.A. van Ruler, "De ambten" [Herinafter "Ambten"], in Van Ruler's course *Kerkrecht*, lectures 1957-1961, Van Ruler Archive, folder III/12, 18.

[96] A.A. van Ruler, *Reformatorische opmerkingen in de ontmoeting met Rome* [Herinafter *Reformatorische*] (Hilversum: Paul Brand, 1965), 114.

Second, Graafland comments on the report on ecclesiastical office that was to bear Van Ruler's name and imprint and claims that the report was more "concrete" in its discussion of what the existing offices look like than was so for Van Ruler.[97] That is not the case, however. This study intends to show, in the chapter on particular offices, that Van Ruler spoke and wrote extensively not only on the concrete reality of the offices of elder and deacon (as well as that of the minister) but did so resolutely within the context of his theology of the kingdom of God.

Third, and perhaps most importantly, is Graafland's hesitation in his discussion of whether the office comes from God or from within the congregation. Van Ruler's claim that the office comes from God but emerges from within the congregation sets up, for Graafland, a false dilemma, one not found in scripture.[98] If we bracket for a moment the question of the warrant in scripture for Van Ruler's understanding, Graafland's claim that Van Ruler's approach is confusing misses Van Ruler's shift of emphasis from Christ to the Spirit. We shall show below that Van Ruler's notion of theonomous reciprocity allows that the congregation itself decides and judges with God as God calls persons to office. While one may not accept Van Ruler's formulation, he is clear in his understanding of the relation of office to congregation.[99]

A second and more extensive study on Van Ruler's theology of office is offered by A.N. Hendriks's dissertation of 1977, *Kerk en ambt in de theologie van A.A. van Ruler*.[100] Hendriks's work is a historical development of Van Ruler's doctrine of church and office, set within the immediate history of the Netherlands Reformed Church of the mid-twentieth century. Hendriks does great service by showing the development of Van Ruler's thought through three stages, what he calls the "unfolding of the theocratic vision of culture," the "explication of the apostolate of the church," and the "accentuation of the peculiar gestalt of the church," respectively. He then sets Van Ruler's changing ecclesiological understandings within that framework and consequently views office within that developmental scheme.

---

[97] Graafland, 174.

[98] Graafland, 185.

[99] See below, 5.5. Graafland's main criticism of Van Ruler is that Van Ruler does not sufficiently support his doctrine of office exegetically. Graafland, 181-184. This, however, is an argument of method. We address Van Ruler's theological method in the following chapter.

[100] Buijten en Schipperheijn: Amsterdam, 1977.

As will be clear below, this study works within that developmental scheme, albeit with some adjustments. While our inquiry surveys much of the same area, it differs in a number of significant ways. First, this study emerges from a different context. It asks the question of office from within an ecumenical framework that has paid continuing attention to ministry and office as central to the process of unification of the church. That in turn sets the stage for a second difference. This study is more analytical and systematic than is that of Hendriks. That is, the ecumenical discussion forces us to ask about the nature of office itself. Subsequently we turn to the question of the particular offices and how they are set within Van Ruler's theological framework. Furthermore, our approach will encourage the ecumenical discussion to consider the theological commitments of the varying approaches to office. Third, this study is far more detailed as to the nature of the offices themselves and how they are to be envisioned theologically within the world of the congregation of believing Christians. This is possible in part because we review archival material of Van Ruler's unpublished work not taken into account by Hendriks.

CHAPTER 2

Theology of the Kingdom: An Outline of the Theology of A. A. Van Ruler

It is imperative that the first part of this study review the broad outlines of the theology of A.A. van Ruler for two reasons. First, since we intend to show that his understanding of office is itself expressive of a theological understanding of God's actions with the world, we must perforce bring that broader theology into view. Subsequently, we must review that theology for the simple reason that Van Ruler's notion of office is not understandable without the larger framework of his theology firmly in mind.

A major theological voice, Van Ruler did not write a systematic theology. His theology can be traced from several major early works, most signally his doctoral dissertation, *De vervulling van de wet* ("The Fulfillment of the Law"), and a significant number of occasional writings that engaged theological themes in a systematic manner. It is difficult to find a starting point by which to enter his theology.[1] However, Van Ruler himself offered a clue when he remarked late in his career that "the Trinity, the Kingdom and Predestination are the widest and thus the real viewpoint of systematic theology."[2] We shall

---

[1] "...on the one hand Van Ruler's thinking fascinates and intrigues me, while on the other hand I have the feeling that I have not found the right entrance to his thinking." G. van Leeuwen, *Christologie en Anthropologie* ('s-Gravenhage, 1959), 206, n.4, quoted in W.H. Velema, *Confrontatie met Van Ruler* (Kampen: J.H. Kok, 1962), 9.

[2] A.A. van Ruler, "Christocentriciteit en wetenschappelijkheid in de systematische theologie" in *Theologisch Werk* 5 (Nijkerk: G.F. Callenbach, 1972), 200. See also Hendriks, 46.

indeed see these themes as central for Van Ruler's thinking. An overview of his theology is complicated by a development in his theology that moved from an early more christocentric, Barthian stage to his later theology where, with his emphasis on creation, he stands clearly over and against Barth.[3] While we shall remark on the development of his thought where relevant, particularly when we look at his ecclesiology, we shall maintain that in the broad outline of his thought he remains sufficiently consistent for our purpose. Thus, for example, while he places greater emphasis on creation in his later years, that same concern was present already as early as his doctoral dissertation in 1947. And while he would give greater emphasis to a theology of the apostolate in the late 1940s and through the 1950s, the church retains its apostolic nature in his later writings even as he will give a greater emphasis to the liturgical character of the church. Rebel remarks that "Van Ruler's thinking is to be compared with a spider and his web." The spider does battle with what he catches in the web, moves to the center, and moves outward yet again. "From the center, the constructed web appears to be a unity."[4]

---

[3]Pieter van Hoof, *Intermezzo: kontinuïteit en diskontinuïteit in de theologie van A.A. van Ruler* (Amsterdam: Ton Bolland, 1974) argues for a "phase-theory" in Van Ruler's theology. He identifies an early, christological phase (1930-1947), a pneumatological phase (1947-1965), and a protological phase (1962-1970). While rejecting a development that follows such strict lines (and many of the conclusions that accompany Van Hoof's evaluation of Van Ruler's theology), Hendriks, *Kerk en ambt*, agrees that Van Ruler's theology developed from an early christological stage to a later, patrocentric stage. For a critical review of Van Hoof's assessment see Jacob Jan Rebel, *Pastoraat in pneumatologisch perspektief: een theologische verantwoording vanuit het denken van A.A. van Ruler* (Kampen, J.H. Kok, 1981), 27-32 and *passim* where he rejects Van Hoof's strict division of Van Ruler's development, rightly in my opinion. A. Hennephof, "Christus, de Geest en de werkelijkheid in de theologie van A.A. van Ruler," Scriptie (n.p., 1966) offers an earlier version of a similar "phase-theory" of Van Ruler's thought, one that claims less than does Van Hoof. Christo Lombard, *Adama, thora en dogma: die samenhang van de aardse lewe, skrif en dogma in die teologie van A.A. van Ruler* (unpublished dissertation) University of the Western Cape, rejects a "phase theory." However, he offers a detailed account of Van Ruler's development and the shifting accents in his theology, 56-85. Lombard's earlier master's thesis, *Kontinuïteit en diskontinuïteit in die denke van A.A. van Ruler. 'n Kiritiese gesprek met P. van Hoof oor die aktualiteie van die "Intermezzo"* (Universiteit van West-Kaapland, 1983), is a sustained argument against Van Hoof's reading of Van Ruler.

[4] Rebel, 33.

While it is difficult to encapsulate Van Ruler's theology in brief compass,[5] it can fairly be understood as a theology that centers on the kingdom of God. All of creation and history moves toward its end or goal, the kingdom of God. Because it moves toward that end, Van Ruler understands that history comes "from the end." Our theology shall need to be a "thinking from the end."[6] Because it is the kingdom of *God*, Van Ruler will denote his theology as predestinarian. Predestination will mean for him fundamentally that the kingdom originates in the living God who will use humans and institutions as instruments in the realization of Gods ultimate (*uiteindelijk*—literally, "out of the end") intentions. And because it is this *particular* God who acts in a particular way—in the Son through the Spirit—it will be a trinitarian theology.

It will not be our intention to offer a full analysis of Van Ruler's theology. That would exceed our purpose.[7] It will be sufficient to grasp the broader outlines of his theology. Likewise, we will not raise critical questions except in those places that affect our study of office within the kingdom.

---

[5] Rebel rehearses the various attempts to typify Van Ruler's theology, 33-37. He elects to use the awkward phrase "eschatological-trinitarian kingdom theology" which nevertheless accurately describes the main thrust of Van Ruler's theology.

[6] Velema subtitles his study of Van Ruler's theology "*Denken vanuit de einde*" ["thinking from out of the end"]. Van Ruler's theology does not begin with either the beginning or the middle but "he begins with the end" (p. 6). Van Ruler says just that in *De vervulling van de wet: een dogmatische studie over de verhouding van openbaring en existentie* [Hereinafter *Vervulling*] (Nijkerk: G.F. Callenbach, 1947), 26: "...in dogmatic thinking we must begin with the end." In the superscription for the first part of his dissertation, he cites J.H. Gunning, Jr.: "We are deeply convinced that even as the entire confession of faith in the first century was formed with a backward directed movement from eschatology, the renewal of our dogmatics and preaching that is demanded in our time will also have to emerge from eschatology." *De prediking van de toekomst de Heeren* (Utrecht, 1888), 87.

[7] There are no full studies of Van Ruler in English. Fries, *Religion and the Hope*, gives a very detailed account. The entire number of *Reformed Review* 26:2 (Winter, 1973) is devoted to the theology of Van Ruler. John Bolt, "The Background and Context of Van Ruler's Theocentric (Theocratic) Vision and its Relevance for North America," in A.A. van Ruler, *Calvinist Trinitarianism and Theocentric Politics: Essays Toward a Public Theology* (Lewiston: Edwin Mellen Press, 1989), ix-xliv, offers a brief background for English readers. T.J. Hommes, *Sovereignty and Saeculum: Arnold A. Van Ruler's Theocratic Theology*, Ph. D. diss., Harvard, 1966, offers an early summary of Van Ruler's thought but is only available in manuscript.

We shall, then, begin our summary of Van Ruler's theology from the end or the goal—the kingdom of God. Indeed, Van Ruler himself indicates that the kingdom of God forms the proper starting point for theology: "Must we not search for another system-forming orientation point, for example, that of the kingdom of God about which both the Old and the New Testament are concerned, albeit in very different ways?"[8] However, having begun to understand God's goal, it will be crucial to exploit Van Ruler's understanding of time and history. Only in this way shall we be able to locate God's work in creation, in the Messiah, and through the Spirit. For only as we grasp that God works "backward" into history and "forward" within history will we begin to comprehend how God works in history. We shall discover that God not only works "with" creation and "in" history, but that creation is itself the expression of God's original love for reality as God's own counterpart. The appearance of sin, however, brought ruin to the good creation. History is more than a stage on which God works, but is established by God as the time in which the Messiah and the Spirit work to meet the reality of sin and to restore creation to its original intention. It is this restoration that will, as we shall see, include a "plus" as the kingdom of God.

By beginning at the end, with the kingdom of God, and working toward Van Ruler's conception of the trinitarian nature of God, we can begin to grasp the scope of Van Ruler's theological commitments. For, as we shall see, God's intentions are not limited to Christ, or even to God's own self, but extend to include the entire created order, the human, culture, and society included.

Only after we have gained a full notion of the scope of God's intentions will we be in a position to understand where and how both the offices and the church are used by God to further God's intentions.

2.1 Van Ruler's Theological Method

However, before we turn to Van Ruler's theology proper, a brief look at his method is in order. In fact, his method is itself reflective of his theology. This is most easily seen in what might be called his trinitarian aversion to monistic thinking. He will, for example, claim in a late writing that "theology must be neither christological nor pneumatological. They are only parts. In its total reach it can only be described as trinitarian theology, as eschatological kingdom theology,

[8] Van Ruler, "Methode en mogelijkheden van de dogmatiek vergeleken met die van de exegese," in *TW* 1 (Nijkerk: G.F. Callenbach, 1969), 83.

and as predestinarian theology."[9] Arendshorst can describe his theology as "*twee-polig*" ("two-poled") that executes itself not as a circle around one focus, but as an ellipse around two foci.[10] Reduction to one principle is simply not possible for Van Ruler.[11] In a number of places, he will use the image of a skater who must continually move from one leg to another, in order both to maintain balance and to be able to skate.[12]

That this is methodologically the case can be seen from within Van Ruler's theology in at least two ways. First, in a remark in the context of pneumatology, he states that "every monism appears to me to be death for pneumatology. In this view as well a leap is characteristic for the Spirit. As certainly in the mediation of salvation as in the appropriation of salvation the Spirit leaps over and again from one gestalt[13] to another in a continual and never ending round

---

[9] Van Ruler, "Christocentriciteit en Wetenschappelijkheid," in *TW*, 5:212-213.

[10] J.W. Arendshorst, "Woonsteden van God: A.A. van Rulers pleidooi voor een relatief zelfstandige pneumatologie" (Doktoraal skriptie, Rijksuniversiteit Utrecht, 1978), 9. On this as a structural leitmotiv of Van Ruler's theology, see also P.F.Th. Aalders, "Religie en politiek, de theocratische gedachte bij prof. Dr. A.A. van Ruler," in *Woord en werkelijkheid: Over de theocratie* (Nijkerk: G.F. Callenbach, 1973), 13-15. Aalders even detects something of the relation of love in this *tweepoligheid*. More to the point, he sees Van Ruler's understanding of the church as an example of this way of thinking. Van Ruler himself uses the notion of *tweepoligheid* in "De kerk in een zich mondig noemende wereld," in *TW* 2 (Nijkerk: G.F. Callenbach, 1971), 126-128.

[11] A telling example of this refusal to think monistically can be found in Van Ruler's *Droom en Gestalte* [Hereinafter, *Droom*] (Holland: Amsterdam, 1947), 162, where Van Ruler resolutely maintains a distinction between revelation and culture, salvation and existence, refusing to allow either to collapse into the other. Gerrit Immink judges the notion of *tweeheid* ["two-ness"] to be typical of Van Ruler's thought. "Openbaring en existentie–De betekenis van A.A. van Ruler voor de theologie beoefening in Utrecht" in *Zo de ouden zongen...: Leraar en leerling zijn in de theologie-beofening (tussen 1945 en 2000)* ed. Jurjen Beumer (Baarn: Ten Have, 1996), 173.

[12] E.g., Van Ruler, *Droom*, 96

[13] The Dutch term *gestalte* has found its way into ordinary English usage by way of German. It has thus been understood in the popular psychological sense of a constellation of perceptions or symptoms that cannot be analyzed in more discrete parts. However, here it must be understood in its Dutch sense. That is, a *gestalte* is a concrete expression of a particular form. It could be translated as "configuration" or "manifestation."

dance."[14] Second, he will write about the "necessity" of a trinitarian theology. Theology is necessarily trinitarian not only by its content, as we shall see, but theology as a practice, in the doing of theology, is trinitarian because the persons of the trinity are not only related to one another [*op-elkaar-betrekken*] but are *distinct* from one another [*uit-elkaar-houden*].[15] We cannot reduce theology to any of the persons but will also go back and forth from the one to the other, much as movement happens back and forth within God.[16]

There is a certain *playfulness* to theology, according to Van Ruler. There must be room for experiment. Theology must exhibit a certain gymnastic flexibility. He asks: "Does one have one firm starting point?" And he answers: "[The theologian] has starting points, a whole series, at least of viewpoints to which he orients himself."[17] Van Ruler's way of moving from one side of the matter to the other thus includes the sources to which he appeals in his theology. While scripture will remain the final court of appeal, he will exploit church history, dogmatic history, the history of Europe, philosophy, experience, to name a few.[18] These methodological notes are important as we proceed for we shall have to hear Van Ruler speak first about one matter and then another. The loci of his theology will be related, but that cannot always be seen from within the matter that is under discussion. His theology must be seen as a whole.[19]

---

[14] Van Ruler, "Hoofdlijnen van een pneumatologie," [Hereinafter "Hoofdlijnen] in *TW* 6 (Nijkerk: G.F. Callenbach, 1973), 29.

[15] See Rebel, 41-47.

[16] Van Ruler, "De leer van de Drieëenheid," in *Elsevier's weekblad*, May 26, 1956, 4.

[17] Van Ruler, "Methode en mogelijkheden," 62. In the same article, Van Ruler notes that there is a loneliness in theological experiment that can be difficult for the theologian to bear. He then remarks that this has been so for him personally in his notion that the incarnation is an emergency measure that will be reversed in the eschaton, 66.

[18] See "Methode en mogelijkheden," 58. In *Gesprek*, Van Ruler answers the reproach that his dogmatic work (in contradistinction from his biblical meditations) displays so little exegesis by claiming that there is a "leap" between exegesis and dogmatics. But then, he goes on, one must not take dogmatics with such deadly seriousness. It is, for example, a Protestant mistake to confuse doctrine with gospel (61, 62).

[19] See Lombard, *Adama*, 132-167 for a detailed discussion of Van Ruler's theological method. His discussion of Van Ruler's use of scripture, 132-140, is particularly important as it responds to the criticism of some that Van Ruler is not sufficiently scriptural.

2.2 The Kingdom of God

Van Ruler can summarize the goal of God's actions in history in the phrase: "the kingdom of God."[20] In one place, Van Ruler will describe the kingdom of God as "the ultimate and salvific actions of God with this world."[21] It is "nothing other than the penetration of God in history." [22] The kingdom of God is an *eschatological* reality; it exists both in the future toward which history tends, and in the present. But it is crucial to understand just *how* it exists in both the future—and how one is to understand "future."

The kingdom of God is *eschatological*. It is not to be understood in a static-ontological sense, as though the kingdom represents a higher order of being that exists in an eternal now and that touches human history by one means or another.[23] Were that so, the manifestation of God could be sought in the essence of reality, however approached and howsoever hidden. Van Ruler sees the kingdom of God as a liberation of all reality from its essential character; reality finds its center in the God who comes.[24] The kingdom of God is eschatological in that it presses from the end to the present.[25] That sets history in motion as it moves toward God's ultimate intentions.

In this way, eschatological does not mean that history presses from the past or the present to the future. It is not an unfolding of a grace that, for example, has been infused. Nor does it press in on the present because the time is ripe.[26] While the kingdom is immanent in

---

[20] Van Ruler is fully cognizant that *baseleia* can be understood as either "reign" or "kingdom." Translating it as "kingdom" is indicative of the area under the rule of the king. Van Ruler does not choose between the two, but instead leaves the ambiguity in place. However, given the importance of the *scope* of the kingdom in Van Ruler's theology, I choose to retain the phrase, "kingdom of God." See Van Ruler, *Religie en politiek* [Hereinafter *Religie*] (Nijkerk: G.F. Callenbach, 1945), 57, 58.

[21] *Vervulling*, 40.

[22] Van Ruler, "Het koninkrijk Gods en de geschiedenis" [Hereinafter "Koninkrijk"], in Van Ruler, *Verwachting en Voltooiing* [Hereinafter *Verwachting*] (Nijkerk: G.F. Callenbach, 1978), 35.

[23] "Koninkrijk," 33.

[24] *Vervulling*, 52. See Hendriks, 51, where he observes that it was particularly in Van Ruler's early years that he rejected every metaphysical notion of being. God creates history from out of the end. There is no "being" to which one can appeal in its protological state.

[25] *Vervulling*, 46.

[26] *Vervulling*, 46.

the sense that it is not displaced either to the future or to a reality separate from creation, it is not to be understood anthropologically or in a spiritualist way. In other words, one cannot probe created reality from whence to discover the seed of the kingdom that can subsequently be projected into the future. "The future may not be projected out of the present."[27] In scripture, the kingdom of God is nowhere described as either a natural development of created reality or as a product of human work. It is always a gift from God.[28] "The idea of the kingdom of God has its deepest roots in the notion of God."[29] It is the action of God within history. But it is God as the "coming one."[30] There is a certain "power and violence [*geweld*] of eschatological reality" that "create history." "The eschatological action of God is a historical action."[31] And because it is God who acts out of the future of God, history will be drawn toward a future that is not yet fully disclosed. The kingdom of God is "an action of God from out of the end."[32] "...[T]he kingdom of God is radically understood from the end, from the future of God approaching us."[33] Hence, the kingdom presses toward a future that is yet to be fully disclosed even as it determines the shape of the present.

The kingdom of God is *transcendent*. Its transcendence is not ontological, but eschatological. The kingdom presses in from the future. God's actions overwhelm the present: it is an "overpowering [*overmachten*] by which God acts with his world."[34] Transcendence, for Van Ruler, is to be understood as horizontal rather than vertical. It is a *historical* transcendence, from out of the future.[35] God's ultimate intentions cannot be contained in the present. They transcend the present.[36] The kingdom of God exceeds everything. It doesn't simply embrace everything, but extends beyond the sum of all reality. For all

---

[27] *Vervulling*, 37.

[28] *Religie, 61.*

[29] *Vervulling*, 38.

[30] Hendriks, 52.

[31] *Vervulling*, 49.

[32] *Vervulling*, 49.

[33] *Vervulling*, 26.

[34] *Vervulling*, 38.

[35] Van Ruler observes in one place that "transcending" can be translated as "going above." But a better translation is "crossing a border." "Then one does not intend this as vertical but horizontal." *Waarom zou ik naar de kerk gaan?* [Hereinafter *Waarom*], 2nd ed. (Nijkerk: G.F. Callenbach, 1970), 29.

[36] *Vervulling*, 35.

things are subject to the actions of the God who is future[37] and whose essence is Will.[38]

But if transcendent, God's kingdom is *bodily*. Van Ruler tilts against the notion that the kingdom might be ideational[39] or a moral utopia, or that it is to be described in the decisional language of one like Bultmann.[40] In any case, Van Ruler will maintain an "absolute identity" between this world and the coming world.[41] The kingdom of God is not a reality divorced from creation and history as it is created by God and experienced by the human. God's actions are directed toward this world.[42] This can be observed in Jesus' miracles as they are illustrative of Jesus' preaching of the kingdom of God. In the miracles of healing, for example, we see the bodily nature of the kingdom.[43] Van Ruler can go so far as to claim that the goal is not simply the kingdom of God *tout court* but the *experience of the world as the kingdom*.[44]

Nonetheless, this transcendent, immanent, eschatological kingdom is *hidden* in the present era. No one knows why God's good favor turns toward this world, when it will fully break into history, or even what the kingdom is.[45]

Still, this hiddenness takes a certain form for Van Ruler. He distinguishes the kingdom of God from *the kingdom of Christ*. The kingdom of Christ is the kingdom of God in hidden form.[46] Or said another way, the kingdom of Christ is the kingdom of the Father in a particular way—that of hiddenness in the flesh.[47] He can go so far as to

---

37 *Vervulling*, 61, 62.

38 *Konijkrijk*, 33.

39 Van Ruler maintained an allergy to philosophical idealism. See, e.g., *Religie*, 96.

40 *Vervulling*, 35.

41 *Vervulling*, 56.

42 *Vervulling*, 38.

43 *Religie*, 59.

44 "Hoofdlijnen," 13.

45 *Vervulling*, 39.

46 *Vervulling*, 89.

47 *Vervulling*, 90. In "Toekomst des heils" (sermon preached on October 8, 1939, at Kubaard on Amos 9:11), Van Ruler Archive, Folder IV, 316, p. 2, Van Ruler claims that "all of reality is messianic: brought into contact with the Messiah, judged by the Messiah, saved in the Messiah, so that it receives sense, standing, content, salvation."

state that Jesus Christ is the kingdom of God himself. [48] Christ is the *autobasilia*.[49]

Van Ruler can even claim that the kingdom of God is equivalent to salvation in Christ. This is most clearly seen in a set of words that the New Testament uses in a linguistic world that describes the kingdom: peace, gladness, salvation, life, knowledge, joy, promise, glory, power, authority. All these have come into this world in Christ. They offer provisional content to the kingdom of God. And yet, even as they are descriptive of the one reality that is our world, they retain their eschatological character. The miracles, for example, remain miracles; that is, they point to what is not fully present.[50] The kingdom of God is both manifest and hidden.

The bodily nature of the kingdom is expressed in the fact that Jesus is the fulfillment of the law. For Van Ruler that means that the law has received its "body," its gestalt and its content, its reality and its substance. Fulfillment is "giving embodiment to the kingdom, the future, and the essence of God and to the shadows that fall on existence." Jesus is the bodily content of Mosaic law.[51] Genuine fulfillment of the law lies in the historical reality of love, the love of God, set within the reality of this world. In this original sense, Jesus Christ is the love of God. The law is fulfilled in the Messiah.[52]

It is the place of the *law* in the divine economy that enables us to see the kingdom of God as established in the flesh in Jesus Christ. Van Ruler understands law within the context of the biblical story. That is, the law is not a natural law to be abstracted from the structure of being, but a law given by the living God. The law expresses the will of God and the will of God emerges from the essence of God. The law, in fact, is an expression of the essence of God.[53] This is so much the case that Van Ruler can claim that the law is eternal in a way that not even

---

[48] *Vervulling*, 85.

[49] Van Ruler, "Christusprediking en rijksprediking" [Hereinafter "Christusprediking"], in *Verwachting*, 47. One can see Van Ruler distancing himself from Barth here. If Christ is the *autobasilia* and if this kingdom receives its gestalt in this world, then Van Ruler would no longer be able to concur in Barth's explosive "No!" to all "points of connection" between God and this world. The point of connection does not arise from the human, nor from this world. It comes from God's side for Van Ruler. But the point exists and is earthly. This fact will be crucial for Van Ruler as he works out his doctrine of church, sacraments, and offices.

[50] *Religie*, 59-61.

[51] *Vervulling, 483.*

[52] *Vervulling*, 484.

[53] *Vervulling*, 470.

the Messiah, in his work as Messiah, is eternal. The law, then, is the law of the kingdom. Van Ruler can conclude: "God has expressed the entire of his actions, and thus all actions, and thus in essence the entire of reality, in his law."[54] If, then, the law is fulfilled in the Messiah, then the Messiah can be seen as the kingdom, and the kingdom of Christ in turn can be understood as a modality (or gestalt) of the kingdom of God. Furthermore, the law is this kingdom *embodied* as the law of God tells us "what marriage, parenthood, kinship, state, in short, what true human existence is and must be."[55] It is the kingdom present in its provisional form in this one, earthly, reality.[56]

The kingdom of Christ does not, however, coincide with the kingdom of God.[57] As we have seen, the kingdom of Christ is a modality of the kingdom of God. One might be tempted to describe it as a stage along the way. That, however, is to import the category of "stages" and that does not fit for Van Ruler. We shall turn to Van Ruler's understanding of time and history below. While the kingdom of Christ is not a preliminary historical stage or preparation for the kingdom of God, nonetheless it takes a subsidiary position within the kingdom of God. The kingdom of Christ is, however, provisional[58] as it stands in relation to the kingdom of God. The kingdom of Christ will be about salvation, and salvation, while a mode of the kingdom, points beyond itself to God's greater goal, expressed and embodied in the kingdom of God.

It is crucial to keep Van Ruler's clear distinction between the fulfillment [*vervulling*] and completion [*voleinding*] in view. While the law is fulfilled in Christ, the completion is reserved for the eschaton. The kingdom of God is present, but under the form of the kingdom of Christ. That means on the one hand that the kingdom is hidden. It is

---

[54] *Vervulling*, 472.

[55] *Vervulling*, 526.

[56] That we have to do with reality as *one* Van Ruler makes clear in his sermon "Toekomst des heils" (see above, n. 46), p. 5. Salvation takes place within one reality. It is described in earthly terms. "In all of prophecy the promised salvation is described in earthly terms. And not only in prophecy. Also in the fulfillment salvation appears to be taken up in the earthly; the flesh of the incarnation of the Word, the body at the cross and the grave in resurrection, the flesh in heaven." "The salvation that I expect, that I believe, of which I have part–it is not something completely different than this my life, but it is the salvation thereof."

[57] "Christusprediking," 47.

[58] *Vervulling*, 189.

not present in its completion. On the other hand, however, it *is* present. Coming from the end, God elects and sanctifies both humans and "things" to be signs of the kingdom that is coming. [59] The fulfillment happens in this one reality, this *ordinary* reality. The demonic is exorcised from the everyday and "we not only see things in the light of eternity. We see the light of eternity in things."[60]

While the kingdom of Christ gives expression to salvation, the Messiah plays a particular, functional role in relation to the kingdom of God. God's goal is not Christ, but the kingdom, and Christ acts in service to the kingdom: "...in the Bible, the New Testament included, it has to do not with the Messiah and the Spirit, but with the coming of the kingdom of God on earth, however much the coming of Jesus Christ and the work of the Holy Spirit are unconditionally necessary within that purpose."[61]

Christ's role in the kingdom is salvation, and salvation is concentrated on the work of the atonement. Sin has disturbed God's good creation and interposed itself in God's good intentions. Christologically understood, salvation is atonement for sin, or more specifically for guilt.[62] The guilty human can neither perceive nor participate in the creation as God's kingdom. The human is saved in order that he or she might experience the world as the kingdom and the self within that world. Fulfillment is the action of God in Jesus Christ by which the creation is exorcised of demonic powers, and where the human need no longer live under the memory of guilt. The human is set within a history where he or she is set within the "play" of moral and historical freedom.[63] As Paul Fries remarks, Van Ruler "depicts the eschaton as the restoration of creation to the original purposes and purity intended by the creator."[64] So Van Ruler: "...the eschaton is nothing other than the unfolded, and on account of sin saved, proton."[65] Van Ruler can also speak of this as a breaking open of the "coherence of being," of life imprisoned within the bonds of a

---

59 *Vervulling*, 73.

60 *Vervulling*, 78. In *Vervulling*, Van Ruler summarizes the characteristics of the fulfillment as (1) historical, (2) hidden, (3) signifying, (4) pluralistic, (5) combative, (6) ecclesiastical/sacramental-political/cultural, (7) universal, (8) cosmic, (9) ordinary, and (10) plerophoristic and realistic. 72-78.

61 "Koninkrijk," 33.

62 "Christusprediking," 45.

63 *Vervulling*, 465.

64 Fries, *Religion and the Hope*, 92.

65 *Reformatorische*, 151.

metaphysical order.[66] The human can live in history as it is, where God's Spirit creates history from out of God's future.

This is love, the love of God, that will enable the fulfillment to occur which Van Ruler describes as the "round dance of the actions of God."[67] He concludes his dissertation by claiming that everything lies within guilt and atonement: "the riddle of history, the justification of God, the mediation of salvation and existence, the establishment of the kingdom in the flesh, the coincidence of the law and the council of God, the realization." And this leads to the "final word": love. This is a "love that includes all that the living God has said and done on the earth, and thus love that includes the entire reality."[68]

If the kingdom is established in a particular modality in Christ, it is the Spirit who expands and extends this kingdom. "The Spirit...creates around the gift and the work of the Messiah the room to maneuver of history in so far as the Spirit holds apart the walls of existence between the first and the second coming of Christ and in the Christian centuries God's torah expands around the cross in the ordering of existence."[69] Van Ruler maintains that a Reformation understanding cannot remain with the "eternal now," a *nunc aeternum*. There is a genuine expansion around this "eternal now" in the form of time in existence.[70]

The Spirit is not itself, however, to be understood as the kingdom of God. It is not even a beginning stage of the kingdom.[71] The "genuine" promise is of the kingdom, of God who comes to us out of God's own future. The Spirit is a moment, an aspect, a first-fruit, a pledge, a seal. "The Spirit is the kingdom in the modality of promise," it is the "way of being of the approaching kingdom."[72]

The Spirit is related to the Messiah. The Spirit takes what has been established in Christ and through the work of the Spirit, Christ receives a gestalt within human beings.[73] In that way, Christ's

---

66 *Vervulling*, 24.

67 *Vervulling*, 42.

68 *Vervulling*, 535.

69 *Vervulling*, 141, 142.

70 *Vervulling*, 523.

71 *Vervulling*, 159.

72 *Vervulling*, 138.

73 In *Vervulling*, Van Ruler discusses extensively whether it is the Spirit who precedes Christ in the divine economy or it is Christ who precedes the Spirit. He offers compelling reasons for each order and decides finally for the traditional order of Christ-Spirit. However, in confirmation of his method, Van Ruler finds the two approaches a "beautiful dissonance" and

kingdom finds a gestalt within humanity. But again, this must be understood within the broader context of the kingdom of God. For this gestalt breaks in from the eschatological kingdom of God.[74] Van Ruler can describe the kingdom of the Messiah in one place as "the expansion which the Spirit gives to the offering of the atonement, in Christian existence which [the Spirit] creates."[75]

The Spirit is poured out from the glorified Christ. The Spirit is the *power* of the kingdom in that it expands the kingdom of Christ into the gestalts of history. "The Spirit is not the stuff, but the power of the kingdom."[76] In an oft-repeated phrase in his dissertation, Van Ruler speaks of the Spirit as "expanding and representing" [*uitbreiding en uitbeelding*] the kingdom of God.[77]

The place and the work of the Spirit are crucial to Van Ruler's theology, and we shall examine the place and work of the Spirit more closely below. For the present, it is sufficient to note that the Spirit, like the Messiah, works toward God's ultimate intentions of the kingdom of God. This is dramatically expressed when Van Ruler will claim not only that the work of the Messiah is provisional and that the Messiah will abdicate his messiahship in the eschaton (see below), but that the work of the Spirit, outpoured and dwelling within the human, will also cease.[78]

God's final goal is not directed toward Christ but toward the human. But what is the content of this goal? Is it human participation in the immanent-trinitarian life of God? Not at all, according to Van Ruler. "In the eschaton it is only the triune God and the naked existence of created things in their *vis-à-vis* as the *vis-à-vis* of mutual joy."[79] The final goal is not that we give ourselves to Christ, but to our pure humanity.[80] The goal is the creaturely existence in God's presence and in accord with God's will. "When the whole earth sings praise to

---

refuses a reduction to one scheme. See 169-173, his remark on "dissonance" on p. 172, and his refusal to reduce to one scheme on p. 173.

[74] "Hoofdlijnen," 19, 20.

[75] *Vervulling*, 187.

[76] *Vervulling*, 161, 163.

[77] See, e.g,. *Vervulling*, 494. *Uitbreiding* and *uitbeelding* literally are expansion and representation (nouns). However, they are *acts* of the Spirit and can be expressed as participles.

[78] Van Ruler, "Structuurverschillen tussen het christologische en het pneumatologische gezichtpunt" [Hereinafter "Structuurverschillen"], in *TW* 1, 190. See also *Vervulling*, 189.

[79] "Hoofdlijnen," 27.

[80] "Hoofdlijnen," 37.

God it finds it true life."[81] Or Van Ruler: "The original destiny is also the ultimate. It exists exclusively in that it rejoices in itself, before his [God's] face, praising him....The genuine spiritual life exists in the natural life lived in the right way."[82] This realization includes the kingdom of God and the eschaton. The consequence of this is that God in Christ enters the gestalts of human existence through the Spirit. That, in turn, implies on the one hand that all of human existence is to be "Christianized" [*gekerstend*], and on the other hand that God be expressed in the gestalts of human existence so far as possible in order that existence can be what it is in fact, the image and the kingdom of God.[83]

The human, as human, takes a particular place in God's ultimate intentions as the human is set in an "open reality"[84] where God and created reality—the human and his or her neighbor—meet. The *church* will be important at just this place. For God uses the church in God's work of the salvation of the human. We shall return to a much fuller discussion of the church in the following chapter. Here, however, it is important to note that the work that God does through the church is subservient to God's greater intentions:

> ...[T]he notion of the kingdom is not to be completely superseded by the notion of the church. Christ focuses himself in the church. But the church is not the last of God's intentions. That is theocracy. [God's] final intention is and remains the kingdom of God on earth. Where the mission to the peoples took place, the atmosphere of the kingdom is present. The experiment of Galilee repeats itself here and there on earth....It is necessary to see everything in the dim light of God's intentions.[85]

Before, then, we can turn to the human, we must engage in a brief discussion of Van Ruler's notion of theocracy.

---

[81] Fries, 165.

[82] Van Ruler, "Ultragereformeerd en vrijzinnig" [Hereinafter "Ultragereformeerd"], in *TW* 3 (Nijkerk: G.F. Callenbach, 1971), 143.

[83] "Hoofdlijnen," 28.

[84] *Vervulling*, 348, 504.

[85] Van Ruler in W. Balke and H. Oostenbrink-Evers, *De commissie voor de kerkorde (1945-1950): Bouwplan, agendastukken en notulen van de vergaderingen ter voorbereiding van de nieuwe kerkorde (1951) van de Nederlandse Hervormde Kerk* [Herinafter, *Commissie*] (Zoetermeer: Boekencentrum, 1993), 179-180.

2.2.1 Theocracy

God's goal with humanity takes provisional form in a theocracy. It is beyond the scope of this study even to begin to explicate Van Ruler's notion of theocracy.[86] It is important to see, if however briefly, its place in Van Ruler's theology for two reasons. First, a summary of his theology would be incomplete without acknowledging the place of theocracy in the breadth of his understanding of reality. Second, no inquiry of his doctrine of office is possible without understanding the nature and place of theocracy for Van Ruler. The offices will find their location not within the church, but within the kingdom. Hence, so the argument will go, the offices will address and work within the framework of church and state, church and culture, theocratically understood.

H.W. de Knijff claims that the notion of theocracy in itself is simple: "...it is simply identical with the fact that through God's revelation God makes himself present in the world." This "making present" includes the expansion of the gospel collectively as well as individually.[87]

But if simple, the notion of theocracy has multiple meanings for Van Ruler.[88] In *Religie and politiek*, he offers a three-fold description. First, one can conceive of theocracy as "giving political form to life and thought in the ordering of the world by the church so that life comes to be seen as an ellipse with two foci–church and state–or–Lord's Supper and civil law."[89] The kingdom of God is the goal toward which God works, and uses the church to that end. Second, one can understand theocracy from out of a theology of the Word that includes all of life and does so "critically, not ontologically, predicative and not phenomenologically; it only proclaims and does not constitute."[90] This is theocracy as it engages life as event. But it is the third notion that one senses has Van Ruler's fuller passion. One can conceive of theocracy as

---

[86] See on theocracy, e.g., the entire book of essays, *Woord en werkelijkheid*. Van Ruler works his notion of theocracy out most fully in *Droom en gestalte* and *Visie en vaart*.

[87] H.W. de Knijff, "A.A. van Ruler anno 1995," in *De waarheid is theocratisch: bijdragen tot de waardering van de theologische nalatenshap van Arnold Albert van Ruler*, Gerrit Klein and Dick Steenks ed. (Baarn: G.F. Callenbach, 1995), 20.

[88] I am indebted to Christo Lombard for this insight. See his "Van Ruler se nalatenskap en relevansie vir vandag," in Kempers, *Inventaris*, xxxix-xl.

[89] *Religie*, 153.

[90] *Religie*, 153.

> ...an all-embracing notion of life and thereby think of an entirely peculiar *Seinsverstandnis* and penetrate to the last and deepest roots of existence, so far that no concept remains that is not touched by biblical doctrine. Moses and Aristotle do battle in our European consciousness. The gestalt of a Christian philosophy rises before us.[91]

Here we see the eschatological kingdom at work in this world in its widest sense. It is clearly inclusive of political authorities, but it is not limited to them. It is inclusive not only of a way of thinking, but of a way of being, of reality.

2.3 The Human

As became clear at the end of the previous section (2.2), "The telos of the human lies not in the essence of God, but in his peculiar life in God's presence according to his will."[92] The goal is that the human find his or her humanity not in becoming united with God in God's being, but in becoming fully human. True humanity is an "eschatological good."[93] As Van Ruler puts it, it is that the human as *mannetje*[94] can stand over and against God, as human.[95] He concludes his inaugural lecture upon becoming a professor at the University of Utrecht by stating that the kingdom of God finds its goal in the human. The final sentence of that lecture reads: "For however much the kingdom of God is eschatological in nature, it is nonetheless soteriological and thereto has as its intention that the human is saved

---

[91] *Religie*, 153.

[92] Van Ruler, "De verhouding van het kosmologische en het eschatologische element in de christologie" [Hereinafter "Kosmologische"], in *TW* 1, 172.

[93] Rebel, 108.

[94] *Mannetje* is a Dutch idiom, and one crucial in Van Ruler's theological anthropology. In Dutch the phrase has the meaning that the human can do something without giving way. It is the human who can "stand his or her ground," who can "stand up to" another, in this case, God. It is Van Ruler's way of saying that the human is truly a human being before God. It is not to be understood as gender specific, relating only to the male of the species. In any case, we remind ourselves that we are working in an era where inclusive language was not at issue.

[95] *Reformatorische*, 190, 194. It is one of the burdens of Fries's dissertation, *Religion and the Hope for a Truly Human Existence*, to show how Van Ruler's theocratic vision sees God's actions as directed toward a "truly human existence."

in his historical existence."[96] Van Ruler sets this in contrast to a Roman Catholic notion that understands that the human at essence needs to be transubstantiated or elevated to a "higher" way of being. Such an understanding reflects a vertical structure of being. Behind this notion Van Ruler detects a latent hellenistic, gnostic, or neoplatonic influence. The Reformation, in contrast, with its doctrines of *iustitia originalis* and *iustificatio impii*, maintained that God desires for the human this earthly, temporal existence.[97]

Christ's atoning work makes human existence possible as it undoes what has been done, and so removes guilt from the sinner. In this way the sinner is "saved." The human can exist again *as* the human he or she is within created, historical reality. It is the Spirit, however, who gives the human its full place in the future of God now present. It is in the Spirit, for example, that I find my hypostasis not in God, but instead in myself. Furthermore, it is the work of the Spirit, who makes me his dwelling place, that I exist in full reciprocity with God.[98]

While it is central in Christological thinking that human nature, flesh, is united with the being of God, this is not so when we think from the perspective of the Spirit. Christology works with the notion of assumption; Christ assumes human flesh. Neither humanity itself nor individual humans are added to God.[99] The case is quite different in pneumatology. Here the category that applies is adoption; the human is adopted.[100] Humans retain their creaturely existence. In being united with Christ, I am not made to be identical with Christ. I retain my identity. I have already been born; I am not created afresh.[101] Furthermore, I am the object of salvation. Salvation is not as much about the savior as it is about the saved. "The essence of belief exists, then, in assent to self, acceptance of the world, passion for being."[102]

Still, the place of the human is not simply that of acceptance of salvation, of an acknowledgment that the human has a place. The Spirit works in such a way that the human is much more active. Van Ruler introduces the notion of *theopoiesis*. Through the Spirit I know, will and do all things with God. There is even a certain identity of God's judgments and my own, and that occurs not only in the

---

96 "Koninkrijk," 38. Emphasis in original.
97 "Kosmologische," 172.
98 "Structuurverschillen," 178.
99 "Structuurverschillen," 178.
100 "Structuurverschillen," 180.
101 "Structuurverschillen," 179.
102 "Structuurverschillen," 180.

eschaton, but in the present. As one would expect from his aversion to the notion that salvation entails elevation of being, Van Ruler hastens to add that this does not mean that we are ontically elevated beyond our creatureliness.[103] God retains a certain priority, but with the Spirit, there exists an "essential and full reciprocity" between the human and God, which includes the fact that God allows and, through the Spirit, enables the human to share in judgment.[104] The human knows genuine existence in this reciprocity: "genuine existence as human *is* to praise God into eternity."[105]

One can even go so far as to talk about the deification of the human: "God has, in Jesus Christ, become human, in order that we humans can become deified, as God."[106] That can only be understood, however, in a trinitarian-pneumatological perspective. It is not to be understood Christologically in that the human is ontically "elevated" to a new way of being. The human is met within salvation history, and there the Spirit indwells the human, the Spirit being fully the third person of the trinity, God now is present within the human. This "deification" is not then identity with God, but, as we shall see below, rather that the human can "think with," "act with," and even "judge with" God.

The outpouring of the Spirit is a historical event that, like the incarnation, happened at a particular time. But in contradistinction from the Messiah, there is continuity in the presence of the Spirit. In an image he uses a number of times, Van Ruler says that the coming of the Spirit is not like a seagull that lands upon the water only to return to the skies again. The Spirit poured out extends into history as it indwells the human (albeit not limited to the human—see below, 2.7).[107] The Spirit then frees the human in such a way that the human is the subject of his or her own conversion. She obtains a certain autonomy, by which she knows that the atonement is for her, thereby not only appropriating salvation, but also participating in her own salvation.[108] In the work of the Holy Spirit, a divine decision takes place; however, it is not only a decision about us, but in us. It is God's decision in such a way that it is also our own decision. That is the

---

[103] "Structuurverschillen, " 189.
[104] "Hoofdlijnen," 12.
[105] *Waarom*, 46. Emphasis in original. This is a "theonomous reciprocity." See on this Rebel, 142-144.
[106] "Hoofdlijnen," 27.
[107] "Structuurverschillen," 184.
[108] "Structuurverschillen," 181, 182.

work of the Spirit.[109] The human then can enter full reciprocity with God, and, furthermore, can enter the mystical union with Christ[110] and experience the world as the kingdom.[111] Put another way, the Word of God spoken to me becomes my word spoken back to God.[112]

This is the person in his or her individuality. Under the rubric of adoption, Van Ruler claims that the Spirit respects the person in his or her individuality. The human is taken seriously in his uniqueness, as an unrepeatable historical individual.[113] Nonetheless, the human is never isolated, but lives always in communion. Van Ruler can ask, for example, about the essence and the destination of the human: "Do they really live in the personal, individuality and personhood? Do they not live, for Christianity, much more in communion (the communion of saints!) and its tradition and history?"[114]

The human as goal has several implications. First, this will mean that the human is integrated into the life of the church.[115] Second, however, we shall see that the church is not the goal, but a means toward the realization of the kingdom of God. The communal nature of the human is realized in family, society, and culture. And third, because the human is now autonomous (within communion), and because the human shares in God's judgment not only concerning the self's relation to God in Christ but shares in God's judgment in all of life, Van Ruler can introduce the notion of theodicy. Since the human participates with God in the shaping of communal life, a "great thesis" emerges for Van Ruler: "The Spirit begins to throw light on theodicy."[116] The human becomes a full partner in the presence of the kingdom as it breaks into the present.

---

109 "Hoofdlijnen," 24. This insight has direct relevance for Van Ruler's understanding of the dynamics of election in the individual's appropriation of salvation. God takes initiative, but God's free election is reflected in the individual's choice and confession. "The free election of God intends to be mirrored and realized in the choice of the human." *Heeft het nog zin, van "volkskerk" te spreken?* [Hereinafter *Volkskerk*] (Wageningen: H. Veenman, 1958), 5.

110 "Hoofdlijnen," 14.

111 "Hoofdlijnen," 13.

112 "Hoofdlijnen," 33.

113 "Structuurverschillen," 180.

114 *Volkskerk*, 5.

115 "Hoofdlijnen," 34.

116 "Hoofdlijnen," 35.

2.4 Time in an Eschatological Perspective

God's ultimate intentions point toward the future of the kingdom of God. God works in and through history toward the kingdom. It is crucial, however, to understand how time and history work for Van Ruler. For he does not understand time and history as unidirectional as it moves from a chronological past, through the present, and toward a future.

In fact, time works from the future and so history is created by God, particularly through the work of the Spirit. As we noted above: "In dogmatic thinking we must begin from the end."[117] Theology will have to consider the end or the goal as history moves toward that end.[118]

One can envision eschatological thinking in different ways. One could think toward the end from out of the past as it contains the future within itself. Alternately, one could think from out of the present as it either participates in the development of history toward a future or contains the seed of the future within itself. Van Ruler takes neither of these options. Instead, for him the future finds its way into the present and so creates the present. The movement is *from out of the future* toward the present. In discussing fulfillment, he states that the "kingdom of God is to be radically understood from the end, from out of the future of God approaching us."[119]

This God who comes approaches from the future. There is a "historical essence" of God,[120] but this historical essence is not to be understood as God sharing in something like human history and development, but as God who "...is only to be understood as coming."[121] In this sense we can say that there is an "eschatological essence" of God.[122]

This is the future of God, but not a future to be understood chronologically, for this is God's future that implodes into the present. Since it is *God* who acts, the present stands open to the new; that is, the present is not the product or function of the past. The future continually "overpowers" [*overmachtigt*] or "overwhelms"

[117] *Vervulling*, 26.
[118] Rebel, 66.
[119] *Vervulling*, 26.
[120] "Koninkrijk," 32.
[121] *Vervulling*, 49.
[122] *Vervulling*, 50.

[*overstelpt*] time. The present is to be understood from the future, but particularly from *God's* future.[123]

God then creates history. This happens particularly through the Spirit. The Spirit did not enter a history already existent; history is not a stage on which the Spirit acts. Rather, the Spirit creates history. The Spirit calls forth or creates history as a particular gestalt and does so from out of the kingdom of God that itself is coming. "History is a predicate of the Spirit."[124] The Christian centuries came into view, as did the "christianization" of culture and the theocratization of the state: "In a word, the baptism and the education of the peoples and the course of the gospel of the kingdom throughout the earth."[125]

History is a fundamental category for Van Ruler. He titled his inaugural address, "Het koninkrijk Gods en de geschiedenis" ["The Kingdom of God and History"] because it expresses and coordinates two foundational themes in his theology. If the kingdom is the eschaton of history within which creation exists and in which God, having created, works, history is a gestalt of the kingdom.[126]

It is a genuine *history* in all its temporality, provisionality, and unrepeatability. Jesus Christ lived in a moment in history; the work of the Messiah was *ephapax*.[127] Created existence moves toward the eschaton; therefore a genuine *past* exists that also affects the present and the future. God creates history through the Spirit as the end breaks into the present. Time moves from the future to the past. But time also moves from the past to the future. There is a "double action" in time. Fries states that "on the one hand, time is 'filled' with eschatological salvation originating and hidden in the kingdom of God; on the other hand, time is 'taken up' into eternity."[128] Velema also identifies a "double content" in Van Ruler's eschatology as it moves not only from out of the end to the present, but from the present to the end.[129] The "arrow points in both directions from eschaton to time (filled time) and from time to eternity (time taken up into eternity)."[130]

---

123 *Vervulling,* 50.
124 *Vervulling,* 145.
125 *Vervulling,* 186.
126 *Vervulling,* 186.
127 "Structuurverschillen," 184.
128 Fries, *Religion and a Hope,* 86.
129 Velema, 14. According to Velema, we move *toward* the end because, after all, we have not yet reached the end.
130 Fries, 89. Van Hoof notes that "end" has a double meaning for Van Ruler. It can mean both "completion" and "starting point" (45). Rebel (78) also

It is with this understanding that Van Ruler can claim that there is no surprise in discovering the Spirit in the Old Testament chronologically prior to the outpouring of the Spirit at Pentecost, itself a historical event. The Spirit enters history from the future and could find its way into a (chronological) past with Israel.[131] Indeed, the first Christian community experienced the outpouring of the Spirit as taking place in the "end of days."[132] In the same context Van Ruler can assert that the atoning work of Christ happened in a past (once for all) but from out of the future.[133]

The role of the Spirit is central as it works not only from out of the future onto the present as the power of the kingdom breaking into the present,[134] but as making the past to be present. Furthermore, Van Ruler intends this in a full ontic sense. The Spirit works not only noetically, bringing the past into memory, but makes the past present in the most real sense.[135] In this way we can claim that the Spirit can take what is Christ's (what happened in Israel centuries ago) and make it our own. We can note here that the Spirit works in a manifold way in the realities of God's creation, our world, and indeed of the cosmos.

It is, then, the creation, or the cosmos, that is caught up in a history that moves toward the completion. And God acts in Christ through the Spirit for the sake of creation. "The work of salvation in Jesus Christ has happened only that creation can again exist in God's presence."[136] It is not as though in Christ's coming and the Spirit's work the old creation is set aside. God's "creation is no fiasco."[137] As we have noted, salvation is to restore creation to its original intention. Nonetheless, Christ's saving work does not bring about a return to the original creation. That simply cannot be so, argues Van Ruler, given that historicity, the substitutionary work of Christ, and salvation are central constituents in Christian thought. Sin has entered history and has disturbed the creation. It must be come to terms with, and God

notes the same phenomenon in Van Ruler's thought when he states that Van Ruler's eschatology "is not only futuristic but 'present-pleromatic.'" Each are reading Van Ruler in a slightly different way but all perceive that the eschaton works both toward the past and the present from the future and from within the past and the present to the future.

131 *Vervulling,* 146.

132 *Vervulling,* 132.

133 *Vervulling,* 150.

134 *Vervulling,* 125.

135 *Vervulling,* 182.

136 "Kosmologische," 165.

137 *Vervulling,* 58.

uses atonement and sanctification as means. What has changed? The Messiah and the Spirit are God's presence saving the creation, making it *vuurvast* [fireproof].[138] In his discussion of new creation, *kaine ktisis*, Van Ruler argues that the phrase is not to be understood as *nova creatio*, but exclusively as *recreatio*.[139] The old creation is not thrown away to be replaced by the new; the new creation is the old creation saved. Nothing falls away, save sin.[140]

The proton (creation) is given a "plus" in salvation. With Christ, this "plus" is of a "purely synthetic character."[141] What is added? In the *Vervulling van de wet*, Van Ruler identifies this "plus" as the law of God.[142] The law, of course, must be understood in its broadest sense, as coming from God, and as the law of the kingdom as we have seen. Van Ruler can also claim that the law is not to be reduced to laws or prescriptions found in the Torah, but the law *is* the Old Testament.[143] For our purpose it is sufficient to note that creation is set in an eschatological context and that it participates in a genuine history that includes creation in salvation and more, in sanctification, that points toward the completion in which God's original intention is shaped by history that comes from God's future.

The category of *sign* allows Van Ruler to talk about time as eschatological. The reality of this world as known and experienced by humans is fully real, but it is not final. It is but a sign of the true reality of the kingdom. The "secret of signs lies in the overpowering presence of the kingdom of God; and the essence of the signs lies in the matter of which it is the sign, that is fulfilled in a hidden manner."[144] "Reality is freed from all demonic depth and influence, stripped of the definitive character of its being, and broken apart into signs of the time." And that "is the real messianic action of God and stretches to save and maintain the reality of the world for the original

---

[138] "Kosmologische," 170, 171.

[139] See Lombard, *Adama*, 174-178 for his discussion of Van Ruler's rejection of the notion of *nova creatio*.

[140] "Kosmologische," 168.

[141] "Kosmologische," 171.

[142] *Vervulling*, 286.

[143] *Vervulling*, 466. Hendriks describes the "plus" in the following words: "The torah makes it clear to us that the living God has to do with the commonwealth in which he is served and praised. Van Ruler sees here the emergence of the 'visions of the holy life of the people' under ecclesiastical and civil authority" (69).

[144] *Vervulling*, 66.

and ultimate intentions of God."[145] We come to the same conclusion as we have above, that time, historically, participates in the (divine) future of God's kingdom in its present modality, the kingdom of Christ as present in the power of the Spirit.

2.5 Creation

We have seen that God's kingdom, as God's ultimate intention, is not divorced from this world; it is not spiritual in a nonmaterial sense. God's goal is the kingdom of God and the experience of this world as kingdom.[146] If the creation is "not a fiasco," the kingdom, as eschatological, is not to be thought of as a denial, or even a remaking of the creation. Indeed the creation, as proton, plays a central role in Van Ruler's theology.

The cosmological—another way of speaking about the creation—has to do with what he calls the "deepest question": what is God about? What is the sense of being?[147] He answers that God's intention, the goal for the human, and the sense of being is found by pointing to the covenant, to salvation, and to communion with God. Nevertheless, covenant and salvation are *means* and not the end or goal. Van Ruler points to the fact that created reality is "there," in God's presence, by virtue of God's eternal good pleasure. "Communion with God" must be understood as the pleasure that God has in God's world.[148]

Creation is relative, not absolute. It is not divine in itself; nor does it rest in itself. As creation, it is clearly to be distinguished from God.[149] But if distinct, creation nevertheless emerges from the goodness and freedom of God. It is the first of God's works, and more, it is God's most characteristic work.[150] God takes pleasure in creation.[151]

That is the case in the proton. But the proton tends toward the eschaton. Being and pleasure in being, existence as joy—that remains

---

[145] *Vervulling,* 110.
[146] "Hoofdlijnen," 13.
[147] "Kosmologische," 165.
[148] "Kosmologische," 166.
[149] Van Ruler, *Ik geloof: de twaalf artikelen van het geloof in morgenwijdingen,* 7th ed. (Nijkerk: G.F. Callenbach, n.d.) 32, 33. [Hereinafter *Geloof*]. Velema, noting Van Ruler's early relation with Barth, writes in this context that for Van Ruler, "the Word creates" (26). See *Religie,* 188.
[150] *Geloof,* 32.
[151] *Geloof,* 40.

the goal.[152] "...[I]n all God's actions the created world as such remains the goal to be worked toward."[153] The work of salvation is to enable the creation to become again what it was intended to be: "The work of salvation in Jesus Christ has taken place only that creation can again exist in God's presence."[154]

Still, it is the things of the created, material world that will exist in their naked reality in and with God (and they do so already as saved). One must, Van Ruler claims, "value matter [*stof*] as the true opposite [*tegenpool*] of God."[155] By this Van Ruler does not mean that matter is "not-God" in a neoplatonic sense, but that matter is that which stands over and against God to be engaged by God. The "earth" that God creates is the ordinary earth, the field, the entire of the material and visible reality.[156] Things [*dingen*] are important in Van Ruler's world. Matter does not occupy a "lower" order, but is to be valued as creation.[157] Such are the things of this created world. In discussing Ephesians 4:10, where Christ has ascended to fulfill all things, Van Ruler understands "all things" as created realities. "All things now become transparent as they shine from within themselves." "Reality has become messianic."[158]

Creation returns but now as saved. Salvation is set toward God's original and ultimate intentions. What is crucial is not salvation itself, but the saved.[159] The process is not what is important; it is only the means. It is the created reality, the "saved," that is of final importance. Van Ruler illustrates this in one place with the metaphor of a photograph. Creation is the photograph. Salvation comes to give meaning to the photograph, to rescue it from ruin. The point is not the "salvation itself" (the process) but the photograph, or in this case, creation.[160] Salvation (and sanctification) are the work of the Messiah and the Spirit, now in service of God's intentions in and for God's beloved creation. And this is manifest in the created world as humans experience it in their humanity. For, as Van Ruler claims, pure humanity, social justice, and political rights (as created and saved realities) are to be found in the Spirit as the principle of divine

---

152 "Kosmologische," 167.
153 "Hoofdlijnen," 40.
154 "Kosmologische," 165.
155 Van Ruler, "Hoe waardeert men de stof?" in *TW* 5, 10.
156 *Geloof*, 69.
157 *Blij zijn*, 28.
158 *Vervulling*, 113.
159 "Structuurverschillen," 189.
160 *Waarom*, 52.

immanence in God's created world. "In the spring, the fields and the flowers do not become green without the Spirit." And further, "In the Spirit, the world is God's pleasure."[161] And that pleasure is to be experienced as well by the human. This world is his home. The human belongs here, in this world; she is at home here, not in another, "higher," world. When the human so experiences the created world, "precisely then the service of the Creator becomes fully praise: when the human enjoys the whole of life and each day as a juicy peach."[162]

To arrive at that point of the joy of the humanity in creation, and to enter communion with God, salvation was necessary.[163] And we can, finally, speak of God's work in the Messiah and in the Spirit.

2.6 Messiah

We have seen that the goal or end of God's work is not human salvation in Christ. Christ is a means to a further end. "The work of the Spirit is to be seen in relation to the work of the mediator as the goal and the work of the mediator as the means."[164] As we shall see, Van Ruler's qualifier here, "in relation," is important as the Spirit, too, is God working toward God's ultimate intentions. The point is made, however, that Christ is not the end and goal toward which all history tends. That would, in fact, be to conflate history into a singular point of "call and election."[165] Christ effects the kingdom of Christ in his primary work of atonement. Said another way, the salvation of the human and of creation comes through Christ.

Salvation is to be understood, "centrally and radically" as atonement. Existence is saved.[166] The incarnation is exclusively to be thought of as reaction to sin.[167] And atonement is Christ's offering of himself, in fulfillment of the (ceremonial) law, to remove the guilt of sin.[168] Consistent with the Reformation, Van Ruler understands

---

161 "Hoofdlijnen," 38.
162 *Geloof*, 40.
163 "Necessary" here is not to be taken in an absolute sense. It is, if you will, a subsidiary necessity. That is, in God's free decision to act in love a certain necessity arises: neither the human nor creation could conform to God's original and ultimate intention without an intervention that we designate with the shorthand "salvation."
164 "Hoofdlijnen," 23.
165 "Koninkrijk," 31.
166 *Vervulling*, 213.
167 Rebel, 103.
168 *Vervulling*, 218.

atonement as primarily under the category of "substitution." The Messiah acts in our place, on behalf of the human. The mediator brings the offering of atonement in our stead; he takes our place as the guilty party.[169] In just such a manner, the guilt of sin is removed and the ruin of death annulled.[170] The human can now exist, freed from the crushing burden of a past that cannot be atoned outside the work of God in Christ. And more, the human can live in and enjoy existence to the full; he or she can experience the world as the kingdom of God.

As we might expect, given the eschatological character of the kingdom of God and the end toward which salvation bends, salvation also bears an eschatological character. In a sermon entitled, "The future of salvation," preached on a text from the prophet Amos, Van Ruler argues that prophecy is not only about judgment but also about salvation. This salvation, however, is future, it is the "over and against" of the future, a future we cannot see in the darkness of the present.[171]

Furthermore, in the eschaton our access to God is no longer hindered by our weakness. We enter into pure relation with God, God in his majesty. The boundary between creature and Creator will continue to be respected, but there is no longer anything between God and the "naked existence of created things." This is so because God has acted in the Messiah to remove that which has arisen between God and the human, sin with its consequence, guilt.[172]

Nor is atonement accomplished only for the human.[173] All reality is included in the offering of the atonement: "...The universe is thereby borne, history is thereby determined, cultures are formed thereby, existence is thereby ordered, the human is thereby saved, and the entire law of God (the Torah) is thereby established."[174] In one place, Van Ruler can speak of creation being "borne" while completed salvation remains outstanding. For salvation is only to be reached in the eschaton. In the meantime, existence is not yet saved. It is only

---

169 "Structuurverschillen," 181, 182.

170 *Vervulling*, 218. Velema, who makes much of Van Ruler's doctrine of atonement, puts it a bit differently: "The justice [*recht*] of God is rent in sin and restored in the offering of Jesus Christ. This restoration of justice as atonement through satisfaction can even be called the kernel of salvation. Through this restoration guilt is removed" (32-33).

171 "Toekomst des heils," 1.

172 *Vervulling*, 93.

173 Arendshorst (76) summarizes Van Ruler's theology in part: "Jesus Christ came exclusively as mediator of salvation to lift created reality out of the guilt of sin and the lordship of the powers."

174 *Vervulling*, 172.

borne in Christ and his offering of atonement. "And it is preserved, in the Spirit, until the day of salvation."[175]

Atonement has happened once for all. That is the nature of the case in Christology. What happened in Jesus of Nazareth occurred in Israel of the first century (so designated because Jesus is a historical personage and because it was an event of such history-determining significance.) It is, in this sense, "hidden." It is not immediately available to contemporary human experience. But it is hidden in a more profound way. Atonement happens more before God's eyes than it does before ours. Something happened that removed guilt from before the presence of God. Van Ruler maintains that this hidden act is "revealed," made manifest in history.[176]

But atonement *happens* (or perhaps more accurately, happened). It is a historical event. Something new has occurred. Hence, one cannot arrive at the reality of atonement through the analysis of being, of what eternal reality *is*.[177]

The historical nature of Christ's atoning work has implications for how Van Ruler understands the incarnation and subsequently the Messiah's relation to the kingdom and indeed to reality. For the Messiah's historical work has to do with offering, and offering with death. It is of the essence of the Messianic work that the Messiah gives himself up to death. That will be so profoundly the case with the Messiah that the real act of the Messiah is to cease to be Messiah, and so allow all things to be saved.[178] "Then it is clear that it is not about revelation but about existence, not about the Son of God in the flesh but about the human, and finally, not about salvation, but about culture."[179] That is to be the case in the final completion. Nonetheless, while we still live this side of eschaton, it remains that the Messiah

---

[175] "Hoofdlijnen," 40. Technically, it is the human who is saved. Creation is not guilty. One might put it for Van Ruler that creation takes part in salvation as the human is saved.

[176] *Vervulling*, 98.

[177] *Vervulling*, 99.

[178] *Vervulling*, 187. This is one place where major criticism has been leveled against Van Ruler. Velema, in his early summary of Van Ruler's theology, criticizes this notion for its lack of exegetical support. He cites, e.g., the presence of the Lamb in Revelation 21 and 22 as exegetical ground for the existence of the Mediator in the eschaton. He makes that point with Van Ruler in *Gesprek*, 60-64. Van Ruler responds, in part, by challenging how exegesis functions as warrant for dogmatic thinking. See his "Methode en mogelijkheden," cited in n. 8.

[179] *Vervulling*, 130.

died for the sake of the atonement, and hence for the sake of the kingdom.[180]

This has two implications. First, the incarnation doesn't "expand" or "extend" into history to become the foundation of all of life. What "expansion" or "extension" occurs is the work of the Spirit. Second, the work of Christ transcends "being." That is, being, as a continuing substrate to existence, is not and cannot be eternal. Something *new* or historical has occurred.[181] This shatters a certain charm that "being" has for the creature. And for Van Ruler it negates the Roman Catholic notion that being is structured vertically. Such a notion holds that while created reality is good, it is still not the full work of God but must be elevated or transubstatiated,[182] a doctrine that we have seen over and again as uncongenial to Van Ruler.

At the same time, the incarnation is not an event that has been abandoned, or given up. In the incarnation a contraction of everything that is of God and that is of the world takes place in the one name.[183] Humans must be engrafted in this person, and that through the real presence of Christ, contemporarily so. This engrafting occurs within the tension of the eschatological reality of God. In this way, the human is not "elevated" in Christ, but is incorporated in the Christ coming from the future. A. Hennephof remarks that the development of Van Ruler's theology includes a "fierce rejection of the thought that the destination of reality would in any way include an elevation to a higher reality."[184] The relation is not vertical but horizontal. After all, this contraction, while real, is not normal. It is, in fact, an "emergency measure."[185] We live in a "messianic intermezzo," the time of fulfillment, which is not yet the time of completion; we live in what was described above as the kingdom of Christ.

The "intermezzo" is characterized by the ascension of the incarnate Christ. Christ's ascension is that of the rule of the living Christ. This reign, as that of the kingdom of Christ, is both hidden

---

[180] *Vervulling,* 100.

[181] *Vervulling,* 100.

[182] "Kosmologische," 172.

[183] "Kosmologische," 173.

[184] Hennephof, 12.

[185] "Kosmologische," 174. Van Ruler is criticized for his notion of Christ as "emergency measure." Velema, e.g., remarks that it is "unthinkable" that "...Christ stands so central and his work so fundamental, that one simply cannot think that God has waited as long as possible with the emergency measure" (52). Others agree, as e.g., I. John Hesselink, "Contemporary Protestant Dutch Theology," *Reformed Review,* 26 no. 2 (Winter, 1973), 86.

and set against an eschatological horizon.[186] It lives in expectation. Nonetheless, it is the rule of Christ, the establishment of the kingdom in the flesh. In just that way, Van Ruler never tires of the phrase, "fulfillment is an act of God in Christ through the Holy Spirit."[187] The prepositions are crucial: God acts *in* Christ *through* (by means of) the Holy Spirit.

Christ comes *to* the creation from out of the future. Understanding how time and history function in Van Ruler's thought, we can acknowledge that Christ comes *both* out of the future and has lived and lives as a historical figure. The Messiah is a figure in the past even as he came from God's future. As one who comes from God and God's future to the human, Christ is the office-bearer par excellence. Christ is the future that posits the church and the world in the present.[188] Or said within the context of the ascension, "The ascension is only to be understood as a moment in the regnum Christi. And the regnum Christi is not to be understood except as a modality of the regnum Dei. And the regnum Dei finds its core in the future of God and in the completion of all things."[189]

God acts in Christ, but through the Holy Spirit. Salvation, fulfillment, extends toward completion. It is God who works not only in the way of the Messiah, but, as we have repeated perhaps too often (if only reflecting Van Ruler's repetition of the notion), it is the Spirit who expands and represents the kingdom of Christ in its provisional gestalt.

2.7 The Spirit

It will not do for Van Ruler either to conflate or to identify the work of the Messiah and the Spirit. The Spirit cannot be understood only as the Spirit of Christ.[190] The Spirit has its own work in God's

---

[186] *Vervulling,* 105. In "Hemelvaart - en wederkomst" (a sermon preached on 30 May 1935 at Kubaard on Acts 1:10,11), Van Ruler Archive, Folder IV, 95, p. 5, Van Ruler maintains that ascension is not a feast of remembrance but of expectation. "Ascension intends to teach us not so completely to turn to what has been and is now past but to look forward to what still comes in the distant and deep future, in unimagined possibilities."

[187] E.g., *Vervulling,* 17.

[188] *Vervulling,* 86.

[189] *Vervulling,* 108.

[190] Van Ruler will reflect on the notion of *filioque* in a number of places. In "Hoofdlijnen" (22) he hesitates to come to definitive judgment on the issue. He calls it a "school question." He is clear, however, that there can be

economy. The outpouring of the Spirit is an event or fact of salvation that occurred in Israel at a particular time. But, as we have seen, the work of the Spirit extends into history.

In this claim, two aspects of the Spirit come to the fore. The first is that the Spirit *enters* history, and indeed, as we have seen, creates history. The Spirit is God in the particular mode of the Spirit, God the third time. The Spirit does not emerge into history from out of a Christ who was present in the past, but from out of the future of God.[191] The Spirit, then, bears an eschatological character; the Spirit is poured out not so much in the last days as from out of the last days.[192]

Secondly, the Spirit, now having entered history from out of the future, nonetheless works "forward" from the historical presence of Christ. As such, it extends Christ's work of establishing the kingdom in the flesh into the gestalts of created reality, time included. Van Ruler can articulate that in different ways. He can say, for example, that the Spirit takes what is in Christ and communicates that to the human. Since atonement happens not before our eyes, but before God's eyes, it must be made manifest to us. It is the Spirit at work in the institution of the office of the apostle and in the calling of the confessing congregation that accomplishes this work.[193] More, Van Ruler will claim that the Spirit also takes what is in Christ and gives Christ gestalt within the human.[194] At still other times, he writes that the Spirit expands and represents salvation in history.[195] In his discussion of the fulfillment of the law, Van Ruler will aver that "the law is fulfilled in the Messiah as the *foundation* of salvation in the world and it is fulfilled through the Spirit in the *expansion* of salvation in the world."[196]

---

no sense of the Spirit only proceeding from the Son, no *ex filio solo*. See also *Vervulling*, 166-169, where Van Ruler claims that the Spirit is a fully objective historical act of God, 167.

[191] *Vervulling*, 121. Velema puts it this way: "The gift of the Spirit is never and exclusively to be understood from out of the Messiah. It must primarily be understood from out of the kingdom." 58.

[192] *Vervulling*, 134.

[193] "Hoofdlijnen," 11.

[194] "Hoofdlijnen," 23.

[195] E.g., *Vervulling*, 219.

[196] *Vervulling*, 499, emphasis in original. In "Verscheidenheid in de gemeente" (sermon preached on June 26, 1938, in Kubaard on 1 Corinthians 12:4) Van Ruler Archive, Folder IV, 249, p. 1, Van Ruler says that the "Spirit is expansive—he expands, now this way, now that." This in contrast to human inclination to "...force the stream of the Spirit into one channel."

This expansion extends beyond that moment in history where the kingdom was established in Christ. The foundational notion in pneumatology, according to Van Ruler, is that of *indwelling*. The Holy Spirit, God's own self, dwells in us.[197] But who is this "us"? It includes the human. I am the intended dwelling place of the Spirit.[198]

But indwelling is not limited to the individual human. It includes the church and Christian peoples: "The dwelling place of the Holy Spirit is the peoples of the earth who in the course of the apostolic Word are engrafted into the covenant of God with Israel." And more, indwelling will include the generations, the structures of society, cultures, and the political shape of life.[199] The kingdom, which comes in the power of the Spirit, extends to peoples, nations, and cultures. "The kingdom is established in the gestalts of the flesh and existence is made historical."[200] The *inhabitatio* of Christ is not only in us humans, but in cultures.[201] In fact, one can go further and claim that the Spirit is "absorbed" [*opgaan*] in the ordinary forms of existence.[202]

Van Ruler articulates the notion of indwelling under the rubric of *gratia interna*, internal grace. "In the *gratia interna* the kingdom of God, in one way or another, is established in the flesh."[203] Theology has been inclined to understand *gratia interna* as something that happens with the human. However, Van Ruler emphasizes over and again that *interna* means "internal to this world." It includes the anthropological but is more all-embracing, extending to the entire cosmos.[204] The Spirit is at work mystically and sacramentally to be sure, but is also at work politically and culturally. *Gratia interna* works historically.[205] "The politics of Christian kings and emperors of Europe are equally as much forms of *gratia interna* as are the songs of Jocodus van Lodenstein." [206] By means of the *gratia interna*, the Spirit

---

[197] "Hoofdlijnen," 14.
[198] "Structuurverschillen," 178.
[199] "Hoofdlijnen," 15.
[200] *Vervulling*, 516, 517.
[201] "Structuurverschillen," 187.
[202] *Vervulling*, 219.
[203] *Vervulling*, 206. Cf. "Hoofdlijnen," 25.
[204] *Vervulling*, 204.
[205] *Vervulling*, 212.
[206] *Vervulling*, 228. Van Lodenstein was a seventeenth- century pietist and a leader in the *nadere reformatie*, or "further Reformation" in the Netherlands.

creates gestalts of the kingdom in the communal existence of the human, specifically in state and in culture.[207]

Gratia interna as the indwelling of the Spirit stands within the eschatological nature of the Spirit. *Gratia interna* is not to be understood as a something, as a substance added to or poured into the human. Salvation remains a *corpus alienum* in existence.[208] The internal nature of the human, and indeed of created reality, is not to be understood from out of itself, not by analyzing the nature of being, but eschatologically from out of the future of the kingdom of God.[209] As we have seen, this is transcendence as horizontal. Said another way, this is transcendence at work, but transcendence now not understood in an ontological-quantitative sense, but in a qualitative-dynamic sense. Transcendence is what approaches from the future.[210]

The Spirit's work in the world is that of *sanctification*. While the Messiah's primary work is atonement, atonement is not the goal but the means. Sanctification, with glorification, is the goal.[211] The glory of God is not primarily the self-justification of God, nor is it the justification of the human, but first of all the sanctification and the glorification of the *world*.[212] In sanctification, the human does not find Christ and God, but the human finds himself and the world. Just so, the work of the Spirit moves from salvation to creation.

Sanctification is not yet glorification. The Spirit works to sanctify; but neither the human nor creation are yet glorified. Here again the law enters the picture.[213] The law is a gestalt of the kingdom of God in the flesh. In the law the entire of existence is ordered and formed.[214] "The law indicates what functions the gestalts have in the entire of the historical-eschatological actions of God. The sacraments and the offices [n.b., the plural], experience and good works, the 'christianized' culture and the theocratic state are 'shadows of the law' that fall along the walls of existence."[215] The law is fulfilled *through* the Spirit. This is the law that is the law of the kingdom of God.

Still, if the Spirit enters the present from out of the kingdom of God, it is not itself the kingdom. The Spirit is the *power* of the

---

[207] *Vervulling*, 258, 259.
[208] *Vervulling*, 209.
[209] *Vervulling*, 224.
[210] *Vervulling*, 225.
[211] "Structuurverschillen," 183.
[212] "Hoofdlijnen," 24.
[213] *Vervulling*, 272.
[214] *Vervulling*, 209-210.
[215] *Vervulling*, 500.

kingdom. The full breakthrough of the kingdom has not occurred. In the intermezzo, we live between the first and the second coming of Christ. This between-time is the characteristic locus for the Holy Spirit.[216] "The Spirit...creates around the gift and the work of the Messiah the room to maneuver for history insofar as the Spirit holds apart the walls of existence, between the first and the second coming of Christ and in the Christian centuries God's torah expands around the cross in the ordering of existence."[217] The Spirit is, then, the kingdom in the "modality of promise"; the Spirit is the "way of being of the approaching kingdom."[218]

Van Ruler uses the category of *sign* to say the same thing. The Spirit is to be understood as "*the* great sign of the kingdom coming to us."[219] It is imperative, however, to keep in mind what Van Ruler means by "sign." A sign is not arbitrary, established by convention or contrivance. In discussing signs in the context of the kingdom of God, he claims that "the essence of the signs lies in the matter, fulfilled in a hidden way, of which it is the sign.[220] The Spirit, as power of the kingdom, then participates in the kingdom. Thus, while the kingdom of God transcends the present, if only because the forms of the present cannot hold the fullness of the kingdom that is yet to come, nonetheless the kingdom takes shape in the historical forms of the present as well.[221]

In contradistinction to the Messiah, the Spirit expands into the full plurality of the created order. This is because the work of the Spirit is broader ranging, more inclusive than that of Christ.[222] The work of the Spirit takes up and embraces all the cosmos, all reality. Christologically, one cannot talk about *plurality*.[223] But there is no monism in the Spirit. Plurality, instead, is at the heart of the Spirit's work.[224] Because the Spirit effects plurality, unity as understood in the Spirit is not unity of being which is a unity that derives from an essential identity. Rather, unity effected by the Spirit is a unity in love.

---

216 *Vervulling*, 136, 137.
217 *Vervulling*, 141-142.
218 *Vervulling*, 138.
219 *Vervulling*, 161.
220 *Vervulling*, 69.
221 "...the Spirit requires forms and instruments of expression. Men could never bring the Holy Spirit into their field of vision apart from the reality of these instruments and *Gestalten*." Fries, *Religion and the Hope*, 109.
222 *Vervulling*, 185.
223 *Vervulling*, 193.
224 "Hoofdlijnen," 32.

Such unity will be expressed through mutuality and reciprocity. In discussing the appropriation of salvation through the Spirit, Van Ruler asserts that the central thought is that what concerns God will also become the concern of the human. The two enter mutual partnership. God's Word spoken to the human becomes the human's word spoken back to God. And this mutuality of love is the goal of the Spirit.[225] We discover what we had discovered earlier in discussing the human as God's goal: the human enters a full communion with God where he or she stands on her own feet and even shares with God in the judgment of this world.

This mutuality or plurality is not, however, limited to the mutual relation between God and the human but extends into the gestalts of church, culture, peoples, governmental authorities. The Spirit comes as first-fruit, pledge, and seal of God's coming kingdom. As such the human learns that there is more to come and so learns to expect. Indeed, the human will expect more than can be contained in the present forms of existence.[226] Plurality, while existent in the present, tends toward an eschatological overflow.

This being the case, Van Ruler must maintain that the gift of the Spirit and its indwelling are provisional. The gift of the Spirit comes up against an eschatological boundary. For the Spirit "is a particular gestalt in the actions of God, but a peculiar, separate gestalt, and not the final gestalt, not even its beginning stage."[227] As the Messiah cedes his messiahship in the eschaton, so will the outpouring of the Spirit and its indwelling come to an end.[228] The Spirit, too, participates in the intermezzo. The Spirit as the power of the kingdom of Christ, then, tends toward the kingdom of God.

2.8 Trinity

We have followed Van Ruler's prescription to think "out of the end." We began with the eschatological reality of the kingdom of God and thought "back" into God's actions creating a history in which God works in Christ and through the Spirit to establish the kingdom and to set it toward its completion. In so doing, we have heard Van Ruler articulate God's work and God's presence in the persons of the Trinity. Only now are we prepared to reflect on the trinitarian nature of God.

---

[225] "Hooflijnen," 32.
[226] *Vervulling,* 160.
[227] *Vervulling,* 142.
[228] *Vervulling,* 189.

While Van Ruler's theology is resolutely trinitarian (and as we have seen, he intended it so), he gives little energy to working out a full theology of the trinity as such.[229] He does not disavow the importance of such a theology, but his fuller theological interest is to be seen in the trinitarian nature of God's work. We have seen the centrality of the work of the Father as creator,[230] of the Son as Messiah, and the Spirit as the one who indwells creation, sanctifying and expanding and giving image to the kingdom of Christ.

For example, in discussing the kingdom of Christ, Van Ruler can state that "the Messiah in the power of his work of salvation and in the power of the Holy Spirit dwells through all things and frees them from their own 'divine,' demonic coherence of being, in order, electing and sanctifying them in the play-room of history to be signs and seals, to be first-fruits and pledge of the glory of God...."[231] Here we see the triune God at work: Father, Son, and Holy Spirit. Indeed, Van Ruler comments further: the truth of the final days gives knowledge of the glory of God; it "enlightens" the truth of fulfillment in the knowledge of God the Son and the truth of the first fruits and pledge of the knowledge of God the Spirit. This does not remain noetic, however. As we have seen, atonement takes place, and further, the Spirit indwells the human and creation. This has ontic significance as it draws the human into a new relation to God.

Since God has manifest God's self as Messiah and as Holy Spirit, we are forced to the "necessity" of a trinitarian theology. God presents God's self as trinitarian. Nonetheless, even as Van Ruler's interest emerges from the economic action of God in history, he claims that trinitarian thought needs to keep two movements in mind within the immanent trinity, that of relation-to-each-other [*op-elkaar-betrekken*] of the persons of the Trinity and that of distinction-from-each-other [*uit-*

---

229 Van Ruler, "De noodzakelijkheid van een trinitarische theologie" [Hereinafter "Noodzakelijkheid"], in *Verwachting.* There he declines to offer a fully developed trinitarian theology, "for I know it not" (9). For a short but profound treatment of the doctrine of the Trinity, see Van Ruler, "De leer van de Drieëeinheid." The essay is also found in *Blij zijn,* 92-94. See as well, "Het mysterie van de drieëenheid" (sermon preached January 5, 1947, in Hilversum on Sunday 8 of the Heidelberg Catechism), Van Ruler Archive, Folder IV, 1016, and "De drieëenheid" (sermon preached January 9, 1955, in Rotterdam), Van Ruler Archive, Folder IV, 716.

230 Van Hoof claims that Van Ruler's theology is, finally, patrocentric (44). Hendriks cautiously agrees. He claims that for Van Ruler the original priority of God as Father will bring Van Ruler to place the patrocentric in the foreground of the idea of the kingdom of God (48).

231 *Vervulling,* 24.

elkaar-houden] of the persons.[232] This double movement also has profound effects economically. For example, creation and salvation can neither be identified nor conflated. They are to be related to each other and held in a certain tension. As we have seen, creation is not to be understood for the sake of salvation, but salvation for the sake of creation. They are related but distinct. Likewise, salvation stands in a particular dynamic relation to the kingdom.[233]

Similarly, the work of Christ and that of the Spirit are not to be identified. Van Ruler advocates, for example, the necessity of a "relatively independent pneumatology."[234] Even in that case, however, pneumatology is only *relatively* independent. The persons are distinct from one another but are also bound to each other. We have seen, e.g., that the Spirit takes that which is Christ and establishes a gestalt of Christ in the human. Put another way, the kingdom of Christ comes to its full present reality only through the Spirit.[235]

Van Ruler will interpret the human's mystical union with Christ from a pneumatological perspective as mystical union with the triune God: "Through the Spirit I understand myself as elect from eternity to an eternal salvation."[236] Even here, though, one needs to be cautious, for Van Ruler resists the notion that the human and creation are "absorbed" into the trinitarian life of God. God works "trinitarianly" to the end that communion with God includes the creature in his full creatureliness.[237] Van Ruler understands this from the trinitarian place and function of the Spirit. Like Augustine, Van Ruler understands the Spirit as the bond of love between the Father and the Son.[238] The Spirit is the "principle of immanence immanent" in God. Thus, the bond of love is mutual, in the way of the Spirit (*viz.*, indwelling), and imaged less as a circle than as a progress.[239] Further, communion with God is not elevation above creaturely existence.[240] We arrive yet again at the conclusion we have come to previously in our inquiry, now from

---

232 "Noodzakelijkheid," 9.

233 "Noodzakelijkheid," 10.

234 "Hoofdlijnen," 11.

235 *Vervulling*, 193.

236 "Structuurverschillen," 189.

237 "The human is only human when he moves within the play-space of the work of the triune God." "Het mysterie van de drieëenheid," 1. Now, Van Ruler argues, this is not only a *vis à vis* of the human as God's partner. The human is "embraced" by God. *Ibid.*, 2.

238 See Van Ruler, "Leer van de Drieëenheid," 2.

239 "The triune God is no longer a circle but a way." Arendshorst, 47.

240 "Hoofdlijnen," 27.

the perspective of the trinitarian nature of God: the Spirit enables the human to be human before God. Just so, the God draws creation and the human forward to the eschaton where it is "only the triune God and the naked existence of created things in their vis-à-vis as the vis-à-vis of mutual joy."[241]

2.9 Summary

We have attempted to sketch Van Ruler's theology in broad strokes. A fuller theological exposition and analysis would include, for example, a description of the place of the Old Testament in theological understanding, his theocratic vision in its fullest extent,[242] and would attempt a closer view of Van Ruler's Christological and pneumatological commitments, particularly from a trinitarian perspective.[243] Such an exposition exceeds our purpose of understanding his theology of office, even as we shall have to understand his ecclesiology as part of that effort. We can summarize the important discoveries as follows.

1. God comes to humanity from the future. God's revelation is not to be discovered by an analysis of being, particularly of the human being. The priority of action belongs with God. This is the predestinarian kernel of Van Ruler's thought.

2. God's original intention emerges from God's ultimate intention, the kingdom of God, which is none other than creation experienced as that kingdom. This is the eschatological import of Van Ruler's theology.

3. God intends human flourishing, which means that the human becomes human as human and not as raised above humanity to participate in divinity. The human's flourishing is in its essence

---

241 "Hoofdlijnen," 27.

242 On theocracy in particular see Benjamin Engelbrecht, *Agtergronde en grondlyne van die teokratiese visioen: Inleiding tot die teokratiese teologie van prof. A.A. van Ruler.* Dissertation (n.p., 1963). Tjaard G. Hommes, *Sovereignty and Saeculum: Arnold A. Van Ruler's Theocratic Theology.* Dissertation (Cambridge: Harvard, 1966); *De waarheid is theocratisch: bijdragen tot de waardering van de theologische nalatenschap van Arnold Albert van Ruler,* Gerrit Klein and Dick Steenks, eds. (Baarn: G.F. Callenbach, 1995); and *Woord en werkelijkheid: over de theocratie. Een bundel opstellen in dankbare nagadachtenis aan Prof. A.A. van Ruler* (Nijkerk: G.F. Callenbach, 1973).

243 One can find the beginning of work at such a task in C. Lombard, "The relevance of Van Ruler's theology," in *The Relevance of Theology for the 1990s,* ed. J. Mouton and B.C. Lategan (Pretoria: Human Sciences Research Council, 1994), 549-569.

communal in nature even as it respects the particular integrity of the unique person. The human finds its goal as he or she enters the great round dance of heaven, a full human now as partner and counterpart of God.

4. God's kingdom intentions are realized in the gestalts of culture, society, government, and art as the communal loci in which the human flourishes.

5. As sin has disturbed God's original and ultimate intentions, God acts to atone guilt, and so effect salvation, through the Messiah. Salvation as brought by the incarnate Son, the Messiah, restores creation in order that the Spirit can effect God's ultimate intentions for that very same creation.

6. The Spirit extends and represents salvation, even as it effects sanctification. The Spirit does so both as it enables the human to know and to receive salvation, and as it creates both the history and the gestalts in which the kingdom of Christ receives gestalt within history.

7. Salvation or fulfillment is not yet the completion. The goal is not salvation, but the kingdom of God, the restoration of creation to its original purpose. The light of all eternity is now seen in all created things.

8. God is trinitarian as God discloses God's self in creation, in the Messiah, and in the Spirit, a relation in which the distinction must be honored. It is as this trinitarian God acts that we shall see God at work in Christ and through the Spirit in the church and in the offices of the church.

The church takes an important place within Van Ruler's theology, as do the offices. However, they find their place *within* the expansive space of the creation as God acts in history with creation.

CHAPTER 3

The Church as Bearer of the Gospel and as Gestalt of the Kingdom

The previous chapter has made clear that Van Ruler's theological vision is of the trinitarian God acting in history from God's future to establish and to realize the kingdom of God. Salvation is God's action in the Messiah to make creation "fireproof"; thus this world can be experienced as the kingdom of God. The kingdom of Christ is the gestalt of God's kingdom in the "intermezzo." Christ, as Messiah, acted historically, *ephapax*, in the offering of the atonement, the fulfillment of God's intentions, and did so in the presence of the triune God, in order that the human might live guiltless before God, and so fully human. Through the work of the Spirit the human now shares in delight, being sanctified in order that the human is established as human and so can work together with God in the realization of God's intentions. In the intermezzo, under the reign of the ascended Christ and through the work of the Spirit, the kingdom of Christ extends to all creation, including the political, the economic, the social, and the cultural life of the human family.

The church will find its place within the "double movement" of history we have outlined above (2.4). God comes to the church from the future, but from a future that establishes a history in the human past. More specifically, the church is used by God to effect salvation. The church shares in the fulfillment, but the church is not the final goal and indeed will fall away in the time of completion. It is the burden of this chapter to articulate just how this is so.

We will need to keep in mind two movements in Van Ruler's thought as we consider his understanding of the church. One is diachronic, the other synchronic. His thought is diachronic in two senses. The first is theological. The church exists in a diachronic movement as *God* uses it in history. That is, it stands within a history that moves toward the goal of the kingdom, where the human and creation can exist in the full joy of creaturehood ("being") in the presence of the triune God.

More importantly for our purpose is the diachronic movement in a second sense, that is, within Van Ruler's *thought* itself. His doctrine of the church will develop throughout his theological career. A.N. Hendriks, in his thorough study of Van Ruler's understanding of the church, sees three phases in this development. According to Hendriks, Van Ruler first understands the church as *sign* within the framework of the development of what Hendriks calls his "theocratic vision of culture." The second phase is that of an "explication of the apostolate of the church."[1] The third phase is that of "accentuating the peculiar gestalt of the church." We shall take note of this development. However, even as Van Ruler's emphases will shift, his core theological commitments will remain consistent.[2]

The second movement is synchronic. That is, Van Ruler's thought will exhibit the same double movement we have observed in his theological method. A certain duality (or *tweepoligheid*) will find expression in various ways when Van Ruler writes about the church. This is evidenced, for example, when Van Ruler talks about the church as "communion and institution,"[3] or as office and congregation.[4] In a relatively early essay (1941), he views the church in a "binocular" fashion, seeing the church through a series of pairs of images: time and eternity, above and below, visible and invisible, and institution

---

[1] Hendriks, *passim*.

[2] René Suss, "Theocratie: koen presens of zacht futurum van de hoop?" (1), *In de waagschaal*, 14 (1985), no. 1, 21, calls Van Ruler's theology "astonishingly consistent." This is clear from a lecture Van Ruler delivered in 1949 where he maintained that there is a close connection between the mystic and the apostolic in the church: "The mystical emotion that one has with God gives fervor to the apostolic vision of the world." "De prediking en het persoonlijk geloofsleven: Aantekeningen van een lezing op een conferentie van de kerkeraad van Rotterdam," August/September, 1949, Van Ruler Archive, Folder I, 247, p. 5.

[3] *Religie*, 87.

[4] *Reformatorische*, 81. "The church is on the one hand sacrament and office and clergy. It is on the other hand, and that equally essentially, congregation, believer" (25).

and organism.[5] We shall view his doctrine of church from two angles: that of the church as the bearer of the gospel,[6] and that of the church as a gestalt of the kingdom of God. The church is, on the one hand, a "vehicle, a cart" on which the Word of God, the gospel of the kingdom, moves itself through the centuries.[7] On the other hand it is, as Van Ruler will describe it in his later works, a "cathedral of love,"[8] "embodied joy,"[9] or "tent in the carnival of life."[10] It is not only that Van Ruler will move from one side of the matter to the other in his thinking; he sees the church itself as existing not around one center, as around the center of a circle, but with two foci, as with an ellipse.[11]

---

[5] *Religie*, 15-26. I owe the notion of "binocular" to P.R. Fries in an unpublished lecture, "Theology in a Binocular Perspective," delivered July 4, 1996, in Doorn, the Netherlands. B. Plaisier, in his *scriptie* on Van Ruler's doctrine of the church, also claims that it circles *tweepolig* around the relativization of the work of the church within God's kingdom actions on the one hand and the separate configuration, or gestalt, of the church on the other. He will agree with us, however, that Van Ruler's ecclesiology displays a consistency throughout: "...a constant in all periods [of Van Ruler's thought] is on the one hand the vision of the church as intermezzo and means; preaching as the *spil* [axle] of the church and predestination as the heart of the church....On the other hand we detect in all periods a great valuation of the institutional moments in reality and in the church in particular. The great emphasis on the (particular) work of Christ and the Holy Spirit play a central role here; both are unavoidable means. Consequently the church is necessary in her separateness." "Instrumenteel tussenspel: Van Rulers ecclesiologie onder het gezichtpunt van het apostolaat" (University of Utrecht, 1977), 90.

[6] In "Gemeente en ambten" (sermon preached May 18, 1941, in Hilversum on Acts 1:8), Van Ruler Archive, Folder IV, 388, p. 1, Van Ruler states: "The church is the bearer of the gospel."

[7] Van Ruler, *Het apostolaat der kerk en het ontwerp-kerkorde* [hereinafter *Apostolaat*] (Nijkerk: G.F. Callenbach, 1972), 155. See also Van Ruler, "De orde der kerk," lezing voor de Pastorale Conferentie in De Horst, spring, 1948, Van Ruler Archive, Folder I, 233, 11.

[8] Van Ruler, "De kerk in een zich mondig noemende wereld" [Hereinafter, "Mondig"], in *TW*, 2, 127; *Geloof*, 132.

[9] *Geloof*, 133.

[10] *Blij zijn*, 194.

[11] Van Ruler himself articulates our two-fold approach when he is writing in a different context and in passing notes that the church is both a "pointing to and sacramental—that is, provisionally!—realization of the ultimate salvation of the total reality." "Vragen door Bonhoeffer aan de orde gesteld," in *TW*, 5, 185.

This will be especially crucial as we look forward to the place of the offices as offices of the kingdom.

We acknowledge that this two-fold approach does not coincide with Hendriks's scheme of three phases.[12] We will speak less of the church as sign. It is clear that Van Ruler did indeed understand the church as sign in his earlier works, or more correctly as the "totality of signs" of eternal life, of the kingdom of God in Christ.[13] Indeed, in one place he calls the church a "divining rod" [*wichelroede*].[14] In a full explication of the development of Van Ruler's theology we would need to give more space to this notion. However, for the purpose of this study, we will treat the notion of church as sign as subordinate to Van Ruler's later, and fuller, doctrine of the church, a doctrine which will continue to express both the apostolic nature of the church and its reality as a gestalt of the kingdom of God.[15] Van Ruler never abandons the notion of church as sign. Rather, on the one hand he deepens the notion in ways that are consistent with the sign-character of the church. On the other hand, the church is not *only* sign.

Van Ruler is a Reformed theologian and as such never strays from the fundamental Reformed confession of Word and sacrament as the marks of the church (although he rarely uses the vocabulary of "marks"). He will claim, for example, that it is the "ur-Reformed" notion that the core of the church is preaching, although he will hasten to add that there is more to the church than preaching.[16] The Word of God brings "the church into existence."[17] The "core" of the existence of the church is Word and sacrament.[18] Van Ruler never backs away from his fundamental theological commitment that it is

---

12 Van Ruler himself gives warrant to our two-fold approach when he comments at a session of the Commission on Church Order that there is a dialectic in the notion of church: the church of the Word *and* the *communio fidelium*. *Commissie*, 205.

13 *Religie,* 17.

14 Van Ruler, *Visie en vaart* (Amsterdam: Holland Uitgevermaatschappij: 1947), 161. See on this Eugene Heideman, "Van Ruler's Concept of the Church," *Reformed Review* 26/4 (Winter, 1973), 136-143.

15 It is important to recall Van Ruler's notion of sign as that which embodies that which it signifies. See above (2.4). Hendriks, in his criticism of Van Ruler's notion of the church as sign, appears to forget this. Hendriks, 268.

16 *Apostolaat*, 27.

17 *Reformatorische, 79.* In "De prophetische taak der gemeente" (sermon preached July 12, 1936, in Kubaard on 1 Thessalonians 5:20), Van Ruler Archive, Folder IV, 148, p. 5, Van Ruler claims that the congregation of Christ is built by prophecy.

18 *Apostolaat*, 101.

God's Word that establishes the church.[19] Just how that is so will engage us below.

More to the point, and at the center of Van Ruler's doctrine of the church, is that the essence of the church is the apostolate. This claim stands at the center at the outset of his theological thought, already in his dissertation.[20] This notion is reiterated and expounded in a number of Van Ruler's major writings through the mid-1950s. And while he rarely describes the essence of the church as "apostolate" in his late writings, the substance remains. For example in his most "liturgical" work, *Waarom zal ik naar de kerk gaan?*, he continues to claim that the point of it all is, finally, the salvation of the world.[21] The church exists to "Christianize" the world, which is, as we shall see, at the heart of the apostolic task of the church.[22] It is, then, to the apostolate that we first turn.

3.1 The Apostolic Essence of the Church

Writing in 1948 to promote the apostolic character of the proposed church order for the Nederlands Hervormde Kerk, Van Ruler argued that the quintessence of the church is not liturgy, sacrament, or office, but is to be found elsewhere, in the "apostolate."[23] Where, he asks, is the center of gravity in the actions of

---

[19] In a very early lecture (given while he was still a theological student) Van Ruler asserts several times, "Jesus Christ is the church." "Kerk en kerkorganisatie," lecture for the youth organization "Daniel" in Apeldoorn, August 15, 1930. Van Ruler Archive, folder I, 35.

[20] *Vervulling*, 75.

[21] *Waarom*, 163.

[22] *Waarom*, 167.

[23] Van Ruler was tireless in his defense of the apostolic character of the new church order. He strongly defends, for example, the placement of the article on the apostolate before the article on the confession of the church in the new church order. See Van Ruler, *De belijdende kerk in de nieuwe kerkorde* [Hereinafter *Belijdende*] (Nijkerk: G.F. Callenbach, 1948), 15-17. See also J. van der Graaf, "De kerkorde en het apostolaat," in W. Balke, et. al., eds., *De kerk op de orde? Vijftig jaar hervormd leven met de kerkorde van 1951* (Zoetermeer: Boekencentrum: 2001), 94-97. Hommes, *Sovereignty and Saeculum*, offers the only full-length reflection on Van Ruler's ecclesiology in English. It is limited, however, to Van Ruler's understanding of the church as apostolic and does not take into consideration his later writing. Eugene Heideman, "Van Ruler's Doctrine of the Church," is a short treatment of Van Ruler's doctrine of the church. B. Plaisier's doctoral

God? Is it in the church or in the world? The question is rhetorical, as are those that follow: is the apostolate the extension of the church's roof over ever more areas of the world, or is it the expression of the truth of the kingdom over all things? Is the apostolate about the "churchifying" of the earth or the "eschatologizing" of the world?[24] Apostolically, the church is used by God in the realization of God's eschatological intentions with the human and with the world.[25] The church is used by God in mission, "understood as the confrontation of the world with the kingdom."[26] The church is not the end or the goal. "The church is not there for itself and not something in itself. It is there only for the world and it is something only in the hands of God."[27] Christ "sets it [the church] in the world. He sends it into the world."[28] In fact, in the eschaton, the church will fall away. What remains will not be the church, but the kingdom of God. In this sense, the church is not essential. That is, it is not an expression of the fundamental reality of the universe, a way of being toward which the human intends, nor toward which God is bending or leading the world.[29] To be apostolic is to be incorporated by God in the furtherance of God's kingdom intentions.

From his earliest publications, Van Ruler was intent on rescuing the church from its introversion. In an article on the "missionary task of the congregation," written in 1934, he argues that the missionary task of the congregation is not secondary; it is not derived from whatever is essential to the church. It *is* the task of the church. The western church, he claims, has been characterized too much by an inward turn. It has treated the gospel as a "possession," something it has and must protect. Just so, it has attempted too little, believed too

scriptie, "Instrumenteel tussenspel," also views Van Ruler's ecclesiology from the "viewpoint of the apostolate."

24 *Apostolaat*, 15, 16.

25 *Apostolaat*, 21.

26 *Bijzonder*, 22. Commenting on Matt. 10:22, Van Ruler claims that the apostolate of the church is sketched in the history of the sending out of the twelve disciples. And "where the church appears with this message from God, there the signs of the kingdom of God are present at the same time." *Sta op tot de vreugde* (Nijkerk: G.F. Callenbach, 1947, 61 [hereinafter *Sta op*].

27 *Bijzonder*, 22. See also Van Ruler "De orde van der kerk," *TW* 5, 5 [hereinafter "Orde"].

28 "De nabijheid van Jezus Christus bij zijn gemeente in het ambt" (sermon preached April 24, 1938, in Kubaard on John 20:19-23), Van Ruler Archive, Folder IV, 237, p. 3.

29 Van Ruler, "De kerk is ook doel in zichzelf" [hereinafter, "Doel"], in *Verwachting*, 55.

little, and rejoiced too little. At this point in his theological career, Van Ruler argues for the "missionary" essence of the church from the foundational claim that the church must always return to the "great moment of God's good favor in which He speaks his word of grace and freedom to us."[30]

In his dissertation (1947), Van Ruler finds the motive for apostolicity in the mission of the church. The church is a sign of the coming kingdom, but a sign that emerges from mission. Mission, he claims, is the fullest notion of what the church is about.[31] It is the "key" to the New Testament: the apostles were convinced that the living God not only had acted but had done something essential and had done so in the historical reality of this world. This alone, he remarks, explains the irresistible missionary impulse that they experienced. They had a message for the peoples and nations and cultures.[32]

However, two qualifications of the notion of mission must be noted. In his discussion of *gratia interna* as a means by which the Spirit creates gestalts of the kingdom in human communal arrangements, Van Ruler perceives the agreement of the history of mission with the apostolic nature of the church. Mission had to do not only with individual human souls, but included even more, all peoples, continents, cultures, and nations as the target of the apostolic kerygma of the kingdom.[33]

Van Ruler would describe the history of missions as the confrontation of the world with the kingdom of God. That is the destiny and the goal of the world: to become the kingdom of God.[34] However, too easily the church could understand that it "has" something that it brings to the world on God's behalf. This is the second qualification: the world is in God's hands. God is busy with the world, and God *uses* the church to be about God's work in God's world.[35] It is not about the ministry of the church *to* the world, but rather ministry *in* the world.[36] In discussing the Spirit, Van Ruler puts it this way:

---

30 Van Ruler, "De zendingstaak der gemeente," *Cheribon*, November 24, 1934. The influence of Barth on the early Van Ruler is clearly in evidence here.

31 *Vervulling*, 67. Cf. Van Ruler, "Theologie van het apostolaat," in *Verwachting*, 101.

32 *Vervulling*, 462.

33 *Vervulling*, 260.

34 Van Ruler, "De pretentie van de kerk" [hereinafter, "Pretentie"], *TW* 5, 70.

35 *Apostolaat*, 20. See also "Gemeente en ambt," 2.

36 *Apostolaat*, 19.

> [The Spirit] posits the church with its preaching, sacraments, and liturgy, with its offices and ministries, with its called believers, with its communion of saints. But much more, it posits the kingdom, the proclamation of the gospel of the kingdom, mission. Therein it goes out to the peoples, the nations, and the churches, baptism and confession take place, confession and education happen, Christianization and exorcism take place.[37]

Van Ruler maintains that mission is not to be limited to something that occurs between humans, as though mission were the handing on of the gospel from person to person.[38] Mission occurs in the "tensive space" [*spanruimte*] between Christ and the kingdom. Nor is it a matter of establishing new churches alone; that would too easily fall into the trap of attempting to bring the entire world within the walls of the church.[39] Rather, mission takes place under the Lordship of the ascended Christ. Christ goes forth from his elevated state through Word and Spirit onto the earth. Mission goes from Christ to the kingdom.[40] The mission of the church is "no more than the vehicle on which the Word of God as the gospel of the kingdom completes its course through the centuries and the peoples of the earth."[41] The church then, understood within the framework of its apostolic essence, is the bearer of the gospel, pointed outward to the world where God's intentions find their aim or mark.

This is the church of the apostles. The apostolic task[42] is rooted in the founding work of the original apostles. The apostles brought the original Word and established the original congregations in the Word. It is the apostles who form the church's connection with the Bible, with a book that reports divine history. And it is the apostolic

---

[37] *Vervulling*, 516. In "Wat God doet en wat de menschen doen" (sermon preached May 28, 1944, in Hilversum on Acts 2:1), Van Ruler Archive, Folder IV, 501, p. 2, Van Ruler says simply, "The church is the Spirit-bearing body of Christ."

[38] *Apostolaat*, 130.

[39] *Apostolaat*, 131.

[40] *Aposotlaat*, 132.

[41] *Apostolaat*, 132. Cf. "Theologie van het apostolaat," 108.

[42] Van Ruler would find the term "mission" too constricting to embrace the full range of what God intends for the church. He would see mission as *part* of the larger apostolic essence of the church. See e.g., *Apostolaat*, 125-142, where he discusses conversation with Israel, mission, and Christianizing as components of the apostolic essence of the church.

tradition that worked its way out through the history of the church.[43] It is as though the church carries a baton in a relay race as it hands on the apostolic Word through time and space. The strange message of the particular historical reality that happened in Palestine is brought to the world through the church.[44]

3.1.1 *The Predestinarian Heart*

Foundational to this notion that the church is turned outward to the kingdom of God, and that God uses the church as instrument in God's intentions, is the doctrine of *predestination*. Van Ruler understands Reformed theology as an articulation of the relation of God and the human from within the framework of predestination, by which Van Ruler means that there exists not only the duality of God and the world, but that God is busy and active with the world.[45] Van Ruler will claim that "this is the apostolate, that the church and the Christian are *used* by God himself in his activity with the world."[46] This, for Van Ruler, is what at core predestination is about; predestination is to be "used [*gebruikt worden*] by God."

While he never rejects the Dortian notion of divine decrees, Van Ruler does not understand predestination primarily from an individualistic perspective. Rather, predestination is to be understood ecclesiastically: "The object of predestination is the congregation, is the covenant. That is the pure spiritual context of predestination and covenant."[47] The doctrine is intended to articulate the fundamental reality that God is primary, that all emerges from God. Election is, according to Van Ruler, "God's omnipotence, that out of all pagans God called just Abraham and that he has begotten for himself a people to bear his name on the earth."[48] The human is elect, not for

---

[43] Van Ruler, "Het apostolische en het apostolaire karakter van de kerk," a lecture held in Barchem, September 19, 1959, Van Ruler Archive, folder I, 526, pp. 6,7. See also *Reformatorische*, 80.

[44] "Institutaire," 183.

[45] "Theologie van het apostolaat," 105.

[46] "Theologie van het apostolaat," 116 (emphasis in the original).

[47] *Religie*, 78.

[48] *Sta op*, 48, where Van Ruler comments on John 4:22b: "For salvation is from the Jews." In "De waarheid der verkiezing" (sermon preached April 7, 1940, in Hilversum on Ephesians 1:4), Van Ruler Archive, Folder IV, 344, p. 3, Van Ruler says that the essence of election is "...that grace, salvation in the Lord Jesus Christ, is wholly and completely from God, by God and to God. The initiative lies wholly and completely with God....In us there is no particular ground, no particular occasion, no particular connecting point for grace."

his own sake, but to "minister, to be used, to be the bearer of the luster of the name of God in the world."[49] Election is not about a "few individuals," but of a "royal priesthood...a communion, a nation, a people...."[50] Van Ruler make this claim in 1936, in his earlier writing, when still expressing affinities with Barthian theology,[51] but the notion of God's initiative in using the church (and the offices, as we shall see), continues throughout his theological career.

The predestinarian heart of the church is illustrated in the church's relation to scripture. Scripture stands over and against the church. It must be seen first not in "connection with the church but in that of the kingdom."[52] It is not a book that emerges from the church but comes *to* the church. Indeed, it can be called the "constitutive tradition of the church."[53] The Word of God wakens belief in the world. "It brought the church into existence."[54] In this way, God is primary. The church is not of itself; it is not its own creation. It is not the creation of the human, although, as we shall see (4.5), the human is in a very real sense "co-constitutive" of the church.

The church is called into existence by the Word, and is used by God; this fact gives the church its apostolic character as the church is used to a particular end or goal. And that end is the honor of God's name as the coming of God's kingdom on God's earth comes into view.[55] This is the other side of the church's relation to scripture. Scripture is not the possession of the church, a "something" that it has to bring to the world. And yet the church is the bearer of

---

On election, see also "De dubbele predestinatie" (sermon preached February 6, 1944, in Hilversum on Mark 4:25), Van Ruler Archive, Folder IV, 495; and "Eerste steenlegging der gemeente" (sermon preached January 15, 1939, in Kubaard on Mark 1:17-18), Van Ruler Archive, Folder IV, 280.

[49] *Sta op,* 78, where Van Ruler comments on 1 Peter 2: 9.

[50] *Sta op,* 79.

[51] Indeed, his Barthian affinities are evident when in the same article he defends his notion that predestination is to be understood ecclesiastically by arguing that we are elect *in Christ*. The Christological focus will shift for Van Ruler as the Spirit moves to the fore in his later ecclesiological considerations, what we have called the diachronic movement of his thought. *Religie,* 78.

[52] *Reformatorische,* 78.

[53] *Reformatorische,* 78.

[54] *Reformatorische,* 79. Van Ruler writes this in 1965. Later, in *Waarom,* he will also claim that where scripture and the Spirit come together, there the church originates (149). It is God who takes the initiative, and indeed who establishes the church.

[55] *Apostolaat,* 69.

scripture's story. The church lives by the message that has come out of Palestine, Israel: "Only and exclusively because there is this history which is told by the evangelists and the apostles in the framework of Moses and the prophets is there the church."[56] The church is used in the telling of this story, that the world is to be experienced as the kingdom of God; "that is and remains the vision that stands burning at the horizon of all Christian interpretation and experience."[57] But that can only be so as salvation breaks into existence, and the church bears that story of salvation, that is, of atonement and justification and sanctification. It is this way that the church is *used* by God.

God comes *to* the human. Salvation cannot emerge from human trial or self-discovery; it is not present "somewhere" in this world. "The living God does not emerge spontaneously from our inward self-consciousness." "In his strangeness, God appears over and against us."[58] We have seen that atonement happens from God's side and in God's presence and hence can only be announced or told to the human. It comes via the message, the kerygma, and that, claims Van Ruler, comes only with the authority of office, or to say it another way, with the authority of story.[59] Or put still another way, the heart of the church is the Word of God. It is the Word that comes to the church and the Word that creates the church. The church lives from revelation, from that which does not emerge from reflection upon the world. Van Ruler contrasts the missionary/preacher and the mathematics teacher. The teacher instructs her student that two plus two equal four. The teacher is no longer needed because the "authority" that reminds the student that two plus two equal four is in human reason itself. It is not so with the story of God's historical action with this world. It must be told again and again. It comes with the authority of the story.[60] The predestinarian heart of the church articulates the reality that at the core of the matter, God initiates.

3.1.2 The Eschatological Reach

If predestination, so understood, is at the heart of the church, it is set within an eschatological framework. The church is eschatological in nature. If the essence of the apostolate is not simply that the church turns itself outward to God's kingdom in the world,

---

56 "Mondig," 107.
57 "Mondig," 102.
58 Van Ruler, "Het gezag in de kerk" [hereinafter, "Gezag"], in *TW* 5, 78.
59 "Mondig," 114.
60 "Mondig," 120.

but also that it is used by God, then the reach of God's work extends beyond the church:

> The living God does more than to use his church! He continues his peculiar wrestling with every human heart and, as one most deeply interested, he shares in the great play and the great struggle of the nations over a political, social, economic, and cultural shape of life.[61]

To understand the essence of the church, the theological starting point, according to Van Ruler, is to bring the end to the fore.[62] Mission is set between the ascension and the second coming of Christ. It is the proclamation of the kingdom of God in its gestalt as the kingdom of Christ.[63] As such, the church is set against the horizon of the kingdom, God coming to the church out of the future, directing the church toward the future as it is used toward God's purposes that remain outstanding. The church as a "gestalt of salvation"[64] points toward the kingdom of God.

The church is an eschatological figure, but it is eschatological in a particular way. It is not the final community [*de Endgemeinde*]; it is not to be identified with the kingdom of God. At most it is a sign and prefiguration of the community that is to be.[65] Here Van Ruler's notion of the church as *sign* of the coming of God's kingdom comes into play. While, as we shall see, his notion of the church develops beyond that of the church as sign, how he understands the church as sign is crucial in his ecclesiological commitments. For it signals the peculiar relation of the church to *being*.

He claims that the church is not an essential reality in the strong sense of that notion. That is, the church does not enjoy a permanent ontological status. It is a historical and eschatological act of God and will disappear in the kingdom of glory.[66] He contrasts this with his understanding of the Roman Catholic notion in which the church emerges from the Incarnation and is understood as a synthesis in being between the divine and the human. This new ontological reality occurs in Christ and is extended in the church.[67] In turn the church

---

61 "Theologie van het apostolaat," 106.
62 "Theologie van het apostolaat," 103.
63 "Theologie van het apostolaat," 103.
64 "Doel," 55.
65 *Vervulling*, 60.
66 *Vervulling*, 53.
67 E.g., *Vervulling*, 529.

instantiates and continues that synthesis of the divine and the human nature, of the natural and the supernatural.[68] This will not work for Van Ruler if the church is used by God for God's further purposes; it is not the (or even an) *eindegemeente.*

The church is set within the interplay of time and eternity. Time and eternity are not set over and against each other. Rather, eternity has entered time, the Word has become flesh, and in that sense time is fulfilled. The human Jesus is now with God. "In the incarnation of the Word time is 'accepted' and in the ascension time is 'taken up' and in the second coming our lives will be 'manifested'....[69] Within this "intermezzo," the church is sign, or as we have seen, the "totality of the signs of eternal life." That is to say, the church is not the matter in itself. Instead, on earth we have only signs of the kingdom. Scripture's story is of signs. Miracles, for example, are signs and the supreme sign is the resurrection. However, certain signs "remain." Van Ruler identifies such signs as the people of Israel, the Bible, preaching, the sacraments, the offices, confessions, the communion of Christians, and the pluriform activity of the congregation in the world.[70]

These signs do indeed point to being, but not to the essential nature that the world or humanity possesses. Only God *is*. In eternity, I too will exist, be, as a child of God alongside created reality or being that is itself now saved. The church points toward and is used by God to bring about that salvation that will enable the human to delight in being.[71] Given the understanding we have gained of Van Ruler's notion of time and eternity in the previous chapter, we can appreciate that the church so understood as sign does not simply point to another, future, reality that awaits the church, the human, or the world. We recall that Van Ruler uses the notion of "sign" in what he considers its biblical sense: as an earthly, temporal reality that not only points to but at the same time is fulfilled with the divine matter.[72] The church participates in the eschatological kingdom; it is the body of Christ.

The eschatological character of the church shapes its apostolic essence. Van Ruler works this out in his understanding of how the Reformation viewed the office of the apostle. The Reformers limited the office of the apostle to the twelve and conceived the apostolicity of the church as residing in the preservation of apostolic doctrine

---

[68] *Apostolaat*, 57.
[69] *Religie*, 16.
[70] *Religie*, 17.
[71] *Religie*, 19.
[72] *Religie*, 18.

(scripture). Van Ruler does not desire to contest this notion, but he adds the crucial provision that the office of the apostle is not an office of the church but of the kingdom. Viewed as an office within the church, the apostle emerged as an extension of the Incarnation, according to Van Ruler. The office of bishop emerged as the result, ultimately personified in the person of the pope. The apostle extends from the past into the present. But this, Van Ruler argues, does not give sufficient place to the *ephapax* of the gospel. As such the "sacramental or mystical church sets everything in an organic stream, in a continual duration in which one gestalt gradually merges into another." The apostle as set within the kingdom is set in the eschaton.[73] As we have seen, the eschatological character of the gospel in turn honors and emphasizes its *historical* nature. The church emerges from is past only as it is set within the "double movement" of time.

The problem for Van Ruler is that while the church is set within history this way of doing so is in error. For then it is set as an extension of a past event, and not as a gestalt rooted in the one-time historical event pointed to and determined by the future. In the notion of the bishop, the church is not turned outward and forward. That is so as well, by the way, when the notion of the church as apostolic resides in apostolic doctrine. For then, likewise, the church is turned toward the teaching of what once took place, to the past. Nor is the turn Van Ruler has in mind so much to the world as it is to the "kingdom of God and thus to the world."[74] This is central for Van Ruler. For apostolicity is not, he says, like the trailer of a tractor-trailer truck, a sort of appendix, albeit a very important one, of the church.[75] Van Ruler prefers a different image, that of the candle that burns and is consumed as it burns. It is not only of the essence of a candle that it burns, but that in being consumed it lightens up the world. So too the apostolic nature of the church; it is of its essence.[76] The church, he will

---

[73] *Apostolaat*, 52.

[74] *Apostolaat*, 68.

[75] This was precisely the argument that took place over the relative placement of the apostolate and confession in the new church order of the Nederlandse Hervormde Kerk. Proponents of an amendment that would have placed confession before the apostolate argued that the apostolic task of the church was indeed central to the life of the church, but is to be added to what is more essential. It is first church, then apostolic. Van Ruler and others argued that the church is *essentially* apostolic. See Van der Graaf, 94-97.

[76] *Apostolaat*, 68.

claim in a later work, is about the revelation of God, which finds its center in Christ and in Israel, and is "the great streaming light in which the entire reality comes to the fore, can be seen, and so also can be experienced as that which it is, namely, as creation and kingdom of the same God whom we know in Christ."[77]

But Van Ruler's notion of apostolicity differs from the Roman Catholic in a more fundamental way.[78] As we have seen, Roman Catholic theology, as Van Ruler understands it, sees the church implicated in the structure of being, and that in turn is expressed in that church's notion of the sacrament. In the sacrament, in the church, and in the liturgy one finds the true reality of the world into the orbit of which all is to be drawn. This is so because the sacrament is identical to the offering of God in Christ. Bishops appeared who were to be the true representation and continuation of the divine human reality of the incarnate Word, according to Van Ruler.[79] The church is the extension of the Incarnation into history. Van Ruler cannot accede to this understanding, primarily because he cannot view the Incarnation as an absolutely new ontological reality. This would be to violate his understanding of the place of Mosaic law in which, as we have seen, God has given and gives shape to the contours of the kingdom. And the kingdom does not have to do with a reality other than this world. In Roman Catholicism, the liturgy, sacraments, and offices are heavenly, eternal, "Christian" realities and not, as Calvin has it, earthly and temporary Mosaic "shadows."[80] The cross as the fulfillment of the (ceremonial) law is planted on this earth in every nation. For the Reformed, the liturgy, sacraments, and offices are understood more soberly, more horizontally, if you will. The "liturgy is found more on the street, in the symphony of public life as it is conducted by governing authority."[81] This is the church set within a history drawn toward God's eschatological intentions. But those intentions have to do with, among other things, the political form of

---

[77] *Geloof*, 139.

[78] It is important to note that Van Ruler works out his theology against his understanding of Roman Catholic theology. It is of course incumbent to allow Catholic theologians to have their own say. However, to understand Van Ruler's theology, the reader must work with his notions. He was, of course, very engaged with Catholic theologians. Perhaps the most insightful instance for the purposes of this study is the "Briefwisseling" with H. Weterman.

[79] *Vervulling*, 529.

[80] *Vervulling*, 530.

[81] *Vervulling*, 531.

Christian existence.[82] One of the most important moments in the church's apostolic life is the "proclamation of the law of God to the authorities."[83]

3.1.3 Christianizing

If the apostolic nature of the church is such that the church is turned toward God's kingdom intentions, those intentions include, as we have seen, the world. Just so, the church's apostolic task cannot be limited to concern for souls of individual persons: "This apostolate is not only to be understood in the sense of evangelization, in which we turn the gospel to the individual human, his heart and his concrete existence, but also in the sense of christianizing [*kerstening*], in which we attempt to see the communal nature of the human being, the ordering of his society, and the gestalts of [his existence] in the light of God's Word."[84] Christianizing belongs to Van Ruler's theocratic vision of culture and as such is the task of governmental authority as it fulfills its role in the establishment of the kingdom of God in the gestalts of the flesh. Here Van Ruler's notion of theocracy is relevant insofar as he sees the church's apostolic task from within this framework. For governmental authority can only execute its task when the church stands over and against it with the apostolic message.

> The Word of God creates *history*. Revelation would have cultures come into view around itself. It is not only and not in the first place about God's actions in the world with the individual human and his salvation. It is about the name of God: that it is found on a piece of the earth. So that there will be a memory of the living God. That is, that a commonwealth exists, and cultures in which this God, the God of revelation, is named and known and praised. Thus, the entire social, economic, cultural, and political life is liturgy, the service of this God.[85]

The church's task is to bring the message of salvation. Salvation is, as we have seen, the salvation of created reality, of this world. This salvation "is historically realized in the apostolic process of Christianization from century to century and from nation to

---

82 *Droom*, 7-42. "Politics is what Christendom is really about" (23).

83 *Vervulling*, 532.

84 Van Ruler, *Kerstening van het voorbereidend Hoger en Middelbaar onderwijs* [hereinafter *Kerstening*] (Nijkerk: G.F. Callenbach, n.d.), 7.

85 *Visie*, 44.

nation."[86] According to scripture (the Old Testament), the living God is interested that the communion of humans takes a particular shape. God's kingdom has social and economic, moral and judicial, cultural and political aspects.[87]

Christianizing is to be understood as the work of the Holy Spirit. As we have discovered, for Van Ruler the Holy Spirit is not rightly understood if it is limited to God's work with individual persons. Of course, the Spirit will use human beings in this work, as full participants. We have seen that the Holy Spirit works in such a way that the human shares God's work fully, so far as to share in God's judgments (2.3).[88] But the Spirit also works in culture, government, society, and institutions.

Christianizing, for Van Ruler, is present already with the apostles in the New Testament. "With the apostles the gospel went out from Palestine from the people of Israel to enter the peoples of the world." This is not simply proclamation of salvation. In a lecture from 1956 entitled, "Christianizing public life," Van Ruler writes in his notes that among the peoples of the earth we find: people—society—state—law—reason—custom—art—science—philosophy.[89] This, in turn, is rooted in the notion of the kingdom of God. God gives himself to be known by the human, but at the same time intends to be known in the world and with society.[90] One can even say that "the gestalt of Christ is impressed on the whole of life." Or put perhaps more clumsily, but appropriately, the "human is to be 'israelitized.'"[91] That is, the human is shaped by the reality that shaped Israel: law, covenant, community.

The church's apostolic task, then, commits it to a public concern that includes politics, culture, law, state, art, education, etc. Above all, politics is involved. Van Ruler would claim in 1946, in an article on the Reformation, that "politics is always the way in which the human gives gestalt to his experience of the life of God in the world." "A reformation of religion is very essentially also a political reformation."[92]

---

[86] "Theologie van het apostolaat," 119.
[87] "Theologie van het apostolaat," 118.
[88] *Kerstening*, 9.
[89] Van Ruler, "Kerstening van het openbare leven; Wat kerstening eigenlijk is" [hereinafter "Openbare"], June 1, 1956, Van Ruler Archives, folder I, 392, p. 1.
[90] "Openbare," 1.
[91] "Openbare," 2.
[92] *Visie*, 9.

But between the apostles and this societal reformation comes the church as the bearer of the Word. There is not a direct line from scripture to culture. It finds its way through preaching.[93] The Word is gospel and law, but the law is "not simply *lex naturae* or even the structure of creation. It is much more the sanctifying power that streams out from God's particular presence with Israel and in Jesus Christ in the chaos of sin."[94]

Preaching is thus understood as taking place within the framework of the apostolic task of christianizing. Preaching is the "calling out from the kingdom in appeal to the kingdom."[95] The intention of preaching is clear: that we experience the world as the kingdom of God. Indeed, the goal of preaching is not that humans come to know and praise God, that they participate in the life of faith, but that life be "isrealitized and christianized." It is for this reason the Van Ruler can call preaching a public event.[96]

In christianizing, the church is then used by God for God's intentions that extend beyond salvation. The "emergency-measure" is respected, says Van Ruler. "It is not about Christ and salvation in him. It is not about Israel and God's particular revelation. It is about God and—this 'and' is essential—his world, as about his kingdom and his image."[97] Here Van Ruler sees a crucial break that occurred with the Reformation. For the Reformation does not read in the Bible a *gratia elevans* whereby there exists a higher reality to which humans are to be "elevated." The relation of the human with God is not vertical but horizontal. In Christ the human is not given a supernature, but atonement from guilt, and sanctification is not the "streamlining" of earthly life to heavenly life, but the "ordering of the chaos of sin to become the kingdom and image of God."[98] God has entered our reality to save us from the guilt of sin. That is atonement. Further, when

---

[93] *Kerstening*, 20, 21.

[94] *Kerstening*, 21.

[95] "*uitroepen van de rijk in oproepen tot het rijk.*" Van Ruler, "Het wegen en de betekenis van de kerk." 19 November 1958. Van Ruler Archive, folder I, 481f., p. 7.

[96] "Het wegen en de betekenis van de kerk," 7.

[97] *Kerstening*, 35. It is the "christianizing" task of the church that helps make clear that "mission" and "apostolicity" are not equivalent for Van Ruler. For while the apostolicity of the church includes mission, the goal of the church is "christianization." "The ultimate meaning of mission is not the appearance of the church, that the people become church, but that they be christianized" (*Commissie*, 263).

[98] *Kerstening*, 35.

> ...this salvation streams out in the gestalt of *sanctification* in our created, fallen, and reconciled existence, a new configuration of the elements of existence finds a place, an ordering, representation and form, in which the order of the law, the image of God, the form of his kingdom is established, but so that the world is always more itself, which is and displays the world itself, the human himself, which is and displays his image, existence itself, which is and displays his law.[99]

3.1.4 Volkskerk

The apostolic task of christianizing brings with it the notion of the church as *volkskerk* and its importance for Van Ruler's understanding of the church. In a series focused on the 1951 church order, he wrote a pamphlet that asked in its title, "*Does it still make sense to talk about a "volkskerk"?* In it, he claims that the core question has to do with "whether things concerning the *volk*, the state, etc., lie purely on the margin of the church or closer to the heart of the church's existence":

> Is the gospel solely and above all about the life of the church, either in the sense of the institution, liturgy and sacraments or of communion, confession and discipline? Is this ecclesiastical life added to the already existing life, either in the sense of the life of the heart, the moral act, and the family or of life in society, culture, and the state? Or has ecclesiastical life come to replace this already existing life, at least in principle? Or must one ask neither about this existing nor this ecclesiastical life, but only about Christ and say of him that he is the end of all because it is saved by him? Or must one say and that most deeply that it is neither about the church nor about Christ, but about the kingdom of God that has broken in in the coming and the work of Christ, and about the confrontation of this world with this kingdom?[100]

God's concern is not only with the life of the individual. It is not about salvation from this world, but the salvation *of* this world. God never intends life for the human without the life of creation. "Is God not interested in the tables of the tax collector or with the

---

[99] *Kerstening*, 37.
[100] *Volkskerk*, 10

establishment of the state with the goal of freedom or of society with the goal of justice?"[101]

The church is not a *volkskerk* because it is a church *of* the people, as though it emerges from the popular religion of the population. Such an idea would be strange to Van Ruler, who sees the church as emerging from outside itself, from God. Neither is it a *volkskerk* because it is the church that is embraced by a nation or a cohesive population (either transnational or intra-national). Van Ruler was criticized because he was seen as maintaining just such a romantic ideal of the Netherlands.[102] In fact, he rejected the notion that the *volkskerk* includes within its membership of a majority of the population of a *volk* precisely because the church does not include the majority of the population of the nation.[103] Rather, the church is a *volkskerk* at its heart because it is a church *for* the people, and for the people not simply as individuals, but as they live together, in culture, society, and state.[104]

The church will speak *to* the culture, society, and state as bearer of the Word. That means that the church has certain *pretensions* over and against the world around itself. These are "enormous" pretensions, and Van Ruler lists three. First, the church must maintain that it and it alone knows the true God who is also Creator of heaven and earth and "whose knowledge is inescapable for the pure experience of reality and right shaping of life." Second, the church must maintain that it and it alone has the true morality in the sense that "it knows from its knowledge of God what the good is," and that in the indwelling of the Spirit it has the power for the realization of this good. And third, it must maintain that with its knowledge of God and morality it and it alone has the true understanding of the essence

---

[101] *Volkskerk*, 11.

[102] See Hendriks, 280.

[103] In fact, the plurality of churches within a nation was not so much a problem for the notion of a *volkskerk* as it was a challenge to the ecumenical task of the church. It was just *because* it is essential for the church to be a *volkskerk* that it is so urgent that the churches become united, and numerically so for Van Ruler (*Volkskerk*, 20-22).

[104] Commenting on Mark 3: 14, 15, Van Ruler finds the notion of *volkskerk* in the fact that Jesus did not withdraw from the crowds. The apostles remained "in the midst of the crowds; they remain *volkskerk*" (*Sta op*, 55). In "Roeping der leiders" (sermon preached August 13, 1939, in Kubaard on Amos 6:1), Van Ruler Archive, Folder IV, 312, p. 1, Van Ruler comments: "The congregation is the salt of the earth, the light of the world, the leader of the *volk*; it is the real circle, the center of the *volk*."

of things, at least of the essence of the human in its individual and communal nature.[105] The church does not shape the life of the community or state (or more correctly does so only in a paradigmatic way), but in its pretension speaks to that which is outside the church [the *buitenkerkelijke*]:

> Social justice and the universal brotherhood of all humans are the real visions on which all the Bible and all Christian faith focuses, but they are not received and in the meantime not maintained without the knowledge and confession of the God of the Bible.[106]

In fact, that which is outside the church, the *buitenkerkelijke*—politics, economics, social life, cultural life—are to remain outside the church, there to be modeled on the gestalt of Christ.[107] As church for God's people, the people of a nation, it is the bearer of this gospel from Israel and Palestine.

Furthermore, the notion of a *volkskerk* is unavoidable for Van Ruler, given his theological commitments. For him, after all, the church is not the extension of the Incarnation into history, but the work of the Holy Spirit active in history and tradition. Van Ruler argues that it is of the essence of the human to be communal in nature, and so rooted in the very history and tradition through which the Spirit works. The *covenant* is a summary notion that includes just these commitments. The covenant does not, Van Ruler argues, coincide with Jesus Christ, with the Incarnation, or with the union of the two natures. It is much more within the compass of the doctrine

---

[105] *Volkskerk*, 12. Van Ruler's claim here echoes that of Karl Barth, "Christian Community and Civil Community," in *Community, State, and Church: Three Essays by Karl Barth* (Garden City: Doubleday, 1960), 149-189, viz. 169-170. It is noteworthy that Van Ruler's essay dates from 1958, well past his earlier, Barthian, inclinations. It is also worth noting that Barth's essay was first published in 1946, contemporaneous to the time when Van Ruler was publishing his earlier writings on the apostolic essence of the church. Indeed, an analysis of Barth's essay would be crucial in explicating both the similarities and differences in the ecclesiological commitments of both theologians.

[106] "Pretentie," 77.

[107] *Waarom*, 167. Van Ruler distinguishes between *persons* who are outside the church who are drawn within there to enjoy their full humanity, and *het buitenkerkelijke*, by which he describes the world beyond the church, particularly in the institutional gestalts in the world.

of the Holy Spirit.[108] It is the Spirit who bears the Word beyond the first century to the nations of the earth. Van Ruler reads Matthew 28 in just this way; when the risen Jesus commands his apostles to "baptize the nations," the emphasis was on the nations of the earth.[109]

All humans are born into a culture, a society that has already been shaped by its particular history. Certain cultures, particularly European cultures, were deeply and profoundly shaped by the work of the apostles, the apostolic preaching in the world. The Spirit has been active forming that culture. As one born into that culture, the human participates in a life shaped by the Spirit. Van Ruler can even claim that the individual Christian is a "piece of the *volkskerk* in miniature."[110] This allows for Van Ruler's notion that the borders of the church have become "hazy." One cannot build a "Chinese wall" around the church. For God's covenant is wider than the church. The church exists within the broader reaches of God's work.[111]

The communal nature of the human includes his or her life in the state. The church as apostolic, as bearer of the Word, has to do with all the moments of life and of the life of all people. Again, it is not within the scope of this study to investigate Van Ruler's understanding of the relation of the church and the state. Nonetheless, it is important to note that that relation exists in a particular way. The church and the state are to be respected as distinct in their separate tasks. The church respects the freedom of the human, of society, and of culture in their independence. It respects the state in its responsibility and authority.[112] Still, the state has certain spiritual commitments. A neutral state is, in Van Ruler's opinion, an impossibility.[113] And where, he asks, can one find the spiritual foundation of the state except from the communion of faith and love which comes through the Spirit in Christ?[114] "On behalf of what can the church appear in the present situation of the culture and the world besides theocracy, in a biblically Reformed sense, than for the state with the Bible?"[115] Or, he asks rhetorically, "...is this all nonsense?

---

108 *Volkskerk*, 6.

109 *Volkskerk*, 15.

110 *Volkskerk*, 9.

111 *Volkskerk*, 7.

112 "Mondig," 127.

113 E.g., *Droom*, 45-48.

114 *Volkskerk*, 19.

115 *Volkskerk*, 19. The phrase "state with the Bible" is a clear reference to Ph. J. Hoedemaker. Van Ruler acknowledges his debt to Hoedemaker in his article, "Wat ik aan Hoedemaker te danken heb," *Blij zijn*, 227-233.

Has the gospel no meaning for the world? Is Christ not really the hope of the world?"[116]

3.1.5 Confessional

The *volkskerk* is also a confessing church in Van Ruler's understanding. It is, in fact, a "Christ-confessing *volkskerk*."[117] The question of the nature and the place of the confessions within the church was a burning issue in the development of the 1951 church order, and since Van Ruler was not only active in the formation of that church order but wrote extensively in its defense, the matter of the nature and place of the confession found its way into a number of his writings in the late 1940s and early 1950s. It is relevant to this study for three reasons. First, a summary of Van Ruler's ecclesiology would be incomplete without mention of the place of the confessions in the life of the church. This is particularly the case for a theologian from within the Reformed theological tradition. Second, the confessional nature of the church finds its location within an apostolic understanding of the nature of the church. Since many Reformed church leaders would argue just the other way around—that the apostolic, while crucially important, is found within the confessional nature of the church—it is helpful to see the sharper counters of Van Ruler's notion of the church as apostolic set within his explication of the confessional nature of the church. And third, the place and content of confessions themselves will contribute to the object of this inquiry, the offices of the church.

As we have seen, the relation of the confessional and the apostolic in the 1951 church order was a matter of particular contention. The proposed order placed the article on the apostolate before the article on confession. While admitting that he could not choose whether the apostolate or the confession was the more important, Van Ruler himself would defend the placement of the article on the apostolate before that on the confession. There can be no order in rank, he argued. It is not possible to probe clearly the relation of the two within the church. Nonetheless, he could claim that the apostolate is anterior to the confession. It is the outward side,

[116] *Volkskerk*, 19.

[117] Hendriks considers this a contradiction in terms (280). A *volkskerk* cannot be a confessing church since it has blurred the boundaries that would be established by confession. Hendriks confuses the notion of a *volkskerk* as consisting *of* the people rather than *for* the people. A confessing church, by his definition, cannot be a *volkskerk*. Van Ruler, as we shall see, disagrees.

the direction in which the church is taken up in the hands of God.[118] It is the church as caught up in the course of the Word of God through history, in the reign of Christ over all the earth.[119]

This is the church in the hands of a living, acting God. It does not enter history with a truth that it has received in a past age. It is not a school of philosophy, but the body of Christ. Or stated more passionately by Van Ruler, the church is "the historic, living, moving, speaking, and acting body of Christ."[120] The church stands in history as the work of the Holy Spirit, "determined and ruled by the course of the Word."[121] It is this church that will have no choice but to articulate not only what it, the church, is, but the truth it is called to proclaim.

And that is the truth as it is revealed. It is the truth of salvation that, as Van Ruler is at pains to point out, cannot emerge from the human him or herself. It emerges from the act of God's own self, God's self-revelation. The confession of the church shares in the particularity of God and in the particularity of God's revelation. This is the triune God, wholly other than the gods of our blood and of our spirit.[122] This comes *to* the church, as a matter of authority. It appears to us from without.[123] "The God we confess is strange to the soul of our race."[124] Hence, it can only be attested, given witness to. The church confesses when it attempts (and it will always be a failed attempt) to articulate the truth of God's revelation.

The church knows and confesses the world as the kingdom of God. The church sees "the entire world from beginning to end; it sees the sense and the destination of the world and everything in it; it sees God's actions with the world, his original and ultimate intentions and all the counter-moves which God makes in the play of being in the establishment of the free human being."[125] The church not only knows, but has seen the meaning or significance of the historical process:

> The sense [of history] lies in the establishment of the kingdom of God on earth, in the social ideal. That has begun in Israel, in

---

[118] *Belijdende*, 70.

[119] "Orde," 134, 135.

[120] *Belijdende*, 8-9. See also *Visie*, 70.

[121] *Belijdende*, 71-72.

[122] *Belijdende*, 15.

[123] *Visie*, 68.

[124] *Belijdende*, 13. See *Visie*, 68, "Gezag," 78.

[125] Van Ruler, "De kerk in de komende cultuur" [hereinafter "Komende"], in *TW* 5, 97-98.

> the formative reality of the law and the critique of the prophets. It is—in extreme concentration—realized in Jesus who is the Christ, in his cross and resurrection. In the work of the Spirit, in the course of the apostolic Word, in the work of the church of the centuries it is worked out, applied and hidden in all instances and times....[126]

The confession of the church does not coincide with the nature of the church. It is but one task of the church alongside other tasks: preaching, sacraments, offices, and the like. And yet it does not simply exist side by side these other tasks of the church. Instead, it *functions* through them all. All the tasks of the church will reflect the confessional commitments of the church.[127] But how does it function? Here Van Ruler borrows a phrase from O. Noordmans: the confession is *"zoowel een stok om te slaan, als een staf om te gaan"* ["is both a stick to strike as well as a staff to guide"].[128] While Van Ruler will cautiously support doctrinal discipline, for example, he is leery of using the confessions as a judicial measuring stick for doctrine.[129]

A third image is more to Van Ruler's liking. The confession is the "voice to sing praise." "Something out of the depths of an existence touched by God sings, an echo of the Word in the midst of forlornness, an immeasurable joy over a salvation that can never be fully comprehended. The confession is the language of love that wells up of itself from the deepest emotions of the heart."[130] It is the "expression of the language of love from the heart of the church to God."[131] So understood, Van Ruler can go on to claim that "in the confession it is not about human concepts, understandings and principles, but about the truth of God's Word. There is something of poetic and childlike emotion behind all true confessing."[132] Further, Van Ruler sees confession in this way as part and parcel of the apostolic nature of the church: "The confessing of the church as an

---

[126] "Komende," 105-106.
[127] *Visie*, 52, 53.
[128] *Visie*, 65.
[129] See, e.g., *Visie*, 62-65. Van Ruler makes note of two dangers that threaten doctrinal discipline from the Reformed side. First, one is inclined to place too heavy an accent on doctrine in the nature of the church. Second, by the promiscuous and incautious use of doctrinal discipline, the church too easily degenerates into a sect (64).
[130] *Visie*, 66.
[131] *Commissie*, 154.
[132] *Visie*, 67.

expression of praise of the truth and goodness of God is the entire apostolate of the church in essence and in seed."[133]

Van Ruler adds still other images to describe the place and use of confession in the church. The confession is a set of "grammatical rules" for the church.[134] Or to use yet another metaphor, it is like a "beacon in the sea" that guides us in the journey of interpretation of scripture.[135] The confession is not the speech of the church itself. It is the guide ("a staff to guide").

The church's confession is an expression of truth that is apostolic in still another aspect relevant to our study. Confession has a public character. It is not only a matter internal to the church. The confession, according to Van Ruler, is an articulation of a religious way of being. And religion is the communion of the human with the living God. Furthermore, this communion of the human with the living God realizes itself as it actively engages the "stuff" of creation. Here we find ourselves in the arena of culture. How the human relates to the stuff of creation betrays the God he knows and serves. Van Ruler cites as example the different way in which a Buddhist relates to the created order from that of a Western European.[136] In its confession, the church offers its understanding of the nature of reality. In the public character of its confession, it stands over and against the state, as *volkskerk*, giving witness to the very reality in which the state intends to function as it does its work within God's eschatological intentions.[137]

So the church speaks a truth. The eschatological reserve that characterizes the church perforce also characterizes the confession as well. The church is itself an intermezzo. It lives after the fall and this side of the last judgment. It is always a struggling church.[138] It is not the kingdom and is not to be confused with the kingdom. This has implications for how the church will understand the offices in the church. For, argues Van Ruler, in the bishop the church understands itself as the kingdom and its dogma as the final truth. Not so for the Reformed church with its elder. The elder functions not so much in the church as *around* the church and witnesses the emergence of a christianized commonwealth. The kingdom stands at the horizons of

---

133 *Belijdende*, 71.

134 *"Spreekregels der kerk."* The phrase is from O. Noordmans, *Visie*, 71.

135 *Visie*, 71.

136 *Visie*, 74. One notes Van Ruler's commitment to creation already in this writing, published in 1947.

137 *Visie*, 75.

138 *Visie*, 84.

the church. Confessionally, the church points beyond itself to the more inclusive reality of the kingdom of God. For, finally, the gospel, and consequently the church, is not about confession, but about God's actions in God's world.[139]

3.1.6 The Church as a Peculiar Gestalt

We proposed at the beginning of this chapter that Van Ruler's understanding of the church as both bearer of the gospel and a gestalt of the kingdom presents itself not only synchronically but diachronically as well. We are now at the point of supporting this claim. While, as we shall see, the gestalt-nature of the church will become more evident in Van Ruler's later works, it was present from the outset. Furthermore, the church as gestalt of the kingdom is itself a bearer of the gospel.

This plays itself out in the relation between the institutional and the communal aspects of the church. Both aspects are, we might observe, gestalt-like in their character. Both are necessary, and both stand as bearers of gospel, albeit in differing ways.

The apostolic essence of the church brings into view the institutional nature of the church. There is a "particular apparatus" necessary to bring the gospel, and this takes form and shape in the institution. Van Ruler uses the term "institution" in a broad sense. It can mean, e.g., the church as it gathers in its various assemblies, establishes its church order, and provides for various bodies that assist in its ministry. It can also mean the tradition that finds its way from generation to generation. It means as well the Holy Scripture, the office of the apostles, and the church of history.[140] All these institutions "bear" the gospel. Without synods, consistories, church orders, the church could not proclaim the gospel. Without the tradition of the past, without a church and a scripture that reaches from the past to the present, we would have no gospel to proclaim.

This institutional character is not accidental to the church. It is not, as Van Ruler says using one image, the "scaffolding" on the church building, but it is the "crossbeams" or the "rafters" on the building. Scaffolding may assist in the building or repair of the church, but it is taken down when the work is done; it is not essential to the building. Or to use another image, the institution is not a "corset" on the body, but the "skeleton" of the body. A body cannot

---

[139] *Belijdende*, 17.

[140] "Institutaire," 183.

exist without its skeleton.[141] The institutional is expressed in the church order, among other gestalts. In fact, the "order of the church rises from its essence."[142] In its order, the church participates in the just divine ordering of the world. Its order is not a "definitive cosmic harmony," but is a paradigm of the "great order of the kingdom of God, a paradigm of the eschatological ordering of the world."[143]

This is the work of the Spirit. The Spirit does not work (only) vertically, but horizontally, in history. "The Spirit is a materialist," claims Van Ruler. It is implicated in such material matters as the sacraments; the elements are bread and wine and water, matter all. But the material exists beyond the sacraments. The offices and the assemblies of the church are material as well, and they are institutional. It is the institution that brings the reality of the one-time offer from the time that was—and from the time that will be—into the present reality of the world.[144] Or, we might add, it is the institution that posits the future of the kingdom of God in the present in the gestalt of the kingdom of God that the church is.

Nonetheless, Van Ruler will claim that the church is not only institutional. It is also communion. From one perspective we still remain in the context of the institutional. For the communion of the church is not only a communion of persons, but of "things" [*dingen*]. Among the "things" to which Van Ruler refers, he includes preaching, the sacraments, and the offices.[145] "These three: preaching plus sacraments plus offices are the institutional elements of the church that make the church more than a communion of believers, namely an institution in Christ."[146]

Still, the communal character of the church cannot be exhausted in the institutional. The human is set in communion, as we have seen. This is the human in all his or her selfhood, his "I-ness." "Am I not intended to become the dwelling place of God in the Spirit [*woonplaats van God*]?" Van Ruler asks. And he intends more. As we have seen above (2.3), the human person needs not only to receive salvation, but to will salvation. He becomes a partner with God. He enjoys a freedom and this freedom of the human in the kingdom of God is an "end-goal" of God.[147]

141 "Doel," 58.
142 "De orde der kerk," 1.
143 "Orde," 124, 126.
144 "Doel," 58.
145 *Religie*, 87.
146 *Religie*, 24.
147 "Doel," 60-61.

This finds expression in the confession in and with the church. In confession, the human is no longer simply an instrument of God, furthering the apostolic task of the church, but is a partner with God, now standing in full humanity over and against God, as *mannetje*. Indeed the human reaches his or her full height in praise, in the liturgy. "Is hymnic praise not the highest point of existence and humanity?"[148] Here the church is used by God to further God's kingdom purpose of bringing humanity to its true humanity.

The characteristics of communion and institution tug the doctrine of the church in different directions. The first tends toward an understanding and experience of the church as sect. However, that direction leads toward the humanization of the church in the sense that the offices or the institutional emerges from the communion itself. Consequently, the identity of the church is sought in the faith of the believer. On the other hand, exclusive focus on the institutional nature of the church, to understand the church as a "delivery system" for divine grace, leads to the divinization of the church. That is the way of Roman Catholicism. Van Ruler refuses to choose between the two. Instead, he opts for both, the institutional and the communal. The two characteristics are related in a particular way: "...the church as communion *is* present only around the church as institution."[149]

The counter-side to his notion that institutional and the communal stand in mutual relation is the claim that two forms of idealism must die off, that of the sectarian and that of the Roman Catholic. The sectarian ideal is that of an elevated and holy inwardness that is to be found within the human heart. All holiness is drawn from within. By extension, the church emerges from the faith of the individual, or individuals gathered in collective enclaves. The Roman Catholic idea in contrast has holiness outside the self, now to be found in the celibate clergy. It, too, is idealist. And both are idolatrous and both miss the point that Christ intends to dwell with sinners.[150] That is, God in Christ comes to traffic with the human *qua* human, fully human. Both forms of idealism live from the notion that reality is found in an (existent) ideal, and both lose the eschatological reserve that characterizes the church. Both tempt the church to escape history by finding its identity in the nonhistorical ideal. By fleeing history, the church misses the very locus of God's activity.

The relation of the institutional to the communal is made irrelevant by the old distinction of the church as visible and invisible.

---

[148] "Doel," 61.
[149] *Religie*, 90. Emphasis in the original.
[150] *Religie*, 96.

While Van Ruler does not deny the distinction,[151] he is careful to argue that we do not have to do with two churches, one visible and one invisible, nor do we have to do with the notion that the invisible church carries greater theological weight. The visible church is genuinely church. Preaching, sacraments, and offices are holy matters, for they are holy to the Lord. Furthermore, what is gathered around these visible matters share in their holiness: "An elect, regenerate soul is in no degree more holy than the first child that is baptized...."[152]

That said, the church as institution "*is* present only in the church as communion."[153] The institutional is present in the organic. There is no higher and lower order of the church. Nor is there a *vis à vis* of the communal and the institutional.

> Because the church as communion exists only around the church as institution, thus the visible communion of the congregation is holy....And because the church as institution exists only in the church as communion, thus all the visible things of preaching, sacraments, and offices are not worldly gestalts, but together are signs, holy signs of the kingdom.[154]

The communal, the gestalt of the church, finds its institutional expression in the liturgical and the sacramental. This stands in contrast to the preaching of the gospel as the apostolic representation of salvation. And here we move beyond the diachronic interplay in Van Ruler's theology to the synchronic, and so stand at the edge of the next section in our inquiry into his doctrine of the church. From the outset, however, Van Ruler would see sacraments, for example, as distinct from preaching. He would say in a later writing that preaching is the "fountain from which the water of the holiness of the church springs." And around that fountain are liturgy, sacraments, and offices.[155] Already in 1941 he could say, for example,

> In the sacrament the riddle of salvation of our existence is demonstrated [*voorgespeld*] letter for letter and we can also follow and understand letter for letter, already eating and drinking...but we grasp it more with the Holy Spirit than with

[151] E.g., *Religie*, 23.
[152] *Religie*, 91.
[153] *Religie*, 92. Emphasis in the original.
[154] *Religie*, 93.
[155] *Geloof*, 135.

our own reasonable spirit, and thus more bodily than in our thinking.[156]

However, the emphasis does shift, and it is to this shift that we now turn as we examine more closely the gestalt-character of the church.

3.2 The Cathedral of Love – The Liturgical Gestalt of the Church

Van Ruler presents the case for the apostolic essence of the church so persistently and so compellingly that the conclusion would appear to be justified that the church's task is exhausted in its service to the world beyond itself. However, he resists this as a consequence from his argument that the essence of the church is apostolic. It is not the business of the church to efface itself in pure service to the world, as though it has no particular reason for its separate existence, or so Van Ruler claims. In fact, the church has an institutional place as a particular gestalt. Its task in history is not to disappear in order that the kingdom of God might appear. The church's task is not exhausted as it provides a vehicle for the Word. The church bears a particular structure. This will be, as we shall see, important to keep in mind as we turn to the offices themselves as skeletal for this institutional gestalt.

In an article from 1958, Van Ruler argues for the "pretension" of the church's existence. He continues to maintain that the church stands apostolically in the world; it goes out from itself to all the world and to all in the world. But this is not "selfless service" to the world and it is not all that the church is about. The church calls the world to repentance.[157] The church can and must do so because it is itself rooted in the particular revelation of God in the world as it occurred in Israel and centrally in Jesus Christ. But the matter does not end there. In this particular revelation, the pure relation and communion between God and the human is given to it. The church is the continuation and representation of that communion.[158] From the outset, Van Ruler will describe this as the *unio mystica cum Christo*, and he will in any number of places write of this mystical union with Christ as the essence of the church.[159] And that will take on form, shape, gestalt.

---

[156] *Religie*, 23.
[157] "Pretentie," 76.
[158] "Pretentie," 67, 68.
[159] E.g., "Doel," 62, *Geloof*, 143.

Here one sees the two images of church (what we might call the "apostolic" and the "liturgical") synchronically in Van Ruler. It is important, then, to keep in mind that the two ways of thinking were not separate for him. It his article on the pretension of the church, he argued that the church is a form of religion in which the creature gathers to praise the creator. But the church is not *only* a form of religion. It is particular; it is Christian. He uses the image of a *palimpsest*. A palimpsest is a document in which the original writing has been erased and over which a new text is written. The original document in this case is the ground text of creation. The human is creature and as creature is drawn into relation with its creator (religion). The second text, that which is written over the first, is that of revelation. This is the story that gives meaning and sense to the first text. Because it is revelation, it can only be told, or preached.[160] The church cannot simply disappear in silent service. It is used by God for the salvation of the world. Only as the revealed story is proclaimed does the world become really the world, for only then is it understood and experienced as creation, as creation saved, we might say.[161] That is the apostolic task of the church.

We see Van Ruler's theological commitments to creation[162] find their purchase in his ecclesiology as his apostolic understanding of the essence of the church takes on a more liturgical character. One notices this shift in the language that Van Ruler uses to describe the essence or the heart of the church. By the 1960s, he rarely uses the language of "apostolate" to describe the essence of the church, but instead uses phrases like "embodied joy," or "cathedral of love."[163] The church is the "world experienced and celebrated as the kingdom of God."[164] "The church *is* the communion with the mediator, with the triune God and with each other in Christ."[165] If the church and its history is about mission, it is not *only* about mission. The church is also something in and of itself, that is, it is about partnership in the life of God in the Mediator.[166] In other words, the church is an institution

---

160 "Pretentie," 66, 67. Van Ruler also uses the image of the church as "palimpsest" in "Geloof en prediking," een voordracht voor Rooms Katholieken en Protestanten, De Brug, Amsterdam, February 17, 1961, Van Ruler Archive, Folder I, 591, p. 1.

161 "Doel," 66.

162 What Van Hoof and Hendriks call the "protological."

163 *Geloof*, 133, 132.

164 *Geloof*, 133.

165 *Waarom*, 87. Emphasis in original.

166 "Pretentie," 70.

and communion that bears a certain shape and in which the believer lives or dwells.

Against the notion that the church gives itself up completely to the world in service, Van Ruler holds "emphatically to the church as a peculiarly separate gestalt. I would want to speak of a 'liturgical pluck.'" There is in the church, he claims, a service, a worship that is to be experienced as nowhere else. It has a certain malleable shape, "plasticity" is his term; it is visible; and it emerges from the foundation of salvation.[167]

3.2.1 Liturgy

In the church as "cathedral of love," the church is equally about liturgy as it is about the diaconate; it is turned inward as well as turned outward.[168] He will maintain this even as he argues that the goal still lies in the kingdom, the eschaton as the saved proton.[169] For the heart of the matter, for the church, is that church is the "place where Christ intends to dwell with sinners."[170] Now, however, this cathedral is "filled with an immeasurable streaming light." It sparkles with the knowledge and the joy in God as Creator, Savior, and Glorifier of all, and who is the "one who is communion and love in itself." It is this light that falls over the entire world, the light of the kingdom of God.[171] Here the church is taken up in God's kingdom intentions in a new way, that of the worshiping human within the gestalt of the church.

Van Ruler himself admits to a development in his understanding of liturgy within the church. Indeed, liturgy is no longer only what happens in life, on the street.[172] It has, at least in some ways, moved indoors. In his early days, he had compared liturgy to the orange crate on which the preacher stood, or the farmer's wagon from which preachers in the Dutch Reformation held their "hedge preaching."[173] The farmer's wagon and the orange crate gave the preacher a place to stand, and thus they were vehicles for the

---

[167] Van Ruler, "Het einde van een huishoudelijke twist," in *TW* 2, 216.
[168] *Geloof*, 132.
[169] *Reformatorische*, 150.
[170] *Geloof*, 132.
[171] *Geloof*, 133.
[172] As Van Ruler would put it in 1947: "But liturgy is most fully developed outside the church, on the street, in the home and in the state" (*Droom,* 40).
[173] See, e.g., *Apostolaat*, 28,

apostolic Word.[174] Later he would compare it with the decorative carving that embellished the area around the pulpit in Dutch churches [*rankwerk*]. In his latest writing, he understands liturgy as the "malleable thickening [*plastische verdichting*][175] of the practice of godliness."[176]

Liturgy is, for Van Ruler, a sort of "socio-drama." It is a place where humans communally play out the whole of reality. This "play" is utterly serious, indeed the highest form of seriousness, for it expresses the essence of the human, which is to live in praise of the creator.[177] For to be human "...*is* to praise God into eternity."[178] In liturgy, the human knows the self, not only as creature, but as saved creature. And so the human can exist fully in the presence of God and of fellow human beings.[179] This is salvation: "That the Eternal has pleasure in me and my pleasure. This joy works itself out then that the human rejoices not only over God and his works, but also over himself and his active existence." Salvation is "the existence that rejoices in itself in the presence of the Eternal and thus with an eternal joy."[180] Here the church, as communal gestalt, is used by God to achieve the divine intention that became evident in Van Ruler's understanding of the salvation of the human.

The human participates in this socio-drama as a full partner with God. In prayer, particularly in intercessory prayer, we "play ball" with God. We toss matters back and forth. We present the world before God as though the world were a candidate in need of salvation. The worshipers share with God in the judgment of the world.[181]

In this way, the human is brought to a certain "maturity." The human becomes "the love partner of God himself. This is the highest form of maturity."[182] The church's task is to nurture maturity within itself to the highest level, in liturgy and sacrament, preaching and

---

[174] "Orde," 131.

[175] This is a very difficult phrase to translate into English. A *verdichting* is a thickening–rather like a "thick description." It can be compared to a poem [in Dutch *gedicht*. The adjective, *dicht*, means "thick"] that expresses reality in a condensed way. The poem, too, is *plastisch* in that it can take new form as it expresses life in differing ways. The liturgy, then, is not life itself in all its forms, but life experienced or expressed in a concentrated manner.

[176] *Reformatorische,* 179-180.

[177] *Waarom*, 53.

[178] *Waarom*, 46.

[179] *Waarom,* 34, 35.

[180] *Waarom,* 41.

[181] *Waarom*, 55, 60.

[182] "Mondig," 123.

confession, not only to effect salvation, but salvation for the sake of the essence or *being* of the human. In so doing, the church invites others to become members of the church because those who do not celebrate the liturgy and who do not sing the Credo are not adult and are not mature human beings.[183] The human, being brought to full humanity, in this way becomes co-constitutive of the church.

The church in its liturgy is a gestalt of the kingdom of God as it enters from the future. The human experiences, albeit in hidden and temporary form, something of his or her eternal destination. It is as though, says Van Ruler, we sit at the piano to play a prelude of the eternal Sabbath. It is not the full song that we play. It is only a prelude [*voorspel*]. But the essence of eternal joy can touch our hearts, "at any rate as the church building echoes." So when we go to church, we "play" that we have entered the kingdom of eternal glory. Nonetheless, we do "not lose ourselves like a drop that returns to the ocean. We hold fast to ourselves in all the temporality that is so characteristic of our existence."[184]

Having made such lyrical claims for the "mystical" side of the liturgy, Van Ruler does not take "flight from the world" into the church.[185] The liturgy is still turned toward the world. Indeed, the entire world is present in the liturgy. The church is that gestalt in which the world, in miniature, experiences itself as the kingdom of God. The entire world becomes creation "not enclosed in itself, but open to God, his will, his counsel, and his kingdom."[186] And the worship of God in the church is not so much the human's full service of God as it is a *practice* for the service of God. We serve God in our entire existence.[187] We are not saved from the world, but from our lostness and ruin. Van Ruler keeps the kingdom within view.

Still, we remain this side of the eschaton (see above, 3.1.2). Because God's ultimate intentions remain outstanding, we continue to talk about particular Christian existence, and do so within the separate, particular gestalt of the church. It is in this framework that Van Ruler can claim that in his opinion, "the mystical-ontic rest is thus the rest of the deepest inwardness over the whole of being in its

---

183 "Mondig," 126.

184 *Waarom,* 116.

185 The phrase is from Van Hoof, 262. Van Hoof accused Van Ruler of being so disappointed in the failure of his theocratic vision to take hold within the church and society that he took flight into the church there to enjoy a mystic-ontic "rest."

186 *Waarom,* 149.

187 *Waarom*, 143.

condition of being saved, the most essential form of Christian existence."[188] He connects this with his theology of the kingdom. For finally it is about the salvation of the world. It is about a new heaven and a new earth on which, finally, righteousness dwells. It is about a social ideal. But it is also where the human can be completely happy, and that in her deepest inwardness. So Van Ruler:

> A human is also reconciled in his deepest inwardness. The soul and body come to exist in harmonic relation to each other. Everyone sits with his neighbor under his own vine. The entire historical process is summed up together and every tear over history is wiped from the eyes. History then presents itself not as a breath on the cold splinter of glass that is nature (E. Troeltsch), nature and history clasp each other as equally harmonically as body and soul. Indeed, the entire universe bathes itself in the luster of divine glory.[189]

The human is saved. She enjoys her being. But this being finds its place with neighbors and in history. This is hardly a liturgy that remains enclosed within the walls of the church.

3.2.2 Sacraments

The church is more than a place where humans gather to receive and to enjoy the delight as God's created beings and to be turned outward to God's world. The church is a place where *God* intends to dwell, and that in the church located on this earth. The "earth must also remain habitable for God. He wants to dwell on the praises of his people. There lies the liturgical and sacramental task of the church."[190] In liturgy, the church is at worship. In sacrament, the church is at worship in a particular way.

We dedicate a paragraph to Van Ruler's understanding of the sacraments separate from a discussion of preaching because sacraments function quite differently for him. He will sound quite Reformed when he maintains that Word and sacrament form the axle [*spil*] around which everything turns in the church.[191] However, sacraments do not constitute the church in the same way that God's

---

188 *Waarom*, 162.

189 *Waarom*, 164.

190 "Mondig," 125.

191 Van Ruler, "Wat doet de kerk? Prediking door Woord en sacrament," lecture, Veenendaal, October 4, 1945. Van Ruler Archive, folder I, 182, p. 9.

Word does. God does not call the church into existence in the sacraments. "God does not come to the human in two ways, the way of preaching and the way of sacrament....He comes only in one way, the way of preaching, and that fully." The sacrament follows on the foundation of the Word.[192] The sacraments are central, but in a different way.

The role and the function of sacraments will evolve for Van Ruler. In an early essay—from 1936—he argued that sacraments are not a means of grace, but a means of knowledge [*kennismiddelen*], and "only a means of knowledge."[193] Sacraments make clear what we cannot know from preaching alone: that salvation begins with the decision of love that God makes for us,[194] that God's goal "lies with the entire, complete human, who is body and soul,"[195] and that the hope for myself and my world is in the world, the earth, that is, that everything does not finally come down to salvation in Christ, and that eternal life is not about another life, but *this* life.[196] This in turn implies that one cannot flee from the church, tangible, bodily, fragile, and breakable as it is. The sacraments are "signs and seals" added to preaching. In baptism I know my justification and regeneration through the blood and Spirit of Christ. In the supper I know the atonement for my sins at Golgatha and the *unio mystica cum Christo,* in heaven.[197] Sacraments are about *knowing.*

In Van Ruler's later writing, sacraments remain separate from the Word. It is still the case that the sacraments cannot be understood as means of grace; it is, however, for quite a different reason. For sacraments are no longer about knowledge, or in any case are not so in an intellective sense. By 1958, he could talk about sacraments as the "holy play in which God and the human celebrate their communion with each other and their mutual joy over each other."[198] Van Ruler uses the image of a couple that becomes engaged and then married. Preaching, he says, is the marriage proposal. But the sacraments are the marriage itself. The sacrament is "the celebration of the union of

---

192 *Reformatorische,* 212.

193 Van Ruler, "Kerk en sacramenten," lecture for the Franeker section of *Kerkherstel,* January 28, 1936, Van Ruler Archive, folder I, 99b, p. 9.

194 "Kerk en sacramenten," 8.

195 "Kerk en sacramenten," 9.

196 "Kerk en sacramenten," 10.

197 "Wat doet de kerk?" 8.

198 "Pretentie," 71.

God and the human, which union comes into existence through and in the Spirit in the way of faith."[199]

In the Lord's Supper, for example, the human is honored in his or her maturity. If preaching comes as the marriage proposal, it does not overwhelm the human. This is not "rape," [*verkrachting*]. One comes to the sacrament willingly. God does not overwhelm the human. Hence Van Ruler can say that there is no violence in the sacrament.[200] The human is not only co-constitutive of the church, he or she is also co-constitutive of the sacrament.[201] The church is the place where God's intentions for the human find purchase as the human enters communion with the triune God.

And the church does so in the sacrament, because in the celebration of the sacrament the church no longer points toward the eschaton. The sacrament is rather a moment in the eschaton, albeit it in a provisional and hidden way.[202] The sacrament is a "concealed" [*verhuld*] or hidden [*verborgen*] eschaton. The sacrament "...already stands in the eschaton; it is the completed communion, albeit in hiddenness."[203] In that moment, God and the human not only celebrate salvation, they celebrate the realization of salvation. In it the human comes to the fullness of communion, communion with God and with one another. As such it is the "feast of perfected salvation, of salvation as communion of God and the human."[204]

In the church, we share in Jesus Christ himself, God's Son in human flesh. We enter a communion of love as a divine, historical

---

199 *Reformatorische*, 183.

200 *Reformatorische*, 212.

201 *Reformatorische,* 210.

202 *Reformatorische*, 61. Van Ruler goes on to add: "So highly the Reformation places the sacrament!"

203 "Geloof en prediking," 10.

204 "Ultragereformeerd," 122. Cf. *Rapport het kerkelijk ambt: Van de commissie Van Ruler – Dokter* [hereinafter *Rapport*] (Generale Synode der Nederlandse Hervormde Kerk, 1974): "Through the sacrament believers experience something of what it is to live as reconciled, sanctified, and saved humans in the kingdom of God. In the mystic communion of God and the human there is something real of the future, in which God will be all and in all." The "Van Ruler report" came from a commission installed by the General Synod of the Nederlandse Hervormde Kerk in 1952, of which Van Ruler was the chair. Its report was received by the Council for Church and Theology in 1965 but was not placed before the General Synod. It was published by the synod in 1974, four years after Van Ruler's death, for information. While it is the report of a commission, its contents can fairly be said to reflect Van Ruler's profound influence.

reality. This is summarized in the sacrament. In the sacrament we come up against the "indispensability of the church—as separate gestalt in life—visible."[205]

In the sacraments, God "uses" the church, then, not as sign, nor as a bearer of the gospel of the kingdom. Rather, God actually comes to share life with the human, and so the church becomes more than it was as sign or as vehicle for the Word. It is still taken up within God's kingdom intentions, but now it shares fully, if provisionally, in the eschaton. Indeed, the communion that the church enjoys is not enclosed within the church; Van Ruler does not lose his apostolic passion. The church enjoys a provisional communion with "the entire created reality in its state of salvation."[206] The church cannot presume to live in the time of completion, but it does live within the time of fulfillment. Within the gestalt of this communion, the human can know fully (in the sense that he or she lives fully) the place that God intends for him or her, as a saved creature now in communion with the triune God. In the words of the Liturgy of the Lord's Supper of the Reformed Church in America, the Supper is a feast of "remembrance, communion, and hope"; the church lives in the past, the present, and the future at the same time.[207]

In discussing the sacrament as the proleptic participation of the church in the eschaton, Van Ruler uses the sacrament of the Lord's Supper as the paradigm. At no place does he speak of baptism as the "marriage" that believers enjoy with God. He does however, leave some hints as to the direction he might take. In "notes for a lecture" on the sacraments, he mentions baptism only in the context of the historical character of the sacraments. However, there he claims that sacraments are "signs, symbols, and images" in which one experiences anew what happened in history. He notes, cryptically, "Israel: pascha,

[205] "Het wegen en de betekenis van de kerk," 5.

[206] *Reformatorische*, 215.

[207] *The Liturgy of the Reformed Church in America together with the Psalter*, Gerrit T. Vander Lugt, ed. (New York: The Board of Education, 1968), 65. The reader might well be struck by the affinities this notion has with Augustine's use of the human mind as metaphor for the Trinity, where the mind with memory, understanding, and will lives simultaneously the past, present, and future. Augustine, *On the Trinity,* trans. Stephen McKenna (Cambridge: Cambridge Univ. Press, 2003), Book 10, Chapters 11 and 12, 57-59. Indeed, this is communion with the God who is communion in God's self, *Blij zijn*, 93-94.

circumcision."[208] This is to live the reality of the covenant in the present. To the extent that the covenant is proleptic life in the kingdom, baptism shares in the communal nature of the sacrament. This is put in a slightly different way in a sermon, "First Stone Laid in the Congregation," where Van Ruler speaks of the covenant of baptism in the context of election. There the call that comes in God's electing love is "so powerful that the one being called also comes." This call, which is what election is about, forms the congregation most clearly in the covenant of baptism.[209] Again, the congregation lives in the new reality into which it is called, communion with God.

3.2.3 Life in Communion

The church as gestalt may find its highest concentration in liturgy and sacrament, but its life as particular communion is not exhausted there. Indeed, as we have seen, it is only "practiced" there. The church lives a "paradigmatic" existence as its very life points apostolically to the future.

As the Spirit gathers humans into the church, they begin to live the communion God intends for all God's creatures. This is a separate place, a space (Van Ruler calls it a "play space") where humans "experiment in love." We are not in the wilderness of the world: "There we are hyenas; here we are brothers." In the church the human finds a deeper communion, one that probes to the roots of existence. This can be found nowhere else in the world.[210]

The church bears its institutional character as a work of the Holy Spirit. The Spirit, as "materialist," concerns itself not only with what is internal but what is external.[211] The Spirit does so as it binds us to the historical Christ. Tradition as the apostolic bearer of the gospel is institutional; it bears a certain shape. But God is at work in the institution of the church as God is served and worshiped in the communion of persons. "The way in which humans relate to each other and in which they set up their society is the real praising service of God."[212] The church is a "paradigmatic reality." And Van Ruler views the church no longer as only a means, but as an end in itself: "The institution is the form of divine love as historic reality in Christ."

---

208 Van Ruler, "De sacramenten," aantekeningen van een voordracht op de professoren-catechisatie, May 2, 1956, Van Ruler Archive, Folder I, 387, p. 1.

209 "Eerste steenlegging der gemeente," 2.

210 "Het wegen en de betekenis van de kerk," 6. See also "Institutaire," 181.

211 "Institutaire," 182.

212 "Institutaire," 185.

The human cannot know him or herself as a child of God in any other way. She "was in no way a child of God when there was no institution."[213]

The communion finds institutional shape in a concentrated way in three places according to Van Ruler. The first place is the *diaconate.* It is in the diaconate that the church offers help and service to society from the source of mercy, that is, from the justice of God. The diaconate propounds a social idea, shaped by the values of the kingdom of God.[214]

The second institutional reality that forms the shape of the communion is *church order* [*kerkrecht*]. Church order establishes this paradigmatic existence in a form that emerges from the shape of God's righteousness that meets the human in salvation.[215] Salvation, as the kingdom of Christ, takes on institutional shape as the offices of the church rule the church according to Christ's will made manifest in the Spirit.

The communal shape of the life of the church expresses its peculiar gestalt thirdly in the *discipline* of the church. By discipline in this case, Van Ruler means the discipline of life in contradistinction from doctrinal discipline. The truth of the gospel "etches" a kind of communal life. There is a conscious stylization of life in the pattern set out by God in Christ and with Israel. The community "sculpts" a particular way of life, of existence. Discipline in the church has as its subject individual persons. But the human is in his essence communal, and thus discipline is in fact the ordering of the congregation, of the communion of the church.[216]

3.3 Summary

Our review of Van Ruler's ecclesiology has not been exhaustive. One could, for example, investigate his understanding of the credal attributes of the church: its holiness, catholicity, and unity in addition to its apostolicity. Nor did our review of the sacraments exhaust his theology of the sacraments. We have, however, followed the main lines of his understanding of the church, and done so sufficiently to place the object of this study, the offices, in proper context.

One point in summary of the development of Van Ruler's doctrine of the church deserves note as it has direct implications for

---

213 "Institutaire," 193.
214 "Het wegen en de betekenis van de kerk," 6.
215 "Het wegen en de betekenis van de kerk," 6.
216 "Het wegen en de betekenis van de kerk," 8.

his understanding of the theological place and content of the offices. We have placed his theology on a grid that moved between the church as the bearer of the gospel and the church as a gestalt of the kingdom of God. This duality exists at all stages of Van Ruler's theological career, but it also developed, as we have seen. Behind this development is a shift from the more Christocentric to the more pneumatocentric.[217] In his earlier writings, he often speaks of the church as the body of Christ. "The deepest essence of the church is Christ himself."[218] Later, however, the church was seen within the framework of the Spirit. The church is the work of God, now however as the work of the Holy Spirit, and thus it is "human in an entirely different way than Jesus Christ is human."[219]

In our inquiry into Van Ruler's understanding of the church, we have been attentive to the development in his theology as it was reflected in his ecclesiology. Within that development, however, we have seen several consistencies that remain into his final writings. Even more, one might claim that his later writings gave depth to his earlier commitments. The church as liturgical reality that embodies the salvific action of God in provisional form is not antithetical to the church's apostolic task. From Van Ruler's perspective, one can argue that it is taken up (*aufgehoben*) in that task and that it gives shape and depth to that task. One can also argue that the Spirit uses the church in a variety of ways. As Van Ruler maintained early on that one need not choose between the institutional and communal nature of the church, so one need not choose between apostolic and the liturgical.

We can summarize the results of our inquiry as follows:

1. In reflecting on the church, we "think from the end" in this as in other theological loci. The church is set within God's eschatological intentions and is pointed toward the end.

2. This eschatological placement implies that the church lives with an eschatological reserve. It lives within the time of fulfillment and not of completion. It lives in expectation of God's future.

3. This eschatological placement gives expression to the fact that the church does not enjoy an ontological status that draws persons to itself, there to be "elevated" into a higher, or more perfect, reality.

---

[217] Hennephof, 46, 47, noticed this already in 1966.

[218] *Bijzonder*, 70.

[219] "Structuurverschillen," 184. It is, of course, the whole import of Hendriks's study to explore the import of this shift and its implications for Van Ruler's doctrine of office.

4. The church is called into existence by God, established by the Word, a creation of the Spirit. The church is not the collective expression of the faith of believers.

5. The church is used by God (predestined) to fulfill God's kingdom purpose. It is not an end in itself but is directed beyond itself to the world, in order that the world might experience itself as the kingdom of God.

6. God uses the church for the proclamation of salvation, which is the atonement of guilt. This salvation embraces all reality, including the human.

7. The church is both institution and communion. It is a communion not only of persons, but of "things," so that the church is both members and offices, the preached Word and the celebrated sacrament, tradition and event.

8. The church is, as the body of Christ, a gestalt of the kingdom of God, as it provisionally and fragmentarily exhibits God's intentions for the world in the communion and institution that is this body.

9. The church is that place where, in worship, the human receives his or her humanity as in liturgy and in the sacraments he or she becomes a full partner with God. As saved, he or she participates provisionally in God's intentions for humanity and for creation.

10. The church as a community of love, bearing an institutional gestalt in this world, nonetheless continues to exist not for itself but on behalf of the world. Van Ruler did not abandon his original apostolic vision of the church but rather deepened it in as the church took on liturgical shape. The church continues, however, to be used by God for God's kingdom intentions.

CHAPTER 4

Office in the Work of the Triune God

The church, for Van Ruler, consists of offices and congregation.[1] That claim betrays the complex significance of office for Van Ruler. Office will be essential for the church, but it cannot be encapsulated by the notion of the church. That is, while office will be central to what God is about with the church in the economy of God's historical action with this world, office will not emerge directly from the church. Hence, while it was important for our inquiry to explore Van Ruler's understanding of the nature and location of the church, Van Ruler's theology of office does not flow directly from his ecclesiology.

In 1957, Van Ruler received a request from the theological faculty in Amsterdam to participate in a disputation on office. In his collected papers is found a single sheet of paper in Van Ruler's handwriting attached to this request and listing seven theses on office:

1. Office is a representation of God and this is a mystical thing.

2. Office is not only in the church, but in a manifold way is also in the world, centrally in the state.

3. Ecclesiastical office is a moment in the work of the indwelling Spirit that mediates between the Mediator and the human.

4. Office functions in no other way than in communion with and on behalf of humans and the congregation and, like the Mediator, is to be understood as an (indispensable) emergency measure.

5. Office and congregation are both serviceable to God's kingdom intentions with his world.

[1] Van Ruler, "Ambt en gemeente," lecture to the Nederlandse Christelijke Studentenraad, together with H. Weterman, Leiden, June 15, 1957, Van Ruler Archive, folder I, 439, p.5.

6. The plurality of office-bearers as well as of the offices, and thus the synodical reality as well, is characteristic and essential.

7. The individual human need never share in office as he or she stands before God and his eternal blessedness, given that the authority in the relation between God and the human is of a theonomous nature.[2]

Van Ruler describes office as "being used by God to do his work." To the question, "what is God's work?" he answers: "It is the work of God in Christ through the Spirit. The sinner must be saved: he must be [saved] from guilt or he must be engrafted in Christ, the power of sin must be broken, he must again see and live as God intends, and that includes the society of humans, marriage and family...city and village, in society and in state."[3] Our inquiry will explore the theological foundations of this description as well as its implications. At the outset we can note in Van Ruler's description of office the predestinarian core—to be "used by God"; the eschatological scope—life as God intends it; and the salvific means in which office will be used. At this point, we note in passing the trinitarian relation within which office operates. Prima facie, Van Ruler's description discloses something of the complexity of his theology of office. In his

---

[2] Letter from the Theologische Faculteit van Amsterdamse Studenten, December 6, 1957, Van Ruler Archive, Folder VI, B. Cf. seven theses around which Van Ruler organized his lecture, "Ambt en gemeente." Those theses read:

1. "Office originates in no manner from the congregation but is the self-presentation of God in Christ in the congregation.
2. Office is only an emergency measure of God (like Christ himself) in the congregation—being is much more important (as the human is more than the Mediator).
3. Office and congregation are both serviceable to God's kingdom intentions with the world.
4. Calling and election to office happen essentially by God by means of the congregation.
5. Given the relationship of God and the human in Christian religion, all the work of office takes place in the communion of the congregation (intercession and criticism, discussion and shared work). Also liturgically and sacramentally.
6. It is not the essence of the believer that he become an office-bearer.
7. Office and congregation together alone are the church."

[3] Van Ruler, "De betekenis van een presbyteriaal-synodale kerkorde - in de practijk" [hereinafter "Betekenis presbyteriaal"], a lecture to the Classis Deventer, June 1, 1960, Van Ruler Archive, folder I, 563, p. 1. See *Sta op,* 35: The work of the office-bearer is to "do the work of God on earth."

description, office stands as an indicator of how God uses men and women in what is called "office" to come "to" the church, to stand over and against the church, albeit within the church.

Furthermore, Van Ruler's description exhibits how deeply his theology of office is rooted in his theological project. It is not an appendix to his theology, an incidental reflection of a theologian in occasional service to the church. "One needs to see all the parts, even the most minute, as they stand in connection with the entire existence of the church, and in each part one needs to feel and to conceive the glowing kernel of the salvation of the Lord."[4] In a number of places, he identifies the ecumenical question of who can be acknowledged validly as office-bearers in the one church as one motivation for reflection on office.[5] Van Ruler's passion for the institutional reunion of the church would not allow him to be silent on this point. He adds that the theological rediscovery of the place of the church in theology also stands as motive for his reflection on office.[6] One must hasten to add that Van Ruler's intense involvement in the development of the new church order, sitting as he did on the Commission for the Work Order and the Commission on the Church Order, writing many articles and books to explicate and advocate for that church order, and leading a later commission on ecclesiastical office, provided a natural context for concentrated theological work on office.[7] Indeed, Van Ruler's doctrine of church would be inconceivable without reflection on office. His theology of the kingdom of God leads quite naturally to an understanding of office in relation to the church. Office plays a crucial role in God's salvific and kingdom intentions.

In *Bijzonder en algemeen ambt* ["Particular and General Office"], Van Ruler sketches a triangular relation among Christ, office, and church.[8] Christ stands at the top of the triangle. He is related both to church and to office. Christ is related to the congregation and Christ communicates through office. The office does not emerge from the believer. It emerges rather from Christ. At the same time Christ does

---

[4] "Orde der kerk," 2.

[5] E.g., *Bijzonder*, 9.

[6] *Bijzonder*, 9.

[7] Hendriks, 16-45, is particularly good on this background. See also J. Bruin, *Kerkvernieuwing: Een praktisch-ecclesiologisch onderzoek naar de betekenis van 'Gemeenteopbouw' voor de Nederlandse Hervormde Kerk* (Zoetermeer: Boekencentrum, 1992). For source materials see W. Balke and H. Oostenbrink-Evers, *De commissie voor de werkorde* (Zoetermeer: Boekencentrum, 1995), and *Commissie.*

[8] *Bijzonder*, 61.

not relate to the church directly through office. Office will have a relation to the congregation—and the congregation to the office. We shall examine that relation further below (4.5). At the same time, Christ is at work with the congregation. And the church is, as we have seen, an instrument in God's kingdom intentions.

Just so, we shall have to examine office from within the context of the kingdom of God. And that, in turn, happens within the context of the kingdom of Christ. For if it is Christ who works through office, it will be the ascended Christ, the Christ who rules as king.[9]

At the same time, Van Ruler's doctrine of office will take account of the relation of office within the church. He will work out his theology of office against two conceptions. On the one hand stands his understanding of an episcopal understanding of office with its singular office of bishop. Van Ruler will resist the theological vision behind that view of office. On the other hand stands a more congregational notion of office (so far as such a "system" holds to a notion of office) that understands the office as particularization of the ministries of the believers or even of the particularization of an essential ministry of the church. Just how and why Van Ruler resists these notions will become clear as we proceed.

A complex picture of how office functions emerges as one examines the several books and the many lectures and essays that Van Ruler has devoted to this topic. In contrast to how his notion of the nature of the church shifted throughout his theological career, his view of office remains consistent throughout.[10] We shall not, then, be following a shift in his doctrine of office. However, office will function in four ways, and it will be incumbent to keep this four-fold shape in view as we proceed. First, office comes to the church from Christ in the Spirit thereby to constitute the church. Office is prior to the church and thus cannot be understood as arising from the church. Second, office (or more correctly the offices) will embody the church. They will function as a skeleton of the church as they govern the church, but even more they will exist as the church *in nuce*. Third, office will be used by God as an instrument of salvation within the

[9] *Bijzonder*, 17.

[10] Hendriks is the only extended study of Van Ruler's doctrine of office. He organized his study around three stages in Van Ruler's ecclesiology. He discusses the offices within each stage, but one finds little fundamental change in Van Ruler's view of office. Instead, one finds a deepening of Van Ruler's doctrine of office; e.g., his greater emphasis on the Spirit in his later theology would provide new support for positions taken earlier. See Hendriks, 209.

church. Fourth, the offices will exist beyond the church; the offices will themselves be active in the kingdom.[11]

4.1 A Preliminary Look at the Notion of Office

The question presents itself: why place so much weight on the notion of "office" itself? Is it not simply another word for the "ministry" of the church? And if so, why not use the more familiar term? After all, "ministry," in the form of *diakoneo* and its cognates, appears in the New Testament. Furthermore, "ministry" has entered the ecumenical vocabulary as a common locution for discussion of the ordered leadership of the church.

These questions emerged when the new church order of the Nederlandse Hervormde Kerk appeared in 1951 as it retained the traditional three offices of the Reformed churches—ministers of Word, elders, and deacons. In fact, Van Ruler can sometimes use office and ministry interchangeably.[12] However, more often he clearly argues that a distinction is necessary, and his reasons are important. Those who resist the notion of office tend to see the ministries of the church as emerging organically and functionally from the church. The entire congregation is in ministry in its essence, and there are ministries that take place within the congregation. Some aspects of the one ministry or *diakonia* are judged to be so important and require such permanence that they are raised to a certain degree of importance and persons are set aside to perform such ministries; they can be called "offices."[13] Against such an understanding, Van Ruler argues that this would "churchify" the Word of God in the sense that preaching would become a function of the congregation's own understanding. In that case, the Word would lose its independence over and against the church. The Word retains a certain eschatological reserve.[14] The church exists only as it is called into existence from without. That is, only as an alien Word comes *to* the church.

---

[11] In at least two places, Van Ruler offers a four-fold function of office in relation to the congregation. *Reformatorische*, 103, *Bijzonder*, 55. We shall consider this below when we examine the relation of office and congregation.

[12] Van Ruler, "Het ambt," A dispute with H. van der Linde and J.A. Oosterbaan before the faculty of the City University of Amsterdam, February 5, 1958, Van Ruler Archive, folder I, 465, p. 1. (This disputation is the occasion for the correspondence cited in note 2 above.)

[13] *Bijzonder*, 11, 12.

[14] *Apostolaat*, 87.

Van Ruler can approach his notion of office from a general use of the term. In its broadest sense, office denotes a circle of tasks with particular competencies (1) that occur within a particular area of life, (2) are of a public character, and (3) take place in legitimated instances.[15] "It is only in an office that someone or something stands over and against something different, or over and against others."[16] The Commission on Ecclesiastical Office opens its report by noting the etymological root in Old German in which *ambachtsman* is a vassal or servant of a prince. The concept developed until it indicated that one with an office is one who serves as one having been given a certain authority, one that derives from and rests upon a higher authority. That report went on to maintain that the church order of 1951 gave preference to "office" over "ministry" because office indicates more than a ministry. That is, it is about the task of speaking and/or acting in the name of another; it is to bear responsibility for a particular group or and "area" (of expertise, for example).[17]

Van Ruler puts it in biblical, or as he puts it at times, a more "israelitic," way when he refers to scholarship that views the office of the apostle as a reworking of the *schaliach*-figure from the Jewish laws of messages [*bodenrecht*]. The *schaliach* is one sent, one who bears the message of another. In this framework, the one who has been sent is received as one would receive the person who sent the messenger. The office possesses an ambassadorial function. It is not the case that the one sent *is* the sender; the one sent functions *as* the sender.[18] In this case the apostle bears the fundamental characteristic of office as one who speaks or acts in the name of another.[19]

In this context Van Ruler argues that the apostle is sent with a task and the authority, and thus "in the name of the Lord." The significance of this is that the one sent acts as the Lord's own self acts. He or she is authorized by the Lord.[20] This reflection on the general nature of "office" signals a foundational notion in Van Ruler's doctrine of office. In contrast to the more general concept of ministry, office stands in a relation *over and against* another. The message borne

---

15 "Ambten," 15.

16 *Bijzonder*, 43.

17 *Rapport*, 5, 6.

18 *Bijzonder*, 28, 29.

19 Van Ruler, "Het gezag van de apostel" (sermon preached September 17, 1961, in Utrecht on Romans 12:3a), Van Ruler Archive, Folder IV, 827, p. 1: "An apostle is a human whom God has elected to be witness of the salvation that God has given in Christ."

20 *Bijzonder*, 29.

by the messenger could not originate within the one who receives the message. If it did, the entire notion would be ridiculous; there would be no need of a message, nor, subsequently, would there be need of a messenger. In the same way, as we shall see below, office will not emerge from within the church but will stand *over and against* (Van Ruler repeatedly uses the term *tegenover*) the congregation. This *over-and-againstness* of the office is essential for office.[21] The office is not only over and against the church, but over and against the human.[22] To probe this remarkable claim more fully, it is necessary to explore the theological foundations of office for Van Ruler.

4.2 The Theology of Office

Van Ruler's claim that office is "used by God to do God's work" presupposes a basic and extensive theological foundation. It is important to insist that at issue is *theology* proper, and not simply ecclesiology. That is, a theology of office is not a subsection of the doctrine of the church. It will certainly be related to a doctrine of the church and inextricably so. We have, in fact, discussed Van Ruler's doctrine of the church prior to a discussion of the offices. We did so in order to place the offices within Van Ruler's full theological project. Nonetheless, as shall become clear, the offices are rooted in the nature and the work of God. They are, in fact, to be found within the trinitarian work of God as the divine activity enters and engages history in the Messiah and through the Spirit. Hence, for Van Ruler, office is very much a theological reality. So too, it is important to pay close attention to the theology of office.

4.2.1 The Predestinarian Heart of Office

The triune God uses the offices on the field of history.[23] When in his lectures on church order Van Ruler advances from a general notion of office to what is specifically Christian in his understanding of office, he states that in its Christian use, office is to be commissioned, or to be given a task [*opgedragen*] by God in Christ through the work of the Holy Spirit.[24] Or as he says elsewhere, the "essence of the office" is

---

[21] Van Ruler, "Is er een ambt van de gelovigen?" [hereinafter, "Gelovigen"], in *TW* 2, 133.

[22] "Gelovigen," 144.

[23] "Mondig," 121.

[24] "Ambten," 15.

"to be used by the triune God himself."[25] For the moment, we shall leave aside the trinitarian content of such claims and focus on what it means to be "used by God." That phrase succinctly states Van Ruler's further claim that predestination is of the essence of office.[26]

Predestination is at the heart of office. This will strike one as odd if one thinks of election as the activity of the divine council as God chooses a certain number for eternal salvation. However, as we have seen above (3.1.1), Van Ruler uses the notion of predestination in a particular manner. It is a way of describing the freedom of God. For example, because for Van Ruler predestination describes the freedom of God the Spirit, he can call predestination as a "pneumatological category par excellence."[27] The Spirit does not work "uniformly and numerically, but thus and so."[28] At issue is not an accounting of the number of souls, but of the free action of the Spirit to take persons, institutions, history, and so forth into God's use. It is in precisely this context that Van Ruler can describe predestination as "God who acts in sovereign freedom and who uses his creatures in his service."[29] That is not only the heart of the church, but of the offices themselves. "This is the essence of the office: that God wants to use you as God's instrument."[30]

It is the *Spirit*, then, who is at work in election. Van Ruler claims that the "main point" of the Genevan doctrine of office is that it "is God the Holy Spirit himself who uses the offices in his divine work of mediation of salvation."[31] That has important implications in a clear understanding of the predestinarian heart of a theology of office. We have seen how Van Ruler's theology of the Spirit establishes the human as human and does not "elevate" the human to a higher (or

---

[25] *Reformatorische,* 90.

[26] *Bijzonder,* 13.

[27] *Bijzonder,* 46.

[28] *Bijzonder,* 47.

[29] *Bijzonder,* 13.

[30] *Waarom,* 104. Cf. Van Ruler, "Gezichtspunt inzake het ambt" [hereinafter "Gezichtspunt"], lecture at Seminary Hydepark, May 27, 1968, in Van Ruler Archive, folder I, 726, 15. [Numbers in reference to this work are to the paragraph.] Van Ruler, "Gezag van het ambt" [hereinafter "Gezag ambt"], *TW* 3, 144. Van Ruler and J.A.M. Weterman, "Een briefwisseling over de theologie van het ambt," [hereinafter "Briefwisseling"], *Vox Theologica* 27 (March 1957), 123.

[31] *Reformatorische,* 100. One notes that Van Ruler returns to Calvin's placement of predestination within the framework of the Spirit. This in contrast to Karl Barth who, in *Church Dogmatics* II/2, developed a doctrine of predestination within a Christological framework.

even different) ontological status. Predestination "brings about no ontological elevation or transferal to a new, supernatural way of existence."[32] In the Spirit, the human comes to his or her maturity.

One consequence of this point of doctrine is that while offices will be used by the Holy Spirit to effect the communion of the people of God, this same communion of mature humans is used in the Spirit's freedom to choose those who are to bear the offices. The human is fully incorporated in the election of persons to office. This finds its shape as the congregation calls and elects its office-bearers.[33] This is the gift and action of the *Spirit.* "In no way does office arise from the general priesthood of believers."[34] The initiative rests with God; the human is taken up in God's action, as represented by the congregation.

But the Spirit's work in electing the human can be seen in the election of the human within a particular office itself. God works with the human as human. An elder, for example, is not an elder because he is an attractive person, or a particularly pious person, or because he can accomplish many good things. He exists as elder because he is set there by God.[35] The minister of the Word is an ordinary member of the congregation.[36] Seen from the human side, this appears almost violent, or so one experiences it, for the office-bearer is called from his or her ordinary communion with the ordinary human.[37]

It is indeed God who uses the human, but God does not "overcome the human by consuming him; God intends that the human freely agree with what God says."[38] God does not silence the human. Indeed, God desires agreement from the human, and that fully from the human side. Likewise, God desires that the human enter God's service freely.[39] "What is human in the person who is in office is and remains fully human, just as the bread in the Lord's Supper remains completely ordinary bread and just so has salvific significance."[40] When God uses the fallible human through the Spirit and so engages the human in his or her full humanity, the

---

32 "Gezichtspunt," 16.
33 *Reformatorische*, 100.
34 *Reformatorische*, 137.
35 *Religie*, 95.
36 *Waarom*, 104.
37 Van Ruler, "Is er een ambt van de gelovigen?" [hereinafter "Gelovigen"], in *Theologisch Werk* 2, 144.
38 "Gezag," 81.
39 Van Ruler, "Het gezag van het ambt," *TW 3*, 21 [hereinafter "Gezag ambt"].
40 "Gezag," 83.

consequence is that the human can be held accountable for his or her action. This is expressed in the church order by the provision for the discipline of an office-bearer.[41] The office-bearer is honored as human fully by God. We see here a genuine "theonomous reciprocity."[42] This is the work of the Holy Spirit.

A further consequence is that as it is the Spirit who elects the offices to act as *schaliach* or messenger, this will take on more of a prophetic than priestly nature. By this, Van Ruler means that predestination happens in the freedom of God. God's free action is, as we have seen, the establishment of the kingdom, which happens on the field of history. It happens "thus and so," not by fixed formula. The Lord gives to this one or to that one gifts, as God wills.[43] For this reason, predestination will play a greater role than does consecration in a proper theology of office.[44] Consecration, with its implication extending an office-bearer permanently in history, gives to the church a "formula" by which it can be tempted to restrict the freedom of God.

Likewise, because God, in God's freedom, uses particular persons in God's service, one must acknowledge that the incumbency of a person in office is of a temporary nature. The living God uses persons in office, but only for a particular period of time. An office-bearer is not called to a permanent office, but for a particular period of service. Such arrangements in a church order express the freedom of God to chose whom God will for the ministry God wills.[45]

The presbyterial-synodical system of church order is not only peculiarly reflective of God's freedom to use whom God will in God's service. It also expresses what Van Ruler calls a "flexible balance" within the church. The presbyterial-synodical system maintains the offices both as a "particular gift of God and organ of Christ and that the particular office is given and functions in an unusually beautiful way" in the church.[46] God does not act by simple formula, but uses *both* the church and the offices, and uses them together to accomplish God's purposes.

Predestination is, finally, a joyous doctrine. It is an expression of God's effecting a good order in the body of Christ. "It is an order—in which one can have joy, where one can rest in the 'peace' of God—that characterizes all the works of God into the eschaton and embraces all

[41] "Briefwisseling," 124.
[42] "Gezag ambt," 22.
[43] *Bijzonder*, 64.
[44] *Bijzonder*, 30.
[45] "Gezag ambt," 20.
[46] *Bijzonder*, 12.

reality, including the political."[47] God will and does choose humans to effect God's work. One can trust in the freedom of God, for the sake not only of the individual and his or her blessedness, but because in that freedom God indeed uses humans in God's work of the salvation of the entire created order.

4.2.2 The Eschatological Position of Office

Predestination summarizes the first half of the formula that office is to be "used by God to do God's work." The second half of that formula indicates that office is set within the action of God. God's work is the establishment of the kingdom, and the kingdom breaks in from the future; it is eschatological. Van Ruler himself makes the connection of predestination with the eschatological in the context of office: "The predestinarian [nature] is only maintained in the context of the eschatological. Election in all its aspects is (synoptic gospels!) related to the kingdom."[48] God engages the human in a task that is, by definition, God's task. We described that task above in the chapter on Van Ruler's theology of the kingdom.

Since office emerges from God's initiative, that means that Van Ruler will find the origin of office in the kingdom of God. That means, negatively, that office will not have its origin either from within the church or from within the faith of those who gather in the church. Put more positively, "The three offices are all more active in the world than in the church: it is about the establishment of the kingdom of God in the world and thus that humans live their earthly life in praise of God."[49] Both the offices and the congregation "are serviceable to God's kingdom intentions with the world." We are not allowed to "lock things up" in the church. Essentially, "God has to do with the world, with his kingdom, with the confrontation of the world of the kingdom, of the world as kingdom."[50]

---

47 *Bijzonder,* 64-65.

48 *Bijzonder*, 13.

49 "Betekenis presbyteriaal," 4.

50 "Ambt en gemeente," 2. Cf. Van Ruler, "Het ambt," 7: "Office and congregation are both particularly serviceable to God's kingdom intentions with his world." Note that office and congregation are coordinate realities in God's action. Neither reality is to be derived from the other. See "Nieuwjaar en ambt" (sermon preached January 1, 1947, in Hilversum on 1 Corinthians 15:58), Van Ruler Archive, Folder IV, 620, p. 1. Van Ruler preached this at the installation (*bevestiging*) of elders and deacons. The

This is a historical, horizontal reality, rooted in the covenant of grace. The three offices exist not only in the church, but essentially and at the same time in the kingdom.[51] Van Ruler's entire theological project comes to bear at this point. The kingdom is of this world; or more correctly, this world is seen as the kingdom, saved by God's salvific work. God's covenant actions and intentions find their trajectory in the everyday life of this world. "The offices do not sit purely enclosed within the holy space of the church. They stand in the midst of the no less holy space of the world and extend to the furthest extreme, to the kingdom of God."[52] The offices are *essentially* in the kingdom because their very existence is to be found within God's eschatological work.

For this reason, office is not positioned within a reality that can be distinguished into levels of "nature" and "supernature." The world of scripture is this world, one world. Reality is one, the reality of this world (see 2.2). To view reality as existing on levels of "being"—the supernatural as more "real" that the natural—is to understand the Incarnation as the elevation of creation (nature) to a supernature, hence to its true destination or reality. Sanctification is then viewed as the streamlining of this life so that it becomes heavenly, divine, eternal life. By contrast, the framework of the covenant, particularly as we read it in the Old Testament, sees the Incarnation as God's faithfulness to God's creation, the reality of sin included, and sanctification as the reestablishment of the order of law within creation. It is horizontal.[53] According to Van Ruler, the Reformation saw things not vertically, but horizontally. The destination of the human is not that he or she rises above earthly life thereby to subsist within the trinitarian life of God. He or she is to live her own life as human in the presence of God. "Genuine eschatological expectation is not heavenly but earthly, not vertical but horizontal."[54]

The offices find their position within the kingdom. The discussion of the task of the particular offices will be taken up in the following chapter. It is illustrative, however, to observe how Van Ruler views the three offices as standing in the kingdom. The minister of the Word in essence "stands on an orange crate and announces the kingdom of God to the world. Think of the apostle! Think of hedge

church council stands "within the great work of God: the kingdom of God on earth."

[51] "Gelovigen," 147.

[52] *Waarom*, 105.

[53] *Reformatorische*, 91.

[54] *Reformatorische*, 26.

preaching! Think of the missionary!"[55] Preaching takes place more in the world than in does within the four walls of the church. The congregation is the "sounding board" for the preaching so that it might find its echo in the world outside the church.[56] Van Ruler puts it more starkly still in his lectures on church order when he states that preaching is eschatological in that it happens neither in the world nor in the church, but in the kingdom of God. In preaching, the kingdom has "broken into the present in Christ and the Spirit: the *musterion*."[57] The elder finds his or her work among the homes and businesses of those who live and work outside the church. The deacon is concerned with the social ideal; he or she comes to help those in need.[58] The gospel "intends to be realized. [It] intends to Christianize life and the world and so to make it what it is, namely (saved) creation, genuine life and genuine world."[59]

In a short essay written in 1969, Van Ruler asks whether "office is only an intra-ecclesiastical matter." Within the framework of his notion of the apostolic nature of the church deepened by his theology of creation, he claimed that the "church is not the goal of the created reality. That goal lies exclusively in the world, as the kingdom of God." And office is, first of all, an "instrument of the triune God in God's kingdom action with the world in the historical process." The church is the first result of this action. But the place or position of the office is in the kingdom.[60]

God works in the kingdom as the reigning Christ, the ascended Christ. This is office not as the representation of the Jesus of a (past) history, bridging the historical gap as a messenger of what once took place. Nor does office represent Jesus as an extension of the Incarnation from the past into the present. It is the ascended Christ who reigns in the world, thereby making the future present.[61] Office as representing Christ is positioned eschatologically in the living work of

---

[55] "Betekenis presbyteriaal," 4. "Hedge preaching" [*hagepreken*] refers to the Reformation practice of preaching outside city limits, amid the hedgerows. It was thus by its very nature public preaching.

[56] *Bijzonder*, 23.

[57] "De ambten," 25.

[58] *Reformatorische*, 92. Cf. "Gelovigen," 147, *Bijzonder*, 23.

[59] Van Ruler "Christocratisch ambtsgezag als kerkscheidende factor" [hereinafter "Christocratisch"], in *Theologisch Werk* 5, 182.

[60] Van Ruler, "Is het ambt alleen binnenkerkelijk?" [hereinafter, "Binnenkerkelijk"], *Woord en Dienst*, September 20, 1969.

[61] *Bijzonder*, 17.

Christ. It is positioned not only or primarily in the church but in the world, the object and place of Christ's reign.

But as Van Ruler has insisted, the work of Christ is represented and expanded by the work of the Spirit. We noted above that it is the Holy Spirit who uses the offices (4.2.1), and we shall expand on the place of the Spirit in the offices (4.2.4). Here we need only remind ourselves that the Spirit's work extends beyond the church, beyond the individual, beyond the heart, to culture, politics, and state. Around the central event of Jesus Christ lies a "wide space, in the field of the Spirit" where occur the eschatological acts of God and the human (see above 3.1.3).[62] The offices, used by the Spirit as they represent Christ, find their place in that eschatological "space."

It is in the context of eschatology that Van Ruler introduces the office of the apostle. We saw the fundamental importance of apostolicity for the nature of the church (3.1). The place and function of the office of the apostle will be crucial for this study, and we shall return to it (4.3), for the offices find their origin in this one office. For that reason it is important to note here that for Van Ruler, the apostle is not an office of or in the church but in the kingdom.[63] The apostles do not form a single chain that connects the historic Jesus with the contemporary church. That was not what Christ was about when he sent the apostles out to the rulers and peoples of the earth. The apostles find themselves in the wider world of God's intentions. Van Ruler was consistent on this matter. In a lecture in 1968, where he offered forty theses on his "viewpoint" on the matter of office, he included one that made the same claim as he did in 1952: the apostles are primarily offices in the *basileia*. Salvation extends to the *world*. This is so, Van Ruler asserts, so that the eschatological perspective can be opened onto genuine reality.[64] Insofar as the offices are rooted in this one office, they are positioned not only in the church, but in the world as God's kingdom.[65]

---

[62] *Bijzonder*, 18.

[63] *Bijzonder*, 20. Van Ruler cites Ph.J. Hoedemaker, *De kerk en het moderne staatsrecht* (Amsterdam: Hollandsch-Afrikaansche Uitgevers Maatschappij, 1904), 137. Hoedemaker remarks that "the calling of the apostles stands not in connection with the church, let alone the Christian church, but with the notion of the kingdom." He adds that the "apostolate was originally the foundation of a new and spiritual Israel." The apostles would be set upon the thrones of glory, judging the twelve tribes of Israel.

[64] "Gezichtspunt," 24.

[65] Hendriks, 284, disagrees that office has its starting point in the kingdom. "The New Testament does not know of an office that has its primary

The eschatological position of office is also to be seen in the relation of the offices to the priesthood of believers. Again, we shall postpone a discussion of the "office of the believer" and its complex place within Van Ruler's understanding of office to a later point in this chapter (4.4). However, the priesthood of believers is itself "not primarily an ecclesiological but an eschatological matter."[66] That is so because both church and office are *means* and not the end. The end is the human in his or her work. But it is also so because the "place" of the believer is not in the cult, not within the church, but within the world, in ordinary life.[67]

Nonetheless, the human does not find his or her full humanity in office. Van Ruler sees that way of putting the matter as an expression of the notion that the human is to be "elevated" to a higher way of being. Our review of Van Ruler's theology disclosed that the eschatological goal of the human is to enter full communion with God *as human* (2.2) In a 1957 lecture on "office and congregation," Van Ruler avers what he has claimed many times, that "existence is the goal and salvation is the means; we are here not to be saved, but that we can be." Office is a means, an "emergency measure" that enables that goal. To be an office-bearer is "unnatural" for the human. The office stands within the eschaton.[68] Office is necessary to bring the human to his or her highest potential. This is so because with office, the human stands over and against the triune God. The premise that remains to be shown is that office is used by God to represent God as God enters communion with the human. As a member of the church, the human does not stand on God's side, but over and against God. The image is that of relations between persons. It is a genuine relationship only as the other remains other. There can be no love when the two do not stand over and against each other. "For insofar as one is an office-

---

position in the kingdom and thereafter in the church." He cites several passages that show the work of pastors and elders as primarily related to the congregation. On the one hand, Van Ruler could respond by repeating that a full and precise doctrine of office is not present in the New Testament. In part, his argument with Hendriks would be over method (see our remarks above 2.2). On the other hand, however, Hendriks's argument is puzzling. Van Ruler could well answer that certainly the *apostle* in the New Testament precedes the church, and is sent into the world; that is the very nature of the apostle. The argument then should take a different tack. Are the offices in a Reformed church—minister, elder, and deacon—founded on the office of the apostle?

[66] *Bijzonder,* 21.

[67] *Bijzonder*, 21.

[68] "Ambt en gemeente," 1, 2.

bearer, one stands on God's side, over and against the human qua human."[69] We shall return to this matter in the following section. At this point it is sufficient to note that the office stands within the eschatological framework as God uses the offices to effect maturity in the human in such a way that "we become the love partner of God himself."[70]

4.2.3 Office as Representing Christ

If the eschatological goal is a full communion of the human with God, then God enters the relation. God is present by means of office as the ambassador of God. Office is, as we have maintained, fundamentally *theological*. But as office represents God, it does so in Christ through the Spirit. The church effects this communion, but does so only as in it and through it Christ is mediated. Or put in other words, only as God establishes this "cathedral of love" does this communion take place. And this takes place as Christ establishes the church. In an article reviewing a proposed new church order in 1938 (quite early in his theological career) Van Ruler comments:

> It is Christ himself who, according to the confession, rules. He is the Head, the church is his body. He rules his church through Word and Spirit. Not only through the Spirit—then you always could and would have to allow everything to run its course in the order and ruling of the church. But also through his Word, through his written *and preached* Word. There you have the root of the idea of office in Christ's ruling of the church. He rules his church through the preached Word and thus through the offices. For the offices are instituted for the preaching of the Word (from scriptures!). They are the organs of the body of Christ.[71]

Just so, the early Van Ruler displays a Christological emphasis in his theology. His assertion that the offices are instituted for the preaching of the Word overstates what he will say later when he will emphasize that the offices of elder and deacon are fully office, and

---

[69] *Reformatorische*, 89.

[70] "Mondig," 122, 123.

[71] Van Ruler, "Ambt, vergadering en werk der kerk," *De Gereformeerde Kerk*, May 19, 1938, 275. Emphasis in original. See also Van Ruler, *Op gezag van een apostel* [hereinafter *Gezag apostel*] (Nijkerk: Callenbach, 1971), 48, where Van Ruler is commenting on Romans 12:6.

that neither are centered in the preached Word. But he will retain his emphasis that the offices represent Christ to the church. In 1970, Van Ruler would claim that the authority of the offices rests "exclusively in Christ." He is the head of his body; he rules the church by means of his offices. The "main thing" is that "office is of the Lord and is so in and of the church. Whoever accepts and fills an office thus in the first instance offers assistance to God, to the Lordship of Christ over his congregation and church."[72] It is the Messiah as the coming king who "rules the church...he maintains his church, he feeds her, protects her, leads her, commands her.... We are his property. No one can snatch her from his hands."[73] It is a matter of what Van Ruler calls "Christocracy."

It is the historic Jesus who is represented by the offices. "It is the historic Christ who must be represented in the present. The particularity and the peculiarity of God in God's otherness is 'condensed' [*verdicht*] in the gestalt of the God-human, of God the Son in human flesh."[74] The Savior has come and he has completed his work. "Thus we do not live and work toward the salvation (of the world). We live and work from it." Christ has overcome the world.[75] "Salvation is given in Christ as a historical reality...that must be mediated."[76] As the "Report on Ecclesiastical Office" (the so-called "Van Ruler Report") would put it: "The historical appearance of Jesus becomes a present reality. The offering of atonement is made present. As the minister opens his mouth to proclaim the gospel, the blood of Jesus drips in the church, according to Calvin....The offices represent the crucified King among humans in order that the people of God be gathered."[77]

This appears clear enough; the events of Palestine of the first century must become contemporary with the present if God is to be present in the world, or it must be so if Jesus is confessed as the Messiah of God. But the offices do not represent the historic Christ of

[72] *Waarom*, 103. Cf. *Bijzonder*, 66: "The ministries or offices must most deeply be understood from this permanent appearance of Christ in his church."

[73] "Christocracy," 167.

[74] "Gezag ambt," 117.

[75] "Christocracy," 175. Cf. "De ambten," 36.

[76] "Ambt en gemeente," 1.

[77] *Rapport*, 33. See also "De ds en gemeente" (sermon preached June 19, 1949, in Hensbroek on 2 Corinthians 1:24), Van Ruler Archive, Folder IV, 657, p. 3. Van Ruler is preaching at the installation of a minister in his first congregation. He preaches that the minister is there "to remind you, over and again, of God in Christ."

the past, but the historic Christ who is ascended. A Christ who is only past would leave us anxious, Van Ruler argues. But in the heavenly Christ we see one who "acts permanently in a divine and spiritual way. When we say that the offices are institutions of Christ, we must think equally of the historic and heavenly Christ."[78] In just this way, Jesus Christ, the historic and heavenly Christ, can speak in the present. Jesus can say to the apostles, and so to office-bearers, "who hears you, hears me!"[79] And the Van Ruler Report can state that "Christ appears and dwells with us through preaching and administration of the sacraments, through pastoral care, through oversight, and through the ministry of mercy."[80] That is, the three offices found in Reformed churches are vehicles or modes of Christ's appearance.

The office as representative of the ascended (and hence contemporary) Christ disallows the notion of office as (only) a continuation of the historic Christ into the present. Such a notion arises when the bishop becomes the office *par excellence*, as Van Ruler sees the matter. In that case, the trajectory of history moves solely from the past to the present. We recall the double movement of history, a history that must be thought out of the end. The risen Christ rules in the intermezzo, as the kingdom of Christ points toward the kingdom of God. The logic, or theo-logic if you will, leads us to conclude that the offices share in the intermezzo nature of Christ's kingdom, and hence both point to the future and are set within the future as they represent the Messiah. We shall return to this below when we consider the role of the offices in God's salvific work (4.2.5).

The representation of Christ through the offices has two very important implications for a theology of office. The first has to do with the fact that the offices are not a particularization of human activity, but stand over and against [*tegenover*] the human. "[T]he work of the Messiah, in whom the kingdom stands founded, is—in its representative and atoning character—a matter that by definition can only be proclaimed, at least originally, and further intends to be celebrated."[81] Van Ruler summarizes a discussion of Christ's presence

[78] *Bijzonder*, 63. Cf. "Christocracy," 168. See also "Hemelvaart - en wederkomst," 7. Christ will come again, and has come again. This coming again is in the Holy Spirit. Christ "has come in the outpouring of the Holy Spirit." He comes to us daily. And just so (p. 8) in the Holy Spirit the ascended Lord gathers and rules his congregation.

[79] "Gezag ambt," 17.

[80] *Rapport*, 33.

[81] "Betekenis," 183.

in the church through office by stating simply "office comes from the other side."[82] He states it as a thesis in *Bijzonder en algemeen ambt* that the "Lord appears in his particularity (thus always in an 'over and against' with his own in his church) in freedom and love."[83]

This characteristic of office cannot be underscored sufficiently. It is fundamental to Van Ruler's understanding that office does not emerge from the church. In this he differs from those who would argue that all believers share in an office. He cites, for example, G. van der Leeuw, who maintains that "all believers are office-bearers in worship." There is, according to Van der Leeuw, a difference in task among office-bearers; some, for example, have leadership in cultic worship.[84] This is rooted in the claim that "office in the church is given to the congregation."[85] Not so, Van Ruler will maintain over and again. "The office originates in no way in the congregation, but is the self-presentation of God-in-Christ in the congregation."[86] In an early lecture on preaching, Van Ruler put it like this: "The particularity of the spiritual office is not in the first place...from the circle of believers; but [it rests] in the first place on the particularity, on the peculiar nature [*eenigheid*] of the Word of God who will be served that he be received as a living voice."[87] The offices come *to* the church; they do not arise *out of* the church. They do not represent the church; nor do they represent the faith of the church. They represent Christ.

In a public exchange of letters with the Roman Catholic J.A.M. Weterman, Van Ruler argued that the question of office is more than a question of church order, more even than a theological question. It is a religious question that comes down to the fact that God is not absorbed in human consciousness. God is more than and something other than a form of human existence. God is God's own self; God stands over and against the human.[88] This provides one of the objections Van Ruler has to consecration to office. In consecration, a human is "lifted" to a new plane of existence. The human "goes ahead"

---

[82] "Gezag ambt," 17.

[83] *Bijzonder,* 61. Cf. 66.

[84] G van der Leeuw, *Liturgiek,* 2nd ed. (Nijkerk: G.F. Callenbach, 1946), 56, 57.

[85] Van der Leeuw, *Liturgiek,* 58.

[86] "Ambt en gemeente," 1.

[87] Van Ruler, "Kerk en prediking" (lecture to *Kerkherstel,* Bethel, Franeker, October 16, 1935), Van Ruler Archive, folder I, 97, 5-6. In "De teekenen van de prediking" (sermon preached January 11, 1948, in Hilversum on Mark 6:13), Van Ruler Archive, Folder IV, 646, p. 2, Van Ruler states that "preaching is the great offensive in the world of demonic powers."

[88] *Briefwisseling,* 112.

of the congregation to the human's appropriate destination. But there is no "over and against" in such a way of thinking; it isn't sufficiently radical. For then the human cannot arrive at the human's proper destination, there to be met by God and so enter communion with God: "It is God himself, who in the freedom of the Spirit, sets him on his (God's) side, who is present in this human [the office-bearer] among his own." [89] Van Ruler would not argue only with Roman Catholics on this point; he expressed his reservation against the so-called "Berkhof report" on office in Van Ruler's own Nederlandse Hervormde Kerk. Berkhof, says Van Ruler, "has it as though the lordship of Christ resides fully in the church as church and the church says, 'Fellows, we must also have an office that can represent Christ.' Over and against that notion I am of the opinion that the New Testament does not have it that first the church exists, but that it is first the ascended Christ and the Spirit who work in history, thus the apostolic Word that goes forth to the peoples. There is the office. Not in the church, but in the world, in the kingdom, in history."[90]

The characteristic essence of office as over and against carries with it a certain institutional element. This is the second implication of office as representative of Christ; it is the mystical or organic nature of office. Christ is head of his body, the church, and appears as such in the church.[91] "The Messiah Jesus himself continues his ministry (to the kingdom of God and thus in the world) and for this purpose he uses his *ecclesia* and its ministries (that is, offices) as his organs."[92] Van Ruler will go on to claim that office is an organ of Christ's own self, "through which he himself builds up his body and actively appears in and through the *ecclesia*."[93] He adds that the image of "organ" is more precise than that of an "instrument." In this more organic way, the ministries outlined in the New Testament can be understood in such a

---

[89] *Briefwisseling*, 116.

[90] *Gesprek*, 21. The "Berkhof Report," formally titled *Rapport over het ambt*, was commissioned by the General Synod of the Netherlands Reformed Church after the synod did not receive the "Van Ruler Report." In contrast to the Van Ruler Report, the new report was commissioned to be written by one writer, Hendrikus Berkhof, with an advisory commission to offer review and suggestions. The Berkhof report was not accepted by the General Synod either. For the "Berkhof Report," see Hendrikus Berkhof, "Rapport over het ambt: aangeboden aan de generale synode der Nederlandse Hervormde Kerk" (Bibliotheek Universiteit Utrecht, photocopied).

[91] *Bijzonder*, 66.

[92] *Bijzonder*, 70.

[93] *Bijzonder*, 76.

way that Christ is the subject of those ministries.[94] Here too, the offices cannot be understood as emerging from the congregation. That which represents the head cannot be confused with the body; it comes to and rules the body—or at least as Van Ruler uses this imagery.

The offices as originating in the representation of Christ represent the Christ of the *munus triplex*. However, it must be clearly stated that Van Ruler resists the Reformed temptation to found its three-fold office of minister-elder-deacon directly on the three-fold office of Christ.[95] Christ's three-fold office is indeed office as Christ acts in the office *par excellence* as the Messiah. The offices of the church, in all their plurality, will each case bear the entire munus triplex within itself, "albeit with special accents."[96] In so doing, the offices are about God's work set within the kingdom.

The "*vis-à-vis* character" of office as representation of Christ could suggest that Van Ruler might lean toward the notion of the office-bearer as having undergone an ontological change. Office represents the "other." It is crucial, however, to keep all of Van Ruler's theological project in mind. The predestinarian heart of office (4.2.1) asserts that God uses humans, as human, in God's work. This is not, as he emphasizes over and again, the elevation of the human but in fact the confirmation of the human in office. The power of Van Ruler's theology of office is as he maintains both a "high" view of office as coming from God and at the same time resists the notion of "ontological elevation."

4.2.4 Office as a Moment in the Work of the Spirit

Our survey of Van Ruler's theology found it to be resolutely trinitarian (2.8). It is to be expected that his theology of office will reflect the same trinitarian structure and content that his theological enterprise displays. This indeed is the case. While the offices represent Christ, they do so through the work of the Spirit. At the outset of this chapter, we cited Van Ruler's definition of office as "the work of God in Christ through the Spirit." We have examined the first two terms of

---

[94] *Bijzonder*, 76, 77. Cf. *Religie*, 92. This stands in contrast to Calvin, *Institutes of the Christian Religion*, IV, 3, 1, where Calvin uses the metaphor of tool or instrument in relation to the ministers of the church. However, Van Ruler uses "instrument" in relation to the offices. E.g., *Waarom*, 104: "This is the essence of the office: that God wants to use you as his instrument."

[95] *Bijzonder*, 70-71; *Reformatorische*, 114; "De ambten," 18.

[96] "De ambten," 18. See *Rapport*, 58.

this claim, "the work of God in Christ," as the offices represent Christ. It is now imperative to turn to the final term, "through the Spirit."[97]

This is fully trinitarian in that while salvation is given in Christ and that the *unio mystica cum Christo* stands at the center of the church, this must be mediated. "This mediation is the work of God the Holy Spirit; it happens in a manifold way, one of the moments of the *pneuma* is the office."[98] Mediation happens through God alone, Van Ruler argues, and that through the Holy Spirit. This is the Spirit as God the third time: "The Holy Spirit is God's self anew, not equal to God the Son and not equal to Jesus Christ."[99] Van Ruler claims that here we are at the heart of the question of office. He asks rhetorically, can this be approached exclusively from Christ? Or aren't we at the foundational structure of the Trinity? The Holy Spirit is the Spirit of the Father as well of the Son. The outpouring and indwelling of God the Holy Spirit form a new establishment of the Word of God in salvation. Church, sacraments, and office stand essentially in the dispensation of the Holy Spirit.[100]

A trinitarian "expansion" occurs in office. We are not simply within the ambit of Christ's presence as it extends into history. For Van Ruler, Roman Catholic theology makes this mistake.[101] The

---

[97] Hendriks, 290, claims that Van Ruler grants too much independence to the place of the Spirit to the detriment of the ascended Christ. "For Van Ruler it is as if Christ himself has no power to be present in his church and in the offices." Hendriks would have it that one must begin with Christ and then proceed to the place of the offices in the work of Christ. But that is precisely what Van Ruler does as he moves from Christ as the one who rules as the ascended one, but who is present through the Spirit. The Spirit is only *relatively* independent, albeit more independent than Hendriks apparently finds justifiable. J. Weterman, "Briefwisseling," 118, agrees with Hendriks that Van Ruler concentrates too much on the presence of God in the Spirit to the cost of the office as the representative of the glorified Lord. Van Ruler would indeed insist that the Spirit who works through the offices is the Spirit of the Father as well as the Spirit of the Son, although he neither belittles nor denies the latter. "Briefwisseling," 116.

[98] "Ambt en gemeente," 1. We note that office is only *one* of the moments in the *pneuma*.

[99] Van Ruler, "Het theologisch verschil tussen Rome en de Reformatie" (notes for a lecture to preachers, Enschede, January 23, 1955), Van Ruler Archive, folder I, 347, 1.

[100] "Briefwisseling," 116. See *Rapport*, 67, where office is described as a "gift of God...an instrument of the Holy Spirit by means of which salvation is mediated in Jesus Christ, our prophet, priest, and king."

[101] "Het verschil," 1.

outpouring of the Holy Spirit is a peculiar and particular salvific fact.[102] Here we move beyond Christ as the one represented to the *representation* (or the *representing*) itself, a new act of God. The Holy Spirit uses the offices in this mediation, this representation.[103] In the use of the offices, the Holy Spirit appropriates to us all his treasures in order that we may be united and engrafted into Christ, that Christ may take on gestalt in us, and that salvation may be worked out within us, sacramentally, liturgically, confesssionaly, diaconally, mystically, ethically, culturally, and politically.[104] This is the representation of God's own self in the historic and heavenly Christ, of the atonement of guilt, of the victory over death, and of the breaking in of the kingdom. These are historical realities.[105] It is not sufficient that these things happened once with Christ. A new act was required. That was to be the work of the Holy Spirit. And the work of the Spirit was not *ephapax*.[106] The Spirit continues to work. The action of the Holy Spirit makes Christ contemporary.[107]

This work of the Spirit is *institutional* as it uses the offices in the work of representation. One senses institutional liniments as the one represented finds expression in new times and places. The kingdom stands founded on the work of the Messiah and that can only be proclaimed, at least originally, Van Ruler argues. There must be a means to make that proclamation contemporary. But that places a heavy accent on the institutional moments in the Christian church. At the outset it is the Holy Spirit at work in such institutional elements as the inspiration of the Holy Spirit, the sending of the apostles, the creation of tradition, and the use of the offices.[108] The Spirit is not to be thought of only as that which is "inward."[109] Thought that way, it is easy to set the spiritual in opposition to the institutional, and hence in opposition to the offices. But, Van Ruler argues, "the institutional and

---

102 *Reformatorische*, 98.

103 *Reformatorische*, 99.

104 *Reformatorische*, 99, 100.

105 *Reformatorische*, 132.

106 To be more accurate, Van Ruler spoke of the Spirit as having been poured out once at Pentecost, but that this is a "singularity in continuity" ("Structuurverschillen," 184).

107 *Reformatorische*, 133.

108 "Betekenis," 183-134. See "De nabijheid van Jezus Christus bij zijn gemeente in het ambt," 6, where, preaching on John 20:19-23, Van Ruler remarks that the Holy Spirit breathes on the disciples so that they could become witnesses to the resurrected Jesus.

109 *Bijzonder*, 30.

the pneumatological, the Spirit and office, do not exclude each other. They do not even stand in opposition to each other. An institutional and a juridical way of thinking is at least equally 'spiritual' as is the organic and the ethical. At least when one derives the word 'spiritual' from the Holy Spirit. This would find its gestalt more in the act of judgment, in order, in the law, and in tradition than in the ongoing stream of life."[110]

One senses that more is afoot than the Spirit's representation of Christ, so far as Van Ruler is concerned. For if the Spirit were only the representation of the one represented, Christ, we could hardly speak of the "expansion" that we found so dear to Van Ruler, as when he talks about the Holy Spirit as both "expansion" and "representation." Van Ruler opens *Bijzonder en algemeen ambt* with the chapter, "Office and the Kingdom," because kingdom stands so centrally in his theological understanding. In that chapter, he claims that the New Testament does not concentrate only on Jesus as the ascended Lord, but includes pneumatological aspects. The Spirit is poured out and the kingdom can be said to consist of "righteousness, peace, and gladness through the Holy Spirit." Around the centrality of the experience of Christ, his historical presence, there exists a "wide space," the "field of the Spirit."[111] The "offices do not exist completely closed within the holy space of the church. They stand in the midst of the no less holy space of the world and extend to the furthest extreme, to the kingdom of God."[112] It is in this space that office is used (although one must hasten to add that this wide space of the Spirit cannot be limited to offices, or to church, for that matter, as we might expect given the theological claims we have heard from Van Ruler).

Van Ruler will in fact speak of the Spirit's work in terms other than that of representation. He employs the notion of *application*. That is, Christ is not simply represented. It is not only a matter of mediation; the human is engrafted into Christ.[113] In his work on office in the early 1950s, Van Ruler would talk about the communion that humans enjoy in Christ as created through the preaching of the gospel of the kingdom. Van Ruler speaks of the Holy Spirit in this way: "...the love, which is taught by the Holy Spirit, that is to say is poured out in our hearts, is more than a moral ideal. It is a reality of salvation history; it is the love of God's self in which we walk."[114] Here the Holy

---

[110] *Bijzonder*, 67-68.
[111] *Bijzonder*, 18.
[112] *Waarom*, 105.
[113] *Reformatorische*, 134.
[114] *Bijzonder*, 59

Spirit has an almost pedagogical instrumentality; we are "taught" by the Spirit. Much later, by the late 1960s, after he sharpened his notion of the Holy Spirit and could write of a "relatively independent" doctrine of the Holy Spirit, Van Ruler would continue to write of the union of the human in Christ, but more boldly. Such is the work of the Holy Spirit that the Spirit unites the human with God in Christ and forms God in Christ within the human.[115]

In this way, office is to be understood as a "moment in the work of the Spirit."[116] It is a "moment" in that the offices are historical instances by which the Spirit "uses" particular persons as office-bearers in the mediation of salvation. As the work of the Spirit, the offices are not only used by God, but in a very real sense God is present through the offices.

Here again, within the work of the Holy Spirit, we must speak of an "over and against" of the offices, and that in two ways. First, there is what Van Ruler calls a "border." The Spirit is God's own self as present over and against the human. The Spirit is not God as God wells up from the human spirit. Van Ruler resists any sort of spiritualism within an understanding of office.[117]

Second, this is an "over and against" that differs from that of Christ to Christ's own, of the Christ who by definition comes *to* the human in the present. This is the "over and against" that stands at the goal, as it were, where the Christian stands over and against, in the presence of, the triune God, the Christian now as fully human. This is an "over and against" in love, as we came across it in the previous subsection.[118] Van Ruler asks: "When God speaks, am I then silent? Or is that just the intention, that I too speak—with God and together with him?" One cannot understand this Christologically, but only pneumatologically. The work of the Holy Spirit is necessary.[119] The offices are used by God as *God* enters the relation with the human.[120]

At this point the structural differences between Christology and pneumatology take purchase in a theology of office. At issue is not the assumption of human nature, a Christological category. Assumption

---

[115] *Reformatorische,* 134.

[116] *Reformatorische*, 128. Van Ruler, "De vreugde van het ambt" (speech to the Classical Gathering of Haarlem, October 8, 1957), Van Ruler Archive, folder I, 445, 4: "Office is a moment in the representation of God in Christ through the Spirit." Cf. also, "Het ambt," 3.

[117] *Bijzonder*, 25.

[118] *Bijzonder*, 39.

[119] "Briefwisseling," 116.

[120] *Reformatorische*, 125.

would take hold if the office not only represented Christ but were in some way the continuation of the person of Christ in history. According to Van Ruler, this would be an expression of office as an ontological elevation of the human, now assumed in Christ. At issue is not assumption of human nature in Christ, but the adoption of human nature in the Spirit.[121] The human has become the dwelling place [*woonstede*] of God in the Spirit.[122] This is the full "over and against" of humanity with God. And this takes place in the *unio mystica cum Christo* (the mystical union with Christ).

The offices are moments in the work of the Spirit as means. It is a means toward the goal, the eschaton. The Christological is the foundation. "The pneumatological is not only the consequence, but also the goal." "God is nearer his goal" in us, at the eschaton: "God all in all."[123]

These few paragraphs may make the dynamic of the Spirit's use of office appear more systematic than it is for Van Ruler. The Spirit is not exhausted by the office; nor can the Spirit be uniformly channeled through the office. The work of the Holy Spirit takes place in a manifold way. It is not limited to office or even to sacrament. Such a way of thinking is not sufficiently catholic. The human is taken up biologically, culturally, historically in the covenant of grace.[124] True catholicity brings with it a pluralistic way of thinking. In one place, Van Ruler lists a series of dualities that suggest this "trinitarian expansion": God and the human, office and the congregation, the Holy Spirit and tradition, the church and Israel, the church and the state, Christ and the Holy Spirit.[125] "The Spirit loves pluriformity."[126]

4.2.5 Office in the Economy of Salvation

Since the Messiah's work is salvific in that he atones for the guilt of the human, and since the Spirit uses the offices to mediate this atonement to the human, the logic of the *necessity* of office in the economy of salvation can now be made clear. Van Ruler says as much, that "office is abundantly necessary for Christian existence."[127] This is not an ontological necessity, one that resides in the nature of being.

---

121 *Reformatorische*, 128.
122 "Briefwisseling," 126.
123 "Het ambt," 3.
124 "Het ambt," 5.
125 "Het theologisch verschil," 3.
126 *Reformatorische,* 113.
127 "Christocratisch," 169.

Office does not enjoy an ontological status in that it can be understood as part of the eternal nature of reality. Office represents God in God's salvific work in the Messiah, as the Messiah effects the intermezzo. If the Messiah is God's emergency measure, the representative of the Messiah, the offices, themselves are but emergency measures.[128] But if they are not ontologically necessary, they are evangelically necessary. That is, God uses the offices to effect salvation. In a sermon on Acts 8:31b, set in the story of Philip and the Ethiopian eunuch, Van Ruler says, "There is no shame that the congregation has the offices necessary to truly understand the scripture. The Ethiopian had Philip necessary. The congregation has the offices necessary; the preacher teaches, the elder rules, the deacon serves—and so the scripture is the Word of God in the congregation."[129] God is free in God's use of office. One can conceive that God might use another way, even if one need not be able to conceive of what this other way might be. God's freedom is, as we saw, the predestinarian heart of a theology of office. Still, something like office will be necessary for human salvation.

As we saw at the outset of this chapter, office represents God in God's work. And as God's ultimate intentions incline toward the kingdom of God, God works in salvation as a means toward that greater end. Salvation is found in the historical Christ.[130] Human justification happens in God's presence and is to be sought completely in the offering at Golgatha.[131] The heart of the gospel is the atonement; Jesus bears human sin and punishment for sin. But this takes place not in our presence, but in the presence of God.[132] Salvation is not about a sanctification that effects a transition from earth to heaven, from time to eternity. Rather, the heart of salvation is atonement from guilt. We are not saved from this earthly life. We are saved from guilt. "Then the order of the kingdom, the law, and creation can be established again within earthly life."[133] We are saved *for* this earthly life.

---

128 "Ambt en gemeente," 2: "...office is only God's emergency measure in the congregation."

129 "Schrift-ambt-gemeente" (sermon preached on March 6, 1938, in Eexta), Van Ruler Archive, Folder IV, 228, p. 3.

130 Van Ruler will claim that this is particularly so for churches of the Reformation because they understood salvation as rooted at Golgatha.

131 "Briefwisseling," 112.

132 *Bijzonder*, 73, cf. 25.

133 "Briefwisseling," 126.

In this way, God's salvific work stands at a double remove from humans. On the one hand it is a historical remove. God works in history, and the historical past (and future) can only be mediated to us. On the other hand, God's works stand at a theological remove. Because atonement happened (and happens) in God's presence, it again must be mediated to us humans. In listing several motivating factors for the particular office, Van Ruler states that as a historical reality, salvation must be handed on through legitimate tradition.[134] That tradition as a gestalt of the Holy Spirit is expressed in the office of the apostle. In anticipation of what we shall see below (4.3), we hear Van Ruler's claim that the apostle is not present in the church as the bishop who continues Christ's presence in the contemporary church. The apostle reports a historic event (or events). In his lecture, "Viewpoints," on office, Van Ruler sets this out in three steps. First, the Savior's work at Golgatha is a completed act. Second, we need not (and cannot) realize the matter of atonement ourselves. It takes place *extra nos*. Third, the Holy Spirit realizes the atonement as the Spirit applies this accomplished work by means of the offices.[135] What has been mediated in the Mediator, between God and the human once and for all, "must now be mediated anew through the Spirit; that happens centrally by means of office."[136]

This historical remove, while real, is only one aspect of the evangelical necessity of office in salvation. Office, as that which stands over and against us, is also necessary because we are unable to conceive either our need or the salvation that God is about. The first motivating factor that Van Ruler lists for the particular office in the list we cited above is that office is necessary because salvation is too great for the forms of human existence to take in.[137] I must be told that I am a sinner; I cannot believe it on my own. It is too monstrous.

---

134 "Gelovigen," 141. Van Ruler lists five motivations for the "particular office." (1) Salvation is too great for the capacity of the forms of human existence to grasp; (2) salvation as a historical reality must be handed on through legitimate tradition; (3) salvation is characterized by particularity and strangeness. That which is strange or other to me must be mediated; (4) salvation is provisional. In the offices we keep hold of this strange and historical salvation until the day of judgment; and (5) the church is a "symbolic play," in which God and the human are engaged in mutual relation.

135 "Gezichtspunt," 36.

136 "De vreugde van het ambt," 4.

137 "Gelovigen," 141. Van Ruler adds that even regenerate existence is incapable of grasping the forms of salvation.

Likewise, I must be told that I am a child of God. "When this is not said to me with apostolic authority, it has to sound like nonsense in my ears."[138] That Christ is salvation from sin, death, and the devil is beyond the human capability of knowing.[139] In reviewing Van Ruler's theological project, we discovered that internal grace was not something to be understood as arising from within the human himself, but that there is a certain *corpus alienum* of salvation. Humans are not in the position to realize salvation themselves. We recall that Van Ruler understands atonement primarily as expiation, and that in turn presupposes substitution [*plaatsvervanging*] (2.6). The human cannot substitute for him or herself.[140] Van Ruler could state this in characteristically aphoristic ways. In one place he claims that the congregation doesn't carry truth "in a pocket."[141] Or more graphically, he can say that "we cannot suck the truth from our own thumbs."[142]

This truth, in itself, offers an additional reason why office is not to be conceived as a particularization of the general office, or said otherwise, of the ministry of the congregation. Van Ruler identifies congregationalism as one form of authority within the church that fails because it does not properly respect the distinction between Christ as head and the body. It cannot do proper honor both to the historical reality of salvation and the historical mediation that takes place through the apostolic office (now expanded in the offices of the church), nor does it appropriately acknowledge the utter lostness of the human sinner.[143] If office were to arise as representative of the congregation, the human could not receive a salvation that must, of necessity, come from without.

The foregoing paragraphs on the necessity of office in the economy of salvation are summarized in the "Van Ruler Report," where the work of office-bearers is described as:

---

138 *Waarom*, 155.

139 "Gelovigen," 141.

140 E.g., "Briefwisseling," 115-116.

141 Van Ruler, "De theologische studie en de ambtspraktijk" (opening lecture, October 3, 1951), Van Ruler Archive, folder I, 270, 4. This is a particular Dutch locution meaning that one possesses the truth and knows it thoroughly.

142 *Gesprek*, 19. This is also a Dutch locution meaning that the supposed truth comes from one's own imagination.

143 "Christocratisch," 169. Van Ruler also comments on the Quakers as an expression of the authority of the conscience. Like congregationalism, it cannot effect salvation of the human for the same reason. The act of salvation must come from God; the human is trapped within human reality.

> ...ministry to Christ's congregation and to God's world. The members of the congregation must be equipped to witness salvation in Christ and the way of God, to place their lives and their gifts in the ministry of God and to the neighbor, to join in the struggle against the powers of evil in their own life and in society, and to advocate justice and righteousness.[144]

Here office is understood within the framework of the apostolic task of the church. Office stands over and against the believers because it brings a certain *message* that the human cannot otherwise receive.

Office is evangelically necessary in another way, and this in parallel with his description of the church as the cathedral of love. Van Ruler would claim that the question of office was about more than theology; it was about religion. By that he meant that it was about the relation of the human to God.[145] In that context, he argued that God is not fully absorbed in human consciousness. God stands over and against the human in an otherness necessary in a relation that is love.[146] When we return to Van Ruler's list of motivating factors for the particular office,[147] we find that he concludes his list with the comment that the church is "symbolic play." This takes place most fully in the sacrament. But who plays? It is the human on the one side, the human as he or she comes believing, confessing, worshiping. On the other side is God. Here we see the provisional nature of salvation as having proleptically been overcome. Here the human arrives at its eschatological goal, life in communion with God. But it is God "as he is represented by the offices."[148] Here one might even claim that the full conversion of the human has taken place, and he or she experiences the world as creation, as the work of God.[149] But the offices are necessarily present because without God as present through the offices, there could be no communion.

Nonetheless, it all remains provisional. Human reality in the present dispensation is lived against the eschatological reserve. The offices, coming as they do over and against the human, represent the strangeness of this salvation. They represent the Messiah whose kingdom is a gestalt of the final kingdom, and so they will appear

---

144 *Rapport*, 67.

145 "Religion" from *religare*, "to tie" or "to bind." Religion "connects" the human with God, or God with the human.

146 "Briefwisseling," 112.

147 See note 134.

148 "Gelovigen," 142.

149 "Christocratisch," 171.

alien to the human—and to the church. "In the offices we best maintain the full, historical, strange salvation until the day of judgment."[150] The offices will press beyond the provisional nature of salvation and will pick up the claim we came across already, that the point is not the Savior, nor is salvation the point, but rather the saved. In this way, Van Ruler can claim that the authority of the apostolic office is not limited to salvation as it moves beyond the atonement and extends to sanctification, to the reality of human life. "The realization of salvation is in many ways also an engrafting of salvation into the true, the good, and the beautiful."[151] God uses the offices in God's work of salvation, which looks beyond salvation to creation. The offices are set within the kingdom.

4.2.6 Women in Office

The issue of whether women were to be accepted as office-bearers emerged contemporaneously with Van Ruler's thinking and writing on office. The General Synod of the Netherlands Reformed Church commissioned a study in the early 1950s. While it will be clear that Van Ruler gave thought to the matter, he committed very little to print. This may well be because he was hesitant on the matter.[152] A brief exploration of his hesitance both helps us to a fuller understanding of his doctrine of office and confirms the theological commitments we have seen come to evidence.

He did some work on a preparatory study for a work on *"De vrouw in het ambt"* ["Woman in office"]. There he claims that office is not the "end" or the goal of the human. One is not *more* human as an office-bearer. Office is "only an emergency measure." For this reason, the woman need not feel "left behind" by omission from office.[153]

His hesitation is also rooted in his understanding that the relation of God and the human is expressed in the relation of the male and female. Van Ruler appears to argue that the male functions rather in the way that God functions, that is, as "other." Van Ruler will emphasize the particularity of the otherness of God, one that expresses itself with a "special urgency." This otherness finds

---

150 "Gelovigen," 142.

151 "Christocratisch," 181.

152 In response to a letter from Annie Lekkerkerker, May 15, 1958, Van Ruler Archive, VI, A, Van Ruler penned a note, apparently to himself, in which he confesses his personal hesitancy about women in ecclesiastical office.

153 Van Ruler, "De vrouw in het ambt," a "voorstudie," Van Ruler Archive, V, 9, p. 1.

expression in apostolic expression. Thus far, Van Ruler seems not only hesitant but resolutely refuses to argue for restricting office to males. But then he immediately goes on to ask: is it so important that the apostles were male? The resurrected Jesus appeared first to women to give to them the message.[154] It is, we recall, the historical message that comes *to* the church that makes for the particularity of office.

It is a matter of tradition, and tradition is important, Van Ruler also maintains. He hesitates to break the tradition of nineteen hundred years.[155] This coheres with his further reservation that this is not something that is to be decided by a "sect," but by the church, the whole church.[156] It is an ecumenical question that includes relation between Catholic and Protestant. Nonetheless, even in this context he can put two questions. On the one hand the church must have the courage to reform if need be.[157] On the other hand, at issue is office and "office is only office."[158] That is, the "possession" of office is not a matter of salvation for the office-bearer.

One other matter was at issue for Van Ruler in the discussion of women in office. He argued strenuously against proposals that would allow women into some offices but not all. He also argued against those who advocated women in office but would refuse them a place in the church council, that is, not in ecclesiastical assembly. There was to be "no splitting in the offices."[159] Office in isolation is nothing; it exists only synodically, with the other offices. You cannot split the minister from the elder and deacon. Nor could you separate the governance of the elder from the service of the deacon. Serving is, said Van Ruler, being "used by God." But then governance comes to the same thing, according to Van Ruler.[160]

4.2.7 Summary

The excursion into Van Ruler's theology of office has shown that office, in its essence, is a theological reality. One cannot

---

[154] "De vrouw in de ambt," 2.

[155] See also Van Ruler's comments to a similar effect as recorded in *Handelingen van de vergaderingen van de Generale Synode der Nederlandse Hervormde Kerk ten Jare 1953/1954* ('s-Gravenhage: Nederlandsche Boek- en Steendrukker, 1957), 558.

[156] "De vrouw in de ambt," 3.

[157] "De vrouw in de ambt," 3.

[158] *Handelingen 1953/1954*, 558.

[159] "De vrouw in de ambt," 3.

[160] *Handelingen 1953-1954*, 557.

understand Van Ruler's notion of office apart from his theology of the kingdom of God. Indeed, office as a moment in the work of the Spirit is to be understood as the work of the triune God. The negative result of this conclusion is that office cannot be construed as primarily a human work, although it engages the human fully in the work of the office. The positive result is that office can be understood within the framework not of the church, itself a vehicle in God's economy, but of the kingdom of God.

Furthermore, this review of Van Ruler's theology of office has begun to authorize the four-fold thesis set out at the beginning of this chapter. We have seen that for Van Ruler the offices cannot emerge from the congregation for both Christological and pneumatological reasons. The offices represent Christ to the church through the Holy Spirit. Furthermore, office is used by God as an instrument of salvation. How God relates to the church through the offices and how God uses those offices to effect salvation in the church will occupy us later. At this point in our investigation, we can observe the theological argument as it begins to come into view. Furthermore, as we see the offices set within the kingdom, we have prepared the theological ground for a discussion in the following chapter of how the particular offices, as such, are active in the kingdom of God.

4.3 The Office of Apostle as the Original Office

Our inquiry has led us to the point where we have seen office as a resolutely theological reality. That is, office is a means, an institution, chosen by the triune God to be used by God in Christ and through the Spirit to effect God's work in a history set in and drawn toward the eschaton. God does not work only through the offices; God's Spirit uses other means as well. But because God does so use humans in the offices, the offices do not simply have a theological rationale; they are themselves of God. Within the framework of the theology articulated above, we turn to the offices proper. Given Van Ruler's emphasis on the apostolate, it is not surprising that he places the office of the apostle at the head of his understanding of office.

The office of the apostle is the original office, for Van Ruler. The term "original" is not Van Ruler's.[161] One is inclined to identify the office of apostle as the root office of the church. And indeed he does

[161] However, *Rapport*, 31: "The office of the apostle is the origin of the other offices."

so at a number of points.[162] But he also warns against the advisability of talking about the office of the apostle as "the root office from which all the other offices of the church emerge."[163] The term "original" expresses Van Ruler's intent if we are careful to guard against an episcopal ecclessiological understanding. In that view, the offices originate in a prior office because they ontically subsist in the prior office; the deacon and the priest exist contemporaneously in the office of bishop. In contrast, one cannot say that the three offices found in Reformed theology and church order subsist in the office of the apostle. Van Ruler will remark, for example, that the elder holds an office integral to itself.[164] For that reason Van Ruler advised against using the notion of "root" in connection with the apostle. In contradistinction to an episcopal understanding of the office of apostle, with its sense of hierarchy and verticality, Van Ruler understands that office as set within a historical-eschatological framework. The offices have their historical origin set within the office of the apostle. We hasten to add that this historical understanding is within the eschatological context we explored in 2.4.

The office of the apostle originates in a particular history. "The apostle stands on the field of history. There he sees—lightning strikes!—the acts of God in his activity with the world. He proclaims them. He goes to the peoples of the earth with the gospel of the kingdom."[165] The apostle has something to report. He witnesses a particular revelation: the presence of God in Israel and in Jesus Christ.[166] This is not a truth spread through the totality of history.

---

[162] "Gezichtspunt," 28. Cf. *Religie*, 89, and "Ambten," 62, where the office of the elder is "rooted" in the office of the apostle. In *Gezag apostel*, 48, he calls the office of the apostle the "backbone" of the church. The offices emerge as "ribs" from this backbone. For the image of "root" see also "De nabijheid van Jezus Christus bij zijn gemeente in het ambt," 5, and "Leiderschap" (sermon preached July 21, 1946, in Amsterdam on Acts 6:6), Van Ruler Archive, Folder IV, 607, p.1.

[163] *Apostolaat*, 56. The context of Van Ruler's claim is that the church itself is *ambtelijk*. That is, the church functions as office. Van Ruler is tilting against the notion that the apostle functions as office in the stead of the church. Does one detect his reservation against the office of the bishop here?

[164] "Ambten," 60.

[165] "Gelovigen," 146-147.

[166] In *Gezag apostel*, 37, commenting on Romans 12:3a, Van Ruler calls the apostle "a human who is elected by God to be a witness of salvation that is given in Christ and specifically in the offering of his death and in his resurrection." See Van Ruler's sermon on the same text, with the same title, "Het gezag van de apostel." See above, note 19.

There is a name attached. Thus it is historically particular. As a historical reality, revelation has something "accidental" about it.[167] We noted above (3.1) that Van Ruler used the image of the relay race where runners convey the baton from one to another. The church is the bearer of the relay baton as it bears the apostolic Word through time and space. In that way the strange message of the particular historical fact is brought through the church: "...it is essential for the structure of the Christian faith that salvation does not lie in and emerge from lived life, existence, or the reality of the world but comes to us out of Palestine, out of history."[168] In fact, Van Ruler comments on the necessity of apostolic succession; since salvation in Christ cannot be grasped by human knowledge, and since Christ's atoning work has happened, it must be passed on. Van Ruler goes on to point out that the Reformation, with its emphasis on the *ephapax*, on the historical nature of God's work, places more emphasis on apostolic succession than does Rome.[169] Because salvation happened and does not continue in an ontic form within historical reality, the issue of the trustworthiness of the witnesses and consequently how the report finds reception in the present is more acute for children of the Reformation.

On the field of history, the apostle is an eschatological figure "who has his place in the last days which proceed according to God's plan."[170] The apostle "goes out" from Israel and in so doing fulfills an office in the kingdom of God.[171] That is, the apostle is no longer located within the sphere where God has acted as reported in scripture. The apostles not only witness history, but they witness from *within* a particular history. It is this particular history of God's actions set toward and determined from the future. In this way, the apostle is an eschatological figure. "The office of the apostle is not primarily an office in the church but an office in the kingdom."[172] If the offices are

---

[167] Van Ruler, "Het apostolische en het apostolaire karakter van de kerk" [hereinafter "Apostolische"] (lecture to catechetical teachers, Barchem, September 19, 1949), Van Ruler Archive, folder I, 526, 3-4.

[168] "Betekenis," 183. Characteristically, the office of the apostle is not the only means by which salvation comes to us. It was one of a "series" of institutions, among which Van Ruler identifies Holy Scripture, the church of history, and tradition.

[169] "Gelovigen," 141.

[170] *Bijzonder*, 26.

[171] *Bijzonder*, 28. In a comment on Mark 3:14, Van Ruler says, "That is the office of the apostle: the sending into the world" (*Sta op*, 53).

[172] "Gelovigen," 147; *Reformatorische*, 146.

set within the eschatological horizon, this placement has its origin in the office of the apostle. Consequently, the office of the apostle finds its place not only with individuals, but with society, family, and culture for such is the arena of God's eschatological activity. It is *reality* in all its darkness that is to be saved. And God does so through the offices. In an article written in 1969, Van Ruler makes just that claim. But he goes on to add that God works through the offices as originating in the office of the apostle, and does so through the church. The church originates around the offices.[173] We see Van Ruler claiming both that the offices come *to* the church, in the same framework as we saw the offices as "over and against" from a Christological perspective, and that the office of the apostle, and consequently the offices, extend beyond the church into the kingdom.

Because the apostle is an eschatological figure, the office of the apostle is extraordinary. "The apostle is an eschatological, once-appearing figure. He has an exceptional and unique position in the kingdom of God and thus in the church."[174] And since the apostle is historical and is set in the kingdom, that office cannot, according to Van Ruler's argument, extend into the church. In this sense the office of apostle as such came to an end with the death of the apostles.[175] This is one reason that the bishop cannot be understood as the continuation of the office of the apostle.[176]

Still, the continuity of the apostles in the church is necessary.[177] "We must have communion with the apostles to be able to have communion with Jesus Christ and the triune God."[178] At issue is the means by which this continued communion is possible. Van Ruler asks: "Do we preach the same gospel? The same doctrine? Is there an apostolic office?"[179] The bishop will not suffice as a means for the historical continuation of communion with God. Van Ruler argues that while originally the bishops functioned as missionaries, this apostolic function was overtaken by the notion that the world is to be "streamlined" through the church to enjoy a "supernature," and the bishop became a sort of "half-way" house by which the lower nature

---

[173] "Binnenkerkelijk," 20.

[174] *Bijzonder,* 80.

[175] See also "Briefwisseling," 123.

[176] See *Rapport*, 31.

[177] In a comment on Jesus' appointment of the twelve, Van Ruler states that they "describe one of the origins of the Christian church as we know it" (*Sta op*, 50).

[178] "Mondig," 120.

[179] "Apostolische," 6.

finds a way to a higher nature by means of grace.[180] This will not do for Van Ruler, given his strong aversion to the notion of the elevation from one reality (lower) to another (higher).

How then, is the relay of the message to occur? One answer is that it occurs through scripture. The New Testament is the written deposit of the apostolic *kerygma*.[181] In one place, Van Ruler says that the apostolic office finds its solidification [*stolling*] in the New Testament.[182] The apostles practice the authority of their office through the canon of the New Testament.[183] This is clearest in the office of the minister, centered as it is in preaching. Preaching has to do primarily not with the internal Word, but with the written, instituted Word. In this office, the office-bearer can say, "Thus says the Lord."[184] Here the apostle, with authority and by means of Holy Scripture, stands over and against the church. We believe on the authority of the apostolic witness.[185] This strange message cannot emerge from the church itself: "Grace in no way emerges creatively from the sinful being."[186] As a result, the apostle functions with a certain "pluck" or "daring" [*durf*]. The apostles lived a certain courage for the world. They could be courageous because they were witnesses of the "lightning strike." And they would meet resistance because they carry the "ridiculous story of the apostolic gospel. Jesus hung on a cross and was raised and therein lies the salvation of life and of reality." But this must be brought by office, by that institution that stands over and against humans, in full divine authority, because this "ridiculous" report could not emerge from the "authenticity" of human existence, the experience of human religiosity, nor from human idealism.[187]

Coincident with this daring or pluck is a certain aggression in the office of the apostle. One can argue that it is the apostle as he is the ambassador of the one name that generates the confession of the church with its strange truth, what Van Ruler can call the "pretension" of the church. There is something "absolute" about the message that

---

[180] "Gezichtspunt, 26.
[181] "Mondig," 120.
[182] *Bijzonder*, 80.
[183] "Mondig," 120.
[184] *Bijzonder*, 83.
[185] *Gezag apostel*, 37.
[186] *Reformatorische*, 51.
[187] "Gezichtspunt," 38.

the apostle brings. Salvation comes from Palestine and it is confessed in the one name, Jesus.[188]

This "strangeness" is, as we have seen, essential to office. But it is not only the case for the office most apparently determined by the report of the events of salvation, that of minister of the Word. "In all the work of the church and in the entire life of the church everything must emerge from and be measured by the Holy Scripture, and this emergence and measure receives its gestalt in the particular office." That includes the elder in his work of sanctification and the deacon in his work of righteousness.[189]

The continuation of the work of the apostles is not limited to the canon of scripture. Others were sent after them—the missionaries. And the missionary continues, claims Van Ruler, in the office-bearers, and that includes, by inference, the offices.[190] It is not a continuation of one office, but of offices, in the plural. Van Ruler remarks that the presbyterial-synodical system with its three offices is a "remarkable expansion of the offices." He calls it a "fanning out" [*uitwaaiering*] of the one office of the apostle into the three offices.[191] Said differently, they are a "branching out" [*vertakking*] of the one office.[192] The three offices are not only the successors of the apostles as the offices are centered around an apostolic doctrine. That is, they are not simply bearers of a particular apostolic orthodoxy. They are successors as offices themselves. We repeat in this context what has already been stated: the office of the apostle "fans out" into the office of the minister of the Word as he or she permanently maintains and announces salvation in Christ;[193] the elder essentially goes forth from the church into the world around the church; and the deacons exist in the world—theirs is the vision of social justice.[194] This "fragmentation"

---

188 "Apostolische," 4, 5. Cf. *Gezag apostel,* 37.

189 *Bijzonder*, 83.

190 "Mondig," 120.

191 "Gelovigen," 146.

192 Van Ruler, "Bisschop of ouderling: De ambtsvraag" [hereinafter "Bisschop"] (a lecture in a cycle of lectures to the congregation following the departure of H. van der Linde to Rome, Middelburg, January 13, 1961), Van Ruler Archive, folder I, 585, 5.

193 Preaching not only announces salvation but includes a "ministry [*bediening*] of the Word." This distinction will be articulated further in the following chapter.

194 "Binnenkerkelijk."

of the one office was taking place already in the New Testament, according to Van Ruler.[195]

Three remarks are in order here. First, this is plurality of the offices themselves, and not simply of office-bearers.[196] God not only uses different persons, with their different personalities and gifts. That would be self-evident. But God uses different organs or instruments in being about God's business of salvation and redemption. This will make for a much more variegated picture of how God uses the offices in the church and the kingdom.

Second, the offices are not derivative of any one of the offices.[197] They find their origin in the office of the apostle; even as that extra-ordinary office does not exist fully either in any one of the offices, nor in the offices together. When the offices are derived from one office—Van Ruler mentions the sacerdotal bishop—then "all the trinitarian music is gone."[198] One cannot, for example, derive the offices of elder and deacon from the one office of minister of the Word. Van Ruler remarks that the office of the elder cannot be understood as an "assisting office" [*hulpambt*] to that of the minister.[199] Nor, in a temptation perhaps peculiar to Reformed theology, can one derive the offices of minister of Word and deacon from the office of elder.

Third, the "fanning" or "branching" out of the office of apostle into offices that are themselves nonreducible is a function of the work of the Spirit. And the Spirit, as we saw, "loves plurality." We see here theological foundation for Van Ruler's insistence that reality, all reality, cannot be reduced monistically.

If the office of the apostle represents Christ to the church through the Spirit, and if it extends beyond the church into the reality that God intends to save, its representations and its extension do not exhaust the function of the office. The office of the apostle functions as the paradigm of the church as well. The church "in its entirety is seen as walking in the missionary, apostolic function as witness to

---

[195] *Reformatorische*, 113.

[196] *Reformatorische*, 113, "De ambten," 19.

[197] *Reformatorische*, 100.

[198] *Reformatorische*, 100. The plurality of offices in the Reformed understanding also stands in contrast to a Lutheran understanding that locates the one office in the minister of the Word.

[199] "Gezichtspunt," 28. This against the notion that the office of elder is a helping office in the Reformed understanding of the offices. Van der Borght, 146, argues that for Calvin the ministry of the Word was the central office and that the elder stood in the shadow and worked in connection with that central office.

God's salvation and kingdom in the need of the world."[200] This is not office, or the offices, as they exist in the church, but the church as seen within the framework of the kingdom. The church, in all its provisionality, takes on an apostolic gestalt.[201] Here yet again, the office cannot be seen as emerging from the church. Were that to be so, we would be trapped within a human circle: the offices that shape the church were shaped by the church. Rather, the law fulfilled takes shape within the gestalt of the church. That is gospel, for that alone is fulfillment that tends toward eschatological completion.

4.3.1 Bishops

The "fanning out" of the office of the apostle into the plurality of the Reformed offices stands in stark contrast to the office of the bishop as the apostolic office *par excellence*. We have noted Van Ruler's reservations to the office of bishop in passing. When we examine Van Ruler's view of the gathering of the offices in synod, we shall discover that he maintains that the synod in all its forms takes up the episcopal function within the church. At this point, we note that the singular, sacerdotal bishop is not the office of the apostle because it is an *impoverishment* of that office.

This is the case because the bishop narrows the field of God's actions. In Van Ruler's view, Roman Catholic church order is "absolute." It stands in a "mystic-organic stream of truth in the tradition" and is summarized in the bishop. "In the bishop God and the human, salvation and existence is condensed in one powerful system."[202] In a lecture entitled, "Bishop or Elder," Van Ruler outlines this impoverishment. First, because the bishop is regional, and because the office of the apostle, constitutive as it is of the church, resides in the bishop, the local congregation is not complete as church in itself. Because the bishop is not physically in place in the local congregation, not all the offices are present. The local church consequently is but a skeleton and a shadow of what it is intended to be.[203] Second, the bishop is monarchical. While this includes several advantages–the bishop exists as a pastor to pastors; the episcopal office is personal; there exists a clear authority in the church; and discipline of the office-bearers is practiced–nonetheless the

---

[200] *Bijzonder*, 32.
[201] So the import of the argument of the previous chapter.
[202] "De orde der kerk," 2.
[203] "Bisschop," 7.

communal nature of decisions is lost.[204] Third, the bishop is sacerdotal. At the center of the church is the offering of Christ. But, Van Ruler asks, what about sanctification? And isn't sanctification the point? We hear what are by now familiar themes from Van Ruler. The church is turned outward, beyond the absolution available through the bishop, to life. The church must reach beyond the pulpit to the home. And there Van Ruler discovers the elder, one of the three particular offices. For it is the elder who is concerned with the stylization of life, with the kingdom as found in family, marriage, vocation.[205] Or, to put it in functions that we shall meet again when we discuss the office of elder in particular (5.1), the elder stylizes life through discipline, home visitation, and church governance, which is in summary the task of sanctification.[206]

Just so, the office of apostle "fans out" as the offices meet the church and move beyond the church, and the church is turned outward. The goal is not a vertical, ecstatic communion with God. Such communion becomes possible in the person of the bishop as the bishop represents the human raised to communion with God. It is not only the case that the *telos* of the human is not that he or she be "raised" to a new sort of being, more like God. This view of office would also have the office trapped within the church.[207] The bishop does not stand over and against the human, symbolic of God's *vis-à-vis* of the human, but is the human *par excellence*.[208] Van Ruler argues in

---

[204] "Bisschop," 8.

[205] Van Ruler remarks that the Reformation did not simply reorient the old three-fold office of *episkopos-presbuteros-diakonos* by shifting the bishop to preacher, the priest to elder, and the liturgical deacon to social deacon. The revolution was more radical. It was the elder who took over the offices of bishop and priest, while the Reformation created a new office, that of minister of the Word ("De orde der kerk," 9).

[206] "Bisschop," 9, 10.

[207] Van Ruler remarks that the system that the bishop represents with its harmonic synthesis of the divine and the human finally leaves the human alone in the world. The church is left to save itself. The church has "neither God nor the world over and against itself" ("De orde der kerk," 4).

[208] "Binnenkerkelijk." Van Ruler goes on to comment that the minister in the congregational system likewise is caught within the church. In that instance he or she is representative of the regenerate life of the congregation. In "Briefwisseling," Van Ruler remarks that the consecration of the bishop is not sufficiently far-reaching. It suggests that the office bearer "goes ahead" of believers to "lift" their existence to a new plane. There is no over and against in this. It is not sufficiently radical. "It is God

contrast that the goal is horizontal, directed toward life, toward society, toward the kingdom of God in the world. The goal indeed has the human in communion with God, but standing *before* God. "That," remarks Van Ruler, "is the life of true catholicity."[209] That demonstrates his understanding that the church includes not only the entire spectrum of persons, but of "things." Genuine catholicity includes the local and the general church, the communion of persons, the assemblies of the church, the ministry of the Word, the sacraments, the diaconate, prophesy to the people and to the authorities, and mission. It is embraced in Van Ruler's vision of revelation as "the great, streaming light in which the entire reality comes to the fore and can be seen and experienced as what it is, namely as creation and kingdom of the same God whom we know in Christ."[210]

4.3.2 The Petrine Office

What little thought Van Ruler gave to the "office" of the pope is appropriately considered within the framework of his understanding of the theology behind the office of bishop in the Roman Catholic church. Indeed, there are few references to the pope in either Van Ruler's published or unpublished writings. One finds, for example, no comment on the Petrine office as symbolic or useable as indicative of the unity of the world church. More typical is his reference to the office of the pope in a single breath with that of the bishop. Van Ruler remarked in one place that he followed the example of Hoedemaker, who resisted the notion that the "apostolate is an office in the church and continually pointed out that this notion unavoidably results in the bishop and the pope: it is the church that contains the apostolate as office within itself and is thus self-sufficient."[211]

Elsewhere Van Ruler views the pope within a five-fold scheme of how the church can be governed. The Lord can rule the church through (1) the pope, (2) the college of bishops, (3) the presbyterial-synodical system, (4) the congregation, and (5) the individual conscience. The real issue, he comments, is how one understands that Christ rules his church. In that case, it makes no difference whether one speaks of the pope at one extreme or the individual conscience (as

himself, who in the freedom of the Spirit sets [the office-bearer] on [God's] side and is present in this human among his own" (116).

[209] "Bisschop," 10.

[210] *Geloof*, 139.

[211] "De orde der kerk," 10.

with the Quakers) at the other.[212] With the pope the issue would remain for Van Ruler of how God acts with the church. And that is not vertically, with the bishop representing a higher order of being, but horizontally. Since the pope is understood, in fact, as *primes inter pares* among the bishops, Van Ruler's reservation against bishops would hold perforce against the pope as well.

He is fully aware of the ecumenical significance of the Petrine office and, given his passion for the unity of the church, he signals that awareness without fully working out the implications. He will aver, for example, that the relation of Protestantism with Rome is the kernel of the ecumenical question for Western Christianity. Then, he says, Protestants stand before the question, "Will Protestants be prepared to accept the pope as a visible sign of the unity of the work of God?"[213] Van Ruler's provisional answer to his own question is that Protestants are not ready to enter the discussion. He goes further when he wonders whether a presbyterial-synodical church order can be combined with an episcopal order or even one that includes the pope. He replies that one must give way to the other. That makes his discussion of office crucially important. In fact the reasons for his hesitance are, as we stated above, a primary motivation for this study.

4.4 The Priesthood of Believers?

Thus far, our inquiry has shown that Van Ruler holds to a "high" view of office insofar as "high" indicates that office is not the particularization of the ministry of all believers. The offices represent Christ through the Holy Spirit. Both later terms imply that the offices are not particular expressions of the life of the congregation or believer. Perhaps surprisingly, we discovered that Van Ruler sees his view as higher than a Roman Catholic understanding. According to Van Ruler, the bishop remains on this side of the divine-human relation as he expresses and represents the goal of the human as he or she is elevated to a new ontological status. One might ask, however, about the Reformation doctrine of the priesthood of believers. Does not the argument against a hierarchical notion of office rest on the foundation of the fact that the true office in the church is in essence that of the believer? Does not God work through a variety of *charismata*? And is not office simply a way of indicating that God uses persons with certain gifts to be about God's work with the church and

---

212 *Gesprek*, 21.

213 "Oecumenisch is: maar één kerk te willen," in *Blij zijn*, 169.

in the world? And furthermore, does not all the fuss about office get in the way of the real task of the church, which is ministry?

Van Ruler himself puzzled over these questions. He spent a great deal of energy discussing the question of what he variously called the "general" office or the "office of the believer" or the "priesthood of the laity." His major work on office, *Bijzonder en algemeen ambt* ["Particular and general office"], written in 1953, is dedicated largely to the question of the relation between the general office of the believer and the particular office of the apostle and, in turn, the offices of the church. He wrote a major article in 1962 asking the question, "Is er een ambt van de gelovigen?" ["Is there an office of believers?"]. And in a study preparatory to a book on office, he dedicated twenty-two pages of notes to the question of the office of the believer.[214] Furthermore, in his major study on the relation of Rome and the Reformation (1965), he devotes a chapter to office and the laity. The question of whether an office of the believer exists and, subsequently, the relation of the believer to the offices was clearly important to Van Ruler.

A survey of his response to this question will further our study. As we probe his answer, certain of his understandings of the nature of the offices will come into sharper relief. This will in turn provide a framework for understanding the particular offices and their relation to the congregation.

Van Ruler accepts the doctrine of the priesthood of believers as a fundamental biblical truth. However, he writes that he wants to think this truth through radically and mystically. For Van Ruler such reflection incorporates his understanding that God intends for the human to become fully human, and as such he or she is drawn to walk with God, to share in God's knowledge and, even more radically, to share in God's judgments.[215] Believers do not become "priests" or office-bearers as a way of becoming human. The office does not represent the apotheosis of what it means to be human.[216] Van Ruler illustrates this notion by describing the Roman Catholic priest, who precedes the congregation into God's presence with the offering of the mass. The congregation follows the priest, who is himself the representative human.[217] By contrast, the minister of the Word

[214] Van Ruler, "Het ambt: een voorstudie voor een boek over het ambt" [hereinafter "Voorstudie"], Van Ruler Archive, folder V, A1.

[215] *Bijzonder*, 37-39.

[216] See note 2 of this chapter.

[217] Theologically, the notion of Christ's assumption of human nature is behind the idea of the priest as the representative human. Humanity subsists "in Christ," the priest as participating in the ontic reality of Christ.

proclaims a completed offering once brought and makes way for God in Christ and his offering as it presents itself to the congregation. Humans "become themselves not in God, but in themselves."[218] Put another way, it is not the essence of the believer that he or she become an office-bearer thereby to become fully human in God's presence.[219]

Office is not an end or a goal, but a means to the true goal—the lay person.[220] The direction is not away from ordinary existence, but toward it. In fact, the offices, like the Mediator they represent, are an emergency measure, and the office, again like the Mediator, are to make themselves superfluous.[221] Van Ruler's theology of the kingdom and the place of the church within that kingdom take full hold here. The human is saved as human to enter the round dance with the triune God. The *nova creatio* is not a new creation, as we have seen, but re-creation. The human is not elevated in an ontological change. The human comes into his or her own. In the church, office comes *to* the laity, and in this way office and lay person "form the relation of God and the human in the mystery of salvation." There are two—God and the human. Office represents God in Christ through the Spirit.[222] It is a relation of mutual love. In his late *Waarom zou ik naar de kerk gaan?* Van Ruler does not even want to talk about the office of the believer. "In my view one must not say of the church member that she functions in an office. Then going to church would be completely ruined."[223] Believers are members of the congregation and as such are partners with God.[224] The office-bearers play a different role. They are the "bridegroom."[225] For the human to find its essence in office would be to deny God's very purpose, that God enters relation with the

It is helpful to recall that while Van Ruler was writing in response to Vatican II, the picture one has is of the priest going *to* an altar *away* from the congregation, and not the later image of the priest standing behind the table, facing the congregation.

218 *Reformatorische,* 139.

219 "Ambt en gemeente," 4

220 Van Ruler, "Het priesterschap van de leek: de grens tussen de verantwoordelijkheid van ambstdrager en leek" [hereinafter "Leek"], notes for a lecture to the Council of Christian Students, Woudschoten, Zeist, March 19, 1955, 2. See also *Reformatorische*, 140.

221 "Het ambt," 6. *Reformatorische*, 140.

222 *Reformatorische*, 125.

223 *Waarom*, 107.

224 Van Ruler is careful to say that the "destination" of the human is not *in* God, so that one's human essence must undergo conversion, but the human's destination is *before* God (*Bijzonder*, 68).

225 *Waarom*, 107.

human and that the justified human might enjoy this same relation. "In my opinion, one grasps the matter clearly when one says that the offices are from God in the congregation over and against believers as God is over and against the human, even as God-in-Christ is over and against the lost sinner."[226]

God uses the offices to enable the believer to exist, to be. As we discovered above, God uses the offices to save the believer. In the sketches for his study for a book on office, Van Ruler proposed a chapter that asks, "How does a believer exist?" His answers point to the essential place of office as it used by God as God comes to the believer from without. The human is believer as she is regenerate and now lives eternal life. She exists as a believer as she confesses and is one with what the church confesses. She depends for her existence upon the Word: "Only thus and only on that basis do I believe. I have it only in this form. Thus it is an eschatological existence." [227] And then to the point: "These words are spoken over the believer. The believer is named Christian." This can only be said. It cannot be said by the person him or herself. Even greater, Christ stands in the stead of the believer, and only so "I am I." This comes from "above" (*van boven af*). I exist as a person, as a human "in the eternal council" and so "written in the book of life."[228] When Van Ruler is provoked to ask whether this is genuine he asks rhetorically whether the believer can exist in and from himself. Does genuineness and truthfulness come from the inside out?[229] And the relevance of the question his chapter poses emerges when he will ask concerning the making of the unbeliever into a believer: "Isn't there something about office in this [*zit daar ook iets ambtelijk in*]?"[230] And he concludes that "office is necessary by virtue of its rootedness in history; it comes from to me from the outside [*van buiten af*], from beyond my deepest self."[231]

We meet yet again the "over and against" nature of office. This time, however, it is not simply because office represents Christ, nor because it is used by the Spirit. Rather it is because the message of salvation is alien to humanity, as we have just seen, and because the very nature of the relation demands an other. Nor is this only a logical move: relation as a concept implies that more than one partner is

---

226 *Reformatorische,* 144.
227 "Voorstudie," 66.
228 "Voorstudie," 67.
229 "Voorstudie," 70.
230 "Voorstudie," 71.
231 "Voorstudie," 74.

present. This is a theological reality, for the other in this instance is God, who cannot be grasped or embraced by a human reality.

So Van Ruler can say yet again that the "particular offices in no way arise from the general office of the priesthood of believers."[232] Van Ruler sees here a distinction between Luther and Calvin. He understood Luther as being inclined to see office as the particularization of the general office of the believer. In contrast, he read Calvin as teaching that office emerges from the office of the apostle and is structured into offices.[233] But Van Ruler wrestles against Calvin's descendants. We noted Van Ruler's difference with G. van der Leeuw above in the context of the Christological representation of the office (4.2.3). He also cites P.J. Roscam Abbing in a contrast that proves enlightening. Discussing the particular offices, Roscam Abbing maintained that "all are office-bearers in the congregation because all stand within the office of believer by virtue of Holy Baptism....All share in the anointing of the Spirit." Roscam Abbing allows for various *ministries* within the congregation, differing ministries with varying authority, but these ministries rest on the variety of gifts given to particular members of the congregation.[234] Office does not determine ministry; the movement goes in the opposite direction: ministry determines office.[235] Van Ruler would oppose this line of thought, first, because the human cannot become human except as God uses the office that comes to the congregation. Second, as we shall see below (4.5), there would *be* no congregation without the office that comes to the congregation. And third, Van Ruler explicitly opposes the notion that to the extent that we can talk about an "office of the believer," it is not to be founded in baptism. That would be to presume that we are or have yet to become something—prophets, priests, and kings. We enter this "office," he argues, in the "manner of the Spirit, by predestination, by virtue of the covenant, in the promise, through the Word...." Baptism is the sign and seal of that covenant.[236]

In fact, Van Ruler argues that not only does the particular office not emerge from the general office of the believer, but the general office of the believer originates from the particular. The "spiritual office" is rooted in "the particularity, the singularity [*eenigheid*] of the

---

[232] *Reformatorische*, 88.
[233] *Reformatorische*, 88.
[234] P.J.Roscam Abbing, *Diakonia: Een studie over het begrip dienst in dogmatiek en praktische theologie* ('s-Gravenhage: Boekencentrum, 1950), 523.
[235] Roscam Abbing, 526.
[236] *Bijzonder*, 41, 42.

Word of God that will be served and will become a living voice."[237] The believer receives his or her "office" as she is set in that office. But she is set in that office as God works through the particular offices in their apostolic work.

The result of this direction of thought within the framework of this study is the conclusion that to the extent that we may talk about the general office or the office of the believer, it does not exist *in the church*.[238] To see the office of believer as an office in or of the church would mean an "ecclesiological narrowing of Christian existence." The human is set as priest, prophet, and king in daily life, in marriage, in family, in culture, in the state.[239] In *this* way, the believer has an office outside the church, in the world. Because the essence of office is that in the office one stands over and against another, Van Ruler can give an affirmative answer to the question whether an office of the believer exists. The locus of the office of the believer, however, is in the world. The believer has an office over and against the nonbeliever. The believer is witness to Christ in the world.[240] The believer does not simply live in solidarity with a fallen world, offering herself in selfless service. "The world must be saved." The Christian witnesses to the truth. There is the same sort of aggression here that we saw with the office of the apostle. The believer is a "spell-breaker."[241] He breaks the spell that the powers of darkness throw over the world. But this means that the believer stands over and against this world; he or she has an office.[242] Nonetheless, despite the truth of this claim, the believer does not find his or her humanity in the office. It is more important that she exists, that she is who she is as a someone, as herself.[243] Once again it must be asserted: office is not the goal; the human in her humanity is.

---

237 Van Ruler, "Kerk en prediking," lecture to the Franeker division of Kerkherstel, October 16, 1935, Van Ruler Archive, Folder I, 97, 5,6.

238 *Bijzonder*, 42.

239 *Bijzonder*, 42. See the *Heidelberg Catechism*, Answer 32, where, as anointed, the Christian shares in the tasks of the threefold office of Christ as priest, prophet, and king.

240 "Gelovigen," 133.

241 "Gelovigen," 134. The Dutch here is *spelbreker*. That is, the believer breaks up the play (*spel*). The believer is a "spoilsport" who disturbs the play of the world. The believer doesn't "go along" but stands "over and against."

242 "Gelovigen," 134.

243 "Gelovigen," 149.

4.4.1 Office and Sacrament

The relation of office-bearer as representative of Christ to the human as one who finds his or her humanity in communion with God in Christ finds liturgical expression in the sacraments. This conclusion sets office in a different relation to the sacraments than is found either with the churches that understand the validity of the sacraments to be founded on (or expressed in) ecclesiastical office or the churches that view the offices as particular expressions of the priesthood of all believers. Van Ruler says bluntly, "I would completely sever the connections between sacrament and office."[244]

He does so because he wants to argue that it is not office that is the subject of the sacrament. It is, rather, the congregation.[245] God has used the offices to bring the human into communion with God's self and so to establish her in her humanity. If the offices are rooted in the apostles, Van Ruler argues, the task of the apostle is to preach, is to bring the full representation of the kingdom of God in Christ. This happens in the present time through preaching.[246] Salvation has already come and the human has received salvation in faith. But that is not yet the sacrament. That is only the "marriage proposal." The "marriage" is the sacrament itself.[247] "...[T]he divine giving and human reception, the communion of God and the human—*that* thickens by virtue of the divine institution of the sacrament: the triune God and the believing and confessing human" constitute the sacrament.[248] And this relation stands beyond the representation brought in preaching. It stands in the eschaton.[249] This is meeting and relation, but it is more. It is communion and union [*vereniging*].[250] The human, thus, is co-constitutive for the essence of the church.[251] The congregation is the subject of the sacrament.

Although not constitutive of the sacrament, the offices are present at the sacrament. They represent God—not the congregation.

---

244 Van Ruler, "De gestalte der kerk," notes for a discussion with the *Gereformeerden*, June 1953, Van Ruler Archive, folder I, 303, 3.

245 "Gezag ambt," 12.

246 *Reformatorische*, 212. "Briefwisseling," 117.

247 In this context, Van Ruler has the Lord's Supper primarily in mind. For baptism, see 3.2.2.

248 "Ambten," 26. Emphasis in original.

249 *Reformatorische*, 213.

250 *Reformatorische*, 217.

251 *Reformatorische*, 210.

God also is necessary as subject of the sacrament.[252] Because God is prior, one can say that God is a prior subject; there is *theonomous* reciprocity at work. So both God and the human are constitutive of the sacrament. For this is genuine communion. Nonetheless, the offices enter the communion as they represent God's kingdom reality. It is not the priest who brings the one offering of reconciliation, but rather the three offices of

> ..the minister of the Word, who says the words of institution and so makes present the entire gospel and the elder who on God's behalf pays episcopal attention to the holiness of life which is included and intended in salvation and is one of the conditions of the celebration of the sacrament and of the deacon who equally on God's behalf looks outward to the kingdom of God in human society that is founded in Christ's offering and is realized from the sacrament in the world. The three offices of the presbyterial-synodical system give to the communion of the sacrament a "fanning-out" over all of life and the entire world. The created reality is not absorbed in the offering but the offering is inserted into created reality. [253]

The offices as representative of Christ, and so of the kingdom, help realize the communion. And more. The sacrament is finally not only about salvation, but as Van Ruler would put it, of "being as saved." "In the Lord's Supper we walk through nature and culture, in paradise and in the city of God" (see above, 3.2.2).[254]

Still, one must put a question to Van Ruler. His claim that the office is not necessary for the validity of the sacrament is an important point in ecumenical discussion with those for whom the whole point of office circles around just this issue. One can grant his claim from within the framework of his thought. Still, because the offices represent God in Christ, can and do the sacraments exist without the office? That is, if in the sacrament it is the human and God together, are not *both* the congregation and the offices necessary for the sacrament to take place? The offices may not be necessary *juridically*, but are they necessary *theologically*? That is, the offices need not be present because they do not share in the constitution of the church in the Supper. Nevertheless because they do represent God, are they not to be present in order that the human gathered in the communion of

---

[252] *Reformatorische*, 217.
[253] *Reformatorsiche*, 218.
[254] *Reformatorische*, 225.

the church can thereby enjoy the eschatological reality of communion with God? In that sense they would be necessary theologically.

4.5 Office and Congregation

Office does not emerge from the congregation but rather enters into communion with the congregation; the particular office does not arise from the general office of the believer. So we have just established in Van Ruler. Office and congregation *together* form the church, as the head and body can only exist together. "In this communion a politia spiritualis is established from God. The mutual play of office and congregation [is] the real elegance and pendant of the existence of the church."[255] There is an "over and against" of the office as it represents God.

This relation, however, is complex. While office represents Christ in the Spirit, the line does not move directly from Christ to the office. We noticed at the outset of this chapter that Van Ruler pictures the relation as a triangle. Christ stands at the apex. One line moves from Christ to the office; another moves from Christ to the congregation. And still another line moves between the office and the congregation.[256] We have seen that Van Ruler is emphatic that the particular office does not emerge from the general office. Nonetheless, the particular office finds its home in the general office. Or as Van Ruler put it, "The office is a seed that is planted in the earth by the triune God and that sinks its roots into this soil in order to cause the sap to arise from the belief and love of the congregation." [257] Van Ruler has used the botanical metaphor elsewhere:

> The particular office certainly "rests" in the general priesthood of believers; in a certain sense it even comes out of it, insofar as it is fed by it; but it is not identical with it, no less than the tree is identical with the soil in which it rests in through which it is fed; the tree itself comes forth from the seed that is set in the soil. [258]

Said another way, the office is from Christ but as such it traffics in the communion of Christ's own.[259]

---

[255] "Het ambt," 6.
[256] *Bijzonder*, 61.
[257] *Reformatorische*, 89.
[258] *Bijzonder*, 44.
[259] *Bijzonder*, 50.

Van Ruler explicates the peculiar relation between office and congregation in different ways. He describes the congregation as the people of God gathered around the office and thus, recalling the representative nature of office, around God. The congregation elects, prays, criticizes, and works together with the offices.[260] "Given the relationship of God and the human in the Christian religion all the work of office happens in the communion of the congregation [*gemeenschap van de gemeente*] (intercession and criticism, discussion and shared work). Also liturgically and sacramentally."[261] There is a deep mutuality at work here. God "speaks with" the human; this is office. "Just everything comes down to this reciprocity." [262]

It is the congregation that chooses office-bearers. But in their action, the office-bearers are chosen "really by God himself."[263] "What is the election and call to office by the congregation other than to share in God's judgment of persons and their gifts which authorize them to office?"[264] Van Ruler can state it in the form of a thesis: "Call and election to office happen essentially from God by the congregation." It is God who calls and elects. But the "human knows, wills, and acts with God" in acknowledging the gifts and by calling and electing persons to office.[265] Here one meets yet again genuine theonomous reciprocity. We have seen that the Spirit draws the human into God's will and judgment. God works in a refractory manner; the line does not go directly from God to the office and on to the church.

The congregation not only calls and elects. The congregation also prays for, intercedes for, the office-bearers. In praying for the work of the office-bearer, the congregation is praying for God's own work.[266] Prayer on behalf of the offices is not simply prayer for the offices as they function within the congregation. Van Ruler can say

---

260 *Reformatorische*, 142.

261 Van Ruler, "Ambt en gemeente" (lecture for de Nederlandse Christelijke Studentenraad Leiden together with H. Weterman, June 15, 1957). Van Ruler Archive, folder I, 439, 4.

262 "Ambt en gemeente," 4.

263 *Waarom,* 103.

264 "Gezag ambt," 21.

265 "Ambt en gemeente," 3. Cf. *Bijzonder*, 53 where Van Ruler maintains that the congregation works together with God in the calling, election, and ordination of office-bearers and in so doing the congregation works together with God. Van Ruler goes on to argue that in this way the offices do not rise from below [*van "onderen" op*] but from God [*van God uit*], although not from above [*van boven af*].

266 *Reformatorische*, 142.

that the congregation exists *for the sake of* the offices, "that they may function in the world."[267] One of the reasons that we go to church is "for the sake of the dominee and the elder and the deacon."[268] Located in the kingdom and not the church, the offices extend beyond the congregation, and the congregation supports God's work in the world as God's kingdom.

The congregation criticizes the office-bearer as well. The believer is given to share in God's judgments. But in criticizing the office-bearer, the believer criticizes God. In just this way, the believer enters full relation with God, sharing in God's judgments.[269]

The congregation also works together with the office-bearers. Together with the offices, the entire congregation "talks over" matters of church life. This occurs in humble gatherings of members of the congregation as they gather to discuss policies enacted or proposed by the church council. Believers share in the synodical and classical work of the church.[270] The offices are not alone the church; they are not even essentially the church. They exist in the church and so in communion with believers. An important distinction is being made. The offices may be essential for the church in that they will, as we shall see, establish the church. But of themselves they are not the church in essence.

Van Ruler describes the relation of office and congregation in another way. "The offices stand within the people of God in a manifold way: realizing, representing, reminding, actualizing."[271] He explicates this four-fold manner of relation as follows.

1. In and through the offices together in institutional form, the congregation is what it is in Christ. It is prophetic, priestly, and royal. This is what Van Ruler calls the *ontic* meaning of office.[272] The offices

---

[267] "Het ambt," 7.

[268] *Waarom*, 98. The book is structured around twenty-one reasons why one goes to church.

[269] "Gezag ambt," 21.

[270] "Leek," 5. This can appear confusing, as though the "laity" participate in the governing councils of the church. Van Ruler is of the meaning that ordinary church members meet together with office-bearers in, for example, "congregational evenings" when the policies of the church can be discussed together. Van Ruler, however, contributes to the apparent confusion in his claim that the elder or deacon does in fact provide the outline of the church. So that in the view of office we have been developing, the office-bearer shares in governance *as human*. Just so, the human shares acts with God. This will be developed in the succeeding paragraphs.

[271] *Reformatorische*, 143.

[272] *Reformatorische*, 102.

establish the congregation; through them the church is something in itself as it stands before God and "does the Lord's work on earth."[273]

The essence of the church is established by the offices. By this point, in our study, the reasoning has become clear. God establishes the church as God calls the church into existence. "Office is the permanent origo originans, the streaming source from which the water of the church wells up....First there is the office, as instrument of the triune God in his kingdom action with the world in the historical process. Then there is the church, as first result of this action."[274] This happens through the representation of Christ through the Holy Spirit. The congregation is generated [*voortgebracht*] by the word of Truth. "Christ builds and maintains his congregation through the offices, through the ministry of the Word and of the sacraments, through pastoral oversight, and through the ministry of mercy."[275]

The church is, says Van Ruler, a "Christocracy," for it is Christ who rules the church. The offices are the organs of Christ's body; together they "display" the church.[276] In "displaying" the church the offices give a picture of what the church is in reality. The "display" is crucial but it does not displace the reality. "The reality of the lordship of Christ is of equally essential significance for the existence of the church as the reality of the genuine, active faith of the human."[277] The offices exercise a certain authority, for it is by means of the offices that God does the work of salvation. If the church's task is to be used as a means to salvation, then the Spirit realizes the mediation of salvation as it applies the work of Christ by means of the offices.[278] The offices are present to the congregation as "instruments and symbols" of God. When they are not present, there is no salvation and no communion with God."[279] The office represents Christ and so the church lives by the real presence of Christ. Van Ruler says that one can acknowledge "one essential and constitutive ministry, which embraces all other ministries and from which all are derived and on which all are dependent, that of the ascended Lord."[280] The offices are essential in the church.

---

[273] *Bijzonder*, 55.
[274] "Binnenkerkelijk."
[275] *Rapport*, 94.
[276] *Waarom*, 103.
[277] "Christocratische," 168.
[278] "Gezichtspunt," 36.
[279] *Waarom*, 99.
[280] *Bijzonder*, 75.

2. The offices offer a visible picture of what the congregation is.[281] In the offices the congregation is given to see that its life is in communion. The communal nature of the congregation is mirrored in he plurality of the offices as they are gathered in synods.[282] As the offices gather in synod (5.4), the synod is to be seen as a reflection of the communal nature of the congregation. The idea of the synod is not only rooted in the essence of the congregation as a communal reality but is connected to the triune God "who is communion in himself (God *is* love) and whose decisions are taken in council."[283] Furthermore, in the work of the minister as witness to the Word, of the elder as centered on the sanctified life, and of the deacon as set within society, the church is given a picture of itself. This is the *illustrative* meaning of office.

The offices also may be called a paradigm of the church. Van Ruler argued that the apostles themselves were a paradigm of the church. The church "in its entirety is to be viewed as walking in the missionary, apostolic function of witness to God's salvation and kingdom in the need of the world."[284] If, as we have seen, the offices of the church are a "fanning" or "branching" out of the office of the apostle, then the logic of the matter would lead us to conclude that in this expansion the church sees itself in the work of the offices as they already function in the kingdom.

3. The offices remind believers who they are. This function emerges from the previous. In a sermon on "Congregation and offices," Van Ruler comments "...that in these offices is given the *plastische* expansion of the congregation: preacher/prophetic, elder/royal, deacon/priestly. Not that the task of the church be taken up and done by the office-bearers. But that the congregation be reminded by the office-bearers of its essence, and that the congregation be brought to work by the office-bearers."[285] "When I see a *dominee*, I recall that I myself am a prophet; when I meet an elder, then I remember that I am placed royally in the world; when I hear from a deacon, then I see my priestly place in the world before

[281] *Reformatorische*, 102.
[282] "Briefwisseling," 122.
[283] *Reformatorische,* 188. Emphasis in original.
[284] *Bijzonder,* 32.
[285] "Gemeente en ambten," 1. One notes that Van Ruler uses the same word, *plastische*, to describe the office-bearers as he does to describe the liturgy. See above, 3.2.1.

myself."[286] This can be called the *disciplinary* or *admonishing*, but also *encouraging* and *evocative* meaning of office.[287]

4. The offices activate the congregation. "Through the dynamic of the work of the offices the congregation and believers are incited [*aangestoken*] and taken up in the course of the work in the kingdom and the world." That, says Van Ruler, is the real point to which the work of the office leads.[288]

> The church council "rules" the congregation as an organ of Christ. That "ruling" is in the widest sense of the word an establishment of the order of the kingdom of God in the whole life and work of the church in the world. In the most central sense it is the pasturing of the flock in the pastures of the Word of God and in the praise of God.[289]

Or as the "Report on Ecclesiastical Office" put it, the work of office-bearers is

> ...ministry to Christ's congregation and to God's world. The members of the congregation must be equipped to witness salvation in Christ and the way of God, to place their lives and their gifts in ministry of God and the neighbor, to join in the struggle against the powers of evil in their own life and in society, and to advocate justice and righteousness. Just so the members of the congregation, in their own way, represent Christ.[290]

This is the work of the offices set within Van Ruler's wider theology of the kingdom. In the following chapter, we shall investigate Van Ruler's view of the relation of the offices in the assemblies of the church. Here it is important to note that their presence together in the assemblies is not incidental to the church. We noted when discussing the institutional nature that the institution functions as the "rafters" of the church (3.1.7). This is true for the offices as well.[291] In that function, the presence of the offices "constructs" the cathedral of love that is the church. Still more, the offices exist together with the

---

[286] *Bijzonder*, 55-56.

[287] *Reformatorische*, 102.

[288] *Bijzonder*, 56. See "Leiderschap," 2, where Van Ruler speaks of the "activating" task of office.

[289] *Waarom*, 106.

[290] *Rapport*, 67.

[291] *Waarom*, 103.

congregation. The particular office is not in "competition" with the office of the believer. The "over and against character" of the office is for the sake of the believer and of the kingdom. And that, itself, is a relation of *love*.[292] It is love between God and the human. God does not stand in hierarchical relation to the human; God stands over and against the human, a relation of an other to the human.[293] The cathedral is constructed of love, the love of God, that love be known, lived, and celebrated. This is the *activating* meaning of office.[294]

4.6 Summary and Conclusions

Having arrived at that stage in our investigation that has probed the complex relation of office and congregation, we are in a position to confirm the theses adduced at the beginning of this chapter and provisionally stated, following a theological review of Van Ruler's theology of office.

The offices do not emerge from within the church but come to the church from Christ in the Spirit and thereby constitute the church. The "over and against" character was displayed in at least four ways. First, because the offices represent Christ, Christ comes to Christ's own (4.2.3). The offices do not represent the faith of the believer, nor do they represent the collective faith of the church. Neither do they represent the Spirit as embodied in the congregation. Second, the offices are the representation in the way of the Spirit. That is, they come as God's own self, a third time, God's Spirit, not simply the Spirit of Christ, but the Holy Spirit, itself an integral person in the Trinity. The offices stand over and against the human spirit even as they are used by God to save the human that the human may become human (4.2.4). Third, salvation is not within the capability of the human to effect, but comes to the human from without as God uses the offices in God's economy (4.2.5). Fourth, through the offices God enters into communion with the human (4.2.5).

In this work, God uses the offices within the church and so establishes the church. God does not use the offices *only* within the church, a point that we shall emphasize below. Nonetheless, the church is called into existence through the Word and in the Spirit; this takes place through the work of the particular offices as they proclaim the gospel, as they govern the church, and as they engage the church

---

292 *Bijzonder*, 51.
293 "Briefwisseling," 123.
294 *Bijzonder*, 102.

in works of justice and mercy. The offices are necessary in the life of the church.

The offices embody the church. Our study has shown that for Van Ruler this occurs already in the office of the apostle, and it takes shape as the church takes on its apostolic gestalt. The particular offices in a presbyterial-synodical system are a branching out or a "fanning out" of that original office. In that way, when one views the offices as they are gathered, one sees the skeleton, the structural shape of the church. The offices are not the full church, but one sees, as it were, the blueprint of the church. The offices do not and cannot replace the church; Van Ruler's view of the church is of offices and congregation *together*. Not only the offices themselves, but the institutional nature of the offices is essential to the life of the church.

The offices are used by God as an instrument of salvation within the church. The offices are so used in a variety of ways. The offices are used by the Spirit to effect a tradition through which the historic events of Palestine are made contemporaneous. They make present the atonement obtained by Christ and so make possible the existence of the person in the created order now seen as it truly is, the kingdom of God. But more, they make Christ present, and in so doing make real the communion of the human with God, which is the goal of salvation. Through the offices, God constructs the cathedral of love in which the human comes to his or her own in the praise of the Father. The offices come to the church from without, but they nonetheless are rooted within the soil of the church. For it is there that the human, the laity if you will, is drawn into engagement with God.

Still, the offices are not exhausted within the church. They exist primarily in the kingdom of God. In fact, it is within that kingdom that they come to the church. But thus as well, the offices exist beyond the walls of the church. How this is so in practice will be a major subject for the following chapter. But that it is so is clear from Van Ruler's theology of the offices. Used by God and set within the kingdom, the offices represent the Messiah, whose business is the kingdom, and the Spirit, who is abroad in the world of society, culture, and politics as well as community, marriage, and family. The fact that the offices cannot be "enclosed" within the church is also clear from Van Ruler's understanding of the office of the apostle as an office not of the church but of the kingdom. This is supported as well as his understanding of the priesthood of believers. To the extent that there is a "general office" of the believer, it is set not within the church, but within the world.

Thus far a *summary*. What *conclusions* are available as one views the offices from within the perspective offered by Van Ruler?

First, the offices are to be understood as theological in nature. Any discussion of office must inquire as to the theological world within which they appear and operate. There can be no discussion of office apart from foundational theological and ecclesiological deliberation, even as one must also insist that the offices do not find their appropriate theological place within ecclesiology. As representative of Christ in the Spirit, the offices do not effect an ontological change in the human, but rather are used in the salvation of the human in order that the human, as human, can experience this one reality as the kingdom of God. This is so because of Van Ruler's Christological and pneumatological commitments. The category of *enhypostasis* functions for Christology but not for pneumatology. For Van Ruler the implication is that the human finds his or her humanity not as it resides *extra nos* in Christ, but in the human his or her self.[295] The offices function within the greater matrix of God's work from the divine future, through the past, in dynamic relation to the church. An alternate view of office (or a view that would eliminate office altogether) would indicate a different theological understanding within which the offices functioned.

Second, one can and indeed must go further and follow the suggestion Van Ruler makes at various points that there are *religious* commitments afoot. That is, how the offices function express not only theological or confessional differences but display how those differences function within the relation of God and the human now expressed in not only liturgy but in the communal and social life of the human community. If the offices are located primarily in the kingdom and this kingdom is in the world, then the matter at hand is religious indeed.

Third, discussion of the offices is unavoidable. This follows from the first two conclusions; if they are theological in nature, then one must account for them because they arise within God's economy. Practically, that means that a church cannot reflect on ministry as a category apart from reflection on office. Office is not a particularization of ministry, but it precedes ministry. Or so it is within a Van Rulerian perspective.

Fourth, this broader theological discussion will place the offices within the kingdom of God. That means that any discussion of the offices must take into full account the kingdom of God, its content,

[295] See, e.g., "Hoofdlijnen," 177.

its foundation, and most of all, the eschatological nature of that kingdom. This places the offices in God's future, and the offices, while they represent the historic Christ, represent the Messiah who tends toward God's future. In a very real sense, the offices come to the church not out of the past, but out of the future.

Fifth, the offices are plural. A theology of office cannot be about one office. The offices are not derived from one office. While they represent Christ, they are not derivative of Christ's office but are established by the Spirit in their particular offices. The offices are a branching out of the original office of the apostle, but they cannot be reduced to that office. When we examine the particular offices, we shall see that the boundaries at times become blurred, but the center of each office remains distinct, and that the offices will function together in their plurality.

Sixth, the offices are set within the congregation. Office-bearers are ordinary human beings who are called by God through the congregation, and they are used by God in ministry both to and through the congregation. The relation of office and congregation is complex in that while the church is established by office, God works through the congregation as well. Just what shape that ministry takes and what that ministry looks like both in the particular offices themselves and as they are gathered into colleges of ministry is the subject of the following chapter.

Seventh, God uses the offices not only in the salvation of the human from guilt, but God is present in the offices, thereby to establish a relation of communion with the human. That relation is one of love. In that love not only does God, through office, meet the human, but God is met *by* the human. In the offices, God and the human unite in the great round dance of mutual joy.

CHAPTER 5

The Offices of Elder, Deacon, and Minister in their Particular and United Ministries

Van Ruler identifies three particular offices—the minister of the Word, the elder, and the deacon.[1] These three, as three, express the "branching" or the "fanning out" of the office of the apostle. As our previous chapter has clearly shown, the particular offices are not, for Van Ruler, particularizations of the general office of the believer. They come *to* the church, but they stand *within* the kingdom. Furthermore, they exemplify the life of the church as it in turn is used by God to effect God's kingdom intentions. One aim of this chapter is to examine just how each particular office finds its place within this framework. A good part of our interest in Van Ruler's understanding of the offices is to see just how the particular offices are eschatologically located.

However, the offices never function by themselves. They always exist together in "synods."[2] The synods themselves possess an "office" character. We can do justice to Van Ruler's conception of office only as we examine the offices as they function together. It is beyond the

---

[1] Some Reformed churches claim a fourth office, that of teacher or professor of theology. Van Ruler will have nothing to do with that. In "Ambten," 19, he brushes that office aside with a curt, "Nothing doing!" The "doctor," he maintained, is more a "function" than an office.

[2] We use "synod" in this context to indicate the assemblies of the church that are constituted by the offices. The phrase in Dutch is *ambtelijke vergadering.* The phrase is untranslatable in English in its intent. It describes the gathering of the offices, or perhaps better, the gathering that itself possesses the character of office.

scope of this study to attempt a full exposition of the presbyterial-synodical system as Van Ruler understands it.[3] We shall, however, pay close attention to his comments as they disclose the significance of office. As we hope to show, the offices together will display God in action in furthering the greater intentions of the kingdom. Thus, as we saw in examining the offices, the offices together express a foundational theological reality. A second aim of this chapter is to show how the offices as they gather in ecclesiastical assembly both exhibit the "rafters" or the "skeleton" of the church and how in this configuration they are also eschatologically located.

The three particular offices are indeed three, genuinely plural. As we have seen (4.3), the offices cannot be derived from one of the offices. Each office possesses a task that is peculiar to that office, the center or hub around which it turns. Van Ruler uses the Dutch word *spil*. A *spil* is an axle around which the wheel turns. The center of the office of the minister of the Word is preaching; for the elder it is the sanctification of life; for the deacon justice and mercy.[4] In preaching, the human is saved; in sanctification we are given to know that life is worthwhile; and in assistance and justice, we see that the world is good and "beautiful."[5] In identifying the center of each office, the locus and work of the offices in the kingdom begins to come into view. As we examine each office, we shall pay particular attention to the center that gives shape to that particular office. Furthermore, we shall see how together they give flesh to the reality that is God's working toward the kingdom within history.

It is to be noted, however, that while it is important to notice the focal center around which each office turns, the offices will blur at the edges. For Van Ruler there is no "job description" in each office that marks it completely from the other offices. This may be because, as we shall see below (5.4), the offices function together. Or to say it another way, the Spirit's expansive work as God's work is refracted into the present does not obey boundaries that conform to human desire for clarity in order.

We shall begin with the elder. The choice to begin with this office is not arbitrary. Van Ruler himself gives some thought to the order of importance of the offices and gives differing answers. He can, for example, suggest that the office of the elder is more important than that of the minister of the Word because, as we have seen,

---

[3] Van Ruler himself offers a fuller exposition in a number of places, perhaps most accessibly in *Apostolaat.*

[4] See "Presbyteriaal-synodale kerkorde," 2. "Gelovigen," 147.

[5] "Gezichtspunt," 29

sanctification is more important than salvation. Using the same logic he can go on to say that the social ideal, represented by the deacon, is in turn, more important than sanctification.[6] Alternatively, it could be argued that the minister of the Word is the central office. The hub of the entire structure of the church is in the "complete office-character of the public ministry of the Word in the Sunday morning gatherings of the people of God."[7] More often, however, he appears to view the office of the elder as at the center. For example, he sets the elder and not the minister as the counter-pole to the Roman Catholic bishop. It is the elder who appears in the Reformed churches and expresses the truth that God's intentions with the human are not primarily in the absolution that the bishop represents but beyond the church, in life, where the elder lives and works.[8] Furthermore, within the configuration of the three offices of minister, elder, and deacon, the elder stands at the center. The elder is the axle, or center, around which matters turn.[9] The elder holds the other offices together. How is that so? Van Ruler claims that unlike the minister, the elder cannot become "clergy." The elder does not make his or her living by practice of office; she or he cannot enter a separate sphere occupied by religious professionals. Nor is it likely that the elder will become a public officer [*burgerlijke ambtenaar*], a bureaucrat who acts on behalf of the state in care for the poor, who, in other words, performs a function that replicates that of the church deacon. The elder stands "a little below" the minister and a "little above" the deacon.[10] The use of terms that suggest verticality is unfortunate, for elsewhere, Van Ruler hastens to emphasize the equality, or the horizontal nature, of the offices.[11] We examine elder first of all because Van Ruler claims that "in the elder lies the *pièce de resistance* of our apostolic church order."[12] Examination of the office of the elder gives us the clearest notion of how the offices fit Van Ruler's kingdom theology with the original office as that of the apostle.

---

[6] *Reformatorische*, 115.

[7] *Reformatorische*, 155.

[8] "Bisschop of ouderling," 10.

[9] Van Ruler, "Het ambt van ouderling" [hereinafter "Ouderling"], notes for a lecture to the Presbytery in Hilversum, Fall, 1951, Van Ruler Archive, Folder I, 277, 2. See also "Bisschop of ouderling," 4.

[10] "Ambten," 66.

[11] "Ouderling," 3.

[12] *Apostolaat*, 56.

5.1 Elder

The elder is the "rudiment and the ornament" of the Reformed understanding of life; "...if he were to disappear, the whole church, the confession, the religion, the feeling of life, and also the establishment of the society would change."[13] This is a pregnant claim, and Van Ruler does not expand on it in its immediate context. Its sense comes into view, however, as we take cognizance of the center around which the office of elder turns. Its axle is the sanctification of life. "Life" is not a locution for a regenerate life, a new creation that leaves the old creation behind,[14] but "life" includes the created life in all its fullness. "Life is something! It is worthwhile!" Van Ruler comments in identifying the central task of the elder as the sanctification of life.[15] "God has established creatures and creation. That has come to light in Christ." As we have seen above, salvation is of foundational importance (2.6), but it does not exhaust God's intention for the human or for the world. It is to be worked out in sanctification.[16] It is the task of the elder "to be and to remain the representation of the divine intention for the human and for the world."[17]

Van Ruler thus claims that the presence of the elder makes for a societal way of being that reflects an understanding of God whose activity is this-worldly, and of which salvation is neither simply union with Christ, but in atonement frees the human for life and work in the world. The elder as "pendant" represents that reality. As "rudiment," the elder begins to make that a societal reality. And indeed, this societal reality was reflected in a societal way of being in places where Reformed churches had taken central place within a society.

Furthermore, the elder is, as with the apostle, located in the kingdom. The elder has a central task in the church, as we shall see (5.1.3, 5.1.4, 5.4). However, he or she finds her central place or locus outside the church as such. In his discussion of office with the Roman Catholic J. Weterman, Van Ruler claims that the "...elder—as office-bearer—is clearly a worldly, eschatological figure. He circulates (his root-function is home visitation) in earthly life within time. He is busy with the world. He forms...history. He establishes the order of the

[13] Van Ruler, "Het ouderling-zijn in deze tijd" [hereinafter, "Ouderling-zijn"], notes for a lecture to the P.K.V. Noord-Holland in Amsterdam, April 29, 1953, Van Ruler Archive, Folder I, 297, 5.

[14] We saw Van Ruler's allergy to such a notion above (2.4).

[15] "Betekenis presbyteriaal-synodale," 3.

[16] "Betekenis presbyteriaal-synodale," 3.

[17] "Ouderling-zijn," 5.

kingdom of God in reality." His task is not the streamlining of human life that it might attain a higher reality. He executes his task within this life.[18] The "real work" of the elder is outside the church, speaking with others of daily matters and how God can be served in the ordinary course of life. The elder's concern is not only for the inner life of the soul, but of marriage and family and education and society and politics and culture.[19] As such, the elder acts within the kingdom, activates the church in its apostolic task, and embodies the church as it finds its goal within God's greater intentions.

The elder is an expression of this concern in his or her own person. As a member of the congregation, she pursues a secular vocation among those with whom she ministers. She is not theologically educated as ministers of the Word are educated; that is, she does not have a seminary degree in theology. The elder is, in himself, a "piece of the congregation."[20] The task of the elder is most clearly seen in his or her role in home visitation. We shall pay a good deal of attention to this task. The elder is also busy in both discipline and the governance of the church, and we shall examine those aspects of the work of the office of the elder in turn.

5.1.1 Home Visitation[21]

The elder embodies the transition from pulpit to home, from the prophetic to the pastoral. When the Word comes to us, it is not about "the confessional with its absolution," but "home visitation with discussion." The minister of the Word proclaims justification, the glorious news that in Christ atonement has taken place; that is the minister's central task. Van Ruler will claim that preaching is about eternal blessedness.[22] It is the elder, in home visitation, who embodies the fact that God is to be served in all of life. This takes place outside the church, in ordinary life. Home visitation makes it clear that the kingdom of God intends to be established outside the church.[23] Van

---

[18] "Briefwisseling," 125.
[19] *Blij zijn,* 154.
[20] "Ouderling," 3.
[21] The Dutch is *huisbezoek*.
[22] In fact, as will become clear when we review Van Ruler's understanding of preaching as the primary task of the minister of the Word, preaching is also about the work of the Word as it shapes the life of believer, congregation, and community. It is here that we begin to notice the blurring of the lines between the offices.
[23] "Ouderling," 2.

Ruler identifies this work as the "pastorate" and claims that such is the particular task of the elder. There is a "broad mildness in the kingdom of God which has us [the church], in the pastorate, apostolically entering the unending pluriformity of persons and of life."[24] This takes place in home visitation. Indeed, home visitation is the "most real" work of the elder.[25]

Theologically, home visitation is rooted in Van Ruler's notion of the kingdom of God. The topics discussed in visitation are not limited to the soul, nor to the Lord's Supper, not simply "about human matters nor the church, but about the kingdom, and thus about the things of God, and then over all the things of God; the soul, the sacrament, and all earthly matters come 'to the table.'"[26]

But home visitation is also rooted in the trinitarian action of God. Jesus, Van Ruler claims, is the paradigm of home visitation. "His coming is the great *huisbezoek*."[27] This is the revealing of God in the world. This is God who "dwells with us."[28]

Home visitation is also rooted in the notion of the Spirit's work as it brings the human to maturity in history. In the Spirit, the alien God becomes our God. God lives among us and in us; God does not overpower us but traffics with us in conversation. The human is invited into conversation with God, there to share in God's own knowing and in God's decisions. God listens to and hears from the human. Here Van Ruler's theology of the work of the Holy Spirit as establishing the human *qua* human becomes actual in the life and work of the office of elder. Van Ruler concludes from this line of thought that the Reformation thus replaced absolution that takes place within the confessional with conversation that occurs in home

---

24 *Apostolaat*, 38.

25 "Ouderling-zijn," 6. While home visitation is primarily the task of the elder, it is not *only* the task of the elder. Two examples suffice to show that Van Ruler also saw visitation within the task of the minister. In a sermon entitled "Huisbezoek" (preached February 21, 1943, in Hilversum on Mark 3:27; Van Ruler Archive, Folder IV, 457, p. 1), Van Ruler states that the central work of the *hulpprediker* is "huisbezoek"! Furthermore, in an article on the figure of the *vicaris*, a figure related most closely to the minister of the Word, Van Ruler mentions as the first task of this ecclesiastical figure that of "huisbezoek." "De vicaris," *Weekblad van de Nederlandse Hervormde Kerk*, November 12, 1949, 174.

26 "De vicaris," 174.

27 Sermon, "Huisbezoek," 1.

28 Sermon, "Huisbezoek," 2.

visitation.[29] The person does not come to the church, there to find his or her goal or *telos*. Rather, the church, in the person of the elder, comes to the person. The human is not understood ecclesiastically—the goal of the church is not to "churchify" the world, we recall—but rather eschatologically.[30] The elder, then, is located eschatologically in the kingdom, where the human lives and resides.

In 1941, Van Ruler delivered a pair of addresses on the nature of home visitation to a group of neighborhood visitors [*wijkbezoekers*] in Hilversum. In these talks, Van Ruler attempts to answer the questions, (1) why home visitation? (2) who visits the homes? (3) with whom do they visit? and (4) how?

Van Ruler answers the first question, *why?* by focussing on what home visitation in fact is. He is clear that it is not another form of preaching; it is "never preaching!"[31] Likewise it is not propaganda; nor is it evangelization.[32] It is conversation. It is more about listening than it is about speaking. "Good listening is a deeper art than good speaking."[33] The conversation is not limited to religious topics, but can include anything: "...every subject is acceptable in the light of the kingdom."[34] The elder is not present to lead the person back to the church, nor to steer the conversation to ecclesiastical matters, but is rather about the service of God.[35] And since God is about the ordinary things of life, the conversation includes not only matters of the soul, but also includes the education of one's children, marriage, one's

---

[29] "Gezag kerk," 83, 84. Hence, yet again, it is the elder in the Reformed churches who takes the place of the bishop. For, first, it is the bishop who is most signally present in absolution. And second, the bishop represents an "elevation" of the human to a higher way of being while the elder meets the human within the plane of the horizontal. Of course, the elder does *not* replace the bishop in a direct sense. The point is, for Van Ruler, that absolution is not what is taking place. Furthermore, in this case, it is the elder who stands in the stead of the bishop in *this* function (one that the priest often does in the name and stead of the bishop). In the governance of the church it will be the elder who replaces the bishop as the elder gathers in council or synod.

[30] *Apostolaat*, 39.

[31] "Ouderling," 4.

[32] Van Ruler, "Wat is huisbezoek?" [hereinafter "Huisbezoek"], two lectures to the circle of neighborhood visitors in Hilversum, n.d. [however, Kempers puts it at 1941], Van Ruler Archive, Folder I, 159, I/3. [Citations to these lectures are noted by the lecture and page number.]

[33] "Huisbezoek," I/8.

[34] "Ouderling," 4.

[35] *Apostolaat*, 38.

position as employer or employee, payment of taxes, radio, film, sport, art, science. "In God's presence all these things are as important as the Lord's Table and the death bed."[36] That does not mean that ecclesiastical matters are out of bounds. In fact, in home visitation, the church takes account of its members and may discover, for example, that someone may require physical assistance in attending church services.[37] Nonetheless, the focus of the conversation is on the full, ordinary life of the person.

But if the conversation is not ecclesiastically centered, the elder does follow the trajectory of the Word into the lives of humans beyond the immediate circle of the church. Van Ruler describes the task of home visitation as to "check [*controleren*] their [the congregation's] reaction in the midst of Christian society to the message that is to be heard and that is heard in preaching."[38] Or as he puts it more colorfully elsewhere: "The seed is sown in preaching, the elder looks to see whether it has sprouted...he pulls the weeds."[39] The elder inquires: how is the Word heard? Has it wakened belief? Has it ordered the personal and public life of the individual? Has it left its stamp on the marriage and the family?[40] This is the elder, as office-bearer, used by God to engage in conversation in ordinary life.

In the context of his answer to the question, "Why home visitation?" Van Ruler mentions ecclesiastical discipline. The discipline in question is not doctrinal discipline, but discipline of life. This is not discipline in excommunication (such discipline exists, but in extremity), but a discipline that is more concerned with helping people find their way through life; this is discipline as it shapes or stylizes life. It includes discussion, the offer of assistance, leadership, and encouragement. While this occurs in the worship of the church as in the proclamation of the law and the ministry of the Word, for example, it also happens in home visitation.[41] Van Ruler compares this to the discipline of a mother in a family. In the person of the elder, the church as "mother of believers" is present in the home. The elder is the "alert eye, the guiding hand, the simple word, the beating heart." But matters are not "forced."[42] In fact, Van Ruler contends that home visitation is not a category in the cure of souls, as it would be in an

---

36 *Apostolaat*, 37.
37 "Huisbezoek," I/12.
38 "Huisbezoek," I/4.
39 "Betekenis presbyteriaal-synodale," 3.
40 "Huisbezoek," I/8.
41 "Huisbezoek," I/5.
42 "Huisbezoek," I/7

episcopal system, but it is rather a matter of discipline. His reason is important to this study, for at issue is not the individual soul in communication with God, but the human in the midst of society. What is of significance is the public face of life, the life of the human as citizen.[43] Again, the elder is actual expression of God's work in history beyond the walls of the church.

As expected, Van Ruler answers the second question posed in his lecture—*who* makes visitation?—by identifying the elder. At the outset, he is inclined to say that it is the minister who engages in visitation, assisted by the elder. But he quickly retracts the suggestion. To have the minister do it would be to clericalize visitation. That would, in turn, alter the nature of what takes place.[44] We recall that for Van Ruler, "clergy" [*geestelijke*] is equivalent to the priest (who in turn subsists in the office of the bishop). The priest stands in advance of the ordinary human, encouraging the human to a higher way of being. In contradistinction, the elder represents God as God meets the ordinary human. The elder is, in himself, an ordinary human, a neighbor, a fellow citizen, who can enter mutual conversation.

Van Ruler here appeals to the notion that in home visitation it is the congregation that engages with itself. The elder represents the congregation in its royal character, as it practices discipline. The office of the elder is a moment in life of the congregation.[45] At first glance, this assertion appears to contradict Van Ruler's emphasis that the offices are *not* particularizations of the ministries of the congregation. We recall, however, that the relation of the offices to congregation is complex. The offices are rooted within the congregation; indeed, the office-bearers are chosen and elected from the congregation. Within that framework we saw how the Spirit works with and through the congregation in the selection of office-bearers in such a way that it is God's own self who chooses office-bearers. In this context, the congregation receives the elder as one who comes *from God* in their very midst. In fact, this is the office of the elder: that he or she comes "not as a human in his piety or in his spiritual power, but as bearer of the office in a commission and with a truth from Christ." The elder is not a substitute for, or representative of, the minister.[46]

---

[43] "Huisbezoek," I/9.

[44] "Huisbezoek," II/1,2.

[45] "Huisbezoek," II/3.

[46] "Huisbezoek," II/7. One recalls that Van Ruler is addressing ecclesiastical visitors, not elders. What then, he asks, about the *wijkbezoekers*? They assist the elders as an "expansion of the office." Otherwise the task would be too onerous for the elders (II/8). This is possible in principle because the

Although Van Ruler never quite settles on the role the minister is to play in home visitation, the minister may well be present; he is there, however, as an assistant to the elder. The elder takes first place. This is, comments Van Ruler, a nice mirror image of what takes place at the Lord's Table where the minister takes the central role and is assisted by the elder.[47]

To his third question—*with whom* does home visitation take place?—Van Ruler indicates that the elders not limit themselves to the houses where church members live. Elsewhere, he remarks that the elder leaves the church not only to enter the homes and the hearts of members of the congregation, but of organizations within society and indeed the society itself.[48] The principle of home visitation has the elder abroad in the kingdom. We shall return to this matter when we consider how the assemblies of the church engage in theocratic work in their witness to society, culture and state (5.4).

Van Ruler's final question—*how* is home visitation accomplished?—appears more technical in nature but in fact continues to emphasize the office of the elder as positioned eschatologically within the kingdom. Visitation, as a way of discipline, happens around the Lord's Supper. In its earliest days, it was envisioned that elders would visit every home prior to the Sacrament of the Lord's Supper.[49] In that way, among others, as we have seen, home visitation replaced the sacrament of confession in that the believer was required to participate prior to receiving the holy Supper. It simply was not possible to visit every home prior to every celebration of the Supper. But the congregation could be divided into neighborhoods, and neighborhoods into blocks, thereby to place the task within reach.[50] Ideally, Van Ruler would have every home visited once every three months. He set an outside limit of once every two years.[51] The sheer weight of the task, particularly since it was to be executed by office-bearers who were themselves not ecclesiastical professionals, indicates the level of importance Van Ruler gives to the elder and her office.

---

congregation and office are not clearly separable. Office is located within the congregation, as we have seen (II, 9).

47 "Huisbezoek," II/6.

48 "Gelovingen," 147.

49 See R.B. Evenhuis, *Ook dat was Amsterdam*, vol. 1, *De kerk der hervorming in de gouden eeuw* (Amsterdam: Ten Have, 1965), 148.

50 "Huisbezoek," I/6.

51 "Huisbezoek," I/11.

5.1.2 Discipline

If home visitation places the elder in the homes and lives where the Spirit is at work engaging humans in the work of the kingdom, then the center of the elder's task is also clearly visible in discipline. Through discipline, elders strive actively to shape the lives of individuals and the life of the community in conformity with the law which is, as we saw, the "expansion of salvation in the world" through the Spirit.[52] Discipline is a work of sanctification.

The proper locus of discipline is not in the church, but in the kingdom. It takes place within the church, of course. It will appear to be concerned with the protection of the boundaries of the church. After all, at its extreme it entails the removal of persons from office or the excommunication of the church member. Nonetheless, Van Ruler argues that discipline is less about establishing and protecting the frontiers of the church than it is about an "aggression on pagan existence with an eye toward and view from the kingdom of God."[53] At issue is the life of the believer lived before God and expressed in society. Discipline intends to shape life in the world.

Van Ruler supports his claim that discipline stands in the kingdom by claiming that discipline relates not primarily to the church but to the sacraments. "[D]iscipline takes place around the Holy Supper."[54] And sacrament itself does not stand "inside" the church. That is, the sacrament is not a function of the church, as though the church "creates" or "establishes" what takes place in the sacraments. As we saw in 3.2.2, the sacrament is located in the eschaton. "Along with preaching and the kingdom the sacrament itself stands in the world. It is an eschatological matter."[55] Elders are given responsibility for the sacraments; together with ministers, they are particularly concerned with requests for baptism, with those who wish to make public profession of faith and so be admitted to the Lord's Table, and with those who by their conduct may be asked to refrain from the Lord's Supper.[56]

The discipline at issue is primarily the discipline of life or of morals. In our description of home visitation, we saw that the elder practices discipline as he or she engages with individuals in discussion of their life in family, marriage, work, society, etc. As the "Ecclesiastical

---

[52] *Vervulling*, 499.
[53] *Apostolaat*, 43.
[54] *Commissie*, 476.
[55] *Apostolaat*, 44.
[56] See, e.g., *Rapport*, 49.

Report on Office" has it, the elder "is called and given the authority to live with others in all of life with all the personal, sociological, and cultural aspects that are part of that life, in order that they might live in gratitude for salvation revealed in Christ, honor God, and live according to his commands."[57] Persons have heard the news of salvation from the minister; the elder "stylizes" the life that has been saved.[58] But the trajectory of discipline extends beyond the individual and his or her relationships to a broader communal existence. The church intends not only to set things under the light of eternity in preaching, but actually helps to make things right.[59] The elder is the office that functions to this end. We are closer to the kingdom of God with the elder than we are with the minister of the Word.

Because Van Ruler is so insistent that discipline be practiced primarily in the conversation of home visitation, we can detect a certain mildness in his discussion of discipline. While exclusion from the life of the church may be necessary in extreme instances, they are the exception. Indeed, he identifies cordiality as a characteristic of the office of elder. The elder does not force matters but rather speaks with another in an attempt to convince. The elder desires the good and the true and the beautiful.[60] This is the elder in office, thus coming from God. So it is God who enters the conversation, God not as domineering, but as partner.

As a result, while in discipline the "church touches the kingdom of God,"[61] Van Ruler is hesitant to speak of the elder when it comes to the discipline of doctrine.[62] The elder participates in the discipline of doctrine, according to Van Ruler, as he or she sits in the judicatories of the church.[63] At issue is the preaching of the Word and the assurance

---

[57] *Rapport*, 64.

[58] "Bisschop," 10.

[59] *Apostolaat*, 47.

[60] *Blij zijn*, 181.

[61] Van Ruler, "Uitzicht in het vraagstuk van de leertucht" [hereinafter "Uitzicht"], in *TW5*, 143.

[62] In fact, while Van Ruler will advocate doctrinal discipline in the church, he remains hesitant. See his "Vragen rondom de leertucht," a lecture specifically for members of the church council in Oudwijk, Utrecht, February 11, 1960, Van Ruler Archive, Folder I, 549, p. 9, where he claims that it is not doctrinal discipline that makes a church to be church: "...a church is not really a church or at least not a confessing church, when it practices doctrinal discipline."

[63] "Uitzicht," 151. "Judicatory" is used here to indicate church bodies as they act as ecclesiastical courts. In Reformed/Presbyterial church orders, those

that the message is founded on the particular revelation in Israel and the Messiah. The place of preaching will occupy us when we turn to the office of the minister of the Word. However, it is important to note that doctrinal discipline occurs within the framework of the kingdom of God. For Van Ruler, true life is possible only when true teaching is present.[64] The upshot is that yet again, the elder is set within the kingdom. We shall return to the elder's place within the judicatories of the church below.

5.1.3 Governance

The stylization of life occurs not only with the church member as the elder meets the member in home visitation and in discipline. The church itself, as a community, is stylized into a way of living in conformity to God's kingdom intentions. As Van Ruler put it in one place, while the elder's life among individuals and society around the church is his or her most genuine task, the elder is also central to the church council. He bears coresponsibility for the right ministry of Word and sacrament; he oversees that everything in the congregation happens according to the peace of God and the order of the kingdom; and he is to tend to the building up of the community as the body of the Lord.[65] The elder is the "pillar on which the building of the congregation rests."[66] Indeed, the congregation sees itself in the gathering of the elders; they are the "skeleton" of the congregation. When the congregation sees the elders as office-bearers, they see God coming to the congregation in a particular way, shaping the congregation as bearer of the gospel and as gestalt of the cathedral of love. God uses those who govern in the shape of the life of the congregation. That is not central to the office of the minister of the Word; nor is it central to the office of the deacon. Sanctification, the shaping of life in accord with God's kingdom intention, is peculiar to the office of elder. Hence, the elder, as office-bearer, functions as the visible pillar of the life of the church.

---

bodies may, in fact, be the "assemblies" or synods as they function as judicatories.

64 "Uitzicht," 148.

65 *Waarom*, 108-109.

66 Van Ruler "Het ambt van ouderling," notes for a lecture to the Presbytery in Hilversum, Fall, 1951, Van Ruler Archive, folder I, 277, 2 [hereinafter, "Ouderling"]. See also Van Ruler, "Het ouderling-zijn in deze tijd," notes for a lecture to the Provincial Church Circle of Amsterdam, April 29, 1953, 9 [hereinafter, "Ouderling-zijn"].

Nor is governance exhausted in the church council as it is charged with responsibility for the local congregation.[67] The task of the elder includes work beyond the local congregation in presbyteries (or classes) and synods. The "greater" assemblies are not allowed to become dominated by ministers and consequently "clericalized." The presence of the office of the elder with his or her locus in the sanctification of the world helps shape or stylize the church as the means to God's greater intention and so to function as a means of protecting the church from ecclesiastical introversion.

It is in the role of governance of the church that Van Ruler most clearly details his argument that the elder is an *office*. In conversation with Van Ruler, F. Haarsma notes the obvious, that the elder comes from among the members of the congregation. He then claims that since the elder emerges from the laity, there is no need for an office of elder in the Van Rulerian sense; that is, the elder does not stand "over and against" the congregation. Van Ruler responds by reflecting on the communal nature of the human; humans live in communities. And communities require a certain authority to lead them. From whence comes this authority? In the church, it cannot come from the laity. Humans are not in a state to know the truth of salvation. It must come from without [*buitenaf*], from Palestine. It is proclaimed by the apostles. It requires office.[68] We encountered this reasoning as we examined the theological nature of office.

Haarsma persists in his reservation that elder need not be considered office. He can, he says, understand Van Ruler's perspective in the case of ministers of the Word. They require education to understand the Word of which they speak. But why the elder? Van Ruler's reply is crucial. The church is, he says, a "pneumatic reality." The issue is neither education nor expertise. Rather, it is the elder as conversant with scripture, the elder who lives with scripture, who is chosen and ordained to promote the sanctification of the community.[69] As a pneumatic reality, it is God who uses the elder to meet the community, with authority, from without. This is the elder with the center of the office in sanctification.

---

[67] In contrasting the elder and the bishop, Van Ruler remarks that since the bishop's office is regional in nature, the local church is incomplete. It has neither all the offices nor all the sacraments. The elder, in contrast, enables the local congregation to be understood as church in the fullest sense. All the offices are present, as are the sacraments. See "Bisschop," 7.

[68] *Gesprek*, 19-20.

[69] *Gesprek*, 20.

Haarsma presses the issue and agrees that from the perspective of the Reformation, office makes sense as God's connection with humans through scripture. He repeats: this makes sense for the minister, but why does this argument include the elder? Van Ruler shifts the conversation to how the church is ruled and so may appear to talk past Haarsma's question. Van Ruler identifies what he sees as five possibilities for how the church can be ruled (see 4.3.2). No matter which option one chooses, and no matter how, the issue remains of how God comes to rule the church.[70] However, Van Ruler does not simply talk past Haarsma; he in fact speaks directly to the point. For if office is about God ruling the church in Christ through the Spirit, then the only question is which option one might choose. In the previous chapter we have seen Van Ruler reject the first two (that governance takes place through pope or a college of bishops) and the final two options (governance by congregation or individual conscience) for reasons adduced there. That leaves only the presbyterial option. So Van Ruler's response. By itself it would appear to be an argument by elimination. However, when one adds that the elder is used by God in shaping the life of the congregation, one comes to a fuller understanding of Van Ruler's claim that the elder is office and furthermore governs *as office*.

It is at just this point where Van Ruler's entire theological enterprise comes to roost, at least as we explore his doctrine of office. The elder is most clearly placed in the kingdom, and thus in a position to act beyond proclamation of the gospel and the ministry of the Word to actually shaping the institution that is the church in the ways of God, and further to speak to those beyond the church of the ways of the kingdom. The elder represents not salvation, which is after all a means to a further end, but sanctification, and so points to the kingdom of God. We also see, however, the complex relation of congregation and office clearly at the fore with the elder. The "ground" or origin of his office is in the congregation and the community. This is clear in the very nature of who the elder is. At the same time, God comes to the congregation. Just so, the human shares with God in the ruling of the congregation. The elder is a *theocratic* figure.

Furthermore, we are in a position to affirm Van Ruler's claim that if the elder were to disappear, not only the church and its confession but religion itself and the "feeling of life" as well as the

[70] *Gesprek*, 21.

"establishment of society would change."[71] It is the elder, placed in society, who embodies the notion that God's intentions are resolutely horizontal. It is the elder in whom the congregation sees God's Spirit abroad in ordinary life, and hence opens the way to a culture, society, and politics that take their primary place not in the church, but in the world.

5.1.4 The Elder Present in the Worshiping Congregation

Although the center of the elder's activity is located primarily outside the congregation, the elder is an office *in* the congregation as well. As an office that shares in the establishment and the activation of the congregation, the elder is present, as office, in the liturgy. Why is this so? Van Ruler remarks that as the office that ascertains that all that happens in the church happens in conformity to God's law, the elder will be visible in this, the central cultic act of the congregation. Indeed, the elder is present because worship is arranged by the church council, itself acting as "office" (see our comments below, 5.4).[72]

More importantly, however, the elder bears coresponsibility for the right ministry of the Word and the right use of the sacraments.[73] Shared responsibility for the ministry of the Word differs from that in the matter of the sacraments. In the first case, the elder wrestles with the minister to ascertain that the "full truth of the council of God as it comes from scripture be fully and understandably proclaimed." The elder who is placed in the world brings a particular perspective to listening to scripture; he or she lives in a context not shared by the minister. In the second case, that of the sacraments, the elder is cognizant of the members who come to the table.[74] The elder, who circulates among the members and the community outside the boundaries of the church, is in a position to care for the members who wrestle with matters of ordinary life.

The elder, then, is a visible sign within the worshiping body of the congregation of the apostolic task of the church. The elder also, and at the same time, makes visible the pillars that hold up the cathedral of love.

---

71 See above, 5.1.

72 "Ouderling-zijn," 9. Cf. a discussion on just this point in the deliberations of the Commission for Church Order, *Commissie*, 239-240.

73 Two "marks" of the church as maintained by the Belgic Confession, Article 29.

74 *Waarom*, 109.

5.1.5 The Elder as Church-warden

It was the particular circumstance of the Netherlands Reformed Church that compelled Van Ruler to entertain the discussion of whether the church-warden[75] be considered a separate office or as subsidiary to the office of the elder. The details of this discussion exceed the reach of this study and need not detain us.[76] However, Van Ruler considered the question, and his reflections further our inquiry as they shed light on his conception of the office of the elder.

The church-warden maintained responsibility for ecclesiastical goods—property, operating finances, and the like. In discussion of the church, we saw that Van Ruler claimed that the church consists of both humans and "things" [*dingen*]. The "things" included the offices and the ministries of the church. Do "things" include the worldly goods of the congregation?[77] But such goods do not belong to the congregation but to God. Still more, he argues that "money is always a holy matter."[78] Money, goods, are the ordinary things of life. But, as we have seen, the elder is about ordering the ordinary things of life, for it is there that the Spirit is at work. If the elder is about the stylization of life, about the holiness of all of life, such life includes the "market" or the "bursary" where the trusteeship of the congregation is administered. If the elder did not include financial matters, Van Ruler argues, something would be missing. Elders are about the "holiness of God and that includes human finances."[79] The task of the church-warden belongs to the office of the elder as the elder orders the everyday life of the church to conform to the holiness of God.

Those familiar with Reformed polity might wonder why Van Ruler would not classify the church warden as a species of deacon. The answer may have a good deal to do with the contextual circumstance noted above. The Dutch church was struggling to find a place for the warden within the structure of offices and synods.

Be that as it may, Van Ruler offers a stout defense when he notes that the figure of the church-warden displays the essence of the office of the elder.[80] The elder is about the building of the congregation as

---

[75] The Dutch is *kerkvoogd.*

[76] See on this *Commissie*, 180-186 and *passim.*

[77] Van Ruler, "De kerkvoogd ambstdrager?" [hereinafter, "Kerkvoogd"], an article written together with H. Wagenaar, Van Ruler Archive, Folder I, 450b, 3.

[78] "Kerkvoogd," 4.

[79] "Kerkvoogd," 9.

[80] For this and what follows in this paragraph, see *Waarom*, 109.

the body of Christ. The elder is the "pillar" of the church building, the "backbone" of the organism. Just here we see the complexity of Van Ruler's notion of office as outlined in our previous chapter illustrated. The elder is not only located outside the church representing the apostolic nature of the church. The elder also helps shape the "cathedral of love" as the congregation expresses God's work and presence in history.

To the objection that the warden has to do with "external" matters, budgets and church buildings, Van Ruler responds as one might expect. Are such things less important to God? Is the Spirit at work only with the "internal"? If matter is holy to God, then such mundane concerns as church buildings are important to God as well.[81]

5.2 Deacon

The office of the deacon centers on help or mercy and righteousness. The deacon "enters the world fully in the needs of families and the society. He is completely active in the ultimate goal of all, the social ideal."[82] The deacon embodies the truth that the apostolic activity of the church is not exhausted in preaching and home visitation.[83] In fact, the deacon stands closer to God's kingdom intentions than does the elder, and so embodies the theological reality that the salvation one experiences through the mediation of the church is only a means to the greater goal. The deacon is, in fact, closer to "the real goal, the kingdom of glory."[84] The diaconate does its work "with its face to the world."[85] It is the deacon who "sees the burning vision of the kingdom of God on earth."[86] It is with the diaconate that Van Ruler can say that the "real liturgy happens not in the church, but in the street, in societal life, in daily work, in the homes of the poor."[87]

Van Ruler insists that, like the elder, the deacon is fully office. That is, it is eschatologically located, used by God, and is caught up in the complex relation with the congregation. Like the other offices, the work of the deacon is not a function of the work of the congregation.

---

81 *Waarom*, 109.

82 "Gelovigen," 147. See "Betekenis presbyteriaal-synodale," 2.

83 *Apostolaat*, 46.

84 "Betekenis presbyteriaal-synodale," 4.

85 *Commissie*, 401.

86 *Reformatorische*, 147.

87 Van Ruler, "Diaconie" (sermon preached March 4, 1943, in Hilversum on Mark 14:7), Van Ruler Archive, Folder IV, 459, 2.

It rests fully in the graceful election of God in Christ who freely uses the ministry of humans in God's work on earth. There exists a direct line from Christ to the office of deacon.[88] This locates the deacon in office as Van Ruler understands that office. The deacon represents Christ. In contrast with the minister of the Word, this is not representation through the Word, but the representation of "God, as the Bible gives witness to him: that he descends into the need of our existence and comes to our help" and establishes our righteousness.[89] Or as he puts it more directly, "God is diaconal. He has come in Christ to help and has established justice [*recht*]. The deacon also comes to assist (that is essentially divine activity!), and he is also on the watch for justice (the social ideal, brotherhood of all humans, justice in the state.)"[90] Van Ruler goes still further. He insists that the deacon reflects the reality that God is not, finally, about Christ, nor about salvation, but about our life, this life. The arrow points from the Communion table to the table that sits in the middle of our living rooms and not the other way around.[91] The deacon embodies the theological reality that God's concern is not, as we have seen, with either salvation or the Savior, but with the saved.

Van Ruler insists that the diaconate originates in the sacrament of the Lord's Supper. That is, the diaconate is the realization of the communion with Christ that is celebrated at the Supper.[92] In this context, it is important to recall that the Lord's Supper is set not within the church, but within the eschaton; it precedes the church. At the Lord's Table we are at the "deepest fundament" of the diaconate, God's act in Jesus Christ in this world. Here the deacon receives the Spirit of mildness and wisdom for the practice of his or her office. This is not, Van Ruler emphasizes, philanthropy; it is not even the presence of a certain social justice. It is, rather, "the radiating of the offering of the atonement into all the needs of humans and the

---

[88] Van Ruler, *Fundamenten en perspectieven van het diaconaat in onze tijd* [hereinafter *Fundamenten*], lecture held at the gathering of the members of the Federation of Deacons, September 23, 1952 (n.p.: Federatie van Diaconieën in de Nederlandse Hervormde Kerk, n.d.), 3. But see *Waarom*, where Van Ruler states it more carefully, and more accurately given his full oeuvre, that it is God in Christ *through the Spirit* who is active in the deacon (110).

[89] *Fundamenten*, 3.

[90] "Betekenis presbyteriaal-synodale," 3-4.

[91] Van Ruler, "Barmhartigheid en gerechtigheid" [hereinafter "Barmhartigheid"], in *Verwachting*, 161.

[92] *Waarom*, 110.

world."[93] As the "Report on Ecclesiastical Office" put it, the assistance that the deacon offers originates at this table: "Deacons help by extending bread and wine as signs of salvation in Christ, who through the offering on the cross became food and drink to eternal life. Among humans they distribute gifts as 'priests' of God's mercy to each as has need."[94] In fact, when writing of the deacon in the context of the Lord's Supper, Van Ruler maintains that "we [from the Reformed side] have sought the reflection of the participation in the priestly office of Christ in the office of the deacon." The deacon is not the only reflection of Christ's priestly office, but the characteristic of the office of the deacon is found here, in the work of justice and mercy to the human in this earthly existence.[95]

In fact, Van Ruler notes that Calvin transformed the deacon from a liturgical figure to a societal function. This move shifted the deacon from a cultic location to that place where God is at work in the kingdom.[96] It further makes clear that God's intentions are not enclosed within the church but are to be found in the kingdom.

The presence of the deacon at the Table is also a reminder to the congregation of what the church is about. The deacon brings the social needs of the world within the liturgy and so reminds the church of the whole world with all its needs. The deacon at the Table signifies God's goal of the kingdom. At the Table the church is reminded of its apostolic nature and so of the peaceful communion of humanity where the salvation in Christ is celebrated and received. And more, the deacon reminds the church of its call to public prophesy as it calls governments and peoples to righteousness and justice on God's behalf.[97]

As office, and so as a branching of the apostolic office, the deacon is located in the kingdom.[98] Because the scope of the kingdom is universal, so too is the reach of the diaconate. Van Ruler argues as follows: the universal scope of the kingdom is possible only in the recognition of the true God and God's Messiah. This universal scope or intention turns about Yahweh and the Messiah where justice and mercy are both displayed and enacted.[99] This is the warrant for what

---

93 *Fundamenten*, 10.

94 *Rapport*, 66.

95 "Briefwisseling," 117.

96 *Reformatorische*, 114. Cf. "Betekenis presbyteriaal," 4.

97 *Waarom*, 110.

98 Van Ruler comments at one session of the Commission for Church Order that the apostles originally practiced diaconal ministry (*Commissie*, 400).

99 "Barmhartigheid," 165-166.

Van Ruler calls the "prophetic perspective" on the diaconate. For it is in the prophetic that a perspective is opened to a new heaven and a new earth. This is the vision of justice, of an earth that is livable for people.[100] This is a *societal* vision. After all, Van Ruler insists, the human is a communal essence. "And God himself is—or so I sometimes think—more interested in the way society is set up than how the individual fares."[101] The deacon exhibits this divine concern in the help extended by that office. This is apostolic in nature. But it is also prophetic in nature, Van Ruler claims, because we see now not with our own eyes, but with God's eyes.[102] We note here again why deacon must be considered office in Van Ruler's understanding; the deacon functions not from human knowledge and vision, but from that of the divine. In the deacon God comes to the human to establish God's kingdom intentions.

The deacon expresses the divine intention in yet another way. We have seen that in salvation the human is relieved of the weight of guilt and in sanctification the human is set on his or her way to enjoy the full scope of her humanity. The deacon meets this person in her humanity. The deacon will not overwhelm the person. The person will be fully respected in her desire to receive (or not to receive) God's diaconal assistance.[103]

How does the deacon represent God's diaconal essence? We can identify three ways of acting. The deacon embodies "justice" (righteousness) and "mercy" (help). But the deacon is implicated in more. The deacon also represents a particular relation to the state, in what might be called the *theocratic* role of the deacon.

5.2.1 Justice

Deacons are not only engaged in the extension of help to the struggling, the oppressed, and the disadvantaged. Justice demands that life be made possible for the weak and the oppressed. This includes two dimensions for Van Ruler. First, the justice that Van Ruler finds in scripture is not the vengeful and demanding justice of the court of law, intent on bringing the offender to curb; it is not retributive justice. As Moses discovered, and Luther later, it is the justice of a giving God and, consequently, a justice that is given.[104]

---

[100] *Fundamenten*, 11.
[101] *Fundamenten*, 12.
[102] *Fundamenten*, 12.
[103] "Barmhartigheid," 166.
[104] "Barmhartigheid," 163.

Deacons, in their work, reflect the God who so extends God's self that the disadvantaged can continue to live and to exist. Second, this sort of justice will reflect God's intention that the creature exist. This is not a justice limited to those who have the means to secure their own existence. God intends that all creatures have a place. In this context, justice works to create such means that socially, culturally, economically, and politically, the weakest has a place.[105] This will include assuring that such basics as food and shelter, work and safety be extended to all.

This is not worked out with the context of Christ alone, nor even of salvation. According to Van Ruler, justice begins with Moses but it extends to Aristotle. "...[E]veryone must receive his/her own. Then we are with Aristotle: the suum cuique as formula for justice."[106] Aristotle is concerned with the right order of society, thought out from the reality of the cosmos. Van Ruler's theological understanding of creation as an act of God apart from Christ and his claim that the Spirit establishes the human as a relatively independent creature provide theological warrant for a philosophical consideration of the nature of justice.[107]

5.2.2 Mercy

If diaconal work extends beyond assistance, it includes help, or mercy, to persons for whom justice does not extend, as well as for persons whose circumstance impairs a fully human existence. The "Ecclesiastical Report on Office" acknowledges that governmental agencies have taken over many tasks that had formerly been the province of the church. Nonetheless, the report maintains, deacons continue to help the aged, the young, the handicapped, and others for the sake of Christ.[108] Van Ruler notes that this concern is made concrete in the church order when it points to medical care as well as pedagogical, social, economic, and social needs.[109]

"Mercy," however, implies more than assistance. In mercy, help is extended to those who have no right to expect a positive result from justice. Diaconal help extends even to the guilty and does so because God has so acted as to take the human's guilt on God's self in the act

---

[105] "Barmhartigheid," 163.
[106] "Barmhartigheid," 163.
[107] "Barmhartigheid," 163.
[108] *Rapport*, 67.
[109] *Fundamenten*, 15, 16.

of atonement.[110] As a representative of Christ, the deacon reaches beyond the atonement to that kingdom reality, the concrete life of the person in his or her dereliction, there to assure him or her that she is not abandoned by God in the concrete needs of daily life, which is, after all the locus of God's intentions.

5.2.3 The Deacon and the State

If the church stands in a particular relation to the state as God works through governmental authorities in the establishment of God's kingdom, then the deacon has a particular role. In fact, Van Ruler could claim that all questions about mercy and justice between church and state have to do with the deacon.[111] The diaconate is not enclosed within the church, but extends its purview to the state.[112] Here the location of the office of the deacon in the kingdom is seen most clearly.

The relation between the deacon and the state, at its simplest, is in the extension of help to those who "fall between the cracks" of governmental programs to assist the weakest in society. Even the just state will lose track of people; it cannot care for everyone. The task of offering help to people who slip through the web of society's "safety net" is a humble one, Van Ruler remarks, but it is necessary.[113]

More fundamentally, the church meets created reality, and hence creation, in the guise of the state. If salvation is a means used by God in the cause of the restoration of creation, the deacon ministers in the creation as it is present in the gestalt of the state.[114] The deacon acknowledges that the state expresses an ordered society, institutionalized in such a way that humans can live as truly human. The deacon delights in the enactment of good laws, for he sees something in them of the social ideal. "The eschaton is also a city, a state, a kingdom."[115]

Van Ruler proposes that there are several possible ways in which the church and the state can relate to each other. First, the church can exist in cultural communion with the state. Second, the church exists in symphonic communion with the state, as is the case with Eastern orthodoxy, or caesaro-papism. Third, the church overarches the state

---

[110] "Barmhartigheid," 164.
[111] "Barmhartigheid," 161.
[112] "Barmhartigheid," 168.
[113] "Barmhartigheid," 172.
[114] "Barmhartigheid," 170.
[115] "Barmhartigheid," 171.

as it did in the medieval world. Fourth, the church and state fall away as the expected kingdom breaks into the present, as with anabaptism. And fifth, the church and state are mutually accountable to God (as articulated, e.g., in Article 36 of the Belgic Confession).[116] It is in the last arrangement where the location of the deacon is to be found. It is at that intersection where the church and state coexist, each as "ministers" in the kingdom.

This is theologically important and relevant to our inquiry. The deacon exists at that place where what Van Ruler calls an "indissoluble duality" [*tweeheid*] exists between church and state. This duality emerges from the creation and eschaton that stand on one side of the matter and atonement and salvation on the other. The two sides of the matter can be related but neither can be derived from the other.[117] The deacon as office at this intersection points beyond the church, but at the same time exists as an office that can only point. It cannot replace the "office" of the state. Nonetheless, it is the deacon who most clearly expresses the theocratic intention of God in "christianization."[118] "With each act which we do in the light of the Bible, we are busy giving fuller form to the *corpus christianum*." Christianization is penultimate to God's real intention, which is the eschaton, the kingdom of God.[119]

5.2.4 The Deacon in the Congregation

The office of the deacon, then, exists with its face turned toward the world, eschatologically located in the kingdom of God. Nonetheless, the deacon is an office with its root in the church and has a role to play within the church as well, albeit one that reminds the church of its apostolic task and God's kingdom intentions. The deacon in fact has a place in the church's liturgy, although one different from the ancient task of assisting the priest in his liturgical duties. The deacon is present and visible at the collection of the church's offering. The collection is for those who are in need, and the administration of those funds—a primary diaconal task—is itself

---

[116] "Barmhartigheid," 167-168.

[117] "Barmhartigheid," 173-174.

[118] Article VIII of the *Kerkorde* of the Netherlands Reformed Church states that the church "contends for the reformation character of nation and people and, in expectation of the kingdom of God, sets itself to the work of christianization to authority and people, to direct life to God's promises and commands." *Kerkorde der Nederlandse Hervormde Kerk* ('s-Gravenhage: Boekencentrum, 1969), 14.

[119] "Barmhartigheid," 169.

liturgical. "Thus we must cease talking about money and goods, administration and oversight, as about worldly matters."[120] Worldly goods are products of creation, what God, in fact, considers holy.[121] In the symbolic play that is liturgy, the congregation is directed to the needs of the world and participates, through the offering, in doing God's work of mercy and justice.

And more. In the deacon, the congregation sees itself at work. The deacon is an organ of the body of the congregation.[122] Or, again, in the diaconate the congregation sees itself in "skeleton" form; the congregation itself is diaconal. The deacon both represents and activates the congregation. Van Ruler uses the image of a stone tossed into a pond. The ripples begin at the center, but they move further and further apart. Soon they disappear. So the work of the deacon "disappears" as it becomes the work of the good citizen.[123]

We recall that the deacon comes *to* the church as office. This work is God's work, but God's work as God engages the human in that work. But it is *God* who engages, and the work would not be possible if God did not work through the Spirit to use women and men in the office of deacon.

5.3 Minister of the Word

As we have already noted, the office of the minister of the Word "...is the hub [*spil*] of the entire existence of the church and even of the kingdom of God."[124] The minister of the Word is a person "of the Holy Spirit," and in that guise God appears in history and is active with the world. The ministry of the Word is necessary for human blessedness, for the building up of the church, and for the establishment of life.[125] The office of minister is not the only thing about the church; it is not even the most important thing. If the church is apostolic at its heart, then the "most important thing" is the kingdom of God which, in turn, stands beyond the church. Nonetheless, Van Ruler's commitment to the centrality of the ministry of the Word is far-reaching. Indeed, what happens as the elder and the deacon minister

---

[120] *Fundamenten*, 14, 15.

[121] See particularly, Van Ruler, "Hoe waardeert men de stof?" in *TW* 5, especially 16: "Matter is holy!"

[122] *Fundamenten*, 6.

[123] *Fundamenten*, 7.

[124] *Reformatorische*, 155. Cf. "Christusprediking," 187.

[125] Van Ruler, "De theologische studie en de ambstpraktijk," opening lecture, October 3, 1951, Van Ruler Archive, Folder I, 270a, 1.

in the world beyond the walls of the church would not be possible without the presence of the Word, who appears in the ministry of the Word.

At the center, or hub, of the ministry of Word, in turn, is preaching, what the minister does on a Sunday morning.[126] The office of minister of the Word exists "for the preaching of salvation and all that is connected with it."[127] The office is not exhausted in preaching; other tasks adhere to this office. The preacher is also pastor, leader of the church council, catechizer, and the like. These other tasks, however, find their center in preaching.

In fact, Van Ruler will argue that preaching is necessary. It is of the *esse* of the church and not of the *bene esse*. The necessity of preaching is to be found, first, in its character as an apostolic-evangelical event in which the living Word calls the human from death to life. Second, the necessity of preaching is found in the common inquiry by the congregation in order that the knowledge of the Lord be deepened and renewed. But third and most importantly, preaching is necessary as "an eschatological event in which the heart of God and the essence of things are disclosed in spoken words in the present hour."[128] This brief summary suggests that an examination of the office of the minister of the Word includes the following attributes: the minister of the Word is (1) apostolic, (2) eschatological, (3) kingdom-oriented, (4) trinitarian, and (5) communal. The last category will present an occasion to inquire about the relation of the office of minister to the congregation.

5.3.1 Apostolic

Preaching is apostolic. "In essence, each Sunday morning an apostle stands behind the pulpit; he has come from Palestine where he witnessed God's decisive revelation and actions."[129] In calling and

---

[126] Van Ruler, "De grenzen van de prediking" [hereinafter "Grenzen"], in *TW* 3, 30. *Reformatorische*, 155.

[127] "Betekenis presbyteriaal," 2.

[128] "Grenzen," 33.

[129] Van Ruler, "De prediker zij zich bewust van de ernst van zijn taak" [hereinafter "Prediker"], in *Hoe vindt u dat er gepreekt moet worden?* ed. A.G. Barkey Wolf, 2nd ed. (Zwolle: La Rivière & Voorhoeve, 1959), 139. Cf., Van Ruler, "De bevinding in de prediking" [hereinafter "Bevinding"], *TW* 3, 75: "Preaching is the apostolic work of the church *par excellence*." See also "Geloof en prediking," speech to Roman Catholics and Protestants, De Brug, Amsterdam, February 17, 1916, Van Ruler Archive, Folder I, 591, 1,

electing the people of Israel and in the work of Jesus Christ, God has acted in ways that are of decisive significance. God has given God's self to be known. In these decisive acts, God has effected salvation from the imprisonment of sin. In so doing, God has established a bridgehead in the world from which God has begun to establish the kingdom of God in the world. The sermon is the announcement of these acts of God.[130] According to Van Ruler, preaching is in essence missionary preaching. The preacher reports the "lightning strike" witnessed by the apostles and reported to others by missionaries.[131] The sermon tells the story of what happened in Palestine with Israel and with Jesus, the story of the breaking in of the shattering of the almighty power of sin and despair.[132] In preaching, the church hands on the "baton" in the "relay-race" that is itself the tradition that links the apostles to the contemporary church.[133] Preaching is the means God uses to communicate past events and so make them contemporary. If God's actions are truly historical, if they happened in a particular time and place, then there *must* be a means that reports to those who live in another time and place. Proclamation is that means.

In fact, Van Ruler can discuss preaching within the context of apostolic succession: "Preaching as the *viva vox evangelii* is the moment *par excellence* in apostolic tradition and succession."[134] The "living voice of the gospel" occurs in the present, but it is a word that gives voice to the first witnesses. The essence of preaching, Van Ruler says in one place, is the passing on of what the prophet, the evangelist, and the apostle say.[135]

But preaching is more than simply the *report* of events that took place in Palestine. Preaching is, Van Ruler argues, the "stream of divine history that flows through time." That is, preaching itself shares in that history. Hence, preaching is more than a vehicle to communicate

---

where Van Ruler describes preaching as "...a *mannetje* comes from Palestine to report what happens..."

130 "Prediker," 139.

131 "Prediker," 139. Cf. Van Ruler, "Continuïteit in de prediking" [hereinafter "Continuïteit"], in *TW* 2, 192, where he claims that preaching can only be understood as "originating from the apostolic office that itself goes back to God in Christ."

132 Van Ruler, "Preekdefinities," *TW* 6, 120.

133 Van Ruler, "De prediking" [hereinafter "Prediking"], lecture to the Classical Gathering of Schiedam, May 15, 1947, Van Ruler Archive, Folder I, 433, 3.

134 *Reformatorische*, 172.

135 "Prediking," 5.

information. It is the representation of Christ, the communication of the Spirit and the establishment of the kingdom.[136] In preaching humans are exorcised of the demonic and are established in a new communion.[137] Something takes place in the *event* that is preaching.

This is to be understood from two perspectives. First, preaching announces a truth that sheds light on all reality. The essence of preaching is, as Van Ruler articulates that essence in yet another way, "an expression of the truth of everything from God's perspective." That "everything" includes more than the eternal fate of the soul. It includes that; but it also includes marriage, the meaning of work, the significance of play, the sense of the historical process, to name but some of what is included in Van Ruler's "everything."[138] He puts it more strongly when he claims that preaching turns all of existence inside out. Everything is seen for what it is. From God's side that includes salvation in gospel, law, Word, as well as the counsel, act, and essence of God. From the human side, the heart of the human is laid bare in preaching.[139]

Preaching sheds divine light because, for Van Ruler, preaching bears an *israelitisch* character. That is, in preaching, the God who reveals God's self in divine activity is the God to whom witness not only can be given, but must be given. For what God is about is to be reported, because the field of God's activity is in history.[140]

Still, preaching as revelatory of reality is only the first thing that is to be said about the event of preaching. Van Ruler can claim boldly, as does the Second Helvetic Confession: "The preaching of God's Word *is* God's Word itself, not only human witness to God's Word."[141] Van Ruler distinguishes preaching from human address. In an address, the preacher speaks to the congregation with the aim of

[136] *Reformatorische*, 172.

[137] Van Ruler, "De teekenen van de prediking" (sermon preached January 11, 1948, in Hilversum on Mark 6:13), Van Ruler Archive, Folder IV, 646, 2.

[138] "Grenzen," 31. See also "De prediking en het persoonlijk geloofsleven," 1.

[139] *Reformatorische*, 170.

[140] *Reformatorische*, 160.

[141] Van Ruler, "Kerk en prediking," lecture to the Franeker chapter of *Kerkherstel*, October 16, 1935, Van Ruler Archive, I, 97. Emphasis in original. See also "Continuïteit," 186: "The ministry of the Word of God *is* the Word of God itself." See the Second Helvetic Confession, Chapter I: Of The Holy Scripture Being The True Word of God: "The preaching of the Word of God is the Word of God." In *The Constitution of The United Presbyterian Church in the United States of America: Part I, Book of Confessions* (Philadelphia: Office of the General Assembly of the United Presbyterian Church in the United States of America, 1966), 5.004.

winning the congregation to the preacher's point of view. Preaching so conceived is a form of propaganda. It is an intrahuman event.[142] In contradistinction, preaching is not something that takes place between humans; no one less than God in Christ comes to us humans in preaching.[143] In a discussion of preaching within the context of Reformed piety and the *nadere Refomatie,* Van Ruler cites A. Comrie and J. van Lodenstein[144] with approval, that preaching is not only the means but the matter itself. That is, that God's own self and Jesus Christ are present *in* the gospel.[145]

Preaching as an apostolic reality makes clear the "over and against" character of office in the case of the particular office of minister of the Word. Preaching cannot emerge from the congregation because it announces to the congregation news that the congregation cannot possess in and of itself. This is so in at least three ways. First, the story of what took place in Palestine, in history, can only be reported. It is not as though the secret things of God are hidden in the cosmos thereby to emerge or to be discovered. God reveals God's self through God's action in history.[146] Revelation history must be reported. In fact, the story the apostles reported is "ridiculous," laughable. It is the report that "Jesus hung on the cross and was raised, and therein is salvation of life and of reality."[147] Second, preaching includes matters that cannot, by definition, be experienced. Such matters include the whole Christ—the Messiah not only as one who dwelt among humanity, but the risen, ascended, and glorified Christ—and the whole of reality.[148] This provides one reason that Van Ruler sees preaching as participating in the apostolic nature of office: "...the office-bearer comes so strongly from the side of God that he can hardly come from the side of the people of God any longer."[149] Third, preaching mediates a salvation that can only be told or proclaimed.[150]

---

142 "Kerk en prediking," 1.

143 "Prediking," 2.

144 Alexander Comrie was an orthodox Reformed preacher in the Netherlands in the eighteenth century. On Van Lodenstein, see above chapter 2, n. 204.

145 "Bevinding," 69.

146 Van Ruler, "Wat doet de kerk? Prediking door woord en sacrament," lecture, Veenendaal, October 4, 1945, Van Ruler Archive, Folder I, 182, 10.

147 "Gezichtspunt," 38. This statement is part of a larger remark that the apostles had a certain "nerve" or "pluck" to announce this "ridiculous" story to all who would listen.

148 *Reformatorische,* 175.

149 *Reformatorische,* 174.

150 "Contituïteit," 197, 198. Cf. *Reformatorische,* 165.

The content of what is proclaimed is far greater than human lostness. It will be the work of God. In fact, preaching will meet resistance from the human; consequently preaching must be somewhat forceful to break through that resistance.[151] We shall return to this last point when we consider the salvific character of preaching.

5.3.2 Eschatological

Because proclamation is apostolic it is, given Van Ruler's understanding of the office of the apostle, perforce eschatological. That is, it happens neither in the church nor in the world, or more precisely, not solely in either the church or the world, but rather in the kingdom of God. The kingdom has "broken into the present in Christ and in the Spirit."[152] The apostolic character of preaching suggests that preaching is the vehicle by which the *past* becomes available to the present. If the office represents Christ from the future of God, what shape does that take in Van Ruler's understanding of preaching as the center and core of the office of minister of the Word?

In *Reformatorische opmerkingen in de ontmoeting met Rome*, Van Ruler articulates the eschatological nature of preaching in several dimensions. On one level, preaching sets all of life under the light of the last judgment. Everything is made manifest. Everything is seen under the light of the kingdom of God. Through preaching, the human is enabled to know "the true, the good, the beautiful in state and in society–through the appearance and the breaking in of the kingdom."[153] Under the light of the kingdom, the true is separated from the false, good from evil, and the beautiful from the ugly. Preaching will include, in an anticipatory way, an "eschatological crisis," and "apocalypse."[154] In preaching, the last judgment, the future, is present in a proleptic manner. Everything is turned inside out; the preacher speaks the secrets of the darkest sinner's heart and the preacher gives expression to the glorious heart of God. Humans stand in the light of the truth, which is in turn the seed of eternal blessedness.[155] Indeed, both the innermost secrets of the heart of God and of the heart of created things are expressed in preaching. The "things" [*dingen*] of this world are disclosed in preaching. The "things" of which Van Ruler speaks include the ordinary things of life

[151] "Preekdefinities," 120.
[152] "Ambten," 25.
[153] *Reformatorische*, 193.
[154] *Reformatorische*, 196.
[155] "Preekdefinities," 124.

including, among others, the human creature, marriage, work, and culture. The content of preaching, then, includes the ordinary creation we meet in our daily life now placed within their eschatological context: "The eschatological reality is identical with the created reality, but in its saved state."[156] We came across this theologumenon in our review of Van Ruler's theological project (2.5). Here it surfaces in the event of preaching. In this way, preaching is a prelude or an overture of eternal judgment.[157]

This is eschaton not deferred to a temporal future, but as having broken into the present. This includes the salvific character of preaching. God uses preaching to effect salvation. On the one hand, preaching includes a call to conversion, by which Van Ruler means that the converted human is "to experience the world as the kingdom of God."[158] It is to live within the light of created reality in its "saved state." It is not to long for an escape from the difficulties of created reality, but to see created reality anew, now against God's blessed future.

On the other hand, preaching as an eschatological event does more than to call, announce, and invite the human to join in the round dance of the kingdom. The human is, in fact, saved *through* preaching. Salvation is announced. Preaching is the announcement of God's decision enacted at Golgatha. Hence, preaching is not the possibility of salvation, but salvation itself. Preaching, Van Ruler comments, raises people from the dead.[159] Preaching is a "fully divine act." It is *itself* an eschatological event: "The preaching of salvation is itself a moment in salvation."[160] It is in the preached moment that the eschaton breaks in and salvation occurs.

This is the preaching of Christ, a kind of preaching that Van Ruler will distinguish from kingdom-preaching.[161] Through the preaching of Christ, Christ is born in the individual soul.[162] In preaching the human is posited as both sinner and as saved. Word and Spirit at work in preaching extend the benefits of the atonement to the individual person; he or she is saved insofar as she is now "fireproof" to the powers of sin, death, and evil. She can stand in the

[156] *Reformatorische*, 191.
[157] "Grenzen," 39.
[158] *Reformatorische*, 167.
[159] "Wat doet de kerk?" 6,7.
[160] *Reformatorische*, 191-192.
[161] The following subsection will clarify Van Ruler's distinction between "Christ-preaching" and "kingdom-preaching."
[162] "Prediking," 6.

world—a *mannetje*. Van Ruler claimed that for Reformed theology, preaching is the "full representation of salvation, the full representation of God in Christ."[163] We have seen that, for Van Ruler, salvation is primarily understood as atonement for guilt. Atonement is made present, actual, in preaching. What happens in God's presence is now made manifest. And more, for salvation is also forgiveness of sins, the power to overcome sin, and participation in the divine life. This is Christological in content; and Christ is re-presented in preaching.[164]

Nonetheless, as we might expect given Van Ruler's theological commitments, Christ-preaching ranges beyond the person whose sins are forgiven and whose sins are overcome. "Life given in Christ is set in the midst of creation in order that it might penetrate everything as leaven and that life again receive its original and ultimate intention."[165] For Van Ruler, it is not only the person who is saved, but the world as well. He adduces the New Testament claim that in Jesus Christ the kingdom of God is established on earth. Van Ruler offers four perspectives. First, Jesus must be approached from within the context of all of scripture; he comes as the Messiah of Israel, its king. The Messiah is not about atonement but about kingdom. Second, God does not enter this world for a short period of time, only to leave it again, as Jesus entered our existence for only a few years at the outset of the Common Era. The coming of the Spirit is also a fact of salvation history. We have become the dwelling of the Spirit. Third, the story of scripture is not about the church, as widely inclusive as the reality of the church might be. The New Testament includes the cosmos. The world has become acceptable to God. Finally, it is gnostic to claim that God is about Christ in such a way that the world is the means and Christ is the goal. In fact, as we have seen, the dynamic works in the opposite direction. God has to do with us, with me, with our society and our history—all as God's kingdom. For the present, the kingdom is found in the gestalt of the kingdom of Christ.[166] This is salvation of the world, the arrival of the kingdom, through preaching.

And this happens in preaching. This is illustrated by how preaching differs from the sacraments in Van Ruler's understanding.

---

[163] Van Ruler, "Christusprediking," 44.

[164] "Christusprediking," 45.

[165] "Christusprediking," 45.

[166] "Christusprediking," 46-47. Van Ruler concludes his reflection on Christ-preaching by repeating his famous (infamous?) claim that in the kingdom of God the Son will hand over the kingdom to the Father, as there is no longer a need for a mediator.

For the sacraments are *not* a means of salvation. God does not come to us in the sacraments. Or more accurately, in the sacraments God does not enter a world bereft of God. God has been with us already, has come to us fully, in preaching.[167] As noted above (2.2) it is not as though God comes to us in two ways, through preaching and sacrament. The sermon is the true representation of God in Christ in the life of the person. In the sacrament, God does not act alone. There are two involved, God and the believing human. In a metaphor we have met before in discussion of the sacraments in the church, the "sacrament is the first kiss, the marriage of God and the human."[168] The human can only come to the sacrament, however, because she or he has already been met by God and set on his feet, that is, has been saved.

The exposition in the previous paragraphs easily leads one to conclude that preaching in its eschatological character is limited to humans. That is not so for Van Ruler. Preaching extends beyond persons to include the institutions in our world that are themselves caught up in created reality. Preaching involves institutions found in society, state, and the culture. Van Ruler illustrates this point by what he calls the "normal marriage" between church and the magistrates. In such a marriage, the magistrates sat in separate pews in the church. Preaching, thus, could address the state as it placed the things of this world under the light of the last judgment.[169]

It is to be remarked that Van Ruler stretches his claim that preaching is an instrument used by God to effect salvation almost beyond its limit. When preaching extends beyond salvation itself to the ordering of life or sanctification, it appears no longer to be simply a matter of salvation. Indeed, Van Ruler may not have been fully consistent on this point. His theological commitment to the kingdom of God trumps the narrower claim that preaching is solely about salvation. However, his larger concern emphasizes the crucial nature of preaching. In a sermon entitled, "The Word and the world," he maintains that the real crisis, the genuine *vis-à-vis*, is between God's Word and the world of humans. But this is not simply crisis; the Word builds.[170] This is the "gospel of the kingdom of God" that "goes out to

[167] "Prediking," 2.
[168] "Prediker," 140.
[169] *Reformatorische*, 197.
[170] "Het Woord en de wereld" (sermon preached in Kubaard September 17, 1939, on Amos 7:16), Van Ruler Archive, Folder IV, 314, pp. 1,2.

humans by means of preaching."[171] Preaching is the "great offensive in the world of demonic powers." In fact, this is the "exorcism of men and communion: the truth is spoken; this makes us free. Thus society cannot be established without the gospel and the church...."[172] Preaching is theocratic. On the one hand, Van Ruler loses simplicity of expression; preaching does not stay within the bounds of salvation. On the other hand, however, his larger point gains strength. Preaching expresses the *vis-à-vis* of God with this world *and* breaks through that distance with God's salvific and sanctifying action as the kingdom breaks into the present.

Van Ruler will take yet a further step. As he concludes his discussion of the eschatological dimension of preaching in *Reformatorische opmerkingen*, he takes a new turn and asserts that preaching is a "simple, lyrical expression to God and in God's presence of the status of the things which God created." Preaching itself becomes an event in which the eschaton breaks in and the human stands before God. In this case, preaching has become a "declaration of love" to God from the human creature, from the congregation, and indeed from the human family.[173] Preaching has become salvific in yet a new dimension. Here, preaching does not communicate the atonement once happened at Golgatha. In the preached moment the human is drawn into the communion that is his or her proleptic destination. That is, the office of minister, in preaching, has, from God, brought into existence the very communion that God intends to enjoy with God's creatures. Furthermore, preaching has become the embodiment of that communion. In this instance preaching tends toward the sacramental as Van Ruler understands the sacrament. This is not surprising given the eschatological location of both preaching and sacrament.

In its eschatological dimension, then, we discover that the trajectory of preaching, while including the congregation, does not rest finally *in* the congregation. With its roots in the office of the apostle, itself an office in the kingdom, it is clear that preaching is set within the horizon of the eschaton which is now, not (only) future, but is set resolutely in the present.

---

171 "De predikers gaan uit" (sermon preached in Hilversum January 5, 1947, on Mark 6:12), Van Ruler Archive, Folder IV, 621, 1.

172 "De teekenen van de prediking," 2.

173 *Reformatorische*, 199.

5.3.3 Kingdom-oriented

The preached moment as apostolic-eschatological is a moment in the kingdom of God. This is so in the first instance in the content of preaching. "Preaching is not about the church, not even about salvation or about Christ, but about the kingdom that is established in Christ, and thus about the kingdom, that is, the world as kingdom, about all of reality that exists and that takes place."[174] In its very content, preaching—and consequently the office of the minister—exists to point the church beyond itself to the kingdom of God.

Nonetheless, it is clear that, as we have seen, the office of the minister of the Word functions within the church. Van Ruler claims that it is precisely because preaching is the representation of Christ that the kingdom of God happens in fact in and through preaching. He reasons as follows. Preaching is about the Son of God in human flesh who brings the offering of atonement.[175] Christ as present in the preached moment is the mediator of the covenant of grace, a historical reality that can only be said, spoken, preached (as we have seen above). Preaching is of "the sacral right relation that God has established in human history between himself and humans."[176] Preaching happens *intra muros* because the kingdom of God is "played out in the church." In the liturgy, in sacraments, and in praise, the activities that accompany preaching, the world is experienced rightly. The service of the church is a sociodrama that exhibits something of the kingdom of God in torso.[177] The kingdom is not enclosed within the church, but it is enabled to be present because Christ's presence and work have become effective. This is the kingdom of Christ which is, as we saw in our review of Van Ruler's theology, a gestalt of the kingdom of God (2.2).

That said, preaching does not reach its final address in the local congregation. Preaching is Christ-preaching, as we saw in the previous subsection, and as such preaching effects salvation. The minister is to preach Christ, but that is not the final goal. "We preach Christ, but we mean kingdom, we mean ourselves and our world as the kingdom of God!"[178] Preaching is not only Christ-preaching, but also kingdom-

---

[174] *Reformatorische*, 169.
[175] *Reformatorische*, 161.
[176] "Continuïteit," 199.
[177] "Preekdefinities," 121.
[178] "Christusprediking," 47.

preaching.[179] And the kingdom does not coincide with Christ. It is true that the kingdom does not coincide with the world either. For that matter, it does not coincide with God; that would be to deny to creation its created nature, that it maintains an integral reality in apposition to God.[180] No, Van Ruler claims, the nub of the matter is that "the human learns to experience the world as the kingdom of God...and in praise of God."[181] While rejecting any sort of dualism, creation exists in a certain duality with God, and in the kingdom creation does not "dissolve" as it loses its nature as creation.

So we have understood from Van Ruler's theology and ecclesiology; in the church the human begins to experience the world as the kingdom of God. The point at issue at this juncture of our study is that the human learns this experience in preaching. The kingdom must be preached. For here we have to do with both Creator and creation, with God on the one hand and the human, as creature, on the other. God acts, and God's acts must be reported, spoken of, said. In fact, they can be communicated only as they are reported. But as we have seen in the context of salvation, it is not only about report. God acts through God's Word. "Preaching is also the kingdom of God in action." The human "learns to experience" the world as the kingdom because the human finds herself *in* that kingdom as it is made present as God enters this ordinary world at the moment of preaching. So that through the proclaimed Word, the human is established in such a way that he must respond to what is set before him.[182] In just this way, the future kingdom breaks into the present, establishing communion with the human who is now set in a position in which he or she is enabled, as (saved) human to respond. Since in preaching "God himself comes to us," Van Ruler can claim on the one hand that preaching is nothing less than a "command" to believe. We stand under the divine demand that we participate in God's kingdom.[183] On the other hand, Van Ruler claims that preaching creates a freedom within the human. The human is enabled to say either yes or no to the marriage proposal offered by the sermon. "Salvation is laid before the doors of the heart."[184] The human, as creature, now participates in the kingdom as fully human.

---

179 "Preaching is the great offensive in the world of demonic powers" ("De teekenen van de prediking," 2).
180 "Christusprediking," 47.
181 "Christusprediking," 48.
182 "Christusprediking," 48.
183 "Bevinding," 66, 67.
184 "Preekdefinities," 124.

Preaching intends to create a certain mutuality, the meeting of God with God's people. The relation is not one-sided from either God's side or the human's, but mutual. Preaching is "centrally" about the human in "his absolute selfhood." Preaching aims toward the world as the kingdom of God, but the world is not the kingdom until it is experienced as such by the human. But the human is not capable of such experience; he or she is a sinner. The human must be set in a new realty—grasped, addressed, turned about, and so set in connection with God and with creation.[185] We see, then, God using the office of minister on the one hand to establish the human in his or her place in the kingdom. This is God at work through the Spirit, using the office of minister as preacher. On the other hand, we see the world itself emerging as the kingdom of God as the human is established in preaching.

And what emerges in preaching? As we have seen, the events of Palestine are reported. But that is more than reportage, and even more than the bare presence of the Christ re-presented in preaching. "Preaching in the first place is a lyrical expression of the mystery of being."[186] Preaching penetrates to the heart of reality and speaks of the essence of things as it sets all in the light of eternity. The things of this world are set within the kingdom of God.[187] Preaching gives sense to reality. Short of the kingdom of glory, preaching is necessary: "Without preaching, in which the essence and mystery of everything is expressed, reality makes no *sense*."[188] Preaching opens the "eyes to see the glory and holiness of God, to see the kingdom of God in all the great and small things in all that exists."[189] One goes to church to "celebrate the salvation of the world."[190] And that is experienced as effected in preaching.

Preaching effects the kingdom in the gestalt of the congregation in a second way. For preaching is not only the proclamation of the gospel, but it is also the "ministry of the Word, which is the expression of God's truth in all things.[191] This is the ordering of life, of ordinary life. The commands of God are proclaimed from the pulpit. The

---

185 "Preekdefinities," 124.
186 "Christusprediking," 48.
187 "Preekdefinities," 122.
188 "Grenzen," 42. Emphasis in original. Van Ruler is also making the point that preaching is not necessary in the kingdom of glory because preaching is, after all, only a means to a further end.
189 "Christusprediking," 49.
190 *Waarom,* 159.
191 "Grenzen," 31.

members of the church find their life ordered in marriage, in play, in work and in how work and play relate to each other.[192] Preaching stands at the center, and humans find their existence "around" that center. In this way, the human stands fully open to a "ministry" that is concerned not only with the person's inner life (although it is that), but with all of one's daily existence.[193] As we saw the place of office in the economy of salvation (4.2.5), it is that the "order of the kingdom, the law, and creation can be established again within earthly life."[194] Preaching enables the believer to experience and to live into this world as the kingdom of God.

More happens, however, in the character of preaching as oriented toward the kingdom. Preaching possesses a certain theocratic dimension, for preaching addresses the issues that face society and government and culture and science—the things of creation. Preaching has a "political aspect."[195] All things have their aim and goal in the kingdom of God. With that understanding, Van Ruler understands the content of preaching, finally, as all of existence in its created, fallen, atoned, and saved reality, now directed toward the future.[196] Even within the congregation, preaching is about the realization of salvation within the reality of life. Nonetheless, while preaching turns on what has happened in Palestine, about Jesus, that story is about the kingdom of God, a kingdom that began at creation and that will reach its goal in glory.[197]

As such, preaching expands beyond the congregation as the issues in the life of the local community are placed under the light of the Word. That includes marriage, education, culture, technology, and politics. Preaching extends to the seat of human power, the halls of government. As Van Ruler sees it, since the synods of the church are to offer prophetic witness to governing authorities, does this not also apply to ministers of the Word? And since the synods do not limit themselves to Christ but have to do with the entire world, including human reasoning, does this not also apply to preachers? "When preaching attains its full eschatological measure, does it then not essentially transgress the borders of salvation and particular revelation?"[198] God desires to be of service socially. So that Van Ruler

---

[192] "Wat doet de kerk?" 11,12.
[193] "Bevinding," 53.
[194] "Briefwisseling," 112.
[195] "Ambten," 25.
[196] "Continuïteit," 199.
[197] "Preekdefinities," 121.
[198] *Reformatorische*, 198.

can say that the government is to listen to preaching so that it can rule "in the light of God's Word."[199] "The good form of the state is only to be found when preaching and sacraments are in the place where they belong—smack in the middle of life."[200]

Preaching moves beyond the enclosure of scripture. Scripture remains the norm of preaching, but preaching is to become fully prophetic, "an expression of the heart of God that reaches God's final intention."[201] The office of the minister is eschatologically located in the kingdom and theocratically addresses not only, and in some senses not primarily, the congregation, but the world beyond the church.

Indeed, the congregation is not the final address of the sermon. The congregation is rather more like the sounding board [*klankbodem*] that projects the notes that emerge as the strings are made to vibrate.[202] The preached word as God's Word "ripples" outward as waves of sound into the surrounding community. Preaching is a public event, not only because anyone can enter the church building to listen to the preacher, but as the sermon is discussed in coffee gatherings and in encounters on the street and even discussed in electronic mail. "The church doors are always open. All ordinary preaching is, in essence, intended for the nonchurched....In principle, it happens in the public square."[203] It is addressed to society, to government, or even, as with St. Francis, to the birds of the air.[204] As a public event, preaching tends toward its goal, which is not only that human comes to know, praise, participate, and anticipate life in the kingdom, but that life, all of life, be "israelitized" and christianized. Preaching is an "announcement of the kingdom in summoning [persons] to the kingdom."[205]

---

199 "Wat doet de kerk?" 12.

200 "Wat doet de kerk?" 14.

201 "Grenzen," 33.

202 *Bijzonder*, 23. Cf. *Reformatorische*, 195, where Van Ruler credits Haitjema with the image, where the sounding board of the violin reverberates from the sound produced by the bow on the strings.

203 *Reformatorische*, 195.

204 "Grenzen," 33.

205 "Betekenis," 7. Van Ruler's words contain a play on words in the Dutch where it is the announcement—*uitroepen*—that becomes summons—*oproepen*.

5.3.4. Trinitarian

The God who uses the office of the minister to further God's activity in history is the triune God, Father, Son, and Holy Spirit. If the minister represents Christ, it is Christ as sent by the Father and present by means of the Holy Spirit. In this way, preaching expresses the heart of the trinitarian God. When, for example, Van Ruler claims that preaching takes place within the kingdom of God, he writes that preaching is "God's messianic and pneumatological activity with the world."[206] God acts in a trinitarian way as God uses the office of the minister to further God's work. And when Van Ruler claims that preaching moves beyond a normative restriction to scripture to become prophetic as an "expression of the heart of God including his ultimate intentions," and that the "completeness of fulfilled time is made more or less transparent in the sermon," he goes on to claim that such is possible only as the Spirit is present.[207] Again, this is at the outer limits of preaching, this time because God is at work in a trinitarian way that is not encapsulated in Christ and Christ's salvific work, but is God fully at work in the kingdom.

The Spirit works in conjunction with the Word in preaching. One can even say that the Word is an "*imago*, a form and gestalt of the Spirit."[208] It is the Spirit who engages the human in such a way that the human retains his or her freedom. What Van Ruler calls the *vocatio externa*, that is, preaching as testimony, mandate, and promise, must become *vocatio interna*. This is the work of the Spirit, and it is the work of the human. We are again in the mode of conversation, the communal setting of preaching. This, Van Ruler comments, is "not a small part of the work of office."[209]

5.3.5 Communal

If preaching is the center or the hub around which the office of minister turns, the office is not exhausted in preaching. Ministry as office extends beyond the pulpit. The preacher is also pastor. Pastoral work is "no small part of the work of the office [of minister of the Word]."[210] That includes a variety of tasks within the scope of his or

---

[206] *Reformatorische*, 195.
[207] "Grenzen," 33.
[208] "Bevinding," 67.
[209] *Reformatorische*, 185.
[210] *Reformatorische*, 185.

her office. She will lead the consistory,[211] visit the sick and their families, lead small groups in Bible study, and function in a myriad of ways in the civil society,[212] as well as sharing with the elder the ministry of home visitation. Such activities are part of the work of the minister as office. The minister represents Christ in these activities; God is at work visiting the sick, leading small groups, etc. Nonetheless, it is crucial to keep in mind that this round of activities is centered on what the minister does in the pulpit, the proclamation of the Word. All the other activity takes place within the centripetal force of God's living presence in the Word.

By this point in our investigation, Van Ruler's theological reasoning has become familiar. The person that preaching intends to engage and indeed to save exists as a social being. Still more, the congregation is brought into communion with God through preaching. While Van Ruler has emphasized repeatedly that preaching extends beyond the congregation, there is something essentially eccelesiological about preaching. It calls the communion and the institution of the church into existence. In the church the office, in this case the minister of the Word, in its character of "over and against," receives its complementary other in the congregation, where the human *qua* human is called to stand over and against God in a new communion of love.[213] The Spirit is active through preaching, establishing this genuine relation between God and the human. Because everything takes place in an atmosphere of freedom, freedom for both God and the human, the duality [*tweeheid*] between God and the human is respected.[214]

That new reality having been established, the preacher steps out from behind the pulpit to become pastor. There, with the elder, he observes how the preached Word becomes incarnate in the hearts and lives of the human creature, in the minister's case, of the humans within the community gathered and living around the local pulpit. The pulpit [*preekstoel*] in the church and the chair [*stoel*] in the home where the minister visits during the week are two *stoelen* and are not to be confused.[215] The human hears the sermon even as she lives a godly

---

211 One notes the blurring of the offices here. One might ask Van Ruler why the leadership of the consistory is not the responsibility of the elder who has as part of his office governance.

212 "Contituïteit," 188.

213 *Reformatorische*, 194.

214 "Bevinding," 68.

215 "Grenzen," 36.

life sanctified by the Spirit.[216] When they leave the confines of the sanctuary, members of the congregation wrestle with the preached Word. This is a struggle, and the minister engages in pastoral work to assist them in this struggle. This work takes place at the limit of preaching as the spoken Word. For the conversation in the living room or the local café is no longer a sermon, no longer a word that comes from without [*buitenaf*], but a dialogue, and thus a genuine duality occurs. Both preaching and conversation are "important in the kingdom of God," Van Ruler maintains.[217] The second, conversation, takes place only because the first has occurred; it is evoked by God's prior Word or address to the human. It can only happen because the human has been saved, has been set on her feet, through salvation mediated in preaching. Preaching thus remains at the center. In the conversation, however, it is clear that we are no longer within the bounds of the church, nor even solely within the context of the inner life; we find ourselves in the full-orbed life of the human in all her concerns and the world which shapes and reflects those concerns.

Here again, we note the blurring of the lines, particularly between the minister of the Word and the elder. The offices differ at the center, not at the edges. It is, however, fair to put to Van Ruler a question from the perspective of the elder. For if the center of the office of the elder is in sanctification, and that expressed primarily in visitation, then further clarification is needed in terms of the office of the minister. Could it be that in the actual practice of ministry, the *vision* of a certain practice of ministry where the elder visited meets the *actual practice*, where in fact ministers *do* more visitation?

It is at this point that the office of the minister works together with the other offices. The office of the minister does not function alone. The office functions with the other offices of elder and deacon in a "pastorie."[218] In preaching, the minister comes with God in Christ, standing before the door of the heart. Then the minister leaves the chancel to visit the home of the church member, there to enter discussion. That, as we have seen, is really the task of the elder. But even there, at the border, the work of elders and deacons is only possible "as the office of the minister of the Word is there as well and as the hub of all the work of his office is found in preaching" and that "in the fullness of preaching as the ministry of the entire Word."[219] The elder's essential task of sanctification of the individual and

216 "Bevinding," 46.
217 "Grenzen," 36.
218 "De theologische studie en de ambstpraktijk," 5.
219 "Continuïteit," 187-188.

communal life turns about God's coming to the human from without [*buitenaf*], and the deacon is "perspectivally at work with the social ideal of the communion of humanity as the kingdom of God."[220] The office of the minister takes place communally, within the church, but from beyond or outside the church, from God's true destination, the kingdom of God. It is an office *in* the church but *of* the kingdom.

Still, it does take place within the church. If the minister is not a minister or servant *of the church*, but rather minister *of the Word*, nonetheless, the office is rooted in the congregation. The minister, like the other offices, is elected, called, and ordained within the congregation, and so by God's own action.[221] In Reformed fashion, Van Ruler can talk about the "external call" that comes to the office-bearer from the church, and the letter of call [*beroepsbrief*] is a concretization of that external call.[222]

5.4 The Offices Gathered

It has been established that Van Ruler understands the offices as resolutely plural. That includes the rejection of the notion that the offices derive from any one of the offices. Indeed, while they originate in the office of the apostle, and indeed that they are apostolic in nature, the offices by themselves are not representations of the office of the apostle. But what about the office of the bishop? Van Ruler himself asks this question. Might we not, he asks, give up the elder for the sake of ecumenicity? Or might one not graft the bishop onto a presbyterial system?[223] One problem, as Van Ruler sees it, is that elders and deacons are retained as "lay elements" in the system or as "representatives of the congregation." This would, he argues, not only reduce the foundational notions of presbyterial polity but to give them up altogether.[224] It would indeed mean that the elder and deacon would not come from God's side to stand "over and against" the congregation. The "otherness" of office is, as we have seen, essential in Van Ruler's understanding of office. He maintained that the presbyterial-synodical system of church order is not accidental, but is "intimately interwoven...with the Reformation's discovery and understanding of the gospel, and thus when one leaves the elder for

---

220 "Continuiteit," 188.
221 "Grenzen," 30.
222 Van Ruler, "De roeping tot het ambt," opening lecture, October 4, 1956. Van Ruler Archive, Folder I, 400, 5.
223 See "Ambten," 20.
224 "Betekenis," 195.

the bishop or pope one is likely crossing into another religion." One would be abandoning the horizontal for the sake of the vertical.[225] And the horizontal, the historical/eschatological breaking in of the kingdom of God, is not only central to God's activity, but the offices are used by God in this divine activity.

Nonetheless, Van Ruler can ask, "What about the bishop?"[226] Where are episcopal functions located in the presbyterial-synodical system? It is beyond the scope of this study to attempt a complete description of Van Ruler's understanding of church order. However, an investigation into his reply to the question of the *episcopos* belongs within this study because it further explicates his understanding of office. The basic reason is simple to state: the offices gathered together in synods function as *episcopos*. Put one way, Van Ruler can say that "the *episcopè* as moment in the office of the apostle lies in the *sunodos*."[227] Said simply, the bishop lies essentially in the church council.[228] The bishop is in the offices together.[229]

Van Ruler is clear that the synod in a synodical-presbyterial system, in whatever guise (church council, classis, provincial, or national synod) is a gathering of the offices and not of the office-bearers. An episcopal system of church order also has synods. They are, however, gatherings of office-bearers who hold the same office. But in Van Ruler's understanding, it is the three offices, as offices, that are together in synod.[230] In this way, the plurality of offices as the expression of the plurality of God's work through the Holy Spirit takes expression. This is a horizontal way of being, and on this plurality depends the entire truth of salvation as it finds gestalt in conversation. It is, as we have seen, the Holy Spirit who establishes the human in the horizontal. This conversation, in turn, is embodied in the synod as the offices come in their resolute "threeness."[231] This

---

[225] *Reformatorische*, 30.

[226] "Ambten," 20.

[227] Van Ruler "Het ambt," a disputation with H. van der Linde and J.A. Oosterbaan before the faculty of the City University of Amsterdam, February 5, 1958. Van Ruler Archive, folder I, 465, 9.

[228] "Ambten," 21. Cf. Van Ruler, "De vreugde van het ambt," address to the Classical Gathering of Haarlem, October 8, 1957. Van Ruler Archive, folder I, 445, 7. Also, "Betekenis presbyteriaal-synodale," 5, where the three offices in the church council form a *sunodos*.

[229] Van Ruler also argues that if the minister is understood as bishop, then the presbyter becomes bishop—an absurdity ("Ambten," 20).

[230] "Betekenis presbyteriaal-synodale," 5, 6.

[231] Van Ruler, "Het theologisch verschil tussen Rome en de Reformatie," notes for a lecture to preachers held in Enschede January 23, 1955. Van Ruler

subsequently gives expression to the theological claim that the final goal of the human is not vertical but horizontal. And behind this lies the further claim that the holiness intended by God is not elevation to enter the presence of God, but life ordered in accordance with the will of God and lived out before God.[232]

The offices gathered in synod, then, are in fact the embodiment of the claim that the offices represent Christ through the Spirit. As the plurality of offices exists, it is clearer that the apostolic witness does not emerge directly from the incarnate Logos, but is the creation of the Holy Spirit. The historic bishop, as existing in the church, is Christologically determined. Synods, by contrast, are not so directly determined by Christ. The synods are pneumatologically determined.[233] This is not to divorce the synods from Christ, but to see them, as we have seen the offices, representing God in Christ through the Spirit.

Van Ruler's theological claim that the Spirit establishes us as humans to share in God's judgments and thereby to work in full mutuality with God prepares us for his observation that the offices together in assembly enter a conversation through which God acts. The assembly "judges together" with God.[234] The offices consult, intending to come to consensus. If necessary, they will vote. "This is the form of the Holy Spirit! The manner of love! So the will of God is discovered!"[235] In just this way, the synod or assembly itself bears the character of office. The assembly is not the deliberation of the church in response to God; rather it represents God to the church and thereby constitutes the church. At the same time, however, the assembly displays God's way with the congregation, for the congregation observes that the Spirit activates the assembly as communion of humans in communion with God. So, too, the human—who is after all the goal of God's work—will be set on his or her feet to work with God, to praise God, to enter the round dance of the kingdom of glory.[236]

Archive, folder, 1, 347, 3. On "threeness," see "Betekenis presbyteriaal-synodale," 5.

[232] "Theologisch verschil," 4.

[233] *Reformatorische*, 57-58.

[234] "Gezag," 84.

[235] "Betekenis presbyteriaal-synodale," 6.

[236] Van Ruler defends the conversational nature of ecclesiastical governance scripturally in a meditation on Zechariah 6:13c: "...a peaceful understanding between the two of them." The "two" are priest and king. In that framework, Van Ruler claims that the "Reformation has brought this notion of consultation into the church. [The Reformers] wanted no

It is in and through synod or assembly, then, that the church is governed. This is not the congregation or the church governing itself through a series of representative bodies. But neither is it the rule of the offices as something inherent to themselves. "The offices do not 'have' the ruling of the church; that would be a hierarchy of clergy over laity....They come together 'to' the ruling of the church—which takes place through God's self, by means of Word and Spirit."[237] Thus Van Ruler can say that the governance of the church is not through the office-bearers, nor the offices, nor even the assemblies themselves, but "by Christ himself, through Word and Spirit. But he uses the offices for this. They gather in session to participate, to function, to be used by Christ in the ruling of the church."[238]

If used by Christ, then the offices together share in the establishment of Christ's kingdom in the gestalt of the church. Governance is, Van Ruler argues, more than administration and more than being in charge of an institution. It is "seeking together the order of God's kingdom in all the work of the church in the world. All of existence is made transparent to God's original and ultimate intentions." In this way life is established, in preaching and the sacraments, in the liturgy and in piety [*bevinding*], in the education of youth and the care of the aged, and as society, culture, and the state are ordered.[239] The governance of the church is "in the widest sense of the word an establishment of the order of the kingdom of God in the whole life and work of the church in the world. At core, it is the pasturing of the flock in the pastures of the Word of God and in the praise of God."[240]

In using the assembly in the governance of the church, the Spirit enters the ordinary things of daily life. For the concerns of the church council are sober and concrete realities. They include administrative matters, such things as budgets and buildings, personnel and office supplies. Many will resist consideration of such matters, thinking them less than spiritual. On the contrary, Van Ruler argues, to be

---

hierarchy in which one stands above the other and decisions come from one side. They desired ecclesiastical gatherings of office-bearers in which one comes to decision through discussion and common consultation." *Heb moed voor de wereld: Zes en dertig morgenwijdingen over het boek Zacharia* (Nijkerk: G.F. Callenbach, 1953), 58.

237 *Apostolische*, 99.

238 "Betekenis presbyteriaal-synodale," 7. See also "Ambt, vergadering en werk der kerk," 276.

239 "Betekenis presbyteriaal-synodale," 7.

240 *Waarom*, 106.

"spiritual is to see concrete and sober things as holy" and thereby to consider, to reflect on, and to work with concrete things as they are ordered by God.[241] It is for this reason that Van Ruler resists notions that the assemblies are to be about biblical reflection or theological discussion. Instead, he asserts, it is important to work through the ordinary items on the agenda of the meeting. It is then, in the concrete locus of history, that the synod will find itself in the presence of the panorama of the kingdom of God: "the genuine spiritual and theological is only in the real and the everyday."[242] The ordering of the life of the humble, local congregation is a matter of God's work, as the congregation haltingly and slowly is led into life as God intends.

Still, the offices together do not simply function in the governance of the internal life of the church. The assemblies, bearing as they do the character of office, are located in the kingdom of God, eschatologically determined. They are, much less than the bishop according to Van Ruler, not inner-churchly. The "dominee, the elder, and the deacon of the presbyterial-synodical system stand and permanently cross over the borderlands of church and state."[243] In the assemblies of the church, the theocractic orientation of the church is made clear. "The offices are not enclosed purely in the holy space of the church. They stand in the midst of the no less holy space of the world and go to the furthest extreme, to the kingdom of God." In just this way, the presbyterial-synodical system is directed toward the union of church with state, society, and culture, in short, with the world.[244]

The synods address authorities at work in the world as a matter of *discipline*. If discipline has to do with God's intentions in the world, with the right ordering of all of life, discipline is a "paradigm of the kingdom."[245] And it is not practiced solely within the confines of the church. Discipline reaches even the government as the discipline of doctrine and of life includes the full communal existence of the human. The synods, as used by God, now do not simply set all things in the light of the kingdom, but actually act to make them right.[246] We can see the work of the elder here.[247] We also see the work of the

---

241 "Betekenis presbyteriaal-synodale," 8.
242 "Betekenis presbyteriaal-synodale," 8.
243 "Is het ambt alleen binnenkerkelijk?"
244 *Waarom*, 105.
245 *Apostolische*, 45.
246 *Apostolische*, 47.
247 This is an extension of home visitation. The church "goes on home visitation in the world. It does home visitation at radio and sport, at science

deacons in the social ideal. The minister of the Word proclaims God's judgments and commands to the magistrate in the pew. But together, in assembly, the offices address the powers that be.

The offices exist in relation to each other not only in the governance of the church and in a theocratic relation to society, culture, and the state. The offices relate to each other functionally. That is, no one office exists or functions in isolation. In reflection on the office of the elder, for example, Van Ruler maintains that one of the characteristics of the office of the elder is that the elder never functions alone. He always stands in conjunction with another. "He is in himself the breakthrough of loneliness." He acts alongside the minister of the Word (the minister is not isolated in his or her office of minister). There always exists a community around him.[248] In examining the elder's primary task of home visitation, we saw that the minister works alongside the elder. But the elder is there for the sake of the minister as well. Van Ruler asserts in one place that the elder humanizes the minister. The minister, with his or her theological education, can become domineering. The elder is "more human" than the pastor. As such, as the elder shares in the ruling of the church, it is not so much from theological considerations as it is from the concrete life lived out between God and the human.[249] Here as well, in the function of the offices together, one comes across the work of God as it finds purchase in everyday life.

The offices as they function together as apostolic and as they work in communion with one another present the church with a picture of itself in skeleton form. The church council, as it functions in the character of office, expresses the four ways of functioning that we outlined at the outset of the previous chapter. The assemblies constitute the church; they embody the church; they are used by God as instrument of salvation within the church; and they exist beyond the church in the kingdom of God.

Here again we are in the realm of religion. The offices as the particular offices of elder, deacon, and minister of the Word, and as they are gathered in assemblies, are expressions of not only a theology, but of a way of life that is expressed in the existence and the function of the offices. This expresses a relation with God and God's kingdom that is more horizontal than vertical, more this-worldly than other-worldly, more kingdom-centered than ecclesiocentric.

---

and art, at professional organizations and political parties, at society and the state" (*Apostolische*, 41).

[248] "Ouderling," 3.

[249] *Blij zijn*, 180.

5.5 Summary

Our review of Van Ruler's description of the particular offices both confirms the more notional understanding outlined in the previous chapter and fills that notion in greater detail. While avoiding unnecessary repetition, it is helpful to indicate how the broader view is confirmed on the closer examination undertaken in this chapter. But the particular is not simply confirmation of the more general, as though the particular offices were themselves instantiations of a "office" that God uses. In fact, office exists only in the particular office.[250] Seen from within their particularity, we may gain new insight into office from Van Ruler's perspective.

First, at the conclusion to the previous chapter, we claimed that for Van Ruler office is resolutely theological. This conclusion is confirmed as we see the elder, deacon, and minister as used by God in particular tasks. Each office with its own center or hub functions in differing, albeit coordinate, ways. They express the work of the triune God; they represent the Messiah through the Spirit to obtain the ultimate purpose of the Father, in which the eschatological completes the original. In fact, the very "threeness" of the offices in itself expresses the Spirit's love of pluriformity.

Second, we see each of the three offices as set within the eschatological framework of the kingdom of God. They are not primarily offices in the church but, as a branching of the office of the apostle, are offices set in the kingdom. That takes concrete form as the elder is not, like the bishop, "seated" within the church, but is located in the community beyond the church. The elder is called to shape or "stylize" life in the contours of the kingdom of God. Even discipline is not the restoration of life within the cult, but the discipline of life in the ordinary world of family, culture, and state. The deacon's function is even more clearly the living out and advocacy of the social ideal of the kingdom of God. The minister of the Word, who lives most clearly within the church and whose proclamation establishes the kingdom of Christ, is him or herself also located in the kingdom. In her proclamation of the Messiah, the human receives salvation and so is set on his feet to live within that kingdom. The message is an eschatological break into the present. The offices together govern a

---

[250] Van Ruler can, of course, speak of "office" in the context of the *munus triplex* of the Messiah, or of the church as "office." The point made here is simply that "office" as understood within the framework of "ecclesiastical office" can only be met as a particular office.

church as institution not to function effectively as an institution among institutions, but to shape a community that proleptically reflects the life of the kingdom of God. The church is not, and is not intended to be, the kingdom; but, as the kingdom of Christ, is a gestalt of the kingdom of God. As such, how it functions in its ordinary life will offer glimpses of that kingdom.

Third, the particular offices are apostolic, and are so in differing ways. In the elder, the church is drawn from its center within itself. As the elder visits the homes and businesses of the community, his work clearly points to the truth that God intends not to bring persons within the cult, but to prepare persons for ordinary life, there to live the law that has been fulfilled in Christ and to be used in the internal work of the Holy Spirit. As the deacon works to serve the community, the work of the apostle that the gospel shape the life of the nations begins to take hold. And as the minister proclaims the gospel, the apostle's message is carried by means of the missionary task of the church. The offices gathered in assembly together engage the church in the multifarious life of the world.

The offices, then, stand first within the kingdom. They are, however, constitutive for the church. This is our fourth point. As we have seen, they are not offices that emerge from the church as particularizations of the work of the believers. They come to the church. This is clearest with the office of minister of the Word. He or she brings the story *to* the church, a story that can only originate without [*buitenaf*]. But the elder comes with a sanctification that does not arise from within a conception of holiness that the human has to offer. The elder will indeed *engage* the human in such a way that the human knows that she is fully responsible before God, for she is indeed fully human. As the elder represents Christ in visitation, the elder invites the human into conversation, and more, into mutual consultation. This mutual work finds its apotheosis in the deacon, as the deacon extends the concerns of God's kingdom into the ordinary world. Together, the three offices make possible the life of the church, and they do so as they are so used by God through the Spirit.

Thus far, we have taken up trajectories developed in the early chapters of this investigation. In this chapter, we have seen that synodical bodies in the presbyterial-synodical system are given to perform episcopal functions. Together, the three offices so represent Christ in the Spirit that they replace the historic episcopate. But they do not simply substitute for the episcopate but transform the episcopate. They are, after all, caught up in the apostolic work in which God uses the church. An example from an episcopal tradition can help to make this clear. Paul Moore, Episcopal bishop of New York, offered as his final charge to the diocese on his retirement the following:

> You are messengers clothed in the beauty of God. Take hope, be strong, be brave, be free, be open, be loving, and hold up the vision of the Heavenly City. Remove the scales from your eyes, so that you can see the City so clearly that you will never cease until you have built Jerusalem in our land.[251]

The three offices are indeed to enable the congregation to be caught up in the beauty, to be strong, brave, open, and loving. But more, they not only enable the congregation to see the Heavenly City—in Van Ruler's words, to experience the world as the kingdom of God—but indeed begin to build that city. The difference for Van Ruler, and it is a profound difference, is that in a Reformed understanding, it is not one office, but three, in full pluriformity, and that office located not in the church but in the kingdom, that is used by God.

The conclusion of the paragraph on the offices as gathered hinted at a fifth, perhaps more profound, conclusion. The particular offices are expressive not only of a certain theological understanding. They have become expressions of "ways of life."[252] It is a life that is experienced more horizontally than vertically, more historically than eternally. The elder, as he or she is about home visitation, has himself become a part of a way that a particular social and cultural community has begun to experience its life. The minister, as he brings the Word of God to bear upon the questions of the day that perplex local governing authorities, has helped to create and perpetuate a way of life quite different from a priest whose homilies remain restricted to the internal life of the congregation. Deacons who express a social ideal as they offer assistance to people left behind by even the most enlightened social democracy live a social ideal quite differently than deacons whose task is executed within a church's liturgy. And as the offices work together to create a certain kind of community, they begin to establish the kind of society that has become familiar to Western Europe and North America. The offices have become expressions of and have in turn helped create a way of being. This is no

[251] Paul Moore, Jr., "His Final Charge," *Cathedral*, September 1989, 7; quoted in Albert Borgmann, *Crossing the Postmodern Divide* (Chicago: University of Chicago Press, 1992), 146-147.

[252] See Stroup, especially 264-265.

longer a matter of theology; it is a matter of life, ordinary life. Or, as Van Ruler might well put it, of the kingdom of God.

Sixth, the offices are implicated in this way of life because individually and together they both bespeak and embody reality. This is the reality of the creation now saved, lived from the future, but the one reality of the kingdom of God as it finds its proper place in history. It is the reality in which the elder converses with people in their homes, the reality of marriage and family and business and play, of art and literature, of culture and government. It is not reality as it is trapped by sin, but reality as it is made "fireproof" and lived before God. In fact, the human is freed to live the reality that he or she is. It is a reality that also finds purchase in the church, not as the church is a higher or better form of reality, but a humble, temporal, provisional form, no less important, real, or joyful for its ordinary nature.

CHAPTER 6

Used By God: Office Within Van Ruler's Theological Project

This study has attempted to display a doctrine of office that emerges from a full theological project, that of A.A. van Ruler. To that end, we began by providing an outline of the scope of his theological intentions, discovering his ecclesiological commitments within that broader framework. Our research into his doctrine of office revealed a persistent pattern of thought in what is sometimes considered the more "practical" areas of church order and ecclesiastical office. It is appropriate at this point to consolidate the results of this research. What does Van Ruler contribute to the discussion of the question of office?

Van Ruler subtitled his doctoral dissertation, "A Dogmatic Study of the Relation of Revelation and Existence," thereby indicating the theological question that captured his attention and evoked his reflection. He articulated the same concern in his inaugural lecture at the University of Utrecht with its title, "The Kingdom of God and History." The title of the lecture, in fact, gives content to the question of "revelation and existence." God's intentions are to make manifest God's kingdom within history. The second chapter of this study is intended to explicate that claim. The theological attention that Van Ruler gives the church is to be seen within the same framework. The historical context of Van Ruler's life and work played a large role in his concern with the church. The question of the nature and purpose of the church loomed large in Dutch ecclesiastical history at the mid-twentieth century. Nevertheless, it can be argued that Van Ruler found his way into the center of that discussion in large part because he was already passionately involved in the question of how God relates to human existence. How does the God who entered human existence with Israel and in Christ continue to act in history? Theology had made large claims for the church as a means that God used and uses in this dynamic. How are such claims to be understood and evaluated? The place of the church in Van Ruler's theology was the burden of the third chapter of this study.

If, as Van Ruler claims, the offices themselves are a means that God uses as revelation engages existence, then the relation of office to the church is of crucial importance. And indeed the offices are constitutive of the church because God so uses them. But the offices are not exhausted as either constitutive of the church or as expressions of the church's ministry. They are themselves expressions of God's economical work in the manifestation of the kingdom of God as the salvation of creation. The explication of these claims was the import of the fourth and fifth chapters of this work.

This summary provides the framework to take cognizance of the results of our study. While it is the nature of the case that these remarks will reiterate what has already been argued in the foregoing chapters, the reader is referred to the final paragraphs of chapters four and five to supplement the summary remarks recorded in this chapter. This summary not only reflects the study thus far but also provides a grid against which one can assess the claims for ministry or office advanced by the churches.

Of the following remarks the first two are of a *formal* or *structural* nature. The remaining remarks are of a *material* nature. They summarily state the content of Van Ruler's doctrine of ecclesiastical office.

6.1 Formal Remarks

First, how one thinks of office reflects not only ecclesiology, but a theology. How office is structured and expresses itself indicates a religious way of being, that religion to be probed theologically. For that reason the discussion on office can only proceed when the deeper ecclesiological and theological commitments are acknowledged and articulated. How the church is ordered emerges from how one understands God's way with the world. One can see that from Van Ruler himself. In a series of lectures to German students in 1955, he put it in terms of church order:

> A church order represents the stylized ordering of community directly and intentionally from the vantage point of God in Christ. As such it has a paradigmatic significance for the whole of society and for the state. One need only think about the very intimate relation that exists historically between the presbyterian-synodical system of Reformed ecclesiastical polity and the rise of the modern Atlantic world in Holland, England and North America.[1]

How one views office is neither accidental nor incidental. It is not accidental in both a weaker and a stronger sense. In the weaker sense, the church does not decide on a notion of office from a purely utilitarian perspective, to ask simply "what works?" How a church comes to its notion of office is not simply an "accident" of history.

But it is also not accidental in the stronger sense of the term. That is, office is not only a predicate of the church, one that can fall away. Rather, office expresses something essential about the church. As we have seen above (4.1) we use the term "office" to mean something different than what is denoted by the term "ministry."

Nor is office incidental. Discussion of office is not about who occupies what position in the structure of the church. Such questions come into play if and when we ask why such persons occupy the positions they do and why the decision that they do so is not only theologically valid but demanded. Why, within the purposes and actions of God, do we have elders and deacons, or bishops and priests? What are we saying about God when we ordain John or Susan as minister of Word and sacrament or as elder? What are we saying about the human as the child of God and the world as God's creation?

This structural comment will provoke us to ask of any statement on office or ministry: is it transparent to the theological and confessional commitments of the church or churches offering the statement? In ecumenical discussions we might ask whether the

---

[1] "Christ Taking Form in the World," in *Calvinist Trinitarianism and Theocentric Politics: Essays Toward a Public Theology*, trans. John Bolt (Lewiston: Edwin Mellen, 1989), 127, 128. This essay is itself a translation of Van Ruler's small book, *Gestaltwerdung Christi in der Welt: Über das Verhältnis von Kirche und Kultur* (Neukirchen Kr. Moers: Verlag der Buchhandlung des Erziehungsvereins, 1956). This essay provides a concise summary of Van Ruler's larger theological project. Its translation into English is thus one of the few documents that provide access to Van Ruler's theology to English readers.

partners have consciously (or surreptitiously) shifted fundamental theological positions.

Second, Van Ruler claims that office is used by the trinitarian God. Office represents Christ through the Holy Spirit in the accomplishment of God's original and ultimate purpose of establishing the kingdom of God. Given that claim one asks: *How* does the trinitarian God engage the church as God's action with the world? How does God rule through the Son and in the Spirit? Van Ruler's claim is that God is at work establishing God's kingdom. As a formal question, however, we can ask of any statement of ministry what it discloses of how God rules. Put another way, we can subject a statement on ministry to the query of whether and how far it is transparent to the purposes of God and how it discloses the ways in which the God of Israel, this trinitarian God, engages the church.

However, this second remark does not remain solely formal but begins to explicate the material result of Van Ruler's doctrine of office. The kingdom of God finds its contours not only, indeed not primarily, in the gospel of salvation in the presence and work of the Messiah, but in the law or Torah where one sees God's purposes as they find their provisional goal in this world. The kingdom of God is not a leaving behind of this world but the salvation of this world, and more the sanctification and glorification of this world. The kingdom is creation saved. It is the work of the Spirit expanding and extending what God was about with Israel and in Christ. Offices are taken up in that work. Office is not the only means that God uses, but it is one means.

6.2 Material Remarks

First, in representing Christ, office is an eschatological reality. It comes to the church from the future. As representing the ascended Christ, office represents the Messiah as he appeared in Palestine. But because it is the *ascended* Christ it is the Messiah who comes to the church from a future/past as well as a future/present.

Standard understandings of office would have office come to the church either as it represents the past or as it represents a present reality, now "above" this worldly reality. The church lives in the present and so needs communication from what once was (in Israel and with Jesus). God uses certain persons to relate the old story. Or alternatively, God uses persons to communicate what is an essentially different (divine) reality, that which cannot in itself be accessed by the mundane.

Van Ruler sees office in neither of these ways. Rather, God comes to the church in Christ and through the Spirit from God's future. That is a future that has arched back into what is, to us, the past. It is a past where God was present to Israel and in Jesus Christ. Those events can only be communicated through office. But it is God coming out of the future of God's kingdom. This is God acting in history, a history driven by what God will be about. Within this framework, office enables the human to see all creation as the kingdom of God already in the present time. The kingdom of God is to be seen only in signs, but the signs are not illusions.

Second, ecclesiastical offices have their origin in the office of the apostle. The apostle is the one sent, *par excellence*, according to Van Ruler. The apostle was sent by God and placed by God in the establishment of the kingdom in the world. The apostle, however, is not a creature of the church. It was God who originally appointed the apostles, calling them through Christ and sending them out by the Holy Spirit. The office of the apostle is not, then, an office in the church.

Because the offices have their origin with the office of apostle, they in turn are set within the kingdom of God. That is their primary "location." Negatively said, the offices are not "of the church." They are, of course, found within the church and function in the church in an important way, as we have seen and shall note again below. But they are not a function of the church. The offices are not the summary expression of the "priesthood of all believers." The offices do not emerge "from below."

Because the offices emerge from the apostle, set within an eschatological horizon, they precede the church. In a very real sense they are used by God in the constitution of the church.

However, as was made clear above (4.5), the relation between office and congregation does not simply exist in a direct relation of God-office-church. Van Ruler pictured the relation triangularly. God's Spirit engages the congregation as they participate in God's action in a certain *theonomous reciprocity*. The human as forgiven and sanctified is established in such a way as to act together with God. Such humans gathered as congregation elect, accompany, and work together with the offices.

This second point, that the offices have their origin in the apostle, can be expressed more positively. The apostolicity of the church is established and handed on for Van Ruler neither by the office of bishop, nor even exclusively with the apostolic message as communicated in the preaching of the Word. The offices themselves both institute and embody the church as engaged in the apostolic task of mission, evangelization, and the christianization of society and culture. This was made clear as the church was characterized as the "bearer of the gospel," and the offices set within that task.

Third, the offices come from without to establish the human creature before God. The goal of human existence is not union with God but communion with God. The goal for the human is not elevation to a higher ontological status. It is not for the human to become more or other than human. The eschatological trajectory is not for the human to share in divinity. Rather, it is that the human might delight in the human's created nature that God may delight in the delight of the human to be human.

The human is caught in sin, trapped by guilt. That objective reality can only be overcome by the action of God in Christ. That wonder was enacted in God's presence by the Messiah on the human's behalf. That reality can only be announced to the human through the offices as they perform their apostolic function. Without this news, the human is left on his or her own, desperate and alone. The God who acts in sovereign freedom uses the offices to effect this communication.

It is here, in Van Ruler's theological anthropology, that his aversion to both the office of bishop (and the adherent Roman Catholic understanding of office) and a more congregational approach to office is made clear. His 1955 essay, "Christ Taking Form in the World," offers a lucid illustration. Van Ruler sees in both a skewed understanding of what God intends for the human. In the Roman Catholic view, creation is itself a duality of nature and supernature. The office represents what the human is to become: "the real goal of humanity, as well as of cultural existence, is still found in modeling and orienting all of life toward God. This is understood in terms of the *visio Dei*, the actual participation of in the inner-trinitarian life of God."[2] Office can be seen as the goal of the human. Van Ruler will admit that God uses office to effect union with Christ, but office is not itself union with Christ.

But Van Ruler is also averse to the notion that the goal of the human is a "new creation" that replaces the old human. This is the Anabaptist option as Van Ruler understands it. In this notion "the old reality which came into being in the first creation is in no way restored, but simply set aside, transcended, let go and abandoned to

[2] "Christ Taking Form in the World," 130.

perdition."[3] This for Van Ruler, is gnostic. This is not the place to argue from Van Ruler's entire theological project. However, the implications for a doctrine of office would withdraw office from the eschatological placement of office outside the church. Paradoxically, both the Roman Catholic and the Anabaptist options "enclose" office within the church.

Fourth, office is the work of the Holy Spirit. God acted fully in the Messiah, but God was also present in the pouring out of the Holy Spirit. This takes place, as we saw above (6.1), within the economy of the trinitarian God. Here it needs to be emphasized that God's work is not only that of salvation, but more importantly, that of sanctification and glorification. The Spirit's work is the extension and expansion of what began in Christ, that took purchase in Pentecost, and that exists in the kingdom of Christ as it is itself a gestalt of the kingdom of God.

God's work is manifold. This is foundational in Van Ruler's view of God's original and ultimate purposes. Salvation is God's work not for its own sake, nor for the sake of the Savior, but for the sake of the saved. It is the Spirit who expands, almost explodes, this reality into the world. The Spirit is at work in history, in institutions, cultures, governments, families. Sanctification extends outward to the human, and indeed to all institutions and cultures that make up our world.

For Van Ruler this means that office is not limited to God's work of salvation. The Spirit's expansive work lays the foundation for an understanding of office that cannot be singular but is plural.

Fifth, office then is not singular but plural. Van Ruler does not see the three offices of the Reformed churches as reducible to one office. The denotation of the particular offices is not essential. An office may appear and disappear in the course of history. Nor is the number "three" important. What is important is that God works in a myriad of ways and the plurality of offices reflects God's multifarious activity.

In this way, Van Ruler's doctrine of office stands in opposition to all approaches that maintain that God really works through one office. That places him over and against both the Roman Catholic understanding in which their *trits* of bishop-priest-deacon in fact collapses into the one office of bishop. It also places him over and against those who maintain that the only office that matters is that of the office of believer. But it also sets him at odds with both Lutheran and some Reformed who would hold that the only office is that of minister of the Word.

[3] "Christ Taking Form in the World," 129.

It is through the Spirit that the human is enabled to see created reality as it is. It is not reducible to a unitary principle. The offices stand rather like a prism that allows the full spectrum of color to become visible. The offices as plural symbolize the plurality of reality as the kingdom of God in which both God and the creature, as well as the creatures themselves, are honored in their integral nature.

Sixth, the offices always exist together. Although plural, they are always related. The plurality of offices finds form in a synodical gestalt. And because the offices cannot be conflated to one office, and because plurality is so fundamental, the three allow the church to live within the kingdom of God in all its irreducible reality. This happens as the synods govern the church. But more is afoot for Van Ruler. They not only "activate" the church. They are the church already in skeletal form.

CHAPTER 7

A Lutheran-Reformed Dialogue on Office: A North American Discussion

The introduction to this study situated our inquiry into Van Ruler's theology of office within an ecumenical framework. Can Van Ruler's exploration of the nature of office contribute to a resolution of the impasse in ecumenical discussion on office (see 1.1)? More specifically, can he offer fresh perspectives to Reformed partners in the conversation, particularly in the United States? This chapter will examine one place where the Reformed have entered a significant ecumenical agreement that includes an agreement on ministry that has in turn enabled the relevant churches to recognize the validity of the ministry of the partners. This agreement on ministry will stand as a case that will enable us to illustrate Van Ruler's contribution to the ecumenical discussion.

In 1997, following decades of discussion, the Evangelical Lutheran Church in America (ELCA), the Presbyterian Church (U.S.A.) (PCUSA), the Reformed Church in America (RCA), and the United Church of Christ (UCC) entered a Formula of Agreement (FOA). This brought together two Reformation traditions, the Lutheran and the Reformed, in a way that allowed the communions to resolve a number of issues that had divided them. Most signally, those included Christology, the Lord's Supper, justification, and ethics.[1] The

[1] The series of multilateral conversations are documented in three volumes: Paul C. Empie and James I. McCord, eds., *Marburg Revisited: A Reexamination of Lutheran and Reformed Traditions* (Minneapolis: Augsburg, 1966); James E. Andrews and Joseph A. Burgess, eds., *An Invitation to Actions: The Lutheran-Reformed Dialogue Series III 1981-1983* (Philadelphia: Fortress Press, 1984);

agreement was entered into after a series of conversations were held. The third conversation resulted in a number of agreements, including a "Joint Statement on Ministry."[2] Examination of this document will provide us a position from which to observe the Reformed partners in discussion on ministry.[3]

We shall examine the statement on ministry paying particular attention to the theological commitments brought by the partner churches. After we note how the discussion on office took place within the larger ecumenical context, we shall then ask how Van Ruler's understanding of office can illuminate the agreement on ministry. Finally, we shall venture a few conclusions on where the Reformed partners find themselves in the current state of ecumenical discussion of office in the United States.

7.1 The *Formula of Agreement*

The FOA[4] culminated decades of conversation among churches of the two traditions, Reformed and Lutheran. At various times the discussions also included, from the Reformed side, the Cumberland Presbyterian Church and, from the Lutheran side, the Lutheran Church–Missouri Synod.

The FOA was not an institutional merger of the churches, nor was it understood as an (explicit) stage on the way to organic church union. A variety of reasons may be adduced why the churches did not work toward merger.[5] The reasons are varied and likely have in part to

---

and Keith F. Nickel and Timothy F. Lull, eds., *A Common Calling: The Witness of Our Reformation Churches in North America Today* (Minneapolis: Augsburg Fortress, 1993).

[2] *Invitation to Action*, 24-36. References to this statement will be noted in the text by SM, followed by the paragraph number.

[3] Of the four partners in the conversation, the Reformed Church in America and the Presbyterian Church (U.S.A.) are both presbyterial in polity. The United Church of Christ is expressly congregational. Hence, while we shall acknowledge the United Church's presence in the conversation and indeed note that church's position at points, our primary focus will be on the Reformed and Presbyterian churches.

[4] The text of the Formula of Agreement (FOA) can be found in *The Acts and Proceedings of the 191st Regular Session of the General Synod of the Reformed Church in America, 1997*, 192-201. [Further references to the actions of the General Synod of the Reformed Church will be indicated by "*MGS*" followed by the relevant year.]

[5] The recommendation and supporting documents for the formula are found in *A Common Calling*. Nowhere in that document, however, is there

do with the historical growth of denominations within the United States. One factor, however, is relevant to this study. As these discussions proceeded, the ELCA was also engaged with the Episcopal Church in a series of conversations that would lead to a "common mission" between those churches. At issue in that conversation was the identity and place of the bishop within the church. It will become clear below that the Lutheran church views office from within the context of freedom. However, how office is understood must clearly be negotiated before institutional merger could occur with the Reformed on the one side and conversations continue with the Episcopal Church on the other.[6] This condition only confirms the claim made at the outset of this study that office stands at the center of the ecumenical task.

The FOA is, rather, a statement of mutual acknowledgment of each church as church and a pledge to a common work that includes full communion in pulpit and around Table. The agreement acknowledges differences but declares that such are not church dividing. Furthermore, the agreement includes the statement that the churches

> Pledge themselves to living together under the gospel in such a way that the principle of mutual affirmation and admonition becomes the basis of a trusting relationship in which respect and love for the other will have a chance to grow.[7]

The principle of "mutual affirmation and admonition" allows and enables the churches to engage one another in confessional, theological, and ministerial differences within the broader understanding that the churches are, at heart, one in Christ. Historic

---

discussion either of why the churches did not desire to discuss merger nor of merger as an ultimate goal of the new arrangement. The statement does talk about a future where the churches grow into deeper union, e.g., 56-64. On expressions of ecumenical relations that attempt to forge new paths see M.E. Brinkman, "A Different Kind of Ecumenism," in *Rethinking Ecumenism: Strategies for the 21st Century*, Freek L. Bakker, et. al., ed. (Zoetermeer: Meinema, 2004), 93-104, where he argues for a "hermeneutic of coherence."

[6] See the text of the agreement between the ELCA and the Episcopal Church, "Called to Common Mission," www.elca.org/ecumenical/fullcommunion/Episcopal/ccmresoursec/text.html. Accessed November 24, 2004. See pars. 6-11, especially par. 9, which includes the "...commitment by the Evangelical Lutheran Church in America to receive and adapt an episcopate that will be shared."

[7] *MGS*, 1997, 193. On this see *A Common Calling*, especially chapter 2.

condemnations were withdrawn as the churches now fully "recognize each other as churches in which the gospel is rightly preached and the sacraments rightly administered according to the Word of God,"[8] thereby acknowledging the historic "marks" of the church as foundational for these Reformation churches.

A central commitment of the churches was that they "recognize each other's various ministries and make provision for the orderly exchange of ordained ministers of Word and sacrament."[9] This is, in fact, being accomplished as ministers of the various communions now serve as ministers in communions other than their own while retaining their ministerial standing in the denomination in which they were ordained. That is, one need neither be reordained nor "change churches" in such a way that, for example, an Reformed Church minister becomes a Lutheran minister when serving a Lutheran congregation. He or she functions fully within the Lutheran communion and does so as a Reformed minister.

The commitment to mutual recognition of ministries was based on the "Joint Statement on Ministry," a product of the series of dialogues that concluded in 1983.[10] That statement concludes: "We agree that there are no substantive matters concerning ministry which should divide us. We urge Lutheran and Reformed churches to affirm and recognize the validity of one another's ministries" (SM, 10). It is the content and analysis of this statement that will engage us in the next two paragraphs of this chapter.

7.2 Lutheran-Reformed "Joint Statement on Ministry"

The agreement among Reformed and Lutheran churches to "recognize each others' various ministries and make provision for the orderly exchange of ordained ministers of Word and Sacrament" was itself based on the earlier "Joint Statement on Ministry" agreed to by the churches. It must be noted that the agreement on ministry mentioned only the ministry of Word and sacrament as an ordained office. Other "various ministries" of the churches are "recognized." Under that rubric, those ministries enjoy at best a subsidiary place in the "full communion." The agreement centers on the one office of minister of Word and sacrament.

---

[8] *MGS*, 1997, 193.

[9] *MGS*, 1997, 193.

[10] Also included in *An Invitation to Action* are a "Joint Statement on Justification" and a "Joint Statement on the Lord's Supper."

7.2.1 The Nature of the Statement

The joint statement is a consensus document, designed to articulate where the churches agree and to state clearly that continuing differences in the doctrine of ministry are not themselves church-dividing. As a consensus document, it makes no claim to be a full statement on the nature of office. Rather it attempts to articulate a common framework within which the churches can share in full ministry at what they consider central to the church.

In fact, the statement is a joint statement on *ministry*. The statement does not use the term *office* until the fifth paragraph, and then only within the broader framework of the church's ministry. Office will take on greater force when ordination comes into view, but a doctrine of office can only be inferred from the document itself. This comment is only to note that questions we place to the statement may ask of it that which it does not itself intend to articulate. Nonetheless, we find the use of language of significance, and we shall return to this in our evaluation of the statement (7.4).

Still, because the statement refrains from a strong claim on the nature of office and in its further claim to be sufficient consensus to recognize the mutual ministry, it implies that it is not essential that the church hold a particular doctrine of office. In fact, documentation from the churches supports this view. There exists a certain *freedom* in how the church—and the churches—order their life. Writing from the Reformed side, Paul R. Fries states, "God freely chooses to employ human agents in the ministry of reconciliation. We are free from the tyranny of an absolute order to shape, under the guidance of the word, government and office in such a way that in each generation God's purpose and mission will be well-served."[11] The 1993 ELCA study on ministry comments on the order of the church that a "Lutheran view, recognizing the variety in Scripture, can set forth its model without expecting others to conform to it and can respect alternative structures for good order in other churches without itself adopting them."[12] While a certain *ministry* may be of the essence of the church, *office* will share in that essential character only to the extent that it reflects the shared understanding of ministry.

---

[11] Paul R. Fries, "Office and Ordination in the Reformed Tradition," in *An Invitation to Action*, 92.

[12] *Together for Ministry: Final Report and Actions on the Study of Ministry 1988-1993*, on-line www.elca.org/leadership/pdf/Together_for_Ministry.pdf, 3.

The vocabulary of office continues to be used by the Reformed churches, albeit with varying degrees of precision. The PCUSA, for example, talks of "particular forms of leadership," which it in turn denotes as "offices." The distinction of office from ministry, however, is more "descriptive than prescriptive."[13] The PCUSA goes on to describe office more fully as a "specific and necessary form of leadership responsibility within the church's ministry of God Service."[14] Further, ordination and office are inextricably linked, since ordination is always to office. For the Presbyterian Church ecclesiastical office is connected with "leadership." The RCA has clearly retained the vocabulary of office. Its 1968 report on office, "The Nature of the Ministry," a statement that took a decidedly functional approach to office, would claim simply that "...the use of ecclesiastical offices is still necessary in the church order of our day."[15] The report did not, however, make any further statement on why the offices remain necessary. The 1980 report to the RCA's General Synod would attempt to make clear the distinguishing characteristics of office.[16] The question of office continues to trouble the RCA, as witnessed by a national conference convened by its Commission on Theology and its professors of theology on the theme, "Spirit, Ministry and Office in the RCA."[17] The question of office will provoke us to ask how it is to be understood as Reformed and Presbyterian churches understand themselves in the ecumenical context of ministry.

The lack of clarity that remains for the Reformed bodies despite the continued use of the vocabulary of office will result in a difficulty in sorting out just what is at issue both within the church when ministry issues arise, and in ecumenical conversation. In the first instance, it will not be clear why certain ministries are to be ordained. That in turn provokes the theological question: how is the church in

---

13 "Theology and Practice of Ordination in the Presbyterian Church (U.S.A.)," in *Selected Theological Statements of the Presbyterian Church (U.S.A.) General Assemblies (1965-1998)* [Presbyterian Church (U.S.A.), 1998] [hereinafter "Theology and Practice], 568.

14 "Theology and Practice," 570.

15 "The Nature of Ministry," in James I. Cook, ed., *The Church Speaks: Papers of the Commission on Theology Reformed Church in America 1959-1984* (Grand Rapids: Eerdmans, 1985), 120.

16 "The Nature of Ecclesiastical Office and Ministry," in *The Church Speaks*, 128-131. The Commission on Theology identified those characteristics as (1) divine appointment, (2) representation of Jesus Christ, (3) authority, and (4) continuity with the early offices of the church.

17 Papers from this conference can be found in the *Reformed Review* (Spring, 2003), 56, no. 3.

fact constituted? We return to this issue below (7.4). The Statement on Ministry discussed below illustrates how the lack of clarity comes to expression in ecumenical discussion.

7.2.2 The Theological Framework

The statement finds its theological center in "salvation through Christ alone" (SM, 1.1) but will describe its theological scope in the kingdom of God (SM, 3). The churches agree that

> Ministry in our heritage derives from and points to Christ who alone is sufficient to save. Centered in the proclamation of the word and the administration of the sacraments, it is built on the affirmation that the benefits of Christ are known only through faith, grace, and Scripture (SM,1.1).

One hears clearly the various *soli* that were the clarion call of the Reformation: Christ alone, faith alone, grace alone, scripture alone. The salvation that comes to the world through Christ is centered in the proclamation of the Word and the administration of the sacraments. Said another way, salvation mediated through Christ finds purchase in the church in Word and sacrament. This will give central place to those persons who are set aside to that particular ministry. With this at the center, the ministry will have a unitary center: Christ as present in the church in Word and sacrament.

The centering of ministry in Word and sacrament has the further implication that the broader ministry of the church itself is centered in Word and sacrament. The plural ministries, whether in further "offices" or in a more broadly understood ministry, are thereby ecclesiocentric. Ministry is a subcategory of ecclesiology.

Further, one might ask at this point in the statement whether the statement's reduction of office to that of the "pastoral office" (SM, 5) does not have its theological foundation at this point. A ministry centered in Word and sacrament will tend to reflect the "one" ministry of Christ. Other ministries will find their center also in Christ. That is so despite the emphasis on the Spirit that we note below.

But if centered in Christ, the trajectory of ministry is to the kingdom of God: "Christian ministry is oriented to the kingdom of God. In the power of the Spirit it serves Christ both in the church and the world by seeking to manifest signs of the salvation to come" (SM, 3). Thus ministry is seen in a trinitarian perspective set against an eschatological horizon.

Ministry is trinitarian. A ministry centered in Christ is set within the original intentions of God's kingdom. And the dynamic that propels ministry is the trinitarian God acting through the Spirit: "The Holy Spirit calls, gathers, enlightens, and sanctifies a people to serve the lordship of Christ (the *regnum Christi*), which will come in its fullness only when Christ returns at the end of history" (SM, 3.1). It is the ascended Christ who rules in the present out of the future and toward the future.

Ministry is eschatological. Ministry seeks to "manifest signs of the salvation to come." The kingdom is future. However, it is also present under the form of *sign*. The "kingdom of God is truly present here and now through signs created when the Spirit of Christ engages the people of God in the servant tasks of the Lord." "These signs are established when the church, in obedience to its Lord and in the power of the Spirit, becomes an agent of justice, mercy, peace, healing and reconciliation in this world" (SM, 3.1). This is ministry that does not look backward so much as forward in the dynamic of the Spirit.

The kingdom that forms the horizon of ministry is a kingdom that is not simply other-worldly. It is of justice and mercy in "*this* world." The statement will go on to say that the signs of the kingdom are present *within* the church. It is clear, however, that these are *signs* and that the church cannot be identified with the kingdom of God. Furthermore, an earthly understanding of the kingdom of God is primary. That orientation is reflected in documents from both Reformed and Lutheran churches. The ELCA's study on ministry says of the mission of the church that the "church is a people who are created, empowered, and sent to bear witness to God's creative, redeeming, and sanctifying activity in the world." Indeed, the church "...like its Lord, lives not for itself but for the world God loves."[18] The Lutheran statement in fact proceeds to set all ministry with the context of mission. This is of such importance that the question of the shape of office must be subsumed to the mission of the church. In reflection on the "threefold office,"[19] the report stated that its authors had discovered "...that for most people in the ELCA the natural starting place for serious discussion is not forms or 'folds' of ministry. The natural starting place is mission."[20] The PCUSA is more explicit:

---

[18] "Together for Ministry," 1.

[19] It is to be remembered that when Lutherans talk about "threefold office" they need not be thinking of the threefold office in the same form as do the Reformed. The "threefold office" is understood from the context of documents like *BEM* to be that of bishop-presbyter-deacon.

[20] "Together for Ministry," 9.

> Ministry is the form the church takes in the service of God's Reign in the world. When ministry is not first and foremost the task of the whole people of God, the church inevitably fails to become what God has called it to be, namely, "the provisional demonstration of what God intends for all of humanity...a sign in and for the world of the new reality which God has made available to people in Jesus Christ."[21]

7.2.3 Ministry as One in Christ

Set within the broader framework of ministry centered in Word and sacrament and against the horizon of the kingdom of God, the statement claims that there is but "one ministry, that of Jesus Christ" (SM, 2). Said positively, this unites the ministry in all the church. From this foundation, the churches expect to meet Christ's ministry in other churches. Said negatively, ministry thus finds no other center, not in the ministry itself, not in the church, not even in the confessions of the church. The ministry of the church participates in the one ministry, the "great ministry of its Lord" (SM, 2.1). As ministry finds its various forms within the church and the world, these forms can only emerge from the one center.

Because it is the one ministry in Christ, it is a ministry of service. The ministry of its Lord is itself that of service. Hence since it participates in the ministry of Christ, the church's ministry will perforce be a ministry of service. The eschatological reality of the kingdom in turn gives the notion of service its positive content. The statement will supply the nature of ministry oriented to the kingdom when it states that the central "office," that of pastor, "finds its meaning in serving others" (SM, 6.1). That ministry does not engage directly in the world but bears "special responsibility for upbuilding the congregation...enabling the baptized members to become a servant community in the world" (SM, 6.2).

Nonetheless one also detects an allergy to notions of ministry that rest on the prestige or power that devolves on those who bear office. In an article that accompanied the joint statement, Warren A. Quanbeck, a Lutheran, states simply that the ordained ministry is a "ministry of leadership in the model of Christ's servanthood."[22] He adds that ordination does not confer higher status or ontological

---

[21] "Theology and Practice," 568. The citation is from the *Book of Order* G-3.0200.

[22] Warren A. Quanbeck, "Church and Ministry," in *An Invitation to Action*, 106.

change in the ordained. Ordination is, in fact, an "appropriate recognition by the church for a position which serves the self-giving God to his people in word and sacrament and which provides leadership and assistance to the Christian community in its mission in the world."[23] The earlier report from the RCA's Commission on Theology was even clearer in its aversion to thinking of ministry in terms of status. "Every variety of ministry is viewed as a service for Christ, rather than as a position of status, power, or privilege."[24]

It is within this one ministry, however, that the various ministries find their place. The statement articulates this fact in two different ways. First, it speaks of the ministry of the church as it participates in that of Christ as threefold. While the statement does not use the vocabulary of prophet, priest, and king to describe the *munus triplex* of Jesus, it describes the content of that ministry in a three-fold manner. In its ministry the church, first, "proclaims this liberating truth [that of the ministry of its Lord] in word and deed." The church engages in prophetic ministry. Second, as Jesus "is the sacrificial lamb offered for forgiveness and reconciliation, so the church announces this free gift of love and acts as an agent of healing and reconciliation." The church shares in priestly ministry. And third, as "Christ is the hidden ruler of the world, the church reveals to humankind its true Lord, calls all people to a life of worship, and participates in the divine acts of justice and mercy which witness to God's sovereign power and majesty." Or the church is engaged in royal ministry (SM, 2.1). This is ministry that while it is centered in proclamation already begins to extend beyond the church in "deed," in acting as "agent of healing and reconciliation," and in "participating in the divine actions of justice and mercy...." The one ministry of the servant Christ begins to expand into a plurality of ministries of the church.

The plurality of ministries is also noted later in the statement when, in the context of a discussion of ordination, it notes that Reformed churches set the pastoral office in a "broader ministerium which includes ordained elders who share the government and oversight of the church and ordained deacons who are given responsibility for ministries of compassion and justice directed to those in need both in the church and the world" (SM, 8.2).[25] Here is

---

[23] Quanbeck, 107.

[24] "The Nature of Ministry," 119.

[25] This is true for the RCA and the PCUSA. The UCC, while entering the conversation from the "Reformed side" is congregational in church order

space for the fundamental plurality that is central in a Reformed notion of office.[26] The statement also noted, however, that Lutherans commission and set apart lay persons for particular ministries of governance and compassion and justice (SM, 8.2). The 1993 Lutheran study on ministry would propose a diaconal ministry. Its rationale was twofold. On the one hand, a diaconal ministry would proclaim important aspects of the ministry of Christ.[27] On the other hand, such a ministry would preserve the traditional Lutheran emphasis on the constitutive nature of the pastoral ministry of Word and sacrament: "...diaconal ministers are now being proposed for greater service in the world and Church so that the crucial ministry of Word and Sacrament can be focused on proclamation of Word and Sacrament."[28]

7.2.4 The Ministry of All God's People

Ministry is not the exclusive province of the ordained ministry. All God's people are called to ministry. "The foundation for this ministry is to be found in the Reformation doctrines of the universal priesthood of all believers and Christian vocation" (SM, 4). This is ministry that is conferred not in ordination but in baptism: "Union with Christ in baptism carries with it the call, power, authority, and promise of gifts requisite for the participation in his servant ministry" (SM, 4.1). "The ministry is the ministry of the entire people of God" (SM, 4.1).[29]

This notion is emphasized in the particular documents of both Lutheran and Reformed churches in their understanding of ministry. The ELCA states that as a church it "needs to recognize and empower all baptized believers to be servants of the Gospel, ministers in the

---

and does not have the offices of elder and deacon as would a Presbyterian church order.

26 On this see Fries, "Office and Ordination," 94-98. The Presbyterian report, "Theology and Practice," is clear that what it calls the "office of Gospel ministry," the office of elder, and the office of deacon are all "essential" to the church's ministry, 571, 587, 602.

27 "Together for Ministry," 18.

28 "Together for Ministry," 16. The ELCA voted to establish a diaconal ministry as "part of the officially recognized, rostered ministries of the Evangelical Lutheran Church in America" ("Together for Ministry," 20).

29 Here the churches echo the consensus articulated in BEM, LM, 1-6. BEM speaks of the "calling of the whole people of God." Interestingly, however, while BEM speaks of this in the work of the Holy Spirit, it does not speak of ministry as rooted in baptism itself.

world."[30] Not surprisingly the ELCA roots this notion in Luther's emphasis on the priesthood of all believers. "The need to enlist laity in leadership roles within the Church should not, for all of its benefits, be allowed to overshadow the indispensable need for the ministry of all Christians in the world."[31] The PCUSA agrees when it flatly claims that "...the church resists completely the notion that ministry is first, or even primarily, the task of its ordained officers."[32] And the PCUSA proceeds to root the ministry of all God's people in baptism: "...all Christians are called by virtue of their Baptism to participate in the ministry of their servant Lord Jesus Christ."[33] The report to the RCA's General Synod in 1988 by special committee on "ecclesiastical office and ministry" emphasized what it called "lay ministries." That report had as a foundational notion that "the primary ministry of the church is the ministry of the members of the body."[34] That statement, in fact, viewed the structures of the church as having become a hindrance to this essential ministry. It quotes with approval the statement that "structure has become the enemy of the church."[35] This has serious theological consequences when the same document claims that "the Holy Spirit is hindered in distributing and igniting gifts among the members of traditional church structures."[36] The implication is that the Holy Spirit is absent in the structure or institution of the church.

---

30 "Together for Ministry," 2.

31 "Together for Ministry," 2.

32 "Theology and Practice," 568.

33 "Theology and Practice," 569. Although as noted the UCC presents a special case, it too roots ministry in the ministry of all believers, as one might expect. Its constitution states that the "privilege and responsibility of witnessing to the gospel belong to every member of the Church." Article V, Paragraph 17, *Constitution and Bylaws, United Church of Christ*, 1976 edition. A later publication on ministry from the same church interprets that paragraph of the constitution when it states the sentence we cited gives expression to the theological conviction "that every member of the church is a 'minister' by virtue of the member's baptism and participation in the Body of Christ." *Manual on Ministry: Perspectives and Procedures for Ecclesiastical Authorization of Ministry* (United Church of Christ, Office for Church Life and Leadership, 1986), 6.

34 "Report from the Committee on Ecclesiastical Office and Ministry," *MGS, 1988*, 132.

35 *MGS, 1988*, 132.

36 *MGS, 1988*, 132-133. One notes a clear divergence from Van Ruler's theological commitments here.

Put more carefully, the report is not clear *how* structure has become the enemy of the church.[37]

The ministry of all God's people finds expression as it is based on both the doctrine of priesthood of all believers and that of Christian vocation. Under the first heading, the statement comments that "[a]ll Christians are called and empowered by the Holy Spirit to be priests to their neighbors. This means that worship, intercession, service, and witness are not reserved for the clergy but are the responsibility of all believers" (SM, 4.2). There exists no *fundamental* difference between the ordained and the laity that would reserve intercessory power to those who have been ordained. Put positively, the church includes all the baptized in participation in the Lord's service to the world (a world that includes the members of the church).

Under the heading of Christian vocation, the statement asserts that "any task that contributes to the preservation of the created order, the well-being of humankind, and the administration of justice is pleasing to God" (SM, 4.3). The church's task is to incite, enable, and encourage this ministry in the world. The church

> ...aids in the identification and development of these gifts both to strengthen the bond of love within its own fellowship and its witness in word and deed in the world. The church also learns from those who work in the secular order about pressing human needs and strategies to address them. Persons at work in the world are equipped by the church for their vocation in the larger society, but they in turn help to shape the church's understanding of its mission (4.3).

This is the church active in the world not as institution, and hence not as the officers of the institution are at work, but the church active through its members. In fact, one can well ask whether it is important that it be the *church* at all that is at work. Instead, the church's task is restricted to an instrumental role.

---

[37] Not only that. The notion of "structure" is itself left ambiguous. To give but one example of ambiguity, churches have "structures" like committees, employed staff, and the like that are of a quite different nature than is the order of the church.

7.2.5 The Pastoral Office

It is only in the fifth paragraph of the statement that the "pastoral office" comes to expression. By speaking of the pastoral office at this place, the statement sets the pastoral office first in the larger framework of Christ's one ministry that is itself set within the orientation to the kingdom of God. And second, the pastoral office is set within the framework of the ministry of all God's people.

The doctrines of the priesthood of all believers and Christian vocation do "not mean that all are called to the same places and tasks in the church" (SM, 5.1). The statement agrees with the claim made by BEM, "In order to fulfil its mission, the Church needs persons who are publicly and continually responsible for pointing to its fundamental dependence on Jesus Christ, and thereby provide, within a multiplicity of gifts, a focus of its unity" (LM, 8). The statement does not claim that the special ministry of the pastoral office is a particularization of the general office of the believer. It is rather set on a horizontal plane, as it were, there to perform a certain, necessary function within the church.

The pastoral office does indeed possess a "special character" according to the statement. "While we do not contend that one particular form of this office has divine sanction to the exclusion of others, we do hold the office itself to be an expression of the will of God for the church" (SM, 5.2). Furthermore, "God deigns to use ordained ministers as instruments to mediate grace through the preaching of the word and the administration of the sacraments" (SM, 5.2). This is God who comes *to* the church. It is for this reason that the statement cannot accede to the notion that this special office emerges from the church. The statement prepared for this notion in its first paragraph where, as we cited above, it is noted that the ministry is centered in the proclamation of the Word and the administration of the sacraments (7.3.2). There the statement did not claim explicitly that salvation comes to the believer from without. However, a salvation that is "through Christ alone" and that is known only through "faith, grace, and Scripture," can only come from without.

This "special character" is further exposed in ordination. The statement does not define ordination. It does, however, refrain from any suggestion that ordination confers any "special character" on the office-bearer. Instead, it describes certain commonalities among the communions simply as "the induction to an office in the church which carries with it certain necessary functions" (SM, 8.1). Included in ordination is a certain *authority*: the "authority of the office is the word of God, and this is also its content" (SM, 8.1). It is this Word that gives to the office not only a special or separate place within the church but makes clear the necessity of the office. The office is used by God both in the church and for the world.

The understanding of ministry as a necessary function among all God's people clearly reflects the ELCA's doctrine of ministry. Its 1993 report cites the Augsburg Confession: "In order that we may obtain this faith, the ministry of the teaching of the Gospel and administering the sacraments was instituted. For through the Word and the sacraments, as through instruments, the Holy Spirit is given, and the Holy Spirit produces faith, where and when it pleases God, in those who hear the Gospel."[38] For the Lutheran church this ministry bears a special character as this teaching is of the gospel as taught by the apostles.[39] Indeed, the report goes on to claim that "congregations were founded 'from the outside' (by the word from apostles and others sent as heralds of Christ to preach)."[40]

In contrast, the Reformed churches, while agreeing that ministry is not to form a special class apart from the whole people of God, place greater emphasis on the "special character." The 1980 report to the General Synod of the RCA is perhaps clearest when it notes among the characteristics of office both a representative and an authoritative function. In representation, the "offices remind us that the church lives from an authority that is over and beyond it, even Jesus Christ."[41] The report further describes authority: "In every age the church lives by and from the Word of God interpreted by the Spirit so that God's people may hear what the Spirit is saying to the church here and now. While all who are in the body of Christ have the Holy Spirit and are qualified to read and interpret the Scriptures, there must be some who are authorized by the church to be its official teachers."[42] When the PCUSA states that the offices as "particular forms of leadership" in which the distinction of office from ministry is more "descriptive than prescriptive,"[43] that church reflects the notion of ministry expressed by the joint statement. When it further denotes as first among core functions of the office of the minister of the gospel the authoritative

---

[38] Article V in *The Book of Concord: The Confessions of the Evangelical Lutheran Church*, trans. and ed., Theodore G. Tappert (Philadelphia: Fortress, 1959). Cited in "Together for Ministry," 4.

[39] "Together for Ministry," 3.

[40] "Together for Ministry," 4.

[41] "The Nature of Ecclesiastical Office and Ministry," *MGS,1980*, 129.

[42] "The Nature of Ecclesiastical Office and Ministry," 130.

[43] "Theology and Practice," 568.

proclamation of the Word,[44] it points to the special character of this office. It is to be remarked, however, that when the Reformed churches talk about office in general, they speak of three (or four) offices.[45]

The trajectory of the pastoral office as the joint statement has it is the equipping of congregation and its members for *their* ministry to each other and to the world. The pastoral office is "exalted by the service that characterizes it" (6). That service of others finds expression in

> ...special responsibility for upbuilding the congregation... enabling the baptized members to become a servant community in the world. Pastors use their gifts and training to assist all the members of the community to grow in faith, to minister to one another in love, to discern their special gifts, and to develop their knowledge and skills for ministry (6.2).

The locus of office is *in* the church, and to the extent that it is shaped by the horizon of the kingdom of God, the office works *through* the church, most particularly through the members of the church. One has little sense that the office itself speaks or functions in the world. This position poses question to the Reformed churches, particularly regarding their elders and deacons. But it also raises question about the proclamation of the Word as an event that takes place in a public that is greater than the gathered congregation.

Nonetheless, it is clear that the Reformed churches share the notion of ministry as primarily enabling and encouraging the members of the church to their ministry. The PCUSA clearly "sets forth an understanding of the office of Gospel ministry focused more around key functions that empower the ministry of the whole people of God than around specific aspects of ministry."[46] Indeed, in discussing the office of minister, the Presbyterians state that "...the litmus test for responsible exercise of office itself is whether the tasks to be engaged in effectively contribute to the building up of the body of Christ and the equipping of the saints for ministry."[47] The RCA makes similar statements. The 1980 report to the General Synod states that the "offices always stand in the service of the church and are meant to illumine and strengthen the general ministry of the

---

[44] "Theology and Practice," 571.

[45] The RCA retains the office of "General Synod professor of theology."

[46] "Theology and Practice," 575.

[47] "Theology and Practice," 573.

congregation."[48] The later 1988 report of the same church affirmed that understanding when it stated that the ordained ministries in the church are, by and large, for oversight and equipment.[49]

7.2.6 The Ministry of Oversight

The joint statement acknowledged the episcopal function of ministry under the broad ecumenical term, "oversight." In so doing it avoided assigning that ministry to a separate office. The traditions agree that oversight is "necessary for the well-being of the church and the prosperity of its ministry" (SM, 9). Because it is necessary for the "well-being," *bene esse*, and not the "being," *esse*, of the church, the ministry of oversight does not rise to the level of office.

Furthermore, given the principle of freedom that had earlier been articulated, the statement agrees that with this particular ministry the "nomenclature, organization and mode of operation may differ" (SM, 9.1). In fact, the "bishop" in the Lutheran church functions in the same way that classes and presbyteries ("corporate bishops") do in the Reformed churches (SM, 9.3). Indeed, Lutheran bishops themselves are held accountable to the synods of the church and all the functions of Lutheran bishops in North America are "carried out in relationship to a synod, district, or church body" (SM, 9.3). As Lutheran bishops *function*, there is little about their presence that would offend the theological sensibilities of the Reformed churches. In fact, Lutheran bishops as presently constituted would put question to Van Ruler's contention that it is impossible to add bishops to a presbyterian system without distorting that system altogether.

7.3 A Van Rulerian Reading of the "Joint Statement"

The conversations that led to the Joint Statement took place as the reception of BEM was finding its way into the life of the ecumenè. As might be expected, trajectories from the document of Faith and Order are reflected in the Joint Statement. The consensus and framework we noted in the introduction (1.1) form the framework of this consensus document. This is the case at the outset with the preference for the neutral-sounding term "ministry" and a consequent reluctance to use the term "office." It is a ministry of the whole people

[48] "The Nature of Ecclesiastical Office and Ministry," 131.
[49] "Ecclesiastical Office and Ministry," 262.

of God, centered in Christ as a work of the Holy Spirit (LM, 1). The church is called to "proclaim the kingdom of God," (LM, 4), the goal of the ministry according to the Joint Statement. This is ministry that is centered in the church, its chief responsibility being the assembling and the building up of the body of Christ "by preaching and teaching the Word of God, by celebrating the sacraments, and by guiding the life of the community in its worship, its mission and its caring ministry" (LM, 13). The Joint Statement clearly moves within this ambit, the pastoral office centered as it is in Word and sacrament, and as it views ministry as that of service. Indeed, as we noted above (7.3.5), the Joint Statement would be in clear agreement with the description of the ordained ministry when BEM claims that the church "needs persons who are publicly and continually responsible for pointing to its fundamental dependence on Jesus Christ, and thereby provide, within a multiplicity of gifts, a focus of its unity" (LM, 8).

However, the Joint Statement does not go as far as BEM in a number of crucial areas. These remaining issues indicate the place where consensus has not yet been achieved.[50] At just these points, our Van Rulerian reading will find its purchase. There appear to be three issues where the churches in question step back from BEM's proposal.

First, the Joint Statement is not clear on the meaning and place of ordination. It describes ordination but must sidestep the issue because the churches ordain to different offices: the Lutherans to one, the Reformed to three. As we have seen, the statement acknowledges this difference. However, do those called to the "broader ministerium" (SM, 8.2) enjoy the authority of office? Or put in the terms BEM uses, do they share in the "chief responsibility" of the ordained ministry? (LM, 13).

Second and related, the statement takes no position on the historic three-fold office of bishop/presbyter/deacon. The statement does not resolve the issue we noted in 1.1.2 of singularity or plurality in office. That matter remains outstanding.

Third, while the statement acknowledges the office of oversight, it takes no position on the theological content of an episcopal office. It rather recognizes that in practice both churches are particularly "collegial" (to use BEM's terminology) in the office of oversight.

This short reflection on the context of the Joint Statement within the larger ecumenical discussion provides an ecumenical

---

[50] I say this in full knowledge that the statement claims that the outstanding issues are not church dividing. It is my contention that just these issues stand in the way of further ecumenical progress. They cannot remain unaddressed.

backdrop against which theological issues in ministry can be seen, given the interpretive framework provided by Van Ruler's doctrine of office in the first chapters. I suggest the following perspectives.

1. The statement reflects our contention that a doctrine of office discloses larger theological commitments. The statement clearly emerges from a theology that expresses the deepest commitments of the Reformation. Ministry can only be understood from within the confession that salvation is from Christ alone. That gracious reality is centrally expressed in the proclamation of the Word and the celebration of the sacraments. This is stated at the outset (SM, 1.1). All ministry emerges from that center. That fundamental theological commitment will and must be conscious in all discussions of ministry. For that reason, Reformed and Lutheran churches must ask themselves when at an impasse in their discussion of ministry: to what extent are the "means" of salvation as found in Word and sacrament at issue in the matter at hand?

2. The theological framework articulated by the statement echoes the trinitarian nature of Van Ruler's own theology. The statement clearly sets ministry within a trinitarian framework. Not surprisingly, the churches begin with a concurrence that there "is but one ministry, that of Jesus Christ" (SM, 2). However, in viewing Christ's ministry as a ministry of service, the statement sets ministry within a historical dynamic. This is not a Christ who only draws humans to himself within a religious space apart from the world. The ministry of the church participates in Christ's ministry in the world.

Ministry, however, while participating in the ministry of Jesus Christ, does so by the power of the Holy Spirit (SM, 3). Ministry, then, is not the extension of Christ into the present, but is the work of the Holy Spirit. The "space" opened up by the trinitarian action of God establishes the church in its ministry in the world, where the church points to the "advent of a new age when all things shall be made new" (SM, 3.1). All discussion of ministry must not only take into account the work of the Spirit, but must expose how the Spirit works in the church and in the world.

3. Ministry is set within the historical context of the kingdom of God. This reality again reflects Van Ruler's theological project (in chapter two, we described his theology as a theology of the kingdom of God). This is ministry oriented beyond the church, a ministry that follows the trajectory of God's intentions in and with the world. When ministry is at issue, Lutheran and Reformed churches will ask how the ministry, or the office, functions in service to the kingdom of God.

Furthermore, as we noted above, this is the kingdom set within an eschatological horizon. Ministry takes place within a history when signs of the kingdom are present and the church in its ministry as it functions as an "agent of justice, mercy, peace, healing and reconciliation in this world" (SM, 3.1) is a sign of that kingdom. This is a ministry that looks not only backward to its founding, but forward as it is drawn by the Spirit to God's future.

The third paragraph of the statement as it sets ministry within the kingdom of God under the power of the Holy Spirit is a "Van Rulerian" perspective set within the joint statement. To the extent that this perspective enters the larger ecumenical conversation, Van Ruler's theology will have found purchase in the ecumenical discussion. In any case, this paragraph of the statement offers perspectives to the conversation on office not often entertained.

4. Thus far Van Ruler's doctrine of office has helped us to see the convergence on ministry under a positive light. His doctrine of office also allows us to pose questions to the Reformed of a more critical sort. While the statement describes ministry within the larger framework of the kingdom of God, the ministry itself extends to the world through the church, particularly through its members. As we have seen above (7.3.4) the churches view all members set aside for ministry in baptism. The statement reads the doctrine of the priesthood of all believers to mean that the ministry of the church in the world takes place through the believers. Ministry as centered around proclamation of the Word and the celebration of the sacraments naturally takes place primarily within the church.

Van Ruler's understanding of the offices as set within the kingdom asks particularly of the Reformed churches: do the three offices exist *only* to enable the members of the church to their ministry? Is the deacon not set in ministry beyond the church? Or is the deacon in ministry only to enable others to engage in their diaconal ministry? Is the elder in ministry only in the governance of the church and the discipline of its members? Does the elder's ministry extend into the community? Does the church council, elders and deacons, have anything to say *to* the civil powers in the community? Is preaching only to the gathered believers, or does it echo from the "sounding board" of the church into the world?

There are two critical questions to be put at this point. First, if office is exercised in and for the church, does God use office in any way in the kingdom? From a Van Rulerian perspective one inquires about the theological root of the office. If office is rooted in baptism, one can indeed say that it rises in Christ and through the Spirit. But if the Spirit ranges, as Van Ruler contends, beyond the church and indeed ahead of the church, then the rooting of ministry in baptism is limiting indeed. Van Ruler suggests that the Reformed might consider the root of the offices in the apostle, and so to understand the apostolicity of the church in a particular way.[51]

Second, when ministry emerges from the baptized, one must ask how the church is sustained from without. One can, of course, argue that every believer is qualified to interpret scripture's story for the church. But the danger of exchanging the human's deepest commitments for God's Word is always present. Office is the claim that it is *God's* Word that comes to the community and that that the community can only live by the presence of the living Other.

5. Put another way, Van Ruler compels one to ask of the joint statement whether it makes a clear that there is a difference in *kind* between the ministry that comes with baptism and the ministry that comes with ordination. That is, the ministry denoted by office is not a particularization of the ministry of all believers. In his discussion of the office of believer, Van Ruler agrees that the believer has a ministry. He can even speak of the "office" of the believer in a qualified sense (see above, 4.4). Even if one refrains from maintaining that ordination entails an ontological change in the ordinand, one must insist that office is more than a function of the community of faith. The office of minister of the Word comes *to* the believer. The joint statement acknowledges this concern when it concedes that the office has a "special character": "While we do not contend that one particular form of this office has divine sanction to the exclusion of others, we do hold the office itself to be an expression of the will of God for the church" (SM, 5.2). We recognized at the outset of this chapter that the joint statement does not pretend to articulate a full doctrine of office. However, the question we put at this point is *how* is the office an "expression of the will of God for the church."

6. In the joint statement office is singular. Only one office is spoken of, the pastoral office. Ministry is plural as it emerges from baptism; all believers share in ministry. But insofar as office can be understood as used by God as God comes to the church, only the pastoral office comes into view. Elders and deacons are acknowledged as "valid" within the statement that the churches "affirm and recognize the validity of one another's ministries" (SM, 10). However,

---

[51] In fact, in one place Van Ruler explicitly rejects the notion that even the "office of the believer" is to be founded in baptism (or even in regeneration). Baptism is but a sign and seal of God's work through the Spirit, through predestination by virtue of the covenant (*Bijzonder,* 41, 42).

as we have seen above, they take their place within a theology of office only within a "broader ministerium." A Van Rulerian doctrine of ministry that resolutely holds to the plurality and the irreducibility of the offices would challenge the Reformed partners to the conversation. Have they ceded not only an office (the elder) or offices that are precious to a particular religio-historical heritage, but in fact have they given up a theological understanding of the work of the Holy Spirit and of the nature of the church? Have they lost a sense of the Spirit's work as irreducibly plural and the expression of that plurality in the offices? And does God come to the church not only in the way of Christ's salvific presence but in the Spirit's work of sanctification and glorification? If the Reformed churches hold to such an understanding of office, it is difficult to see how they could give up their plural offices and how they could progress ecumenically much further than "full communion." This is not to suggest that the Reformed partners are prepared to make that step. It is, however, to ask whether the Reformed partners are fully cognizant of what is at stake.

For example, a Van Rulerian perspective suggests that if office is singular, the inclination is to see it from solely a Christological perspective in such a way that office becomes the goal rather than a means. That is, the goal of the believer is not to be human but to enter union with the divine. I do not intend to suggest that either the Reformed or the Lutheran churches in fact betray such a stance in their theological confessions or commitments. An approach fully aware of Van Ruler's questions would, however, ask that question when the plurality of offices threatens to disappear.

7. Bishops are acknowledged as they are found within Lutheran churches. The joint statement, perhaps carelessly, notes in passing that bishops hold an office (SM. 6.1). However, this can only be understood within the broader Lutheran framework that acknowledges, in fact, only the one office. In the joint statement, bishops are not laden with the character ascribed to them in an episcopal understanding of office. Rather, as being responsible for "oversight," bishops are seen to function in a similar manner as the corporate "bishop" within Reformed church orders. This is not surprising from the Lutheran side, given that the ELCA officially declared that the "ministry of bishops be understood as an expression of the pastoral ministry."[52] In the language of office, this is an expression of the Lutheran commitment to a singular office.

[52]"Together for Ministry," 17.

In this way, the joint statement describes a state of affairs in which it is possible for Lutheran and Reformed churches to acknowledge each other's ministries as valid. However, the "office" of oversight as described in this document leaves unanswered the question of how these churches can and will enter conversation with churches with a fundamentally different understanding of office. This is the case as the churches engage with those churches that hold to the three-fold office of bishop, presbyter, and deacon. For the latter understanding of office emerges from a different understanding of office and hence of the church.

7.4 Van Ruler's Contribution to the North American Discussion

Not only does a Van Rulerian understanding of office put critical questions to a particular ecumenical statement. His perspective can also provide new trajectories for the discussion on office. Van Ruler can also help the Reformed, in particular, clarify their own doctrine of ecclesiastical office. From the outset the way that he situates office within God's original and ultimate purposes signals what is at stake in the discussion on office. While it is likely that he would applaud the convergence that has occurred not only in Europe but in North America between Lutheran and Reformed churches, his theological project would caution against a premature closure of the discussion of "ministry." We can venture the following assessment of the state of the conversation with Van Ruler as a theological guide.

First, the convergence on ministry that allowed the two traditions to declare that their various understandings of ministry were not church-dividing was possible because the two traditions could and did find a theological consensus that formed a framework within which a common doctrine of ministry could be established. This is not surprising given that the two traditions emerge from the continental Reformation and share a fundamental theological commitment around the confession of "salvation through Christ alone." With the related doctrines of an alien justification and *sola scriptura*, the two traditions could concur on the "pastoral office," that of ministry of Word and sacrament. Likewise, a common doctrine of vocation as well as the agreement that ministry is oriented toward the kingdom of God enabled the two traditions to place ministry within the context of this world.

The very fact, however, that it is this theological framework that allows the two traditions to find consensus on ministry suggests that because the discussion must perforce be ecclesiological, discussions with other communions may prove to be difficult. Or, to put it another way, they will be difficult to the extent that the Reformed and Lutheran churches remain faithful to their own ecclesiological commitments. On the one side are discussions with those of a more "free church," or congregational commitment. Van Ruler has allowed us to see that theological matters are at stake. To what extent and how is revelation communicated to the human? Where and how is the Spirit of God at work? And does God's intention take purchase in history, in institutions, in cultures, in states, as well as in the human being? On the other side are churches of an episcopal order. Again Van Ruler reminds us that theological issues are at stake. To what extent is the Christ who comes to the world from a "higher" reality? For that matter, to what extent is creation at issue in God's salvific action in Christ? Such are ecclesiological dimensions that must be kept in mind in the discussion.

This in turn places the limits of the consensus in question. This is our second comment. We noted above that both traditions claimed that God allowed a certain freedom in how the churches shaped the ministry that was entrusted to them. The freedom created by the gospel is indeed a profound heritage of the Reformation church. Nonetheless, one must always ask about the shape of that freedom within God's greater purposes. Van Ruler reminds the church that discussions of office not only must but can only take place within a world of institutions, culture, history. We have to do with "things." And if God uses such "things" as scripture, liturgy, and offices, then how humans use them is not a matter of indifference. For that reason alone it is important to clarify what the church means by "office" and "ministry." And since in the larger ecumenical context those terms are used in profoundly different ways by different communions, it is incumbent upon the partners to the discussion to engage in a theological discussion that may, itself, go beyond the limits of a doctrine of the church. And indeed, it must surpass such limits. At issue is not human freedom. It is God's freedom to use the church as a means in God's hands as God works toward God's original and ultimate intentions. That claim stands at the heart of a Reformation understanding of the church. It is the freedom of obedience.

It is divine freedom that forces the discussion to inquire as to the place of the church in God's economy. This is our third point. Van Ruler's theological understanding that the offices are not a function of the church but are used by God in the accomplishment of God's intentions makes clear that the church takes its place within the divine economy. This provokes us to challenge the vocabulary of the discussion. The use of the term "ministry" allows the churches to talk about both ordained and nonordained ministry. And it is in fact the case that the ministry of the *church* is neither limited to nor coextensive with the ordained ministries. It also enables a discussion of the ministry of all God's people. However, to subsume the more discrete notion of office within the more general idea of ministry does not allow the churches to clarify the theological question that one like Van Ruler raises. I do not intend to enter a special plea for the term "office." But however designated, the question remains whether God uses something like an "office" as God constitutes the church and works in God's world. Such discussion can only be salutary as the churches engage in the broader conversation over the ordained ministry. For it is the case that some churches will argue that the ordained ministry is only a particularization of the ministry of the baptized, while other churches will insist on the three-fold ministry as summarized in the *episcopos*. Van Ruler reminds us that the Reformed churches offer a third, theologically robust, option.

Fourth, as we have continually attempted to show, the question of the relation of the offices will raise fundamental theological questions about God and God's action with the world. We noted in the opening chapter of this work that the contemporary discussion of office is trinitarian at heart. We have seen that Van Ruler's theological vision of office is itself trinitarian. Our analysis of the Lutheran-Reformed joint statement has shown how it advances that notion as it delineates the work of both the Messiah and the Spirit. Van Ruler's notion of office can assist in the unpacking of how this discussion can be advanced. As the offices represent Christ, they express the objective nature of salvation. How God intends to rule the church is freed from human temptation to identify the stirrings of the human spirit with that of God's Spirit. The God who came to the world in the Messiah and the God who reigns through the ascended Messiah is the one who not only saves but who rules. Furthermore, the Christ who comes not simply from the past but from the future to make manifest the kingdom of God will ask the question of the church's apostolicity in a new way. It will set the church as much in expectation of the reign of God as in memory of the ways of God in a past.

However, the matter cannot rest there. Van Ruler pushes beyond the objective, the *extra nos*. His doctrine of the Holy Spirit shows God not only objectively other but "dwelling" in the present. This is not to continue the division of "subjective-objective." It is rather to embrace both ends of that binary description within the active work of God. In fact, Van Ruler's theology compels the contemporary discussion to ask how it is to think of the Holy Spirit. It is not only how the Spirit acts in and with the offices, but the place and work of the Spirit in God's economy. The discussion of office will not proceed very far until the partners in the discussion are ready to expose not only their understandings of the person and work of the Holy Spirit, but also to surface how ecclesiastical life and practice are themselves expressions of a particular doctrine of the Spirit.

Thus far Van Ruler has provided a lens through which one can observe trinitarian commitments within the Lutheran-Reformed conversation and subsequently to expect those commitments to be present in ecumenical discussions of office. But Van Ruler's trinitarian understanding of office challenges the present conversation not only formally but also materially. He resists any reduction of the three persons within the Trinity and consequently insists that the persons of the Trinity are differently implicated in how God uses the offices. For that reason, an approach that takes his view seriously would likewise resist the reduction of office either to the work of the Son or to that of the Spirit. And for that reason alone, Van Ruler would resist an approach to office that sees in the office an *alter Christus simpliciter*. A Van Rulerian approach would, in fact, insist that the Spirit's role be taken with full seriousness not simply as an *alter Christus*, but, he puts it, as God a third time, God's work in the Messiah now extended and expanded, "poured out" into God's created reality. Van Ruler forces the discussion to a serious discussion of the Holy Spirit. And that means, as our previous discussion has shown, not only a discussion of the relation of Spirit to office, but of a full doctrine of the Spirit, and consequently of a renewed understanding of God.

Van Ruler's theology of office would then, fifthly, challenge Reformed participants in the conversation by asking about the nature of the three offices in their plurality. Why do the offices of elder and deacon fade in the presence of the office of the minister of the Word? When they remain in their distinct plurality, the Spirit is understood in a particular way. It is the Spirit's work beyond the work of the Messiah in salvation, the Spirit's work in extending beyond salvation to sanctification, and thus to God's creation. When it is God coming to the church through the three offices, and working through the three offices together, then the church is set within the horizon of the kingdom of God, which is to say in another way that it is set within the creation now saved.

That said, Van Ruler's approach thereby asks whether the doctrine of office takes creation with sufficient seriousness. We remain within the trinitarian dynamic of God's economy, for now it is the

Father as the creator who works through the Son and the Spirit as God uses the offices. If the offices (or more likely office) exists to "rescue" the creature from its created nature, then God would come to the creature in a certain way. But it is quite different when the offices exist and function beyond salvation in the world and history as God's beloved creation.

This challenge from Van Ruler to the Reformed churches poses the question within a historical framework. Reformed churches have understood that God was at work shaping their churches. Their confessions expressed a commitment to the offices of minister, elder, and deacon. Were these offices only accidental, or were they the product of the Spirit working in and through history? Put most strongly, was the religion of the Reformation a mistake? Contemporary heirs to the Reformation must ask that question in the context of office. For office, at least as Van Ruler describes it, opens one to a way of life established by the God in Christ who freely met God's church in Word and sacrament, and who was Lord not only of the life of the individual, nor of the church, but of the entire human community, secular as well as sacral. Was that understanding theologically demanded?

And indeed one might ask whether Van Ruler's understanding does not suggest that the old Reformed notion of the three offices, rooted in a reality that is itself pluralistic, fits particularly well within the so-called "post-modern" culture. The term "post-modern," while notoriously ambiguous, describes at the least a culture that is allergic to unitary thinking and to the uniformity of a single theory. Van Ruler's understanding of the Spirit's work as prismatically expanding to engage the created order in a wide variety of ways is itself reflected in an understanding of office that is irreducibly plural. A Van Rulerian approach would not insist that the offices take any particular shape. There is nothing fundamental about the number three nor the three offices themselves. The sovereignly free God can establish and use any "office." What is essential is that God's Spirit can and does work in ways that are irreducibly many.

Writing from a Reformed perspective in the Netherlands, M.E. Brinkman suggests that the issue among the churches should not be framed by asking how much diversity unity can bear, but instead by asking "how much diversity is necessary in order to be able to guarantee unity."[53] When he goes further to ask, "Who defends this unity in the midst of all this diversity?" his final answer is that "above

---

[53] "A Different Kind of Ecumenism," 104.

all, it is the work of the Spirit of God, which blows where it will."[54] I suggest that this is precisely where Van Ruler has been tacking.

An emphasis on the offices of elder and deacon further challenges the peculiar appearance of a simultaneous growth of both laitization and clericalism in North American ecclesiastical culture. The offices of elder and deacon are not "lay ministries." The Reformed approach understands these offices as fully part of the ordered ministry of the church. They are not, however, part of the professional leadership of the church. Elders and deacons live and work in the secular reality. And yet in Van Ruler's approach, they fully represent the triune God to the church and in the world. Together with the minister of the Word, they form an approach that is personal (elders, deacons, and ministers are persons) but also communal and plural at the same time.

The joint statement under consideration in this chapter contains hints of this approach when it speaks of a "ministerium" that consists of elders and deacons along with ministers of the Word (SM, 8.1). The RCA in a study on "faithful consistories" put it more pointedly when it speaks of a "pastorate" that consists of minister, elder, and deacon.[55] A fuller conversation with Van Ruler's doctrine of ecclesiastical office can encourage a Reformed insistence that the offices of elder and deacon be taken with full seriousness as offices. His thought gives a robust theological framework for the understanding of the offices. For this reason, the offices need not be seen as little more than historical remainders from an earlier, nay even simpler, era.

---

[54] "A Different Kind of Ecumenism," 104.

[55] *MGS, 2000.* The entire report is found on pp. 280-295. The "pastorate" is noted on 290. It is no accident that the principle author of this study, Paul R. Fries, is a student of Van Ruler and is one of North America's foremost interpreters of Van Ruler's thought.

CHAPTER 8

An Evaluation of Van Ruler's Theology of Office

In the final sentence of 1.4 above, I asked whether Van Ruler offered a theology of office that was both usable and theologically valid. The previous chapter answered the first question in the affirmative; a review of the Reformed discussion of office in the framework of ecumenical discussion disclosed how a Van Rulerian understanding of office offered a challenge to the Reformed churches in their discussions of ministry. In this chapter we turn to the second of the two questions: is Van Ruler's doctrine office theologically valid?

This chapter concludes our inquiry. But it can be said to "conclude" only to the extent that it brings this work to an end. It does not conclude by summarizing Van Ruler's doctrine of office; that has been done at a number of points throughout this study. But it also does not conclude in that it does not round off Van Ruler's theology of office by tying up whatever loose ends may have emerged. Instead, I will suggest that this study proposes still more questions to others who desire to probe Van Ruler's theology more deeply or from newer angles.

8.1 Aporiae in Van Ruler's Theology of Office

A number of difficulties present themselves in Van Ruler's theology of office.

First, Van Ruler is not always as clear and consistent as one would like when he presents the individual offices. For example, he will claim in one place that the minister of the Word has as his sole task the proclamation of the gospel. That is clear if it stands alone. But he will maintain, following Hoedemaker, that the minister also has as his task the ministry of the Word. Given Van Ruler's understanding of the place of law and the setting of the office within the kingdom of God, this makes a great deal of sense. But this appears at least to be inconsistent. This would appear to be important in those instances when Van Ruler argues that the office is necessary because it communicates the atonement, and thus salvation, to the believer.

Likewise, Van Ruler will say any number of times that the elder's primary task is home visitation. Still, the minister of the Word enters that discussion as well as Van Ruler reports that the minister assists in home visitation. And he goes so far as to preach at the installation of an assistant minister a sermon that has as its main topic home visitation, thus clearly indicating that visitation is the primary ministerial task of this *minister*.[1]

Does this apparent inconsistency constitute a crippling objection to Van Ruler's theology of office? I think not. While in the first instance Van Ruler is not clear about the preacher's task, and indeed that salvation must be communicated in proclamation, the main thrust remains for Van Ruler. God's Word both of salvation *and* of command comes to the church and to the believer from without. God works with the believer both to save and to sanctify. And the believer, gathered in church, continually needs to hear both. And more, the Word that echoes from the "sounding board" into the world as the locus of God's kingdom, must come from the God who uses humans as instruments to voice that Word in the world.

It is crucial to see what is at stake for Van Ruler when he insists that God works through a variety of offices, each with its own task. This is God who comes to this world in a plurality of ways. It is God in God's trinitarian reality and *as* trinitarian reality who is active both as God constitutes the church and as God acts beyond the church in history. If office could be reduced to one, by any scheme, that would mean that God comes not by means of the Spirit who, as Van Ruler is at pains to insist, not only extends but expands God's work. When the offices come in their particularity, not only to save, as the office of minister of the Word would emphasize, but to sanctify and to glorify, that is, when the offices come in their plural reality, they enable the church to exist as sign of the kingdom of God in the world. Together they constitute the church as a paradigmatic institution that in itself instantiates a community that issues not only from the multifarious

---

[1] See above, 5.1.1, note 24.

reality of creation, but is called into existence from the reality of a God who acts in a multiple manner and does so in a trinitarian way. That is, God acts as Father, Son, and Spirit in, one might say, a perichoretic way.

Second, Van Ruler is clear that the offices belong together. As three they exist in tensile relation. Together, as offices, they form the church *in nuce*. Indeed, the minister cannot exist without the elder alongside, nor the elder without the minister nor either without the deacon. That said, however, Van Ruler says very little about the work of elders together or deacons together. Reformed church orders work with boards of elders and boards of deacons. To what extent is their mutual presence and activity *ambtelijk*, of the office?

This reservation, likewise, seems hardly crippling. It indicates more a lacuna than a theological mistake. One can easily view both elders and deacons both in council and in action as executing the central tasks of their office. A church need only be cautious not to allow the offices, in council, to accede to the temptation to act on their own, apart from the other offices of the church. Otherwise, the offices collapse into a functional singularity, thus violating Van Ruler's commitment to plurality and, consequently, no longer symbolically involved in the Spirit's multifarious work.

Third, it is clear that for Van Ruler the office of bishop cannot be grafted onto a synodical-presbyterial system, for in so doing one violates the very system. It must be noted, however, that it is a particular *kind* of bishop that is in view, the bishop as the office-bearer in which subsists the other offices of presbyter and deacon. In that case, it would be very difficult indeed to "mix" the system.[2] It is just this impasse that is given expression in the ministry section of BEM.

However, the notion of bishop is not unambiguous. Bishops may be, and have been, understood in different ways. The Lutheran bishop, as he or she appeared in the previous chapter, is of a different kind than an Episcopal bishop, or at least as suggested in the Joint Statement on Ministry under discussion there. To the extent that the notion of bishop is not laden with the understanding that Van Ruler places on the bishop, a theology of offices does not necessarily preclude the bishop. In fact, the discussion of the notion of bishop is currently on the agenda of the ecumenical conversation, and although Reformed churches may be reluctant to enter that conversation, the conversation is moving ahead in any case.

---

[2] See J. Kronenberg, "Een episco-presby-gational kerkmodel," in *Geen kerk zonder bisschop?*, 258-265.

This question to Van Ruler's doctrine of office also need not be crippling. In fact, a Van Rulerian approach would put the question of office at the center. Should the bishop be considered an office? Does it meet the criteria for office within the framework of a theology of the kingdom of God? Might not, for example, the bishop function as a symbol of unity, rather like a permanent president of a synod? And might such a figure function in the stead of a synod on occasion? In fact, might not the bishop find its origin in the office of the apostle much like the other three offices? Or might not a bishop be seen as a missionary figure? These are suggestions only, but they offer possibilities that are not necessarily outside a Van Rulerian understanding.[3]

Understood this way, a church might engage in the ecumenical discussion on office that includes discussion of the office of bishop. However, again it is crucial to see what is at stake for Van Ruler. I have indicated a number of times in this study the reason Van Ruler was allergic to this office. A number of central theological commitments are at stake. What, for example, is God's purpose with the Incarnation? Is it to "lift" the human beyond his or her created reality thereby to locate the essence of the human in union with God? Is the Messiah himself the point of God's action in the Incarnation, or is creation the point? Likewise, one asks about the goal of the human. What does it mean to be truly human? Is it to be drawn beyond one's created reality, or is it to be saved as created? These questions point one toward eschatological considerations. What is God's ultimate intention? The figure of the bishop as Van Ruler understood it presented an answer to these questions that he found troubling. The bishop made concrete God's intention to lift the creature above his or her created reality, to be elevated to a new sort of being. In this way, a theology behind an episcopate so understood was, fundamentally, gnostic. Van Ruler's reflections can remind the church what is at stake in the discussion of bishop within the context of office.

A fourth "loose end" in Van Ruler's theology of office has to do with ordination. One would expect that a discussion of office would focus on ordination. Indeed, we saw in the introduction that ordination is one of the issues currently under discussion. It would be ordination that marks the offices from the broader ministry of the church.

---

[3] Kronenberg, *Episcopus Oecumenicus,* 259-267, reviews alternate models of the office of the bishop and proposes, in his conclusion, a "mixed" church order that could include bishops.

Van Ruler does in fact discuss ordination in a few places. For example, in his lecture entitled, "Viewpoints on Office," he notes that ordination is constitutive for office and then makes what is a typical remark: Ordination is the "communication of the Spirit," and it is the Spirit as communicated and received in the form of promise, belief, and prayer.[4] He expands on this notion in *Reformatorische Opmerkingen,* where he notes again that ordination is the communication of the Spirit and then adds that this must be understood pneumatologically.[5] He continues by noting further that the laying on of hands is to be understood as a bodily gesture that is a way of prayer, of faith, and of the Word.[6]

The "Van Ruler Report" on office adds further reflection when it discusses the laying on of hands, *bevestiging,*[7] and the "indelible character" of office. The laying on of hands expresses continuity or succession in office. It is a "link between those who have stood in office and those who are called to office."[8] However, an office-bearer is "confirmed" in office each time. There is no indelibility in the sense that an ontological change has taken place. The only indelibility that one can speak of would be "God's speaking to this particular human in this particular way."[9] There is no "character" impressed on the human soul. This is an expression of Van Ruler's contention that the sovereign God is free to use persons and so uses them for a discrete period of time.

Nonetheless, the question remains as to the link between ordination and office. Are, for example, ministers to be ordained but not elders and deacons? If that is the case, does that not devalue the "office-character" of elders and deacons and place in jeopardy Van Ruler's entire understanding of office? Or, to ask the question differently, does not the Spirit constitute *all* ministry, not only the ministry of office? And if so, what is it about ordination that links it particularly to office? One might note that Van Ruler's discussion of

[4] "Gezichtspunt," 19.

[5] *Reformatorische,* 110.

[6] *Reformatorische,* 110, 111.

[7] "Bevestiging" is a difficult word to translate into English, or at least into a comparable ecclesiastical action. The term itself can mean "confirmation," "induction," or even "ordination." It is not equivalent to "wijding," or "consecration." But an American church might think of it as an "installation" in office - a distinct action from "ordination."

[8] "Rapport," 72.

[9] *Rapport,* 76.

ordination was limited by the practice of the Netherlands Reformed Church. But the theological question remains open.

The questions raised by ordination, however, need not be fatal. In fact, in his claim that ordination is a work of the Spirit that includes prayer, faith, and the Word, Van Ruler has provided material that can be used to construct a fuller doctrine of ordination in such a way that it reflects his fuller understanding of office. Ordination as prayer for the Spirit to use a particular person in a particular task would respect the freedom of God and would designate or "set aside" that person for a special task. The Spirit would use that person as the Spirit used the apostles in announcing the kingdom of God.

In fact, Van Ruler's doctrine of ecclesiastical office makes clear why ordination belongs on the theological agenda. It is ordination that enables the church to talk about the ministry of all believers while reserving ordination for certain particular ministries. His "high" view of office insists that office comes to the church from God. Office-bearers do not represent the apotheosis of human existence. In ordination, the congregation used by God's Spirit sets certain people aside who will be received on the authority of the ascended and ruling Messiah.

Furthermore, the argument about whether office is one or is many is also central. Does God come to the church in only one way or in many ways? How is one to view not only the minister of the Word, but the elder and the deacon? Do they come authorized by God's Spirit, acting with the authority of the ascended and ruling Messiah?

8.2 A Positive Evaluation of Van Ruler's Doctrine of Office

Despite the reservations noted above, we offer, finally, a positive valuation of Van Ruler's doctrine of office. We make this claim for three reasons. First, his theological description of office offers a clear way of talking about ecclesiastical office. Second, his understanding of office can claim theological coherence. And third, his theological reflections on office open the way to further theological inquiry and discussion.

First, then, Van Ruler's doctrine of office quite clearly offers a way of discerning what counts as office in and for the church and why it counts. An office must (a) emerge from the apostolic work of God as God furthers God's kingdom intentions in the world and (b) must have its centered task as that task emerges from God's intentions. It is not crucial that the offices reflect the three-fold scheme that emerged from the Reformed strand of the Reformation. In fact, in God's sovereign freedom, the number could be more or less and the offices could have a different character. The central matter is that the church acknowledge how God has worked in Christ and through the Spirit in a history that is discernible by the church. Furthermore, Van Ruler has described how this takes place without being trapped by a theology that can do little more than repeat what scripture has reputedly stated. He has offered not only the theology but a theological method as well.

Throughout this work we have observed Van Ruler as he worked through a revelation that found its way into existence, that was rooted in God's definitive action with Israel and in the Messiah but was not encapsulated in a past era. Rather, the Spirit enters the present as God draws creation toward its future. In terms of theological method, that means that the Spirit has been at work in history, with institutions, working through a created reality that includes human reason and experience. God's action in history includes what in retrospect we call the "Reformation" with a new understanding of office. He of course honors the Reformation's insistence on scripture. But he also understands the Reformation itself as tradition, and as such a work of the Spirit. Because there is for Van Ruler a "playfulness" in theological method, his theology opens the discussion beyond an ascetic dependence on what stands in scripture and a traditionalism that insists that antiquity lends validity to ecclesial custom.

Second, his approach can claim theological coherence. We have attempted to make the case that his doctrine of office stands within his entire theological enterprise in toto. For that reason, his notion of office must be judged as one evaluates his theological project. That task exceeds the bounds of this work. We have, however, noted several objections to Van Ruler's thought throughout this work and have attempted to respond to those challenges as they presented themselves. We shall also suggest that Van Ruler's theological project remained unfinished and indicate where further questions might be pursued.

Seen from his theology of the kingdom of God, Van Ruler's theology of office is coherent within that whole. In fact, as we saw at the end of the previous chapter, his early project of investigating the relation of revelation to existence finds one, but hardly the only, point of expression in the offices. God uses the offices as a means to establish the church from out of the future of the kingdom, and, more, the offices to act within the kingdom. The offices symbolize where and how God is at work, coming to the human in history.

Indeed, God comes to history in the concrete realities of its created existence.

Furthermore, it is the offices as caught up within the trinitarian action of God. The offices represent Christ in the representing, which is the Spirit. The offices do not "gather" either humanity or creation into the reality of the Son. Creation does not dissolve as it moves to the eschaton. The offices rather establish or save the human in all his or her created reality that she might join the divine in the great "round dance." It is and shall become a community of joy.

This thesis can be put more strongly to maintain that it would be *inconsistent* for Van Ruler to propose an alternate doctrine of office. It would not, of course, be inconsistent for God to have acted differently in the mediation of salvation, sanctification, and glorification to this creation. God is sovereignly free. The thesis points to Van Ruler's theology or understanding of God's actions with God's beloved creation. The trinitarian God did not act in Christ to correct God's work as Creator. Creation was not a "mistake." In the Spirit God uses institutions—themselves creation—and persons to accomplish God's purposes. Given the options that Van Ruler himself proposes, from the "highest" church view, papal authority, to the "lowest," the Quaker meeting,[10] Van Ruler's theology compels him to the view of ecclesiastical office set out in this study.

Third, Van Ruler's theology is heuristic. As we have seen throughout this inquiry, Van Ruler's doctrine of office pushes the theologian to the heart of theology. As such, it provokes further questions. His insistence that office is an instrument used by God and is not in some way paradigmatic of what God intends the human to become rests on his particular theological anthropology. At issue are such matters as the theological status of the creation. Does creation exist for the sake of salvation, as its precondition? Or does salvation exist on behalf of creation, and consequently, in part, the human? Is it the goal of the human to become "Christ"? Or is it to enter union with Christ?

Van Ruler's theological anthropology in turn leads one directly to the heart of his doctrine of the trinity. Indeed, he was clear on the "necessity" of a trinitarian theology. The issues include, as his essay on "structural differences" between Christology and pneumatology states quite clearly, the nature of Christ as enhypostatic and that of the Spirit as adoptive. Where does the human's nature "subsist"? And how is this drawn into the trinitarian reality of God? Van Ruler is clear, it

[10] *Gesprek*, 21.

seems to me, that he has not worked these matters out into a full theological statement. One wonders, given his theological method, whether they *can* be fully worked out, or whether one is left moving from pole to pole, the skater stepping from side to side. The titles of his essays are telling in themselves: "structural differences," "main lines in a pneumatology," the "necessity of a trinitarian theology." The result is that one can offer a positive evaluation of his doctrine of office by granting that it leads to theological work that remains unfinished. It opens rather than closes the conversation.

In the introduction to this study I noted that the Faith and Order Commission's consensus document, *The Nature and Purpose of the Church*, presented ministry within the divine trinitarian action with the world in the realization of God's kingdom. Van Ruler's theology was an early attempt to articulate a theology of office within those parameters. As one pursues his doctrine of office, one soon finds oneself within a trinitarian discussion of how the Father, Son, and Spirit work. How, for example, is one to understand the continuing work of the ascended Christ in relation to the person and work of the Holy Spirit? The recent revival of theological interest in the doctrine of the Trinity would welcome Van Ruler into the theological conversation. His work impels the children of the Reformation to take a new look at their own heritage, there to engage in ecclesiological conversation within the framework of trinitarian discussion.

8.3 Van Ruler's Doctrine of Office in an American Protestant Context

The utility and theological validity of Van Ruler's doctrine of ecclesiastical office suggest that this theologian, lesser known in the American context, has a great deal to contribute to the American ecclesiological discussion. In this final paragraph of this study, I suggest that this is so and how it is so. First, I must venture a few general comments on the current state of American Protestantism. This is, of course, a bold, nearly presumptuous attempt. The study of American Protestantism extends to a variety of fields, and those not only in theology but in religious studies, cultural studies, sociology of religion, and so forth. Nonetheless, the practice of ministry takes place within a larger context that must, in some manner, be sketched. Second, I venture that Van Ruler offers a distinctive contribution from within a theocentric understanding of ministry. Third, I conclude with a few comments on Van Ruler's contribution to the American churches of Dutch Reformed lineage.

8.3.1 Ministry in the American Protestant Context

American Protestantism presents a bewildering array to the investigator. The Protestant branch of Christianity in the United States includes not only denominations that can easily be located within the family tree that emerged in the sixteenth century, but includes a vast number of independent churches that range from the so-called "mega-church" to countless storefront churches to people who gather in "house churches." Nonetheless we can as a working premise divide the Protestant world into the "mainline" churches and "evangelistic" churches.[11] The concerns and culture of these two types of churches are very different. It is beyond the scope of this work, and the ability of this writer, to describe and to analyze these differences. I indicate them to suggest a certain, perhaps surprising, commonality in approach to the ministry of the church.

Mainline churches in the United States are concerned with a decline in membership and a perceived loss of influence in the culture. While they have been historically at the center of the American culture and thereby turned outward in both cultural and political concerns, and while they have also been at the forefront of missions both in the United States and abroad, they have of late become consumed with concerns over their ecclesiastical identity. This rising anxiety has made these churches ecclesiocentric in their concerns.

Evangelistic churches tend to boast a growth in numbers and in cultural influence. If the mainline churches can be described as ecclesiocentric, evangelicalistic churches tend to be anthropocentric. That is, their primary concern is the salvation of the human individual. They tend to be highly experiential in style, although what counts as experience varies widely.

Both families of traditions talk about ministry in terms of "leadership." Both will ask "how does God lead the church?" It is the task of the leader of the ecclesiastical community to set before it a path that can be understood as God's way for the church. How the churches select and view leaders will differ. Nonetheless, leaders are viewed within the broader context of the concerns of the churches. Leaders may be expected to establish the broader goals of the church,

---

[11] This is, of course, rather arbitrary. By the "mainline" I denote established churches organized into larger denominations that can trace a heritage to one branch of the Reformation or another. The term "evangelistic" is a neologism. I use it to avoid the ambiguous term, "evangelical." The term denotes churches that are largely independent in structure. As a rule they emphasize "soul-winning" as the basic imperative of Christianity.

or they may be expected to embody the goals set by the church. In any case, the churches come to their understanding of leadership through pragmatic arguments.[12] Churches will ask, "What works as leadership?" The question "what works" invokes the further question, "What works for what?" At issue, then, is the purpose of the church, and how one understands leadership is to be discovered within that broader framework. Leadership becomes a function of the larger purpose of the church. This formal mode of consideration holds whether one considers the purpose of the church to be the salvation of individual souls or the gathering of the faithful for the praise of God or witness to public morality.

However, the category "leadership" is so broad as to be nearly unmanageable. Indeed, that has become the problem when ministry is described as leadership of the ecclesial community. Professional ministers under whatever name have become burdened either with all the tasks of leadership or they (or their congregations) are left to pick and choose tasks from a long menu of options. Are they to be preachers, liturgists, administrators, pastoral counselors, teachers, entrepreneurs, evangelists, chaplains, priests, worship coordinators, to name a few? Who is to decide? And by what criterion?[13] Congregations are adrift longing for a leadership they can neither define nor describe. Evangelistic churches, independent by definition, may concur on what counts as leadership, but by the nature of the case that can change as fashion changes. Mainline denominations simply looked confused when nothing seems to "work."

8.3.2. A Theocentric Approach to Office

It has been remarked that nothing is as practical as a good theory. I suggest that Van Ruler offers the North American church a practical theology. It must be clear that "practical theology" in this context does not denote courses in a seminary curriculum on pastoral

---

[12] This is not to make the formal argument that American ecclesiology is in any direct way dependent on the American philosophical tradition known as "pragmatism," although it may well be that such a connection can be made.

[13] Alasdair MacIntyre in *After Virtue: A Study in Moral Theory* (Notre Dame: Univ. of Notre Dame Press, 1981), 24-34, suggests three character types are regnant in contemporary culture: the manager, the therapist, and the virtuoso. I suggest that ministers are expected to fulfill one of the three character types. Ministers are pastoral administrators, pastoral counselors (more recently spiritual directors), or preacher/liturgical leaders.

practice—preaching, pastoral care, administration, and the like—that may or may not include a theological rationale for their practice. Indeed, practical theology is not even the theology of a particular practice. Practical theology articulates *God* in "practice." This is a theology that speaks of God's actions in the world *and* how God engages the human in that practice. That will include the work of the church. It will also include, as this entire study has been at pains to show, what we call the "offices" of the church.

Van Ruler comes, of course, from a particular ecclesial and theological tradition, that of the Reformed churches. The vocabulary of his contribution will sound familiar to Reformed ears, even as he intends it for the ecumenical church. His is what might be called a *theocentric* view of office. It is, as we noted in chapter 4, a theology of office that is predestinarian at heart (4.2.1) and eschatological in scope (4.2.2). If the church is to be "led," it is God who leads it and does so in a way that can be identified and articulated.

By theocentric I am, of course, setting this view of office in contradistinction from an ecclesiocentric and an anthropocentric way of understanding "ministry." However, I intend to indicate more. Theocentric indicates a view of office that is trinitarian at heart. I noted at the end of the previous paragraph (8.2) that Van Ruler's understanding of office is heuristic in that it points toward the theological and ecumenical discussion currently underway on the nature of the church and its ministry.

Van Ruler offers a way of thinking through God's engagement of humans in a ministry that emerges not from the church but from God as God comes to the church in Christ and through the Spirit. Because Van Ruler understands the Spirit as coming out of God's future and not only extending Christ's rule but *expanding* it, the church is led in a multiform way. God acts through the Word in a central way, but God also leads the church through the work of sanctification and glorification as they are articulated in separate offices.[14]

A theocentric approach liberates the church from captivity to itself and its own designs. It frees the church from a concern for its

[14] To cite Van Ruler one last time, and in the framework of his explicit work on office: "One shall have to understand [God's] work not as uniform but as pluriform: there is not only the church, there is also Christ; there is not only the historical Christ, there is also the exalted Christ; there is not only Christ, there is also the Spirit; there are -this is the extreme—not only Messiah and the *pneuma,* there is in them and around them and above them God himself, who acts with his world" (*Bijzonder*, 19).

own survival; indeed it frees the church from the necessity of finding its own reason for existence. That is given to it by the God who uses the church in God's greater intentions.

A theocentric approach also liberates the professional ministry from having to accomplish all tasks that are considered necessary. The God who acts in Christ and through the Spirit (indeed the God whose Spirit is more than the "Spirit of Christ") can and does use a variety of persons to do the multitude of work that God is about with the church and in God's world. Ministers of the Word can be freed to do what the church desperately needs: God's active meeting of the congregation as God calls it to ministry. Likewise, others in the ordained ministry, elders and deacons, can be liberated to be about their tasks.

Subsequently, other ministries of the church can also be given their various tasks. If it is clear that certain ministries come *to* the church, entire varieties of ministries can emerge *from* the church without the burden of having to constitute the church. Ordination can take its proper place, and the church need not be burdened with the notion that ordination implies a "higher" valuation of those persons whose ordination has made them office-bearers.

Van Ruler gives the Reformed churches a perspective from which to enter the ecumenical discussion. It does so with a fully trinitarian understanding of the church.[15] The Reformed need not insist that their approach is the only or the final word. But Van Ruler's contribution enables the Reformed to insist that the offices of the church in a Reformed understanding offer a theological perspective that must be taken into account.

A theocentric approach along the lines suggested by Van Ruler offers further possibilities for the American church as it enters the twenty-first century. The God who uses the offices together to lead the church comes to the church in a variegated manner. This presents a way of governing the church that is one in which the church is engaged in continuing conversation among office-bearers and hence among offices. There is always word and counter-word, engagement of a variety of perspectives. This is a human conversation used by the

[15] Miroslav Volf, *After Our Likeness: The Church as the Image of the Trinity* (Grand Rapids: Eerdmans, 1998), presents a trinitarian ecclesiology. However, he discusses churches of an episcopal type and of a congregational type and ignores Reformed ecclesiology. I suggest that a theocentric understanding of office would issue in a trinitarian ecclesiology in a theologically exciting and responsible way.

trinitarian God in a way that reflects the trinitarian nature of God's self.[16]

Moreover, the offices working together as the "rafters of the cathedral of love" model a way of plurality within unity. This is the unity of the church not in one office, not in confession, but in God as the offices themselves are theocentric. Van Ruler offers a way of engaging a world where plurality threatens to degenerate into a violent pluralism by arguing resolutely that God intends a world of the many, and that God intends to redeem that world not by forcing unanimity but by inviting creation into the great round dance.[17]

8.3.3 Van Ruler and the American Reformed Churches of Dutch Heritage

Van Ruler's theology of office has much to offer the Reformed church on the North American continent of Dutch descent. The two largest churches, the Reformed Church in America (RCA) and the Christian Reformed Church (CRC), live from a divide that took place in the middle of the nineteenth century.[18] While the CRC originated from a division from the RCA, it may be fairly said that such "union" was not of long duration. The mutual history of the two churches includes descendents of the nineteenth-century *Afscheiding. Both* churches include descendents of a Dortian piety that was expressed in

---

[16] This conversation includes conversation around the Word that comes to the church. In a widely read book on preaching, Walter Brueggeman rightly claims that the "preaching task is to guide people...into a serious, dangerous, subversive, covenantal conversation, a conversation that is the root of communion." But then he goes on to add that "it is the preacher's task to carry on both sides of the conversation at the beginning." *Finally Comes the Poet: Daring Speech for Proclamation* (Minneapolis: Fortress, 1989), 49. This, I think is wrong. Van Ruler comes closer with the three offices when it is the task of the elder to ascertain how the Word preached is heard and of the deacon to execute the Word become active in the world. The three offices embody a conversation that is already afoot.

[17] On the plurality and unity of the church see the recent dissertation of R. de Reuver, *Eén kerk in meervoud: Een theologisch onderzoek naar de ecclesiologische waarde van pluraliteit* (Zoetermeer: Boekencentrum, 2004).

[18] On this division see *On the Eve of the Dutch Immigration to the Midwest* (Grand Rapids: Eerdmans, Gerrit J. ten Zythoff, *Sources of Succession: The Netherlands Reformed Church* 1987), and Elton J. Bruins and Robert P. Swierenga, *Family Quarrels in the Dutch Reformed Churches in the Nineteenth Century* (Grand Rapids: Eerdmans, 1999).

a certain "experiential" (*bevindelijke*) religiosity.[19] The RCA, however, was itself a descendant of the public Dutch church and experienced itself as an established church in the American colonies (first "politically," later culturally). In the American context, it soon engaged the American revivalist tradition. Nonetheless, the older tradition would experience tension with the newer, more experiential religion.

Van Ruler's understanding of ecclesiastical office within a trinitarian perspective offers a way that includes both a "high" church understanding of God who comes *to* the church, and an experiential tradition of God whose Spirit works in and through the church. His view of office can assist the conversation among those of a common tradition who have been estranged in mutual incomprehension. Because his view of office can only be understood within a broader theology, it will require the churches to open the theological discussion in a new generation in ways that look not backward, but forward.

Van Ruler shifts the discussion of ministry to one of office and in so doing would enable the American churches to engage in robust theological discussion. We recall, however, that for Van Ruler there is something playful in theological work. Could the American churches join in theological play, in the back and forth, in the dance that while always a duality never degenerates into dualism, and that is, finally, the play of the human before God?

[19] On this development see Al Janssen, "A Perfect Agreement? The Theological Context of the Reformed Protestant Dutch Church in the First Half of the Nineteenth Century," in George Harinck and Hans Krabbendam, eds., *Breaches and Bridges: Reformed Subcultures in the Netherlands, Germany, and the United States* (Amsterdam: VU Uitgeverij, 2000), 54-59, and Allan Janssen, "Reformed and Evangelical: New Questions and Old," in John W. Coakley, ed., *Concord Makes Strength: Essays in Reformed Ecumenism* (Grand Rapids: Eerdmans, 2002), 115-118.

Abbreviations

General works:

Commissie	*Commissie voor de kerkorde*
LM	Ministry section of *Baptism, Eucharist and Ministry*
MGS	*Minutes of the General Synod, Reformed Church in America*
NPC	*The Nature and Purpose of the Church*
SM	"Joint Statement on Ministry"

Van Ruler's works:

"Ambten"	"De Ambten"
"Apostolische"	"Het apostolische en het apostolaire karakter van de kerk"
"Barmhartigheid"	"Bermhartigheid en gerechtigheid"
Belijdende	*De belijdende kerk in de nieuwe kerkorde*
"Betekenis presbyteriaal"	"De betekenis van een presbyteriaal-synodale kerkorde—in de praktijk"
"Bevinding"	"De bevinding in de prekiding"
Bijzonder	*Bijzonder en algemeen ambt*
"Binnenkerkelijk"	"Is het ambt alleen binnenkerkelijk?"
"Bisschop"	"Bisschop of ouderling: De ambtsvraag"
Blij zijn	*Blij zijn als kinderen*
"Briefwisseling"	"Een briefwisseling over het theologie van het ambt"
"Christocratisch"	"Christocratisch ambtsgezag als kerkscheidende factor"
"Christusprediking"	"Christusprediking en rijksprediking"
"Continuïteit"	"Continuïteit in de prediking"
"Doel"	"De kerk is ook doel in zichzelf"

Droom	*Droom en gestalte*
Fundamenten	*Fundamenten en perspectieven van het diaconaat in onze tijd*
"Gezag"	"Het gezag van de kerk"
"Gezag ambt"	"Het gezag van het ambt"
Gezag apostel	*Op gezag van een apostel*
Geloof	*Ik geloof*
"Gelovigen"	"Is er een ambt van de gelovigen?"
Gesprek	*In gesprek met Van Ruler*
"Gezichtspunt"	"Gezichtspunt inzake het ambt"
"Grenzen"	"De grenzen van de prediking"
"Hoofdlijnen"	"Hoofdlijnen van een pneumatologie"
"Huisbezoek"	"Wat is huisbezoek"
"Institutaire"	"De betekenis van het institutaire (in de kerk)"
"Kerkvoogd"	"De kerkvoogd ambtsdrager?"
Kerstening	*Kerstening van het voorbereidend hoger en middelbaar Onderwijs*
"Komende"	"De kerk in de komende cultuur"
"Konijkrijk"	"Het koninkrijk Gods en de geschiedenis"
"Kosmologische"	"De verhouding van het kosmologische en het eschatologische element in de christologie"
"Leek"	"Het priesterschap van de leek : de grens tussen de verantwoordelijkheid van ambtsdrager en leek"
"Mondig"	"De kerk in een zich mondig noemnde wereld"
"Noodzakelijkheid"	De noodzakelijkheid van een trinitarische theologie"
"Openbare"	"Kerstening van het openbare leven"
"Orde"	"De orde van de kerk"
"Ouderling"	"Het ambt van ouderling"
"Ouderling-zijn"	"Het ouderling-zijn in deze tijd"
"Prediker"	"De prediker zij zichzelf bewust van een ernst van zijn taak"
"Prediking"	"De prediking"
"Pretentie"	"De Pretentie van de kerk"

Rapport	*Rapport het kerkelijk ambt*
Reformatorische	*Reformatorische opmerkingen in de ontmoeting met Rome*
Religie	*Religie en politiek*
Sta op	*Sta op tot de vreugde*
"Structuurverschillen"	"Structuurverschillen tussen het christologische en het pneumatologische gezichtpunt"
"Theologisch verschil"	"Het theologisch verschil tussen Rome en de Reformatie"
TW	*Theologisch Werk*
"Uitzicht"	"Uitzicht in het vraagstuk van de leertucht"
"Ultragereformeerd"	"Ultragereformeerd en vrijzinnig"
Vervulling	*De vervulling van de wet*
Verwachting	*Verwachting en voltooiïng*
Volkskerk	*Heeft het nog zin, van "volkskerk" to spreken?*
"Voorstudie"	"Het ambt: een voorstudie voor een boek over het ambt"
Waarom	*Waarom zou ik naar de kerk gaan?*

BIBLIOGRAPHY

I. Van Ruler

The fullest bibliography of Van Ruler's writings in print is found in Ellen M.L. Kempers, *Inventaris van het archief van prof. dr. Arnold Albert Van Ruler (1908-1970)*, Utrecht: Universiteitbibliotheek, 1997. That book includes not only the contents of the archives but Van Ruler's entire oeuvre.

The Van Ruler Archive, located in the Bijzondere Collecties of the Library of the University of Utrecht, contains many unpublished lectures, notes, speeches, and correspondence. The location of works cited from this collection are noted by the folder number. Herewith the author expresses his deepest gratitude to the staff of that institution for their gracious assistance.

A. Books

apostolaat der kerk en het ontwerp-kerkorde, Het (Apostolate of the Church and the Proposed Church Order, The). Nijkerk: G.F. Callenbach, 1948.

Bijzonder en algemeen ambt. (Particular and General Office). Nijkerk: G.F. Callenbach, 1952.

Blij zijn als kinderen: een boek voor volwassenen. (*Being Glad as Children: A Book for Adults*). Kampen: J.H. Kok, 1972.

Calvinist Trinitarianism and Theocentric Politics: Essays Toward a Public Theology. Toronto Studies in Theology, vol. 38. John Bolt, trans. Lewiston/Queenstown/Lampeter: Edwin Mellon Press, 1989.

Christian Church and the Old Testament, The. Trans. Geoffry W. Bromiley. Grand Rapids: Eerdmans, 1971.

Droom en gestalte: Een discussie over de theologische principes in het vraagstuk van Christendom en politiek. (*Dream and configuration: A discussion *of the theological principles of Christendom and politics*). Holland: Uitgevermaatschappij te Amsterdam, 1947.

Fundamenten en perspectieven van het Diaconaat in onze tijd: Referaat gehouden op de ledenvergadering van de Federatie van Diaconieën op 23 sept. 1952. (*Foundations and Perspectives of the Diaconate in Our Time: A Lecture Held at the Meeting of the Members of the Federation of Deacons, 23 September 1952*).

Gestaltwerdung Christi in der Welt: Über das Verhältnis von Kirche und Kultur. (*The Configuration of Christ in the World: On the Relation of Church and Culture*). Neukirchen Kr. Moers: Verlag der Buchhandlung des Erziehungsvereins, 1956.

Heb moed voor de wereld: Zes en dertig morgenwijdingen over het boek Zacharia. (*Have Courage for the World: Thirty-six Meditations on the Book of Zechariah*). Nijkerk: G.F. Callenbach, 1953.

Ik geloof: De twaalf artikelen van het geloof in morgenwijdingen (*I Believe: The Apostles' Creed in Meditations*), 7th ed. Nijkerk: G.F. Callenbach, n.d.

In gesprek met Van Ruler (*In Discussion with Van Ruler*). G.C. Berkhouwer and A.S. van der Woude, eds. Nijkerk: G.F. Callenbach, 1969.

Kerstening van het voorbereidend hoger en middelbaar onderwijs (*Christianizing college training*). Nijkerk: G.F. Callenbach, n.d.

Op gezag van een apostel (*On the Authority of an Apostle*). Nijkerk: G.F. Callenbach, 1971.

Op het scherp van de snede: posthuum gesprek met prof. Dr. A.A. van Ruler (*On the Sharp Edge of the Knife: A Posthumous Discussion with Professor Dr. A.A. van Ruler*). Amsterdam: Ton Bolland, 1972.

Reformatorische opmerkingen in de ontmoeting met Rome (*Reformed Remarks on the Meeting with Rome*). Hilversum: Paul Brand, 1965.

Religie en politiek (*Religion and Politics*). Nijkerk: G.F. Callenbach, 1945.

Sta op tot de vreugde (*Rise Up to Joy*). Nijkerk: G.F. Callenbach, 1947.

Theologisch Werk (*Theological Work*), 6 vols. Nijkerk: G.F. Callenbach, 1969-1973.

vervulling van de wet: Een dogmatische studie over de verhouding van openbaring en existentie, De. (*Fulfillment of the Law: A Dogmatic Study on the Relation of Revelation and Existence, The*). Nijkerk: G.F. Callenbach, 1947.

Verwachting en voltooiing: een bundel theologische opstellen en voordrachten (*Expectation and Completion: A Collection of Theological Essays and Lectures*). Nijkerk: G.F. Callenbach, 1978.

Visie en Vaart (*Vision and Journey*). Amsterdam: Holland Uitgevermaatschappij, 1947.

Waarom zou ik naar de kerk gaan? (*Why Should I Go to Church?*), 2nd ed. Nijkerk: G.F. Callenbach, 1970.

B. Articles, Lectures, and Notes

"ambt, Het" ("Office"). A disputation with H. van der Linde and J.A. Oosterbaan at the City University of Amsterdam, February 5, 1958. Van Ruler Archives. Folder I, 465.

"Ambt en bedieningen" ("Office and ministries"). Lecture at a conference of religious educators. Teylingerbosch Vogelenzang, May 30, 1956. Van Ruler Archives. Folder I, 389.

"Ambt en gemeente" ("Office and congregation"). Lecture for de Nederlandse Christelijke Studentenraad Leiden together with H. Weterman, June 15, 1957. Van Ruler Archives. Folder I, 439.

"ambt tussen Rome en Genève, Het" ("Office between Rome and Geneva"). Speech to the Convent Rome-Reformatie in Leeuwarden, December 8, 1959. Van Ruler Archives. Folder I, 538.

"ambt van ouderling, Het" ("The Office of Elder"). Notes for a lecture to the Presbytery of Hilversum, Autumn 1951. Van Ruler Archives. Folder I, 277.

"Ambt, vergadering en werk der kerk" ("Office, Assembly and the Work of the Church"). *Hervormd Weekblad De Gereformeerde kerk*, May 19, 1938. Pp. 275-276. Van Ruler Archives. Folder I, 115.

"Apostolisch en confessioneel" ("Apostolic and Confessional"). *Gooische Klanken*, February 14, 1948. Van Ruler Archives. Folder I, 229.

"apostolische en het apostolaire karakter de kerk, Het" ("Apostolic and the Apostle-like Character of the Church, The"). Speech to catechetical teachers. Barchem, September 19, 1959. Van Ruler Archives. Folder I, 526.

"Barmhartigheid en gerechtigheid" ("Mercy and Justice"). In *Verwachting en voltooiing*, 161-175.

"betekenis van het institutaire (in de kerk), De" ("Meaning of the Institutional (in the Church, The)"). In *Theologisch Werk*, IV, 176-200.

"betekenis van een presbyteriaal-synodale kerkorde - in de praktijk, De" ("Meaning of a Presbyterial-synodical Church Order in Practice, The"). Speech to the Classis Deventer in De Alerdink. Heino, June 1, 1960. Van Ruler Archives. Folder I, 563.

"bevinding in de prediking, De" ("Experience of faith in preaching"). In *Theologisch Werk* III, 61-81.

"Bisschop of ouderling: de ambtsvraag" ("Bishop or Elder: The Question of Office"). Speech in a cycle of lectures for the congregation after the conversion of Dr. H. van der Linden to Roman Catholicism in Middelburg, January 13, 1961. Van Ruler Archives. Folder I, 585.

"briefwisseling over de theologie van het ambt, Een" ("Correspondence on the Theology of Office"). *Vox Theologica*, No. 27:4 (March 1957), 111-131.

"Christocentriciteit en wetenschappelijkheid in de systematische theologie" ("Christocentricity and Scientific Character in Systematic Theology"). In *Theologische Werk* V, 198-213.

"Christocratisch ambtsgezag als kerkscheiding" ("The Christocratic Authority of Office as Church Dividing") (1969). *Theologish Werk II*, 160-184.

"Christusprediking en rijskprediking" ("Preaching Christ and Preaching the Kingdom"). In *Verwachting en voltooiing*, 43-52.

College "Kerkrecht" ("A Course on Church Order"). Lectures, 1957-1961. Van Ruler Archives. Folder III, 12.

"Continuïteit in de prediking" ("Continuity in Preaching"). In *Theologisch Werk* II, 185-208.

"einde van een huishoudelijke twist, Het" ("End of a Family Quarrel, The"). In *Theologisch Werk* II, 209-219.

"Geloof en prediking" ("Faith and Preaching"). Speech for Roman Catholics and Protestants in De Brug, Amsterdam, February 17, 1961. Van Ruler Archives, Folder I, 591.

"Gestalte der kerk" ("The Shape of the Church"). Notes for the discussion with the Gereformeerden, June 1958. Van Ruler Archives. Folder I, 303.

"gezag in de kerk, Het" ("Authority in the Church"). In *Theologisch Werk* V, 78-84.

"gezag van het ambt, Het" ("The Authority of the Office"). In *Theologisch Werk* III, 9-29.

"Gezichtspunt inzake het ambt" ("Viewpoints on Office"). Speech at the Seminarie Hydepark, May 17, 1968. Van Ruler Archives. Folder I, 726.

"grenzen van de prediking, De" ("Boundaries of Preaching, The"). In *Theologish Werk* III, 30-42.

"Hoe waardeert men de stof?" ("How Does One Value Matter?"). In *Theologisch Werk V*, 9-18.

"Hoofdlijnen van een pneumatologie" ("Main Lines of a Pneumatology"). In *Theologisch Werk* VI, 9-40.
"Is er een ambt van de gelovigen?" ("Is There an Office of Believers?"). In *Theologisch Werk* II, 131-151.
"Is het ambt alleen binnenkerkelijk?" ("Is office only internal to the church?"). *Woord en Dienst*, September 20, 1969, 270.
"Kerk en kerkorganisatie" ("Church and Its Organization"). Lecture for the youth union "Daniël" in Apeldoorn, August 15, 1930. Van Ruler Archives. Folder I, 35.
"Kerk en prediking" ("Church and Preaching"). Lecture to Kerkherstel, afdeling Franeker. Bethel, Franeker, October 16, 1935. Van Ruler Archives. Folder I, 97.
"Kerk en sacramenten" ("Church and Sacraments"). Lecture for Kerkherstel afdeling Franeker, January 28, 1936. Van Ruler Archives. Folder I, 99b.
"kerk in de komende kultuur, De" ("Church in the Coming Culture, The"). In *Theologisch Werk* V, 96-106.
"kerk in een zich mondig noemende wereld, De" ("Church in a World that Calls Itself Mature, The"). In *Theologisch Werk* II, 101-130.
"kerk is ook doel in zichzelf, De" ("Church Is Itself Also an End, The"). In *Verwachting en Voltooiing*, 53-66.
"kerkvoogd ambtsdrager, De?" ("Is the Church Warden an Office-bearer?"). Article written with H. Wagenaar. Van Ruler Archives. Folder I, 450b.
"Kerstening van het openbare leven: Wat kerstening eigenlijk is" ("Christianizing of Public Life: What Christianizing Really Is"). Lecture for the old members of the N.C.S.V. in Utrecht, June 1, 1956. Van Ruler Archives. Folder I, 392.
"koninkrijk Gods en de geschiedenis, Het" ("Kingdom of God and History, The"). In *Verwachting en voltooiing*, 29-38.
"leek in het pastoraat, De" ("Laity in the Pastorate"). Panistische calvinische vergadering, Utrecht, March 28, 1962. Van Ruler Archives, Folder I, 632.
"Methode en mogelijkheden van de dogmatiek, vergeleken met die van exegese" ("Method and Possibilities in Dogmatics compared with that of Exegesis"). In *Theologische Werk* I, 46-99.
"noodzakelijkheid van een trinitarische theologie, De" ("Necessity of a Trinitarian Theology, The"). In *Verwachting en voltooiing*, 9-28.
"orde van der kerk, De" ("Order of the Church, The") (1948). In *Theologisch Werk V*, 124-136.
"ouderling-zijn in deze tijd, Het" ("Existence of the Elder in This Era, Het"). Notes for a lecture for the Provincial Kerkkring of

Amsterdam, April 29, 1953. Van Ruler Archives. Folder I, 297.

"prediker zij zich bewust van de ernst van zijn taak, De" ("Preacher who is Conscious of the Serious Nature of his Task, The"). In *Hoe vindt u dat der gepreekt moet worden?* A. G. Barkey Wolf, ed. 2nd ed. Zwolle: La Rivière & Voorhoeve, 1959, 138-147.

"prediking, De" ("Preaching"). Speech to the Classcale Vergadering Schiedam, May 15, 1957. Van Ruler Archives. Folder I, 433.

"Prediking en ambt: beeld, liturgie, evangelisatie" ("Preaching and Office: Image, Liturgy, Evangelization"). Speech to a circle of intellectuals around ds. S.W. de Vries. Hilversum, February 1, 1961. Van Ruler Archives. Folder I, 584.

"prediking en het persoonlijk geloofsleven, De" ("Preaching and the Personal Life of Faith"). Notes for a lecture to a conference of the church council of Rotterdam, August/September 1949. Van Ruler Archives. Folder I, 247.

"Preekdefinities" ("Sermon Definitions"). In *Theologisch Werk* VI, 120-125.

"pretentie van de kerk, De" ("Pretension of the Church, The") (1958). In *Theologisch Werk* V, 66-77.

"priesterschap van de leek: de grens tussen de verantwoordelijkheid van ambstdrager en leek, De" ("Priesthood of the Laity: The Boundary between the Responsibility of the Office-bearer and the Laity, The"). Notes for a lecture to the Christenstudentenraad, Woudschoten, Ziest, March 19, 1955. Van Ruler Archives. Folder I, 351.

"roeping tot het ambt, De" ("Calling to Office"). Opening lecture, October 4, 1956. Van Ruler Archives. Folder I, 400.

"sacramenten, De" ("The Sacraments"). Notes for a speech to catechetical teachers, May 2, 1956. Van Ruler Archives. Folder I, 387.

"Structuurverschillen tussen het christologische en het pneumatologische gezichtpunt" ("Structural Differences between a Christological and a Pneumatological Point of View"). In *Theologisch Werk* I, 175-190.

"Theologie van het apostolaat" ("Theology of the Apostolate"). In *Verwachting en voltooiing*, 101-123.

"theologische verschil tussen Rome en de Reformatie, Het" ("Theological Difference between Rome and the Reformation, Het"). Notes for a lecture to preachers held in Enschede January 23, 1935, and in Binnen-Wijnend January 18, 1961. Van Ruler Archives. Folder I, 347.

"Uitzicht in het vraagstuk van de leertucht." ("Prospects in the Question of Doctrinal Discipline"). In *Theologisch Werk* V, 137-151.

"Ultragereformeerd en vrijzinnig" ("Ultra-Reformed and Liberal"). In *Theologisch Werk* III, 98-163.

"verhouding van het kosmologische en het eschatologische element in de christologie, De" ("Relation of the Cosmological and the Eschatological Element in Christology, The"). In *Theologisch Werk* I, 156-174.

"verhouding van het predikambt en de plaatselijke kerk, De" ("Relation of the Office of Minister and the Local Church, The"). *Woord en Dienst*, January 21, 1961, 21-22. Van Ruler Archives. Folder I, 587.

"vicaris, De" ("Vicar, The"). A series of articles in *Weekblad van de Nederlandse Hervormde Kerk*, vol. 33. Van Ruler Archives. Folder I, 255.

"voorstudie voor een boek over het ambt, Een" ("Preparatory Study for a Book on Office, A"). Van Ruler Archives. Folder V, 1A.

"Vragen door Bonhoeffer aan de orde gesteld" ("Questions put by Bonhoeffer"). In *Theologisch Werk* V, 171-187.

"Vragen over welke de commissie voor het ambt spreekt" ("Questions that the Commission on Office Addresses"). *Woord en Dienst*, May 17, 1958, 151. Van Ruler Archives. Folder I, 467.

"vreugde van het ambt, De" ("Joy of Office, The"). Speech held at the Classicale Vergadering van Haarlem, October 8, 1957. Van Ruler Archives. Folder I, 445.

"vrouw in de ambt, De" ("Women in Office"). A preparatory study. Van Ruler Archives. Folder V, 9.

"Wat is huisbezoek?" ("What is Home Visitation?"). Two lectures for the circle of neighborhood visitors in Hilversum, N.d. Van Ruler Archives. Folder I, 159.

"Wat doet de kerk? Prediking des woord en sacrament" ("What Does the Church Do? Preaching of the Word and Sacrament"). Lecture, Evangelization, Veenendaal, October 4, 1945. Van Ruler Archives. Folder I, 182.

"Welke weg moeten wij gaan terzake van het ambt" ("What Course Must We Take in the Matter of Office"). *Woord en Dienst*, May 31, 1958, 167-168. Van Ruler Archives. Folder I, 468.

"werk van de commissie voor het ambt, Het" ("Work of the Commission on Office, The"). *Woord en Dienst*, April 19, 1958, 119. Van Ruler Archives. Folder I, 466.

"wezen en de betekenis van de kerk, De" ("Essence and the Meaning of the Church, The"). Studium Generale, November 19, 1958. Van Ruler Archives. Folder I, 481.

"zendingstaak der gemeente, De" ("Missionary Task of the Congregation, The"). *Cheribon* (Orgaan voor de classicale zendingsvereeniging binnen de classis Franeker) 24 (November, 1934). Van Ruler Archives. Folder I, 90.

C. Sermons

"Diaconie" ("The Diaconate"). March 4, 1943. Hilversum. Van Ruler Archives. Folder IV, 459.

"dominee en zijn gemeente, De" ("Minister and His Congregation, The"). June 19, 1949. Hensbroek. Van Ruler Archives. Folder IV, 657.

"Dubbele praedestinatie" ("Double Predestination"). February 6, 1944. Hilversum. Van Ruler Archives. Folder IV, 495.

"Eerst steenlegging der gemeente" ("The First Laying of the Foundation of the Congregation"). January 15, 1939. Kubaard. Van Ruler Archives. Folder IV, 280.

"gezag van de apostel, Het" ("Authority of the Apostle, The"). September 17, 1961. Utrecht. Van Ruler Archives. Folder IV, 827.

"Gemeente en ambten" ("Congregation and Offices"). May 18, 1941. Hilversum. Van Ruler Archives. Folder IV, 388.

"Hemelvaart en wederkomst" ("Ascension and Second Coming"). May 30, 1935. Kubaard. Van Ruler Archives. Folder IV, 95.

"Huisbezoek" ("Home Visitation"). February 21, 1943. Hilversum. Van Ruler Archives. Folder IV, 457.

"Leiderschap" ("Leadership"). July 21, 1947. Amsterdam. Van Ruler Archives. Folder IV, 607.

"mysterie van de drieëenheid, Het" ("Mystery of the Trinity, The"). January 5, 1946. Hilversum. Van Ruler Archives, Folder IV, 1016.

"Naar de eenheid van de kerken" ("Toward the Unity of the Churches"). January 22, 1961. Haarlem. Van Ruler Archives. Folder IV, 819.

"nabijheid van Jezus Christus bij zijn gemeente in het ambt, De" ("Nearness of Jesus Christ with his Congregation in the Office, The"). April 24, 1938. Kubaard. Van Ruler Archives. Folder IV, 237.

"Nederlandse Geloofsbelijdenis, Artikel 36" ("The Belgic Confession of Faith: Article 36"). September 22, 1947. Hilversum. Van Ruler Archives. Folder IV, 1010.

Nieuwjaar en ambt" ("New Year and Office"). January 1, 1947. Hilversum. Van Ruler Archives. Folder IV, 620.

"predikers gaan uit, De" ("Preachers Go Out"). January 5, 1947. Hilversum. Van Ruler Archives. Folder IV, 621.

"prophetische taak der gemeente, De" ("Prophetic Task of the Congregation, The"). July 12, 1936. Kubaard. Van Ruler Archives. Folder IV, 148.

"Roeping der leiders" ("The Calling of Leaders"). August 13, 1939. Kubaard. Van Ruler Archives. Folder IV, 312.

"Schrift-ambt-gemeente" ("Scripture-Office-Congregation"). March 6, 1938. Eexta. Van Ruler Archives. Folder IV, 228.

"teekenen van de prediking, De" ("Signs of Preaching, The"). January 11, 1948. Hilversum. Van Ruler Archives. Folder IV, 646.

"Toekomst des heils" ("The Future of Salvation"). October 8, 1939. Kubaard. Van Ruler Archives. Folder IV, 316.

"Verscheidenheid in de gemeente" ("Diversity in the Congregation"). June 26, 1938. Kubaard. Van Ruler Archives. Folder IV, 249.

"Vraag en antwoord 54" ("Question and Answer 54"). February 21, 1937. Kubaard. Van Ruler Archives. Folder IV, 916.

"Vraag en antwoord 55" (Question and Answer 55). 28 February 1937. Kubaard. Van Ruler Archives. Folder IV, 917.

"waarheid der verkiezing, De" ("Truth of Election, The"). April 7, 1940. Hilversum. Van Ruler Archives. Folder IV, 344.

"Wat God doet en wat de menschen doen" ("What God Does and what Humans Do"). May 28, 1944. Hilversum. Van Ruler Archives. Folder IV, 501.

"Woord en de wereld, Het" ("Word and the World, The"). September 17, 1939. Kubaard. Van Ruler Archives. Folder IV, 314.

D. Correspondence

From:

P. Aalders, August 16, 1956. Van Ruler Archives, Folder VI/A.

Annie Lekkerkerker, May 15, 1958. Van Ruler Archives, Folder VI/A.

Theologische Faculteit der Amsterdamse Studenten, December 6, 1957. Van Ruler Archives, Folder VI/B.

II. Secondary Literature on Van Ruler

Aalders, P.F.Th. "De Hilversumse theologenklub" ("The Hilversum Club of Theologians"). *Areopagus* 14, no. 2 (1981), 18-20.

Aalders, P.F.Th. "Religie en politiek" ("Religion and Politics"). In *Woord en werkelijkheid over de theocratie: Een bundel opstellen in dankbare nagedachtenis aan Prof. A.A. van Ruler* (*Word and Reality on Theocracy: Essays in Thankful Remembrance of Professor A.A. van Ruler*). Nijkerk: G.F. Callenbach, 1973, 9-27.

Arendhorst, J.W. *Woonsteden van God: A.A. van Ruler's pleidooi voor een relatief zelfstandige pneumatologie* (*Dwelling Places of God: A.A. van Ruler's Plea for a Relatively Independent Pneumatology*). Doctoraalscriptie, University of Utrecht, 1978.

Balke, W. "Hoedemaker, Gunning, Kraemer en Van Ruler." In *De kerk: wezen, weg en werk van de kerk naar reformatorische opvatting*. Ed. W. van't Spijker, W. Balke, K. Exalto, L. van Driel. Kampen: De Groot Goudriaan, 1990, 202-230.

Balke, W. and Oostenbrink-Evers, H., eds. *De commissie voor de kerkorde (1945-1950): bouwplan, agendastukken en notulen van de vergaderingen ter voobereiding van de nieuwe kerkorde (1951) van de Nederlandse Hervormde Kerk* (*The Commission on Church Order (1945-1950): Plan, Reports, and Notes of the Meetings in Preparation of the New Church Order (1951) of the Netherlands Reformed Church*). Zoetermeer: Boekencentrum, 1993.

Berkouwer, G.C. "Over de theologie van A. A. van Ruler" (*On the Theology of A. A. van Ruler*). *Gereformeerd Weekblad*, April 23, April 30, May 7, May 14, May 21, May 28, and June 4, 1971.

Bolt, John. "The Background and Context of Van Ruler's Theocentric (Theocratic) Vision and its Relevance for North America." In *Calvinist Trinitarianism and Theocentric Politics*. Lewiston: Edwin Mellen, 1989, ix-xliv.

Brinkman, M.E. "Pluraliteit in de leer van de kerk? (Een analyse en evaluatie van enkele kernpunten uit de ekklesiologie van

Bavink, Van Ruler,Barth en Rahner)" [*Plurality in the Doctrine of the Church? (An Analysis and Evaluation of a Number of Central Points from the Ecclesiology of Bavink, van Ruler, Barth, and Brunner)]. Geloofsmanieren: Studies over pluraliteit in de kerk.* J.M. Vlijm, ed. Kampen: J.H. Kok, 198, 127-162.

Fries, Paul Roy. *Religion and the Hope for a Truly Human Existence: An Inquiry into the Theology of F.D.E. Schleiermacher and A.A. van Ruler with Questions for America. N.P., 1979.*

Fries, Paul R. "Spirit, Theocracy and the True Humanity: Salvation in the Theology of A.A. Van Ruler." *Reformed Review,* vol. 39 (Spring, 1986), 206-213.

Fries, Paul R. "Van Ruler on the Holy Spirit and the Salvation of the Earth," in *Reformed Review*, 26, no. 4 (Winter, 1973), 123-135.

Groot, Aart de. "Levensschets van Prof. Dr. A.A. van Ruler." ("Life Sketch of Professor Dr. A. A. van Ruler"). *Inventaris van het archief van Prof. Dr. Arnold Albert van Ruler (1908-1970)*, Ellen M.L. Kempers, ed. Utrecht: Universiteitbibliotheek, 1997, ix-xvi.

Hasselaar, J.M. and Knijf, H.W. de. "Arnold Albert van Ruler (1908-1970): Zijn leven. Zijn actualiteit." ["Arnold Albert van Ruler (1908-1970): His Life, His Relevance"]. *Areopagus* 14, no. 2 (1981), 60-72.

Heideman, Eugene P. "Van Ruler's Concept of the Church," in *Reformed Review*, 26, no. 4 (Winter, 1973), 136-143.

Hendriks, A.N. *Kerk en ambt in de theologie van A.A. van Ruler.* (*Church and Office in the Theology of A.A. van Ruler*). Amsterdam: Buijten en Schipperheijn, 1977.

Hennephof, A. "Christus, de Geest en de werkelijkheid in de theologie van A.A. van Ruler" ("Christ, the Spirit and Reality in the Theology of A. A. van Ruler"). Scriptie, n.p., 1966.

Hesselink, I. John. "Contemporary Protestant Dutch Theology," in *Reformed Review* 26, no. 4 (Winter, 1973), 67-89.

Hommes, Tjaard G. "Deus Ludens: Christianity and Culture in the Theology of A.A. Van Ruler." *Reformed Review* 26, no. 4 (Winter, 1973), 90-122.

Hommes, Tjaard G. "Sovereignty and Saeculum: Arnold A. Van Ruler's Theocratic Theology." Ph. D. Diss., Harvard University, 1966.

Hoof, Pieter van. *Intermezzo: kontinuïteit en diskontinuïteit in het theologie van A. A. van Rule. Eschatologie en kultuur.* (*Intermezzo: Continuity and Discontinuity in the Theology of A A.van Ruler. Eschatology and Culture*). Amsterdam, Ton Bolland, 1974.

Immink, F.G. "A.A. van Ruler: Sytematicus met hoofd en hart." ("A.A. van Ruler: Systematician in Head and Heart"). In *Inventaris van het archief van Prof. Dr. Arnold Albert van Ruler (1908-1970)*, Ellen M.L. Kempers, ed. Utrecht: Universiteitbibliotheek, 1997, xvii-xxvii.

Immink, Gerrit. "Openbaring en existentie - De betekenis van A. A. van Ruler voor de theologiebeoefening in Utrecht." ("Revelation and Existence—The Significance of A.A. van Ruler for the Practice of Theology in Utrecht"). In *Zo de ouden zongen...: leraar en leerling zijn in de theologiebeofening (tussen 1945 en 2000)*, Jurjen Beumer, ed. Baarn: Ten Have, 1996, 165-182.

Jongeneel, J.A.B. "De apostolaatstheologie van A.A. van Ruler in kontrast met die van J.C. Hoekendijk." ("The Theology of the Apostolate of A.A. van Ruler in Contrast with that of J. C. Hoekendijk"). In *De waarheid is theocratisch: bijdragen tot de waardering van de theologische nalatenschap van Arnold Albert van Ruler*. Gerrit Klein and Dick Steenks ed. Baarn: G.F. Callenbach, 1995, 85-94.

Kempers, Ellen M.L. *Inventaris van het archief van Prof. Dr. Arnold Albert van Ruler (1908-1970)*. Utrecht: Universiteitbiliotheek, 1997.

Knijff, H.W. de. "A.A. van Ruler anno 1995." In *De waarheid is theocratisch: bijdragen tot de waardering van de theologische nalatenschp van Arnold Albert van Ruler*. Gerrit Klein and Dick Steenks, ed. Baarn: G.F. Callenbach, 1995,17-24.

Kruiff, G.G. de "Een adembenemend theologisch experiement" ("A Breathtaking Theological Experiment"). *De waarheid is theocratisch: bijdragen tot de waardering van de theologische nalatenschap van Arnold Albert van Ruler*. Gerrit Klein and Dick Steenks, ed. Baarn: G.F. Callenbach, 1995, 68-75.

Kruis, J.M. van 't. *De Geest als missionaire beweging: Een onderzoek naar de functie en toereikendheid van de gereformeerde theologie in de huidige missionologische discussie.* (*The Spirit as Missionary Movement: A Study in the function and sufficiency of Reformed theology in the contemporary missiological discussion*). Zoetermeer: Boekencentrum, 1997.

Lombard, Christo. *Adama, thora en dogma: die samehang van de aardse lewe, skrif en dogma in die teologie van A.A. van Ruler* (*The coherence of earthly life, Scripture and dogma in the theology of A. A. van Ruler*). Diss., University of the Western Cape, 1996.

Lombard, Christo. "Kontinuïteit en diskontinuïteit in die denke van A.A. van Ruler. 'n Kritiese gesprek met P. van Hoof oor die aktualiteit van die "Intermezzo." M.A. thesis, Universiteit van West-Kaapland, 1983.

Lombard, Christo. "The relevance of Van Ruler's theology." In *The Relevance of Theology for the 1990s*, ed. J. Mouton and B.C. Lategan. Pretoria: Human Sciences Research Council, 1994, 549-569.

Lombard, Christo. "Van Ruler se nalatenskap en relevansie vir vandag" ("Van Ruler, his Heritage and Relevance for Today"). In *Inventaris van het archief van Prof. Dr. Arnold Albert van Ruler (1908-1970),* ed. Ellen M.L. Kempers, xxixli. Utrecht: Universiteitbibliotheek, 1997.

Meent, Jaap van de. *Kerkelijke verandering in perspektief: de toepassing van de methode opbouwwerk binnen de kerk en het denken van A.A. van Ruler.* (*Ecclesiastical Change in Perspective: The Application of the Method of Pastoral Practice within the Church and in the Thought of A. A. van Ruler*). Doctoraalscriptie. Universiteit Utrecht, 1982.

Meeter, Daniel. "The Trinity and Liturgical Renewal." In *The Trinity: An Essential for Faith in our Time*, ed., Andrew Stirling, 207-232. Nappanee, Indiana: Evangel, 2002.

Plaisier, B. "Enige gedachten over de actualiteit van de apostolaatstheologie van A. A. van Ruler." ("A Few Thoughts on the Relevance of the Theology of the Apostolate of A. A. van Ruler"). *De waarheid is theocratisch: bijdragen tot de waardering van de theologische nalatenschap van Arnold Albert van Ruler*, Gerrit Klein and Dick Steenks, eds. Baarn: G.F. Callenbach, 1995, 76-84.

Plaisier, B. *Instrumenteel tussenspel. Van Rulers ecclesiologie onder het gezichtpunt van het apostolaat.* (*Instrumental Intermezzo. Van Ruler's Ecclesiology within the Viewpoint of the Apostolate*). Doctoraal scriptie. Universiteit Utrecht, 1977.

Rapport het kerkelijk ambt van de commissie Van Ruler-dokter. Generale Synode der Nederlandse Hervormde Kerk, 1974.

Rebel, Jacob Jan. *Pastoraat in pneumatologisch perspektief: Een theologische verantwoording vanuit de denken van A. A. van Ruler.* (*The Pastorate in a Pneumatological Perspective: A Theological Account from the Thought of A.A. van Ruler*). Kampen: J.H. Kok, 1981.

Ruler-Hamelink, J.A., van. "500 Pastorieën." ("500 Parsonages"). *Areopagus* 14, no. 2 (1981), 8-11.

Sleddens, W. Th.G. and Wissink, J. "De Structuur van de theologie van dr. A.A. van Ruler: Een inleiding tot zijn denken naar aanleiding van de uitgave van zijn "Theologish Werk." ("The

Structure of the Theology of Dr. A. A. van Ruler: An Introduction to his Thought on the Occasion of the Publication of his 'Theological Work'"). *Bijdragen* 36 (1977), 234-249.

Spanning, H. van. *In dienst van de theocratie: Korte geschiedenis van de Protestantse Unie in de Centrumsgespreksgroep in het CHU.* (*In the Service of Theocracy: A Short History of the Protestant Union and the Central Discussion Group in the CHU*). Zoetermeer: Boekencentrum, 1994.

Suss, René. "Theocratie: Koen presens of zacht futurum van de hoop? Enkele grondlijnen in de politieke theologie van A. A. van Ruler." ("Theocracy: Bold Present or Soft Future of Hope? A Few Foundational Notions in the Political Theology of A. A. van Ruler"). *In de waagschaal,* 14 (1085) 1-3. pp. 21-25, 39-41, 83-87.

Velema, W.H. *Confrontatie met Van Ruler: Denken vanuit het einde.* (*Confrontation with Van Ruler: Thinking from out of the End*). Kampen: J.H. Kok, 1962

Zwaag, K. van der. "Een 'vrijage' met de Bond." ("A 'Courtship' with the Bond"). Available on- line..html http:/out.refdat.nl/series/toonzetters/99042709

III. The Reformed-Lutheran Dialogue

Andrews, James E. and Burgess, Joseph A., ed. *An Invitation to Action: A Study of Ministry, Sacraments, and Recognition.* Lutheran-Reformed Dialogue Series III. Philadelphia: Fortress Press, 1984.

"Called to Common Mission: Official Text." Available www.elca.org/ecumenical/fullcommunion/Episcopal/ccmresources.text.html.

Constitution and Bylaws. United Church of Christ. 1976.

Empie, Paul C. and McCord, James I. *Marburg Revisited: A Reexamination of Lutheran and Reformed Traditions.* Minneapolis: Augsburg, 1966.

Fries, Paul R. "Office and Ordination in the Reformed Tradition." In *An Invitation to Action: A Study of Ministry, Sacraments, and Recognition.* James A. Andrews and Joseph A. Burgess, eds. Philadelphia: Fortress Press: 1984, 90-100.

"Joint Statement on Ministry." In *An Invitation to Action: The Lutheran Reformed Dialogue Series III, 1981-1983,* ed. James E Andrews and Joseph E. Burgess, 24-36. Philadelphia: Fortress Press, 1984.

Manual on Ministry: Perspectives and Procedures for Ecclesiastical Authorization of Ministry. United Church of Christ, 1986.

"Nature of Ecclesiastical Office and Ministry, The." In *The Church Speaks: Papers of the Commission on Theology Reformed Church in America 1959-1984.* James I. Cook ed. Grand Rapids: Eerdmans, 1985, 124-137.

"Nature of the Ministry, The." In *The Church Speaks: Papers of the Commission on Theology Reformed Church in America.* James I. Cook ed. Grand Rapids: Eerdmans, 1985, 115-123.

Nickle, Keith F. and Lull, Timothy F. *A Common Calling: The Witness of Our Reformation Churches in North America Today.* The Report of the Lutheran-Reformed Committee for Theological Conversations, 1988-1992. Minneapolis: Augsburg, 1993.

Quanbeck, Warren A. "Church and Ministry." In *An Invitation to Action: A Study of Ministry, Sacraments, and Recognition.* James A. Andrews and Joseph A. Burgess, eds. Philadelphia: Fortress Press, 1984, 101-107.

"Report of the Committee on Ecclesiastical Office and Ministry." The Acts and Proceedings of the 182nd Regular Session of the General Synod, Reformed Church in America. June 13-17, 1988. pp. 261-280, 130-139, 234-242.

"Theology and Practice of Ordination in the Presbyterian Church (U.S.A.)." In *Selected Theological Statements of the Presbyterian Church (U.S.A.) General Assemblies (1956-1998).* Presbyterian Church (U.S.A.), 1998, 568-616.

"Together For Ministry." Final Report and Actions of the Study of Ministry. Evangelical Lutheran Church in America, 2000. Available www.elca.org/leadership.pdf/Together_for_Ministry.pdf.

IV. Other

Abbott, Walter M., ed. *The Documents of Vatican II* (The America Press, 1986).

Augustine. *On the Trinity: Books 8-15.* Trans. Stephen McKenna. Cambridge Texts in the History of Philosophy. Cambridge: Cambridge University Press, 2002.

Baptism, Eucharist, and Ministry. Faith and Order Paper 111. Geneva: World Council of Churches, 1982.

Bartels, Hendrik. *Tien jaren strijd om een belijdende kerk, de Nederlandsche Hervormde Kerk van 1929 tot 1939.* (*Ten Years Struggle for a Confessing Church, the Netherlands Reformed Church from 1929 to 1939*). 's-Gravenhage: W.P. van Stockum, 1946.

Barth, Karl. "The Christian Community and the Civil Community." In *Community, State, and Church: Three Essays by Karl Barth.* Garden City: Doubleday, 1960, 149-189.

Beek, A. van de. "Over protestantse reacties op de ambtsvisie van het rapport over doop, eucharistie en ambt van de Wereldraad van Kerken." ("On Protestant Reactions to the Vision of office from the Report on Baptism, Eucharist, and Ministry of the World Council of Churches"). *Tussen traditie en vervreemding: Over kerk en christenzijn in een veranderende cultuur* Nijkerk: G.F. Callenbach, 1985, 126-132.

Beker, E.J., and Hasselaar, J.M. *Wegen en kruispunten in de dogmatiek: Deel 5 Kerk en toekomst.* (*Roads and Crossings in Dogmatics: part 5 Church and Future*). Kampen: Kok, 1990.

Benedict, Philip. *Christ's Churches Purely Reformed: A Social History of Calvinism.* New Haven: Yale, 2002.

Berkhof, Hendrikus. "Rapport over het ambt: aangeboden aan de generale synode der Nederlandse Hervormde Kerk." Universiteitbibliotheek, University of Utrecht, Utrecht, the Netherlands, 1969.

Blei, Karel. "Gemeente, ambt en oecumene" ("Congregation, Office, and Ecumene"). *De kerk verbouwen: Dingemans' ecclesiologie critisch bekeken.* P.J. Aalbers, ed. Leidse Lezingen. Nijkerk: C.F.Callenbach, 1989, 49-59.

Blei, Karel. "De receptie van de Lima-tekst over doop, eucharistie en ambt in Nederland" ("The Reception of the Lima Text on Baptism, Eucharist, and Ministry in the Netherlands"). *Nederlands Theologisch Tijdschrift* 40 (1986), 14-43.

Borgmann, Albert. *Crossing the Postmodern Divide.* Chicago: University of Chicago Press, 1992.

Borgt, Ed.A.J.G. van der. *Het ambt her-dacht: De gereformeerde ambtstheologie in het licht van het rapport Baptism, Eucharist and Ministry (Lima, 1982) van de theologische commissie Faith and Order van de Wereldraad van Kerken.* [*Office Rethought: The Reformed Theology of Office in the Light of the Report Baptism Eucharist and Ministry (Lima, 1982) from the Theological Commission Faith and*

Order of the World Council of Churches]. Zoetermeer: Meinema, 2000.

Brinkman, M.E. "Het ambt als heilzaam symbool in onze cultuur."("Office as a Salutary Symbol in Our Culture"). In *Geen kerk zonder bisschop? Over de plaats van het ambt in de orde van de kerk,* Martien Brinkman and Anton Houtepen, eds. Zoetermeer: Meinema, 1997, 97-114.

Brinkman, M.E., "A Different Kind of Ecumenism." In *Rethinking Ecumenism: Strategies for the 21st Century*, Freek L. Bakker, et. al., eds. Zoetermeer: Meinema, 2004, 93-104.

Brinkman, M.E. "Ministry and Sacrament in a Dutch Context." In *From Roots to Fruits: Protestants and Catholics Towards a Common Understanding of the Church*, Martien E. Brinkman and Henk Witte, eds. Geneva: World Alliance of Reformed Churches, 1998, 137-160.

Bronkhorst, A.J. *Schrift en kerkorde: Een bijdrage tot het onderzoek naar de mogelijkheid van een "schriftuurlijke kerkorde." (Scripture and Church Order: A Contribution to the Study of the Possibility of a "Scriptural Church Order")*. Den Haag: Zuid Holland Boek- en Handelsdrukkerij, 1947.

Brownson, James. "Elder-Pastors and Deacon-Evangelists: The Plurality of Offices and the Marks of the Church." *Reformed Review*, 56, no. 3 (Spring, 2003), 235-248.

Brueggemann, Walter. *Finally Comes the Poet: Daring Speech for Proclamation*. Minneapolis: Fortress, 1989.

Bruins, Elton J. and Swierenga, Robert P. *Family Quarrels in the Dutch Reformed Churches of the Nineteenth Century*. Grand Rapids: Eerdmans, 1999.

Catechism of the Catholic Church. Liguori, Missouri: Liguori Publications, 1994.

Constitution of the Presbyterian Church (U.S.A.) Part II Book of Order 2003-2004, The. Louisville: The Office of the General Assembly, 2003.

Cornick, David. "The Reformed Elder." *The Expository Times* 98/8 (May, 1987), 235-240.

Decker, Rodney J. "Polity and the Elder Issue." *Grace Theological Journal* 9/2 (1988), 257-277.

Dingemans, G.D.J. *Een huis om in te wonen: Schetsen en bouwstenen voor een Kerkorde van de toekomst. (A House to Live In: Sketches and Building Material for a Church Order of the Future)*. 's-Gravenhage: Boekencentrum, 1987.

Dulk, Maarten, den. "De verzoeking Christus te representeren." ("The Temptation to Represent Christ"). In *Geen kerk zonder bisschop?* 115-129.

Ernst, Margit. "We Believe the One Holy and Catholic Church." In *Reformed Theology: Identity and Ecumenicity,* ed. Wallace M. Alston and Michael Welker, 85-96. Grand Rapids: Eerdmans, 2003.

Fries, Paul R. "Coordinates of a Theology of Office: Footnotes for an Emerging Narrative." *Reformed Review,* 56, no. 3 (Spring, 2003), 197-210.

Gosker, M. "Ambt als Christusrepresentatie" ("Office as Representative of Christ"). In *Geen kerk zonder bisschop? Over de plaats va het ambt in de order van de kerk,* Martien Brinkman and Anton Houtepen, eds. Zoetermeer: Meinema, 1997, 130-145.

Gosker, Margriet. *Het ambt in de oecumenische discussie: De betekenis van de Lima-ambtstekst voor de voortgang van de oecumene en de doorwerking in de Nederlandse SOW-kerken.* (*Office in the Ecumenical Discussion: The Significance of the Ministry Text of Lima for the Progress of the Ecumene and its Importance for the SOW Churches of the Netherlands*). Delft: Eburon, 2000.

Graaf, J. van der. "De kerkorde en het apostolaat" ("Church Order and the Apostolate"). In *De kerk op orde? Vijftig jaar hervormd leven met de kerkorde van 1951,* ed. W. Balke, A. van de Beek, and J.D.Th. Wassenaar, 93-107. Zoetermeer: Boekencentrum, 2001.

Graafland, C. *Gedachten over het ambt: 'Och, of al het volk des Heeren profeten waren...!'* ("Thoughts on Office: 'Oh that all the People of the Lord were Prophets!'). Zoetermeer: Boekencentrum, 1999.

Haitjema, Th.L. *Nederlands Hervormd kerkrecht* (*Netherlands Reformed Church Order*) Nijkerk: G.F. Callenbach, 1951.

Haitjema, Th.L. *De richtingen in de Nederlandse Hervormde Kerk.* (*Schools of Thought in the Netherlands Reformed Church*), 2nd ed. Wageningen: H. Veenman, 1953.

Handelingen van de vergaderingen van de Generale Synode der Nederlandse Hervormde Kerk ten Jare 1953/1954. 's-Gravenhage: Nederlandsche Boek-en Steendrukkerij, 1957.

Heideman, Eugene P. *Reformed Bishops and Catholic Elders.* Grand Rapids: Eerdmans, 1970.

Hoedemaker, Ph. J. *De kerk en het moderne staatsrecht.* (*The Church in Modern Constitutional Law*). Amsterdam: Hollandsch-Afrikaansche Uitgevers-Maatschappij, 1904.

Houtepen, Anton. *Een asymmetrische dialoog: Historische kantteekeningen bij de onderlinge erkenning van de kerkelijke ambten* (*An Asymmetric Dialogue: Historical Notes on the Mutual Recognition of Ecclesiastical Offices*). (Utrechtse Theologische Reeks, deel 22) Utrecht: Faculteit der Godgeleerheid Universeteit Utrecht, 1994.

Janssen, Allan. "The Future of Offices in the Future of God." *Reformed Review*, 56, no. 3 (Spring, 2003), 273-280.

Janssen, Allan. "Ministry in Context." *Reformed Review*, 51, no. 1 (Autumn, 1997), 15-26.

Janssen, Allan. "A Perfect Agreement? The Theological Context of the Reformed Protestant Dutch Church in the First Half of the Nineteenth Century." In *Breaches and Bridges: Reformed Subcultures in the Netherlands, Germany, and the United States*, George Harinck and Hans Krabbendam, eds. Amsterdam: VU Uitgeverij: 2000, 49-60.

Janssen, Allan. "Reformed and Evangelical: New Questions and Old." In *Concord Makes Strength*, John W. Coakley, ed. Grand Rapids: Eerdmans, 2002, 113-129.

Jonge, Otto de. *Nederlandse kerkgeschiedenis* (*Netherlands Church History*). Nijkerk: G.F. Callenbach, 1978.

Kerkorde der Nederlandse Hervormde Kerk. 's-Gravenhage: Boekencentrum, 1969.

Koffeman, Leo. "Het bijzondere van het kerkelijk ambt" ("The Particular in Ecclesiastical Office"). *Gereformeerd Theologisch Tijdschrift* 91 (March, 1991), pp. 28-43.

Kronenberg, J. "Een 'episco-preby-gational' kerkmodel." In *Geen kerk zonder bisschop? Over het plaats van het ambt in de orde van de kerk*, Martien Brinkman and Anton Houtpen, eds. Zoetermeer: Meinema, 1997, 258-265.

Kronenberg, J. *Episcopus Oecumenicus: Bouwstenen voor een theologie van het bisschopsambt in een verenigde reformatorische kerk* (*Building Stones for a Theology of the Office of Bishop in a United Reformation Church*). Zoetermeer: Meinema, 2003.

Leeuw, G. van der. *Liturgiek*, 2nd ed. Nijkerk: G.F. Callenbach, 1946.

Looman-Graaskamp, A. H. "Het ambt, in en uit de tijd" ("Office in and out of Time"). In *Geen kerk zonder bisschop? Over het plaats van het ambt in de orde van de kerk*, Martien Brinkman and Anton Houtepen, eds. Zoetermeer: Meinema, 1997, 146-173.

MacIntyre, Alasdair. *After Virtue: A Study in Moral Theory*. Notre Dame: University of Notre Dame Press, 1981.

Mcleod, Donald. "Deacons and Elders." *Scottish Bulletin of Evangelical Theology* 13/1 (Spring, 1988), 26-50.

Nature and Purpose of the Church: A Stage on the Way to a Common Statement, The (Faith and Order Paper 181). Geneva, 1988.

O'Meara, Thomas F. *Theology of Ministry*, completely rev. ed. New York: Paulist Press, 1999.

Oostenbrink-Evers, H. "Het ambt in de kerkorde" ("Office in the Church Order"). In *De kerk op orde? Vijftig jaar hervormd leven met de kerkorde van 1951 (The Church in Order? Fifty Years of Reformed Life with the Church Order of 1951)*. W. Balke, A. van de Beek, and J.D.Th. Wassenaar, eds. Zoetermeer: Boekencentrum, 2001, 42-66.

Rausch William G. and Martensen, Daniel F., eds. *The Leuenberg Agreement and Lutheran-Reformed Relationships: Evaluations by North American Theologians.* Minneapolis: Augsburg, 1989.

Reid, J.K.S. "Reformed Responses to Baptism, Eucharist, and Ministry: A Commentary." *Reformed World* 39/5 (1987), 683-692.

Reuver, R. de. *Eén kerk in meervoud: naar de ecclesiologische waarde van pluraliteit* (*One church in plural: a theological inquiry into the ecclesiological value of plurality*). Zoetermeer: Boekencentrum, 2004.

Rohls, Jan. "Das geistliche Amt in der reformatorischen Theologie" ("Clerical Office in Reformed Theology"). *Kerygma und Dogma* 3 (April-June, 1985), 135-161.

Roscam Abbing, P.J. *Diakonia: Een studie over het begrip dienst in dogmatiek en praktische theologie.* (*The Diaconate: A Study on the Concept of Service in Dogmatics and Practical Theology*). 's-Gravenhage: Boekencentrum, 1950.

Sell, Alan P.F. "Some Reformed Responses to Baptism, Eucharist and Ministry." *Reformed World* 39/3 (1986), 549-565.

Speelman, H.A. "De zin van het ambt in de kerk" ("The Sense of Office in the Church"). In *Geen kerk zonder bisschop?* 171-184.

Steinfels, Peter. *A People Adrift: The Crisis of the Roman Catholic Church in America*. New York: Simon and Schuster, 2003.

Stroup, George W. "Reformed Identity in an Ecumenical World." In *Reformed Theology: Identity and Ecumenicity*, ed. Wallace M. Alston, Jr. and Michel Welker. Grand Rapids: Eerdmans, 2003, 257-270.

Thurian, Max. *Churches Respond to BEM: Official Responses to "Baptism, Eucharist and Ministry."* Six volumes. Faith and Order Papers 129, 132, 135, 137, 143, 144. Geneva: World Council of Churches, 1986-.

Trimp, C. "De kerk bij A. Kuyper en K. Schilder" ("The Church in A. Kuyper and K. Schilder"). In *De kerk: wezen, weg en werk van de kerk naar reformatorische opvatting.* W. van't Spijker, W. Balke, K. Exalto, L. van Driel, eds. Kampen: De Groot Goudriaan: 1990, 187-201.

Volf, Miroslav. *After Our Likeness: The Church as the Image of the Trinity.* Grand Rapids: Eerdmans, 1998.

Zythoff, Gerrit J., ten. *Sources of Succession: The Netherlands Reformed Church on the Eve of the Dutch American Immigration to the Midwest.* Grand Rapids: Eerdmans, 1987.

Index

N.B. Names are indexed according to Dutch convention. That is, Van de Beek, e.g., is listed as Beek, van de, or Vander Lugt as Lugt, vander.